Counterpoint, Composition,

and *Musica Ficta*

CRITICISM AND ANALYSIS OF EARLY MUSIC

JESSIE ANN OWENS, *Series Editor*

TONAL STUCTURES IN EARLY MUSIC
edited by Cristle Collins Judd

COUNTERPOINT AND COMPOSITIONAL PROCESS
IN THE TIME OF DUFAY
Perspectives from German Musicology
edited and translated by Kevin N. Moll

THE LANGUAGE OF THE MODES
Studies in the History of Polyphonic Modality
by Frans Wiering

COUNTERPOINT, COMPOSITION, AND *MUSICA FICTA*
by Margaret Bent

Counterpoint, Composition,

and *Musica Ficta*

Margaret Bent

Routledge
New York and London

Published in 2002 by
Routledge
29 West 35th Street
New York, NY 10001

Published in Great Britain by
Routledge
11 New Fetter Lane
London EC4P 4EE

Routledge is an imprint of the Taylor & Francis Group.

Printed on acid-free, 250-year-life paper.
Manufactured in the United States of America.

10   9   8   7   6   5   4   3   2

Library of Congress Cataloging-in-Publication Data

Bent, Margaret.
    Counterpoint, composition, and musica ficta / Margaret Bent.
    p. cm. – (Criticism and analysis of early music; v. 4)
    Includes bibliographical references and index.
    ISBN 0-8153-3497-4
    1. Musica ficta. 2. Counterpoint. 3. Composition (Music). 4. Music theory—History—500–1400. 5. Music theory—History—15th century. I. Title. II. Series.

ML174.B46   2002
781.2—dc21   2001048110

Table of Contents

Series Editor's Foreword
General Introduction to
Criticism and Analysis of Early Music
Jessie Ann Owens

Recent years have seen a critical reassessment of our approach to early music. Musicians, scholars, and critics have been searching for ways of talking about and reacting to the music that engage it not from the perspectives of later music but rather on its own terms. These new approaches would not be possible without the scholarship of the previous decades. The discovery and cataloguing of musical sources, the preparation of critical editions, and the investigation of archival documents have furnished important information about composers, performers, patrons, and institutions that supported the creation and performance of early music. Building on this work, the editors of these volumes now seek to develop and explore analytical methodologies for the discussion of early music as music.

Analytic methods are not easily found for early music. The theorists of the time had their own agendas, and they do not provide models that suit our purposes. As a consequence, many twentieth-century scholars have chosen approaches that reflect their own beliefs about early music and its relation to later music. While some continue to rely on common practice tonality as a prism through which to view early music, others have begun to explore methods that respect the integrity and self-sufficiency of the languages of early music.

We offer a forum for exploration of particular topics, from both a methodological and critical viewpoint. Our premise is that we can best develop new methodologies by encouraging debate. We will explore compositional procedures, tonal structures, musical borrowing, and other topics, focusing both on individual compositions and on theoretical systems. We seek to encourage critical writing about music that will be useful to performers, listeners, and scholars.

Preface

Friends and students have encouraged me to collect together thematic groups of essays that represent the various strands of my scholarly work over the past thirty years. This one is the first such collection I have made, and includes essays on counterpoint, *musica ficta*, compositional procedure and some related topics published up to about five years ago. It does not include "The Grammar of Early Music: Preconditions for Analysis," which appeared recently in another volume in this series, nor does it include other studies (currently in press) that may eventually form a sequel to this collection.[1] Most of the essays in this volume present aspects of a still-evolving view of the relationship between notated music and its realisation in sound. They are concerned with how pitch relationships worked, how composers composed, what notation means, how performers dealt with the written notes and words, and how they applied their internalised training to it. There is much more to be said, but it seemed time to take stock, to annotate where revision is needed, or where I have corrected or modified my views or improved their formulation. Much of what I wrote in earlier articles has percolated through to general acceptance, though naturally it is points of disagreement that are most clearly signalled, and I attempt in the Introduction to give an interim reassessment of some points that have attracted criticism. Debates about *musica ficta*, the rationale, provision, and consequences of written and unwritten accidentals, and in general the actual pitch content of early music: all these have aroused strong opinions and feelings throughout the twentieth century, for almost as long as musicology has been a self-conscious discipline. I have tried to address some of the views of those who disagree with the positions developed here, signalling where they proceed from different and sometimes incompatible premises.

Because these essays are in a sense cumulative and show some progression in formulations and vocabulary, it seemed impossible to revise them without radical rewriting, and this I decided not to attempt. They represent successive stages in the evolution of a hypothesis which seeks to place the understanding of *musica ficta* in the context of counterpoint teaching, one of the most fundamental among a range of skills, now in need of reconstruction, by which the performer of late medieval and Renaissance polyphony unlocked the—to us—underprescriptive notation. When advancing new hypotheses, I may occasionally have overstated elements of a case, in order to make quite clear how the new premises differ from existing views. I recognise that some such statements now need refinement. I have tried to adjust the weight that attaches to various parts of the hypothesis; I hope that my critics will see this as an honest attempt to find common ground on which the debate can proceed without rancour, and that those who are new to the issues will approach them in this spirit. This is not a new book on *musica ficta,* but rather, in part, an attempt to clear the way for one; by gathering together my own contributions to the debate, together with a few other related articles, I hope to make clear just what I do and do not claim, and to correct some misrepresentations.

The articles are therefore reprinted without textual change except for the correction of minor misprints and light editing. New additions within text and footnotes are confined to short clarifications and more recent bibliographical references, mostly to new editions of treatises cited. All such additions are in <angle brackets>. To permit easy location of references to the original published version, page breaks in the original printing are shown within the text by ^{||2} at the junction of original page numbers 1 and 2. Original footnote numbering has also been retained. There are many points that I would now state differently, but since each was formulated at its own stage of ripeness I have not attempted to change the substance, partly also to avoid diplomatic confusion. I have confined annotations/comments at the end of some chapters to points with which I now have a clear and substantive difference, or which have given rise to debate.

I am grateful to the many people over many years who have helped me with and constructively criticised my formulations. Many students and friends are not listed here, especially some from long ago, and I apologise for omissions and oversights. Those whose comments have been particularly important, or who have helped in other ways, include J. Michael Allsen, Charles Atkinson, Karol Berger, Alexander Blachly, Bonnie J. Blackburn, Calvin Bower, John Buttrey, Suzannah Clark, Annie Coeurdevey, Harold Copeman, Julia Craig-McFeely, Lucy Cross, Jonathan Dancy, Jeffrey Dean, Giuliano Di Bacco, Theodor Dumitrescu, Lawrence Earp, David Fallows, Iain Fenlon, James Haar, Leofranc Holford-Strevens, Andrew Hughes,

Cristle Collins Judd, Elizabeth Eva Leach, Daniel Leech-Wilkinson, Kenneth Levy, David Lewin, Judith Loades, Edward E. Lowinsky, Thomas Mathiesen, Matthew Mills, John Milsom, Kevin Moll, Robert Nosow, Claude Palisca, Dolores Pesce, Alejandro Planchart, Harold Powers, Joshua Rifkin, Lynda Sayce, Jonathan Shull, Alexander Silbiger, Reinhard Strohm, Peter Urquhart, Jonathan Walker, Thomas Walker, Andrew Wathey, Rob Wegman. I thank Jessie Ann Owens for inviting me to submit this volume for inclusion in her series.

NOTE

1. See Bent 1998a, c; 2002a.

Introduction

I. Musica ficta and related matters: Chapters 1–6

Chapter I started life as an appendix to my unpublished doctoral dissertation completed in 1968 (*The Old Hall Manuscript: a Paleographical Study*, University of Cambridge, 1969), and was slightly revised for its 1972 publication as "Musica Recta and Musica Ficta." That essay was driven by the practical need to formulate a *ficta* policy for the Old Hall edition,[1] and its hypotheses had already initiated a stimulating correspondence with Andrew Hughes as we collaboratively prepared that edition. He was initially inclined to apply the minimum of editorial intervention, but in the course of a spirited exchange he came to revise this view. He went on to develop the theory in his own way in his book *Ficta in Focus*, where he graciously acknowledged the role of my position and arguments in the formulation of his. My article took the debate about *ficta* and editorial accidentals in some new directions: I welcome the fact that, inevitably, some components of the argument have since been superseded or refined, both by me and by others.

Chapters 2 and 3 are hitherto unpublished. Chapter 2 also appeared in my dissertation as an appendix. Its results are incorporated into the Old Hall edition, where they appear in the commentary in abbreviated form. The conundrum posed by this composition has gone largely uncommented, so I include the lightly edited excursus here in the hope that this remarkable device may still engender some interest.[2] Chapter 3 was a paper presented orally in several versions at conferences in the 1980s; it states some of the positions of Chapters I and 4 with formulations that may prove helpful or more accessible. It stresses the contextual nature of solmisation, and the function of anticipations as aural cues for responsive intervallic adjustments; it also draws attention to areas of overlap between *ficta* and *recta*, and to the ways in which the singer need not be aware of a sharp distinction between them unless he needs or decides to solmise. This recognition of a grey area of definition has some consequences for the consideration of clefless compositions and of *recta* transposition.

The term *musica ficta* is commonly used as a shorthand for the whole problem of added accidentals in early music. One thesis of Chapter I is that "*it is . . . not correct to equate* musica ficta *with editorial accidentals*. Manuscript accidentals and added accidentals each include both *recta* and *ficta* inflections, and are therefore not different in kind" (Chapter I, p. 69 and note 13). Berger, Urquhart, and Brothers have since endorsed these distinctions in the use of the term *musica ficta*. I tried to reconcile some apparent conflicts of theoretical and manuscript testimony that had bedevilled earlier debates. Yet Urquhart still maintains that "performers' accidentals" cannot take account of theorists' "harmonic" rules; by thus relabelling the modern practice of *musica ficta*, and by setting aside the possibility of rehearsal and aural adjustment, he disqualifies modern performers from applying the fundamental medieval rule, the prohibition of *mi contra fa* in simultaneous perfect intervals. Thomas Brothers adopts a more literal approach to manuscript accidentals, taking them largely at face value, which is not at all the same thing as taking the notation seriously. Arguments that notated manuscript accidentals are largely complete and sufficient rest on assumptions about the nature of early notation that I reject in Chapter 7. The extent to which Berger and I are on one side and Brothers on the other is brought out at the end of Dolores Pesce's (1999: 286-87) review of Brothers 1997.

The role of theory

Previous twentieth-century writers had tended to stress either evidence derived from theorists, as guidance for the "harmonic" or "vertical" aspect of interval correction, or that of musical manuscripts, for the "melodic" or linear aspect. Hirshberg still considers these two aspects to some extent incompatible, as they had been presented by earlier writers, in part in those articles by Apel (1938, 1939), Lowinsky (1945, 1954), and Hoppin (1953, 1956) that contributed to a heated debate on the meaning of so-called partial signatures. The divide is still with us. Berger's book *Musica Ficta* (1987) gives primary focus to theory and addresses practice only in a limited way, sometimes rejecting a hypothesis on theoretical grounds without taking adequate account of the musical situation that generated it. Other scholars marginalise theoretical precepts in order to privilege more or less literal readings of manuscript accidentals (Brothers, Harden and Hirshberg) or melodic considerations (Urquhart). Hirshberg misattributes to me the view that "each historical period must be examined in the light of contemporary criteria; the application of modern theory to old music is anachronistic. . . . *Musica ficta* is inseparable from the contrapuntal theory and practice of its own period. For this reason, Bent analyses individual works in their regional context strictly from the point of view of contemporary theory."[3] This is not quite right. I heartily endorse the view that "*musica ficta* is inseparable from the contrapuntal theory and practice of its own period," but would continue, as I wrote: "we should beware of assuming that older concepts and terminology are inadequate to their purpose, and of being too hasty to resort to our own theoretical equipment" (Chapter 4, p.119). I do not embrace the position condemned by Leech-Wilkinson (1984: 9), that of *restricting* modern use to old terminology. To prefer contemporaneous terms and concepts where available is not by any means to exclude useful modern extensions of them. Early theorists have sometimes been set aside as inconsistent with practice because they have been misread. Increasingly precise understanding of how relevant theoretical prescriptions are qualified, or their application confined, brings apparently contradictory theory back into play. For example, *mi contra fa* is prohibited not in general, which would be nonsensical, but only "in perfect intervals" (see Chapter 1, p. 82); parallel perfect intervals are forbidden not just anywhere in the texture (where they frequently occur) but in counterpoint—that is, only between the parts forming the basic contrapuntal duet (see Bent 1998a: 36–38). Theoretical and musical testimony need to be reconciled. Apparently competing claims need to be addressed by an appropriate prioritisation of rules extrapolated from both directions, and in particular from those rare cases where theorists cite specific polyphonic repertory (notably in the examples given by Pietro Aaron; see Chapter 5). It is plainly impossible always to avoid all false octaves, diminished fifths, and augmented fourths in linear and simultaneous occurrence; yet all these are variously given by modern editors as reasons for inflection, often without any systematic attempt to set priorities. The problem is exacerbated if the prohibition is extended to oblique false or cross relationships.

My proposals clearly do not solve all problems but try to avoid invoking loosely defined criteria such as "beauty." I assume throughout that, for early musicians, their manuscripts must have sufficed, in conjunction with the training and assumptions they shared with the composers who determined the first notated form of the music. That our only access to their working assumptions is through the combined testimony of the theorists and the music manuscripts is certainly not to say that any theoretical prescription should be imposed if it contradicts the discernible musical sense of an individual piece.

Composer's intention or performer's choice?

Opinions differ about the degree to which *compositional* intent with respect to pitch was fixed, even if under-notated, and the degree to which there was *performative* license of pitch realisation on the part of late-medieval singers. Cross, Leach, Toft, and I all seem to believe that singers with a competent understanding of counterpoint were able to read and construe the notation in the light of aural signals to which they responded. Singers were thus able to realise the composer's intentions therein encoded, at least with respect to the essential correction of perfect intervals and to a suitable approach to such intervals.

Some absolutely essential things must be adjusted; composer and singer by mutual understanding would have taken these for granted when they respectively notated and realised the notation. Those essential things are simultaneous perfect intervals and cadential inflections, which account for most of the initiatives that singers have to take during a piece. But singers are interpreting notation that is by our standards under-prescriptive, and there are cases of ambiguity, just as, in music of any period, a composer might not build his intentions unmistakably into the music (for example, with respect to under-prescribed tempo, pedalling or dynamic markings). Ambiguities whose resolution is not self-evident to us do not mean that the composer did *not* have fixed intentions, and he might well say (as composers sometimes have done, presumably back then, too): "Oh, I hadn't thought of it like that, but what you did makes perfectly good sense."

At the elective end of the spectrum, performers have some freedom with respect to alternative readings and non-essential inflections, and to the resolution of ambiguity. These may be considered analogous to the freedom of inflection exercised by an orator in the rhetorical delivery and intelligible communication of speech, and depend on the internal workings of specific musical grammars to determine appropriate inflections, in the light of theorists' statements, and as a means of extending those statements. I have proposed such language analogies in "The Grammar of Early Music," particularly with respect to the communication of sense and sense-breaks as in verbal language, and I continue to explore them in conjunction with medieval traditions of grammar and rhetoric.

By building intentions into the music, I mean not only the notation of accidental signs, but the way the counterpoint is set up to promote certain solutions or to make one choice more obvious than another in the absence of signs. It is where the composer has left some room for doubt that singers might well come up with different solutions. Aaron negotiates some of these problems in the *Aggiunta* to his *Toscanello*, as I have tried to show in Chapter 5; he urges more explicitness by composers in places where "the singer might first commit a little error." I believe that he is not advocating full notation of all accidentals, only that they should be notated where a sign will resolve ambiguities or pre-empt problems that are not susceptible to normal aural diagnosis; such passages are "not easy for the singer."

Even modern singers reading from original notation can very quickly internalise the musical grammar and make self-evident adjustments from the proposed combination of reading and listening. Notated "accidentals" might be compared to written punctuation, equally variable over the centuries in amount and purpose. Just as a verbal sentence may be generously or sparsely punctuated, so may music. A literate reader who knows the language and the conventions can nearly always get the intended sense of under-punctuated written words, and communicate that sense by speech inflections. But there may be cases where punctuation fails to resolve an ambiguity; written sentences can change their meaning radically when given different spoken emphasis and inflection. A range of different spoken interpretations will be possible within the limits of sense, and so also with musical inflections.

Implicit accidentals

The recognition that some "accidentals" can or indeed must lie at the stronger end of the prescriptive spectrum, and that they are implicit in compositional intention, has been adopted by other scholars, including Cross and Leach. Toft (1992) aptly observes that many theorists advise composers "on the ways of structuring counterpoint properly so that the desired results would be produced in performance" (p. 10). When Cross (1990) writes "that the responsibility for chromatic alteration in most instances in the polyphonic repertoires of the fourteenth century does *not* rest with the performer, indeed that extrahexachordal intervals are almost always either explicitly specified or else clearly and unmistakably indicated by the composers' manipulation of counterpoint" (p. 8), she clearly means that the performer is given enough help to realise the composer's intention. Similar claims are made in several of my writings in this volume, though I would now avoid calling the alterations "chromatic." Cross also concurs with my view of notational synonymy, that "alternate readings are usually not in conflict, being simply alternative instances of inclusion or omission, since it was by no means necessary to notate an accidental that was clearly intended" (p. 10; see also pp. 71–72, reflecting my position). A composer may be playing with or even against the rules by which he and his performers were trained; it would be inappropriate to standardise where the composer may be inviting his readers to recognise and implement a different musical argument. In this sense I agree with Hirshberg (1996) that we should not uncritically flatten out abnormal usages to standard formulas, though in my view his approach accepts too high a threshold of tolerable abnormality, just as Brothers (1997) bases his similar position on too literal a reading of notated manuscript accidentals and their absence, even arguing *against* applying *ficta* in accordance with contrapuntal grammar. But to detect truly deliberate compositional unorthodoxy requires familiarity with the conventions that the composer may have been side-stepping. The notation and its supporting expectations operate in terms of their own conventions, not ours. Some of these conventions may have been so taken for granted that they were spelled out inadequately or not at all in treatises and are accessible to us only by inference from and analysis of the notated music.[4] A strong working-out of the arguments for moderating apparently abnormal progressions in relation to contrapuntal convention is Leach's (2000b) recent essay on Machaut's Balade 31, *De toutes flours*, where she rejects a notated but nonsensical cadential flat in favour of a "normal" reading based on both source evidence and musical sense: "*difficilior lectio potior* requires that all readings considered should first be possible. In a literary text, those readings deemed nonsense against a semantic yard-stick are discarded so as to avoid accepting errors in attempting to privilege authorial exceptionality" (p. 334). I believe she is right to accord the semitone cadential approach this status of fundamental sense. Beauty may stretch the rules, but it cannot be defined in opposition to them. Idiosyncrasy should not be equated uncritically with beauty, especially until editors and performers can more confidently distinguish right notes from wrong, or determine which surviving voice parts may be performed together and which not. Counterpoint is fundamental not only to composition but to performance; analysis, far from being *post facto* autopsy, must always have been an essential stage in the performative realisation of a composition, analogous to grammatical construing prior to the rhetorical delivery of language. The textual status of implicit accidentals is further discussed in part II of this Introduction.

Solmisation

Scholars have disagreed about the role of solmisation in determining *ficta*. I have proposed that, since the solmisation system (and its extension, or condensation, in the theory of *coniuncte*) can be extended to cope even with irregular or forbidden intervals, *any* progression can be solmised, and that inflections are to be determined above all by considerations of counterpoint (see Chapters 1, 3, 4, and 6). Hexachords are intervallically identical, and would have been pointless as tools for classification; pieces are not "in" hexachords, as they may be conceived in keys or classified by modes. The only point of hexachords lies in their flexible mutual relationship. Occasional theoretical injunctions not to change hexachord unless necessary do not oblige a singer to remain in a hexachord beyond the point that will accommodate the notes to be sung. Hexachords are means of articulating decisions made on other grounds; they are descriptive, not prescriptive, as Cross agrees (1990: 181). The practical and pedagogical language of solmisation is the principal or only means by which theoretical writers can specify and name semitone inflections in the context of counterpoint teaching. This recognition was accepted, though with different emphases, by Hughes, Berger, Cross, Hirshberg, and several others. Some have inferred (wrongly) that, because I recognised the importance of hexachords, I was therefore advocating a role for solmisation in determining which notes were to be sung, when in fact I confined it to the articulation and explanation of decisions already made on other (contrapuntal) grounds, and as an important key to the only language available to theorists for the specification of tone/semitone distinctions: "solmisation *ex post facto* is a superfluous chore."[5] It would be unwise to exaggerate the extent to which the *disiuncta* (a device for irregular solmisation, the antithesis of the *coniuncta*) was invoked or systematised.[6] Since the solmisation of any piece must follow, not precede, contrapuntally diagnosed decisions about inflections, experienced singers then and now can bypass the exercise of applying solmisation names. Advanced singers, for whom awkward situations and intervals were most likely to arise, would have internalised the gamut since their elementary education, and the *recta/ficta* distinction was unlikely to be a conscious determinant.[7] Differences of opinion and interpretation on the techniques and operation of solmisation, and about transposed systems and their status, need not impede agreement on the underlying principles that independently govern which notes should or may be sung.

Transposition and signatures

Two related hypotheses to which Hughes and I subscribed in the late 1960s have been criticised. One is that flat signatures effected transpositions of connected groups of hexachords, and the other is to accord priority, where possible, to *recta* over *ficta* inflections. We proposed that such signatures might transpose the networks of hard, natural, and soft *recta* hexachords one degree flatwards for each signature flat. In the case of pieces whose different voice parts are differently signed (usually - ♭ ♭ or ♭ ♭♭ ♭♭), this would reflect the tendency for parts pitched about a fifth lower than the upper part(s) to have one more flat in the signature. This was prompted by practical observation, but we offered theoretical support from Ugolino's presentation of two "hands," the second transposed (likewise) down a fifth from the first, but *both* with *recta* and *ficta* provision, which suggested that the *recta–ficta* hierarchy might still operate when transposed. However, this reading of Ugolino has been questioned by Berger

(1987: 64) and Cross, but without compelling counter-evidence or alternative hypotheses. The transposition hypothesis for signatures does not depend only on this passage.

Such signatures have been called partial, contrasting, or conflicting; I now think that "differentiated" might be a better term. They have been debated by Hoppin and Lowinsky with respect to modal versus hexachordal significance, practical versus theoretical purpose. But to transpose overlapping networks of hexachords also removes the notion of conflict or contrast between signatured and unsignatured parts by emphasising the areas of *overlap* between them (see Chapters 1 and 3), in particular, that *bb* is equally available to parts with and without signatures. As Berger notes (p. 64), Dahlhaus and I independently reached similar views on hexachordal transposition, he in 1968b (p. 208), recognising *eb* as being analogous to *bb* in an unsignatured part. Berger simply asserts that "the assumption, however, is incorrect," without distinguishing between, on the one hand, the transposition of individual hexachords, whether whole hexachords or small segments containing just the *mi-fa* semitone steps (*coniuncte*), and on the other, of whole systems.[8] Berger asserts his own interpretation, of a closed collection of pitches classified as if with reference to a keyboard. Other scholars have accepted the principle of transposing groups of hexachords (e.g., Hirshberg, 1980: 21; Leech-Wilkinson 1984: 18). As Hughes put it: "A consistently applied key-signature can 'deliver' a *recta* series of notes only in a transposed gamut" (1972: 47). Since all hexachords are intervallically identical, any meaningful distinction between them can lie only in their interrelationship, which I believe to be as readily and normally transposable as the hexachords themselves.

Neither Cross nor Berger addresses one problem that provoked my hypothesis in the first place, namely that the gamut or hand, so fundamental in elementary pedagogy, would become pointless for purposes of hexachordal navigation of a signatured part *unless* transposition is invoked; nor does either address the problem identified by Hughes in interpreting Ugolino's *combinations* of *recta* and *ficta* hexachords. I will not attempt to unravel that stubborn problem here, but I do not consider the interpretation of Ugolino a closed issue. In offering a response to my question as to what effect a *bb* signature might have (Chapter 1, p. 87), Cross replies "almost none" (1990: 127), thereby echoing Lowinsky's contention that "from a systemic point of view, conflicting signatures simply make no sense" (1954: 194). Such responses to the notoriously inconsistent notation and transmission of differentiated signatures do not close off the quest for further hypotheses. Berger revives an older modal explanation that looks rather tired in the light of more recent work on mode by Powers, Judd, and others. There may also be further scope for reconsidering Ugolino's transposed hexachordal hand against the earlier medieval background of expedient devices for modal transformation and transposition set out by Dolores Pesce in *The Affinities and Modal Transposition* (1987).

The problem of signatures and transposition is posed in a more pointed form by the phenomenon of "clefless" pieces, or rather, pieces signed only with flat signatures of undetermined and undeterminable letter-name pitch, often with differentiated signatures, whose pitches indeed do not need to be named except for purposes of transcription into modern notation, which requires such definition. Criteria of *recta* or *ficta* and their associated priorities depend on the letter-name anchorage of notes, here absent; clefless pieces share with other flat-signatured pieces an absence of *recta* letter names. In both cases, I still believe that constellations of related hexachords must have provided the performer's primary orientation, corresponding to the *g*, *c* and *f* hexachords of *musica recta*. I find it hard to imagine that the principles which orientated an unsignatured part would have been so drastically different, or indeed absent, for a signatured or partially signatured part, even within the same piece, that the reader of a cleffed or clefless part with flat signature should be cut loose from the procedures of movable solmisation anchored around the three-hexachord system. In the case of uncleffed parts, the linked but unnamed hexachords suggested by the signature would offer no orientation if the operation of solmisation were held to be dependent on letter-names. Both signatured and unsignatured parts would of course then remain open to the projection of isolated hexachords or *coniuncte* to accommodate individual *mi-fa* inflections.

If signature flats function as hexachord signatures, as is now quite widely if not universally agreed, they *must*, at least until the late fifteenth century, involve a short- or long-term flatward transposition of the system, together with its priorities. Hughes and I also proposed that such transposed systems might retain their *recta* status and its associated hierarchies. I still favour the principle that the *recta* constellation of hexachords was to be transposed one degree flatwards for each flat of the signature, and to an unnamed pitch in the case of clefless pieces. But in the absence of clearer theoretical testimony, I would no longer insist on retaining *recta* status for such *congeries* of hexachords when transposed. Whether transposed *recta* remains *recta* or becomes *ficta* is of less importance the more recognition is accorded to the significant area of overlap between the realms of *recta* and *ficta* (see Chapter 1 and, more explicitly, Chapter 3). Indeed, the distinction may be reduced almost to a mere terminological quibble, still important when interpreting the theorists, but further reducing the force of my previous proposal for (qualified) *recta* preference (see below). Berger's account fails to allow for pieces with unnamed notes, yet such pieces sit alongside normally cleffed pieces in the manuscripts.

Until late in the fifteenth century, hexachords were still very much alive as a pedagogical tool. The names *durus, naturalis* and *mollis* applied not to separate scales but to the interrelated, overlapping, and identically constituted hexachords that made up the single gamut. Their *raison d'être* was to provide a basis, or default, for negotiating melodies that exceeded the compass of a single hexachord, or straddled the junction of two hexachords. In early-sixteenth-century terms, three separate scales of *cantus naturalis, cantus mollis* and *cantus fictus* were sometimes distinguished, especially by German theorists, without internal *recta-ficta* distinction and without the earlier emphasis on hexachordal navigation. Ornithoparcus (1517) and Listenius (1533) designated one-flat-signatured parts *cantus mollis*, parts signatured with two flats *cantus fictus*. Was it yet true in the early fifteenth century, as it probably was later in that century and certainly by the sixteenth, that a signatured part, especially a two-flat-signatured part, could be considered entirely fictive? The weakening of the three-hexachord solmisation system around 1500 left little room or need to keep the *recta-ficta* distinction and the operation of a *recta-ficta* hierarchy alive in its earlier functional form. But that hierarchy had undoubted importance at an earlier date when whole parts or scales were no more clearly classified as consisting entirely of *ficta* than were Ugolino's double hands.

Neither Cross, Berger, nor other commentators have come up with a better explanation for the function of signatures. Berger claims (1987: 69) that they "provide an automatic insurance against vertical imperfect fifths," but this is true only over some notes and is not, as he implies, a general remedy. The claim that they "provide automatically leading notes in upper parts at some cadences" does not account for the equally necessary ones they do not provide, nor does it take account of the "accidental" aspects of the notation that did not require such prescriptive provision. Berger then reverts to reconciling this with his earlier assertion "that the function of a key signature was to produce a modal transposition," and invokes the familiar concept of successive composition (now much in need of qualification: see below, under *Resfacta*) to defend the notion that "it was sufficient for one part to be the mode-defining voice." This hardly moves the argument beyond the point reached in the Hoppin-Lowinsky debate.

Recta preference

A second and related principle which has attracted criticism is that of preferring *recta* to *ficta* where the choice of inflection is not otherwise constrained. I proposed this as one possible reading of the common theoretical exhortation not to use *ficta* unless necessary, an injunction that some have taken as an instruction to be sparing in the use of *any* inflections, and as a licence—as some do—to judge many additions of accidentals (visible to *us*) as excessive and textually invasive. Berger dismisses the idea of *recta* preference, which would privilege tenor *b♭* for a cadence on *a*, on the grounds that theorists often preferred cantus *g♯* for such cadences (1987: p. 235 n. 104, and pp. 83–84), reverting to the older reading of the injunction against too much *ficta* as being directed against too many accidental inflections, a reading that presupposes an equation between "accidental inflections" and *musica ficta* that Urquhart and I and indeed Berger reject. I am not sure how we know that theorists "often" preferred *g♯*; the constraints of composed polyphony favour sometimes one kind of inflection, sometimes the other. The theorists do not permit clear and general inferences about differentiated signatures, or applied *ficta* in composed polyphony. Sharp leading notes become more common towards and after 1500 because they often arise at the top of a four-part texture over a fifth, sounding between the tenor and a lower bassus, that would be (illegally) diminished by a *fa-mi* cadence in the tenor. Berger also says (p. 84) that the Bent-Hughes theory does not explain why flats were chosen to correct non-harmonic relations. But this is precisely what it does explain; the choice of flats rather than sharps would reflect the operation of *recta* preference in cases where the choice was otherwise equally balanced, especially if taken in conjunction with the (empirically hypothesised) hexachord transpositions that Berger rejects. *B♭* and *b♮* remain equally available by *musica recta*; in practice, cadences on *a* often favour *recta b♭* over *ficta g♯*, while cadences on *g*, where there is no *recta* alternative, more often use *f♯*.

But even then I did not advocate unqualified *recta* preference: "*Recta* preference takes priority over most other rules, including that of plainsong preference, unless the *cantus prius factus* has a very strong melodic claim to use or to incur *ficta*, or if for some reason it is treated as immutable (as might be the case in certain imitative, canonic, isorhythmic or refrain-like repetitions). It may be impossible to use *musica recta* . . ." (followed by a list of reasons; see Chapter 1, p. 72). Now I no longer regard as a "primary rule for applying accidentals . . . that *musica recta* should be used rather than *musica ficta* where possible." *Recta* preference may still apply in cases of genuinely equal choice, but it easily yields to more pressing considerations, and, as one would expect by the sixteenth century, it has no place among Aaron's priorities. Philip Weller and Andrew Kirkman (1996: 571) observe that Philip Kaye in his Binchois edition eschews cadential *ficta* sharps in favour of *recta* flats at cadences because of "a somewhat misconceived interpretation of Margaret Bent's article 'Musica Recta and Musica Ficta.'" Indeed, Kaye took my prescription too literally, without observing the (insufficient) qualifications I applied even then.

Two points now lead me to lower still more the importance of *recta* priority. One is the aforementioned overlap between the realms of *recta* and *ficta* (emphasised in Chapter 3: not just individual inflections but their hexachordal contexts or at least *mi-fa coniuncte* count as *ficta*); the other is the absolute primacy of counterpoint in governing inflections (whether *recta* or *ficta*). If correct counterpoint can be achieved without unnecessary changes of hexachord—that is, without recourse to *musica ficta*—so much the better. The rationale for preferring *recta* to *ficta* inflections can also be further tempered by two important revisions made by Prosdocimus to the text of his counterpoint treatise. To read the injunction against too much *ficta* as advocating restraint in *writing in* needed inflections now gains support from a clarification: composers are said to err in *notating* the signs of *ficta* where those signs are not needed. In another revision, in order to achieve the necessary interval correction he takes for granted, Prosdocimus advocates applying the signs according to where they sound better (not debating whether to use them at all).[9] If the signs produce better-sounding inflections in the tenor, one should choose those; if in the discant, those; if equal, give preference to the discant, lest it be necessary to apply signs in parts other than the discant and tenor. This clearly suggests that fictive *mi-fa* discant cadences ("leading notes") would often override (tenor-led) *fa-mi recta* progressions. Prosdocimus twice mentions the contratenor (also triplum and quadruplum), showing that he has in mind the consequences of applying his (two-part) counterpoint teaching in a many-voiced composed context. Criteria for better sound must obviously be defined in relation to contrapuntal rules and expectations of the time, not as an invitation to override those rules with modern tastes, schooled by different and irrelevant criteria. There *are* many imperative inflections in this music, but there is also some room for choice. Where there is a choice, it may be constrained, the basis for which Prosdocimus goes some way towards formulating. For both him and Tinctoris (*Liber de arte contrapuncti*, III.5), the judgment of the (appropriately trained and attuned) ears overrides other considerations, including (if indeed that is implicit) *recta* priority. This sounds like a licence for *us* to make such choices, but it could also be explained as the correct discerning of compositional intent by performers (see above).

Terminology

There are several terms in these articles that I would no longer employ, and some need further explanation; see also the notes to Chapter I. They include "accidentals," and the idea of "adding accidentals" (except when talking strictly about written notation). They include "chromatic notes" and "chromaticism," terms not used by medieval theorists except for chromatic melodical intervals, such as f-$f\sharp$; $f\sharp$-g is not a chromatic but a diatonic semitone. They include the notion often described as "successive composition." I now prefer the aural connotations of "simultaneity" to the visual connotations of "vertical." Modern translations of medieval theory frequently and misleadingly use the word "chromatic" where it is not present in the original Latin. The sixteenth-century understanding of "chromatic" in purely melodic terms is emphasised by Haar in his 1977 article "False Relations and Chromaticism." In response to the problem of "chromatic" terminology, Cross refers to such notes as "extrahexachordal," even though she retains "chromatic" quite extensively. Her views reflect many that I have put forward in my own writings, though she does not usually note this. Accidental signs were literally "accidental" and may not necessarily be marked. It may be convenient for us if they are, but musical sense should be judged independently of such markings, just as for verbal sense periods and articulations, and even word divisions, can be judged independently of notated punctuation and at certain periods in the history of writing had to be so judged.

INUSITATA

The word *inusitata* crops up in connection with earlier (fourteenth- and fifteenth-century) definitions of *musica ficta*, inviting several attempts to explain it away as a mis-reading of *mutata* (Russo and Bonge 1999; also Cross 1990: 46–49). In fact, the misreading is the other way round. The printed editions reporting the word as *mutata* are in error; all the manuscripts that they purport to transcribe clearly read *inusitata* and not *mutata*. The treatise of Lambertus was published in Coussemaker, *Scriptores* I, pp. 251–81 from Paris, BN, Lat. 11266 fol. 8v, and Paris, BN, Lat. 6755 (*olim* St. Victor 659), part 2, fol. 75v. Both of these manuscripts indeed have *inusitata*, their readings kindly checked for me in Paris by Andrew Wathey. Sandra Pinegar's transcription of another manuscript version of this treatise (Siena, Biblioteca Comunale, L.V.30, ff. 14r–32r), also with *inusitata*, can be consulted in the *Thesaurus Musicarum Latinarum*.[10] There is thus no basis for claiming mutation *of* places in the gamut; what these passages refer to is mutation *in* unusual or irregular places.

CADENTIA

Misunderstandings of another kind have arisen from my use of the word "cadence." Cross picks up my words in the introduction to the Old Hall edition as betraying a "common but anachronistic and essentially mistaken assumption that it is a cadence . . . that requires chromatic alteration of a 'leading tone'" (1990: 188–89, 323). Although I had not then adequately spelled out the distinction, I never intended to imply cadence in the modern sense of closure; the apparent difference of opinion here lies in the use and understanding of the word. I agree with her that any alteration should be determined by the progression of intervals in counterpoint, and by counterpoint I mean the dyadic process that underlies composition in more than two parts. Some such progressions mark sense-breaks, some mark endings, some may effect a quick change of direction; others cause no discontinuity. Although closure usually requires such a progression, the progression need not imply closure. I intended "cadence" then, as I still do, to connote neither modern tonal definition nor necessarily closure but, simply and neutrally, the progression of an imperfect to a perfect interval, following the fourteenth-century definition of Jacobus of Liège, whose explanation is considerably longer than this excerpt:[11]

> Cadentia, quantum ad praesens spectat propositum, videtur dicere quendam ordinem vel naturalem inclinationem imperfectioris concordiae ad perfectiorem. Imperfectum enim ad perfectionem naturaliter videtur inclinari, sicut ad melius esse, et quod est debile per rem fortiorem et stabilem cupit sustentari. Cadentia igitur in consonantiis dicitur, cum imperfecta concordia perfectiorem concordiam sibi propinquam attingere nititur ut cadat in illam et illi iungatur . . .

> A cadence, insofar as it relates to the present argument, seems to mean a certain order or the natural inclination of a more imperfect concord to a more perfect one. For that which is imperfect is naturally inclined towards the perfect and to that which is better, just as weakness seeks the support of the strong. We therefore speak of "cadence" in consonances, when an imperfect concord strives to attain to the more perfect concord next to it, so that it may coincide with it and be joined to it.

Cadence, therefore, is no more and no less than the two-part progression of an imperfect to a perfect interval, articulated with a semitone progression above or below. I hope that these problems may be solved by adoption of the Latin word *cadentia*. I prefer it to Sarah Fuller's "directed progression," which seems to me even less neutral than cadence and certainly than *cadentia*; moreover, Fuller uses it for progressions of three or more parts, whereas I prefer to retain *cadentia* as a dyadic term that can nevertheless be extended to multi-voice progressions by superimposing dyadic pairs. It is true that "cadence" is not a common medieval term, but modern scholarship has adopted other terms on the basis of one or only few testimonies, and the word is also used in this sense in the late fifteenth century.[12] I see no reason not to use "*cadentia*," avoiding undesirable connotations of "cadence"; neither I nor Jacobus give it connotations of closure; it has a medieval definition by interval progression; and Jacobus uses "*cadat*" in a neutral sense, not necessarily implying descent. I agree with Cross that "sharps and flats in themselves do not function, as they do in later tonal music, as the determinants of focal pitches" (1990: 189).

OPERARE/ OPERARI

My usage "operating" *musica ficta* was once challenged as being a biassed modern term. It is, however, an early term, and one that seemed to me useful in avoiding modern formulations such as *adding* accidentals; it is documented in Chapter 1, p. 72 (see also Chapter 4, p. 127):

> Et ideo quando non possumus habere consonantias per rectam musicam tunc debemus recurrere ad fictam seu inusitatam et eam operari. (Seville treatise, f. 97)

> And therefore when we cannot have consonances by means of *musica recta*, we ought to resort to *ficta*, or the unusual, and apply that.

A similar passage is found in Nicolaus Capuanus: "necessaria propter bonam consonantiam inveniendam et malam evitandam. Et ideo cum non possumus habere consonantias per rectam musicam, tunc debemus recurrere ad fictam seu ad inusitatam et ea operare."[13] I am indebted to Giuliano Di Bacco for clarifying that La Fage's text is a conflation of two different fragmentary texts, and that it is by no means clear that this passage occurs in the portion that belongs with the attribution to Nicolaus. Scattolin considers it to be attributable to Filippotto da Caserta.[14]

VIRTUALITER

In 1972 (and 1969: 411-12) I translated "sed ipsa frequenter sunt in b fa ♭ mi virtualiter licet semper non signentur" (Chapter 1, p. 76; Berkeley treatise, Ellsworth 1984: 44–45, tract I.1) as: "But these are, legitimately, virtually never indicated in b fa ♭ mi [i.e., in practice you almost never find them marked in]." Although that published translation of this sentence was kindly approved by Urquhart, I now disclaim it as a youthful aberration and hasten to prefer that of Holford-Strevens, who places a comma after *virtualiter*, and points out that "virtually" cannot mean, as in modern English, a qualifier allowing that there may be a few exceptions, for which the Latin is *fere*. His translation is: "But they are often virtually [= effectively] present in b fa ♭ mi, even though they are not always written." This clearly supports unnotated convention, even though the writer confines it here to b fa ♭ mi, which is not *ficta* but *recta*.[15] Brothers turns the matter on its head by rejecting the idea of unwritten conventions *then* because they impede analysis *now*: "To assume that the music has been precisely and completely notated facilitates musical analysis. The view that the performer was required to complete the musical text by various conventions of performance practice easily undermines musical analysis." I have frequently invoked the role of aural attention, memory and rehearsal in achieving good contrapuntal results. ("What the singer hears happening around him may, in practice, be the strongest influence upon his own solution," as I say in Chapter I of this volume, pp. 80–81) and have further emphasised this as a contrapuntally specifiable influence (in "The Grammar"), one that works very well in practice, given a little familiarity with early notations. It should be clear (e.g., from Chapter 8 p. 242) that I am not one of those who have allegedly claimed for "successive" techniques any denigration of the mental and aural skills of medieval composers such as draws criticism from Leech-Wilkinson (1984: 9). But Brothers, in the same context as the preceding quotation, asserts that "rehearsal, adjustment, memorization" were "not a normal part of how polyphony was conceived and disseminated" (1997: 44 and n. 66), citing Urquhart: "to expect that Renaissance musicians extensively rehearsed . . . is simply unrealistic" (1993: 22). These surprising statements are the most recent in a long line of scholarship which expresses incredulity that our late-medieval colleagues were capable of using their own notated music; assumptions clearly differ.

Raising and lowering

In Grove VI, s.v. *Musica ficta*, I misleadingly stated "Nowhere . . . up to 1450 is there any direct admission that ♭ lowers or that ♮ raises a note."[16] In the essay that is now Chapter I of this volume, p. 74, I gave examples of two kinds of theoretical statement: on the one hand, direct admissions of raising and lowering, and on the other, circumlocutions that only indirectly admitted raising and lowering by describing affected notes only in terms of changes (tone to semitone, semitone to tone) to their surrounding melodic (linear) context. I over-interpreted *sustineri* as "suppress," here editorially corrected to "raise"; see the annotations to Chapter I. It should still be noted that the affected passage (formerly attributed to de Muris but now dated in the fifteenth century) belongs to the latter category, describing change in terms of melodic context, and is even more striking if the later date applies. I agree with Cross that "there can be no avoiding the fact ... that one pitch has been altered by an accidental and that it is higher or lower than it was in its unaltered state." The passages Cross and I cite from the Berkeley (= Paris) anonymous and those which she cites from Petrus Frater dictus Palma Ociosa and Johannes Boen do indeed express this change in terms of a "vertical" shift of pitch.[17] But it remains striking that many early theorists (including Lambertus and Prosdocimus) talk not of the raising or lowering of individual notes from a normal to an abnormal position, but emphasise the change of horizontal or *melodic* interval from a linear perspective, explaining the power of the signs to turn the approaching melodic semitone into a tone, or vice versa, of raising or lowering the (linear) melodic ascent or descent, without spelling out the obvious consequences for what later theorists (e.g., Aaron, and the few earlier ones mentioned above) would have called the removal of the note itself, the offending component of a simultaneous interval, from its "natural" place, to bring about this result. Cross indeed admits that some theorists (e.g., Anonymous XI) regard "the ineluctable fact of raising and lowering of individual pitches as misleading in their efforts to describe the transposition of whole hexachords," showing a "reluctance to identify the actual nature of the change of pitch" (p. 205). It is an important corollary of such careful circumlocutions with respect to pitch inflection that the "signs of *musica ficta*" do not *necessarily* raise and lower a note, which is why they are often explained in terms of local linear interval relationship. In the later revision of his treatise, Prosdocimus even adds "sometimes" (*quandoque*) to his statement that the signs show the feigning of syllables in places where they are not normally found (ed. Herlinger, 1984: 74–75). *Mi* or *fa* signs often occur on "natural" pitches, and in some rare but significant cases the *fa* or *mi* applies to the *other* note of the pair, the one that, in our terms, is not changed (for example, when g *fa* means f♯).

Role of the lowest voice

I stated: "To some extent an existing part, especially if it is a plainsong tenor, is regarded as fixed. . . .This means that where a chromatic inflection of the written pitch is demanded by the vertical relationship between the two parts, and where there is an equal choice between inflecting the top part, and inflecting the tenor or lowest voice, it is the upper, added part which should be modified" (see Chapter 1, p. 64). I would now put this less strongly (and without the term "chromatic"), especially since chant was not similarly privileged in other aspects of a polyphonic setting, such as text setting (see Chapter 10, p. 282). This statement might at the same time slightly favour semitone cadential approaches in the lowest part (*fa-mi* cadences), by operation of a weakened *recta* preference, but this is easily overruled if raised leading notes in the upper part (*mi-fa* cadences) are judged preferable in a given context. For purposes of strict counterpoint constructed over a given tenor, the tenor may indeed be treated as fixed, the added part adapted to it. But in practice, and in multi-voice polyphony, a plainsong-bearing part may sometimes not be the *contrapuntal* tenor: for an example, see Dunstaple, *Veni Sancte/ Veni creator*, Chapter 8, Ex. 2. I wrote: "The 'harmonic' bias of most theorists must be related to the purpose of the treatise: for it is in manuals of

counterpoint that *musica ficta* is usually given separate treatment, as part of the basic
training not of singers but of composers" (Chapter I, p. 65). I no longer accept this
distinction. Taking into account theorists' own statements about their intended audi-
ences, I now see counterpoint treatises as sources for the musical grammar and common training of both singers and composers; counterpoint was primarily sung, but
could also be made in the mind, or written, and any of these outlets may be explicitly
or implicitly the target of theorists' statements. Brothers (1997: p.27 n. 42) and
Urquhart (1993: 27–28) still subscribe to my older view of treatises as composer-
directed.

"Diatonic *ficta*"

Chapter 4 presented some extreme paradigmatic demonstrations of the fit between
conceptual underpinnings derived from theorists and the musical reality of those
particular cases. In countless other instances, a piece may be so composed that the
musical results differ little or not at all from those produced by the fixed basis advocated by Berger. If my hypotheses were formulated somewhat provocatively, they were
at least not *ad hominem*. I regret that Berger chose to adopt language framed to max-
imise dissent, especially since there is more common ground between my views and
his than one might guess from his criticisms. His book contains much that I admire,
much that tacitly endorses positions I had adopted in the articles he criticises. We
agree, for example, on according priority to vertical or simultaneous correction,
(Chapter I in this volume, and Berger 1987: 166–68), on recognising that the composer's intentions are incompletely notated, on the elementary role of solmisation,
and much else.

   I think it was Urquhart who once characterised "diatonic *ficta*" as a special technique; the apparent paradox of my title was intended, rather, to reflect my demonstration that most normal *ficta* is indeed arrived at by local, melodic progressions that
are not chromatic but diatonic, and that usages that may seem to us "special," like the
Willaert "duo," and the more musically convincing examples of Lowinsky's "secret
chromatic art," are indeed not chromatic at all in any sense understood in the fifteenth and sixteenth centuries (see Haar 1977, in this regard). Berger (1987) does not
explain what he means by "genuine chromaticism" (pp. 174, 188), but the contexts
lead one to suspect that it has slipped to a modern definition, then used to rebut my
very different claim (supported by several sixteenth-century theorists) that "diatonicism, in other words, is defined by the interval content of small melodic segments and
is not affected by transposition. The famous prologue to Lasso's *Sibylline Prophecies* contains only four truly chromatic progressions" (Chapter 4, p. 129).

Lucy Cross's generally excellent dissertation thoroughly investigates musical and theoretical aspects of pitch inflections, which she carefully avoids labelling *musica ficta*. She says however that my "Diatonic *Ficta*" (Chapter 4)

> perpetuates Lowinsky's tradition. These two widely accepted authorities make three assumptions with which I take issue: 1) that a sharp or flat can ever be intended systematically to transpose any more than a single hexachord, 2) that modal rules applicable to unmeasured music should apply also to polyphony . . . and 3) that points of imitation or canon at the fifth or fourth must always duplicate interval species as well as gesture. (Cross, p. 210 n. 1)

This is mistaken on several counts. Cross's three points have nothing to do with the process of interval correction by contrapuntal considerations that underlie both my suggestions and her own presumptions of composed-in intention, diagnosed from contrapuntal procedure. The question of transposition has been, in part, addressed above. Cross's question whether a notated accidental can ever imply the transposition of more than a single hexachord is consistent with her stance on hexachordal transposition. I would say that it sometimes can, she would say not. She and I agree that modal rules devised for unmeasured music are irrelevant to decisions about inflections in polyphony (see section 13 of Chapter 4, where I distance myself from "attempts to reconcile modal theories with musical realities," and from quests for so-called tonal coherence); I do not see how her statement derives from what I have written. Grocheio, in the late thirteenth century, denied that modes were relevant to polyphony; Salomonis related them only to secular monophony. The Berkeley (Paris) manuscript dated 1375 provides the earliest known statement relating modes to genres that are at least sometimes polyphonic—"motets, balades, rondeaux, virelais and the like."[18] But this testimony is far from explicit; the author mentions the principle of judging a mode from the final in the same terms that later theorists (from Tinctoris onwards) apply to tenor or monophonic parts only, giving no hint of how this can be applied to polyphony. This is a very thin branch from which to counter the weightier denials by Grocheio and others.[19] I agree entirely with Cross that "polyphony was not 'modal' in the fourteenth century" (p. 184).

As for imitation, it is Urquhart, not I, who sometimes privileges exactness of imitation over integrity of simultaneities. I wrote: "The case at no point depends on the maintenance of intervallically identical sequence laps, but rather on the independent determination, at each moment in the music, of how the priorities of vertical perfection and cadential subsemitones may be balanced" (Chapter 4, p. 142). Cross and I are again in agreement that context often prevents imitations from being exact.

As for Lowinsky: my premises are quite different from his; he and I disagreed fundamentally about the solutions and interpretations of several paradigmatic pieces, notably the Kyrie of Obrecht's *Missa Libenter Gloriabor* (Chapter 4, section II, and in private correspondence of 2 December 1982). Having failed to find a satisfactory music-theoretical basis for his often sound musical judgments, Lowinsky underpinned them with textual, theological, and symbolic justification. My reasoning is totally opposite to his even though we agree on the solutions for certain pieces; I support such interpretations in purely musical terms, and judge musical sense, in the first instance, independently of possibly anachronistic notions of poetic affect or symbolic word-painting.

Dahlhaus, relative pitch, and "abstract counterpoint"

Berger's premises are determined by a keyboard-based perspective on how pitch materials were construed, rejecting *a priori* the part of my hypothesis that sets out the inherently contextual character of vocal solmisation, rooted in earlier centuries. He misreports the difference between my position and that of Dahlhaus and charges me with "confusion" and "forgetting" aspects that I set out quite clearly (see annotations, and further clarifications in Chapter 6); even if he disagrees with my solutions, Berger has neither fundamentally addressed some of the real problems I raised nor proposed strong solutions to them.

Both Berger and, following him, Urquhart, have mistakenly characterised my view of pitch as an example of extreme relativism borrowed from Dahlhaus, who went so far as to suggest that composers were indifferent to the actual resulting sounds (1969: 15–16). Berger writes:

> It is this strong version of pitch relativism that constitutes the truly original contri-
> bution of the paper [Chapter 4 in this volume] and has to be identified as the essence
> of Bent's hypothesis. All other significantly new ideas presented in this paper (in
> particular its understanding of chromaticism which leads to its claiming diatonic sta-
> tus for Willaert's duo and for the so-called 'secret chromatic' repertoire; its view of
> the relationship between instrumental intabulations and their vocal models; and its
> conception of tonal coherence) depend on this hypothesis and stand or fall with it.
> (1987: 44)

Berger attacks my "radically relative" view of pitch as separate not only from an absolute pitch standard but also as potentially separate from a relatively established standard (1987: 161–67, 43–47, 167);[20] Urquhart charges me with adopting "the concept of an abstract counterpoint not fully specified as to pitch content by the composer" and believing that "composers did not write music with precise intervallic relations in mind"(1993: n. 2, 25–27).[21] I fail to see how my own statements, including specific repudiation of Dahlhaus's view, gave rise to this misunderstanding by both critics. Dahlhaus associated "abstract counterpoint" with "the invariable musical text preserving the identity of a work through various realizations," addressing the problems of conflicting principles for inflection and mutually irreconcilable theorists' rules by minimising compositional intent and leaving performers free to interpret the "abstract" counterpoint. I take a resolutely opposite view, namely that although the notation itself is underprescriptive, the intended pitches are largely determined by the composer through the operation of counterpoint, whose underprescriptive notation singers were trained to decode, just as abbreviated, unvowelled, or underpunctuated verbal text can be decoded by a fluent user of such texts.[22] On the contrary, Berger's rejection of Dahlhaus's distinction between "abstract counterpoint conceived in terms of interval classes and . . . harmonic counterpoint operating with concrete intervals" (1987: 166) endorses my own view (Chapter 4, footnotes 4, 21, and annotations). This was discussed above, under composer's and performers' choices, and under implicit accidentals.

Berger fails to address other parts of my argument, but disqualifies them *en bloc* by a premise that he has not correctly understood (see above). I offer no *view* of "tonal coherence," but rather would ask: Where in late-medieval polyphony is the evidence for such "coherence," in the sense taken as axiomatic, however ill defined, by modern analysts? Berger assumes uncritically that such a concept must have existed, and uses the assumption against me, but the burden of proof lies rather with those who assert its existence. My diatonic/chromatic definition stands independently of other strands of the hypothesis, as does the entirely subsidiary relationship between the conception of vocal works and their later intabulations; I reject the backwards imposition of that different set of constraints while fully recognising the intrinsic interest of intabulations. Berger writes that "she forgets that there is a difference between reading a part and understanding it" (p. 47). It is he, to the contrary, who forgets that my article started out by proposing to study "how what we call pitch was conceptualised in the fourteenth to sixteenth centuries." One has to understand in order to sing, and through singing one understands. Whereas I argue that late-medieval music is sufficiently conceived and notated without the need to name or notate all inflections, Berger reaffirms the conventional view that there was then (as now) a fixed repertory of pitches from which deviations are measured, but he is unable to accommodate certain telling "problem" pieces within this view.

Urquhart is not alone in objecting to the appearance in modern notation of some of my examples: "Bent is simply extending normal editorial practice to its logical limits, thereby demonstrating the illogical grounds on which it, and the theories of Dahlhaus, Harrán and Lowinsky are based: the correction of harmonies found unacceptable to the modern eye" (1993: 27). On the contrary, it is the modern *eye* that finds unacceptable what the *ear* may accept as logical and inevitable. "Neglect of some primary musical facts has led us to tolerate the aural dissonance of intolerable intervals before we accept the merely graphic dissonance of an intolerable-looking modern score" (see Chapter 4, end; see also Chapter 7).

Steps

Berger not only failed to distinguish my position from that of Dahlhaus; when he accuses me of "not keeping constantly in mind that G is not the full name of a step, but merely the name of a 'place' (*locus*) for a step" (1987: p. 45), he did not notice that the position to which he subscribes (that "the full name of a step consists not just of a letter, but of a letter combined with a syllable") is set out in the paper (see Chapter 4, section 3 in this volume). Berger identifies as a "second source of confusion . . . Bent's mixing up the singer's performance of the melody with his understanding of it, in her deriving conclusions concerning the singer's understanding of the music from his way of reading it" (p. 46). He says that "E-fa at the end is a very different pitch (different both as a step and as a frequency) from the E-mi or E-la at the beginning." Certainly it is different as a *frequency*, but this is where Berger's "step" becomes slippery. I used the word "step" to mean a movable point in the gamut or the staff, a movable rung of the ladder (*scala*), a letter that awaits hexachordal definition. The tone or semitone distances between steps (letters) implied by a clef, with or without signature, and providing a default interval set, could be adjusted by redefining those distances, by means of superimposing different (*ficta*) hexachords on the letters. Berger defined "step" as "a pitch defined not in absolute but in relative terms, relative, that is, to other steps of the gamut." For him, a step is immovable, apart from small tuning adjustments, not open to contrapuntally motivated adjustments of a semitone or more. In his construction, while the same or nearly the same frequency within a piece could express different "steps" (1987: 45), the reverse is not true. He separates in principle the terms *step*, *frequency*, and *pitch*, but in fact conflates them as the same modern concept, whereas I show at the beginning of Chapter 4 that many such pitch-words have no modern cognates.

　　If indeed identical "steps" could not, as he says, be expressed by different frequencies, how would he re-name the G*fa* that is two half-tones lower than the identical-*looking* G*fa* earlier in the Willaert "spiral"? There is no evidence that the notation of either would have signalled anything other than "G*fa*" to a reader of the time. Berger's early musician "would also think of the two G's as being two different steps" (p. 45), but that assertion is not built into his own relative definition of a step. If "the correct moment-to-moment operation of the solmization and mutation rules would automatically ensure that the last pitch would not only have a different frequency than the first, but that it would also be a different step" (p. 46), he does not explain how his definition of step accommodates this phenomenon. Indeed, the musician would certainly have recognised them as two different *sounds*, just as a notated *f* might be sometimes *f*♮, sometimes *f*♯, according to context but without differentiated notation. How would he deal in general with naming and labelling in pieces, besides the Willaert "duo," that indisputably weaken the letter-name connection, such as clefless compositions, and other incontrovertibly spiralling pieces like Greiter's *Fortuna* and Costeley's *Seigneur Dieu*? He writes: "the identity, definition and understanding of a step depended, in her view, solely on its relations with steps in its immediate vicinity and would not be affected even if its actual frequency changed (moving, for instance, a semitone or two lower) in the course of the performance of the work. . . . [wherein] the same step could be expressed by different frequencies" (p. 44). Now, this fixed definition of "step" within any one piece is indeed *his* construction, and corresponds directly to no medieval term or concept. It takes no account of the very common pre-Renaissance definitions of *musica ficta* and *coniuncta*, which, by local operation, make a semitone into a tone or vice versa; the availability of two movable positions for each letter-name (*mi* or *fa*), not three fixed ones (flat, natural and sharp) gives rise to ambiguities, at least for us. That mid-sixteenth-century composers were fully aware of the conflict of the old and new systems is signalled, for example, by Greiter's text for his *Fortuna: Passibus ambiguis*. It had long been the case that *mi* or *fa* signs on *g* or *a* could mean either *g*♯-*a* or *g*-*a*♭ (see Chapter I here, p. 75, and Memelsdorff 2000), sometimes even in the same piece, which clearly breaches Berger's more confined definition of "step."

Willaert's "duo," Obrecht's Kyrie *Libenter gloriabor*

The real issue here is that the duo is operating precisely that system, offering two, not three, positions for each note at any given point,[23] with consequences for progressive shifting by semitones. Berger agrees with me that "they had neither a graphic sign nor a name for the double flat" (p. 40), nor, I would say, could they *conceive* a double flat as such. This is so, irrespective of whether the perambulations of this tenor are classified as *recta* or *ficta*. I have presented an interpretation that is diametrically opposite to Lowinsky's view of the piece as a manifesto for equal temperament. Berger turns my argument upside down by saying that "if Bent's hypothesis were correct, Willaert's singers might be able to read his piece, but he himself would have no reason to write it." On the contrary, I think I have shown good reason for Willaert to have written it, as a late and incontrovertible demonstration (even if perhaps a satirical one) of the power of the late-medieval Pythagorean-tuned, gamut-based notational system. For Berger it represents "conquests . . . in order for the gamut . . . to reach its fullest state: non-redundant single flats on c and f and non-redundant single sharps on b and e; and double accidentals" (p. 43). That is to say, he presumes that the double flats are conceived as such (though they are neither named *nor* notated), but does not explain, if it was such a "conquest," why Willaert did not in fact devise a modern way of notating this conceit, or why neither he nor his commentators criticised the notational aspect if it seemed to them wrong. I on the other hand situate the procedure within a system where local operation produces a successive spiral of pitch that would have been just as perceptible to a good musician as a ritardando of tempo in later music, and just as acceptable (Chapter 4, p. 147).

The "duo" spirals inexorably because of the uniquely composed relationship between the two core voices. Remember that it was not only discussed by theorists from Spataro to Artusi (because of its tuning, not its notational implications), but first published alongside "normal" pieces in a printed anthology. Equally ineluctable are the aforementioned famous compositions by Costeley and Greiter, and a few others. Once such pieces are acknowledged to be operating within the late-medieval system and not outside it, there is no reason not to accept that the same notational conceit may also underlie the Obrecht Kyrie *Libenter gloriabor*, Brumel's *Noe noe*, Clemens's *Fremuit* and some thirty other pieces that invite a downward spiral of the kind Berger objects to. Lowinsky accepted the contrapuntal descent of the Greiter and Clemens compositions, but not of those by Obrecht and Brumel, on grounds that there was no textual justification in the latter for what he, from his viewpoint (and Berger's), saw as *departures* from a norm. Berger treats the Willaert as an exception, standing outside the operation of normal notation; and yet he gives very little indication as to how he thinks such pieces were conceived, referring his discussion to modern (transcribed, translated) notation. I treat the Willaert in particular and spiralling pieces in general as extreme manifestations of what could be accomplished *within* a conceptually different notational system, and whose compelling musical testimony corroborates that system. Berger does not tell us at what precise moment he thinks Willaert's tenor departs from a smooth diatonic spiral; there is no one point at which it can be defined as going, in our terms, "off the rails," either notationally or in sound. The "duo" was a principal provocation for my hypothesis, not the other way around; it is not merely "a crucial example in Bent's paper" but a phenomenon demanding an explanation. I try to account for it by offering a model; Berger does not.

"On Bent's account, we moderns notice, and perhaps are bothered by, the change of frequency between the beginning and end of the work. . . . For early musicians, she would claim, the change of frequency would be of no importance whatsoever, since their notion of pitch did not depend on such a standard" (p. 45). Wrong, again. We will be "bothered" by it only if we anachronistically apply a modern and absolute standard. Behind the first of these sentences lurks the assumption that *we will* be bothered; behind the second sentence lurk the further assumptions that *they should* have been bothered—in other words, if they *noticed* change it would necessarily bother them; and that migration or instability of pitch would necessarily—and unthinkably— render pitch unimportant. But it is only our recent extreme privileging of pitch that leads to such assertions. I have offered parallels with rhythm, where we accept and expect flexibility, rubato and ritardando without any sense that a sacred cow has been violated. *Of course* alert singers would have noticed changes of pitch exactly as they would notice fluctuations of tempo. *Of course* the alert singer *can* and could hear and keep track of where he is, though the system no more necessitated or facilitated this than their or our system does with respect to tempo flexibility. What I wrote was that "the singer no more *needs to keep track* of where he was in relation to the original frequency of G than he would need to keep in mind what the original value of a semibreve beat was at the beginning of a piece which has required him to apply a series of proportional relationships" (Chapter 4, p. 124; see annotations to pp. 124, 126). In other words, successive changes are locally defined and, like tempo changes, may not need to refer back to the beginning, which is quite a different claim from saying that musicians would not have noticed or cared about such change.

Josquin, *Ave Maria*

Chapter 6 is a closely related revisitation of Chapter 4; the two should now be read in conjunction for correctives to "Diatonic *Ficta*," particularly with respect to the Josquin example. Roger Wibberley graciously agreed to this publication of my part of our exchange. It was decided that it was not appropriate to include his contribution here: references are given in the bibliography. A major remaining difference of perspective that Wibberley identifies concerns "the perception of interval (and its status) between higher voices when supported from beneath, and the nature of the evidence (viewed alongside all the two-voice-only examples) that bears upon this: a difference that seems inexorably to have dictated diverging routes of exploration and argument" (private communication). The question of perception and of how we hear interval progressions has arisen in several discussions. I would answer that there is indeed a difference between supported and unsupported intervals, and ample theoretical tes-timony to document such cases. (For an example, see Tinctoris's documentation of the consonant status of the fourth in Book I of his Counterpoint treatise, a conso-nance that can nonetheless not be used as such in the basic contrapuntal relationship unless it has appropriate support from beneath; see Bent 2002b).

The rising sequence from Josquin's *Ave Maria* discussed in "Diatonic *Ficta*" is of a different kind from the downward spiralling terminal sequences represented by Obrecht's Kyrie. I am pleased that most recent performances seem at least to accept the multiple logic for a bass *bb* in bar 48 (see Chapter 6, ¶ 21) absent from many ear-lier editions and performances; this always did and does seem to me essential, what-ever one chooses to do about the consequences. I have nothing further to add to my discussion in Chapter 6, ¶¶ 19–22, except to say that, of the various possible compro-mise solutions for performance (as apart from Josquin's provocative one that he might have expected us to consider and reject), I would favour Urquhart's, sounding *b♮* in the treble, as in Ex. 1, measure 3.

Such false relations usually arise by lateral displacement from an underlying dyadic contrapuntal structure, or from the superimposition or overlapping of pro-gressions or cadences between different pairings of parts. I am not at all concerned to avoid false relations wherever they may arise on the musical surface, but they can often be accounted for by some such contrapuntal displacement or superimposition.[24]

Tuning

Jonathan Walker points out that what I say about shifting (Chapter 4, p. 117) refers not to the Pythagorean but to the syntonic comma.[25] The situation arises in the case of triadic sonorities that I believe may in practice have been tuned as just, not as Pythagorean thirds. He writes:

> Frequent (or even occasional) shifting by syntonic commas would not have arisen until pervasive triadic sonorities became the stylistic norm during the second half of the fifteenth century ["triadic *sonorities*," in order to avoid implying that triads had any theoretical status at this time]; before then, the pervasive movement from imperfect to perfect consonances in all parts meant that Pythagorean intonation was appropriate and easily intuited by singers, and the syntonic comma does not arise, of course, in Pythagorean intonation. While some non-cadential imperfect conso-nances, when held over longer durations, would indeed have invited just intonation, their infrequency meant that tuning conflicts leading to syntonic-comma shifting were most unlikely to arise.

EXAMPLE 1: Josquin, *Ave Maria*

Further, with reference to my mention of Prosdocimus and infinity, he writes:

> There is no direct evidence that Prosdocimus recognised any role for the syntonic
> comma in the music of his day; but since he would have been aware of contemporary
> schismatic monochord schemes (i.e., keyboard tunings, in this instance), it is plausi-
> ble to assume that he did. (The schismatic schemes attempted to accommodate a few
> justly tuned imperfect consonances within the customary arithmetic of Pythagorean
> tuning, by approximating just ratios, which require a factor of 5 in the numerator or
> denominator, with high-number ratios using only factors of 2 and 3.)

My "surely" should therefore be softened to "perhaps." Walker continues:

> Since Prosdocimus speaks of "diversi modi cantandi . . . quos scribere foret valde
> difficile et forte impossibile," he isn't able to give any examples, nor does he try to
> explain how this "infinity of sounds" arises. As no performance can avail itself of this
> infinity, he ought to be speaking of a potentiality rather than an actuality, and tuning
> would then seem to be the candidate; unfortunately, the context of the passage pro-
> vides nothing to support this conclusion, and much to render it unlikely. Perhaps his
> "infinity" is mere hyperbole. In any case, the set of possible ratios available within the
> arithmetic of Pythagorean tuning (i.e., ratios with prime factors of 2 and 3 only) is
> likewise infinite, so we are not forced to resort to just intonation in our struggle to
> interpret the passage.

My statement "And even if two monochords were tuned with true Pythagorean
ratios . . ." (p. 118) is incorrect, as Walker points out:

> There are no "different routes" through the "spiral" of fifths: one can only move
> sharpwards or flatwards from a given point. The notion of a "spiral" is unmotivated,
> since the ratios of Pythagorean tuning are endowed with a strict linear order (to use
> the mathematical term) under the relation "a fifth sharper than" or "a fifth flatter
> than," i.e. for diagrammatic purposes, only one dimension is needed, and there is
> no reason why this should not simply be a straight line. The ratios of just tuning,
> however, require a two-dimensional diagram, since there is no relation which will
> place them in such an order; this is because of the two prime factors in the ratios, 3
> and 5, as against the single prime factor, 3, of Pythagorean tuning (we leave aside the
> prime factor 2, since octaves are not our concern here). For diagrammatic purposes,
> we therefore require a lattice, with, say, powers of three increasing upwards along the
> vertical lines, and powers of 5 increasing rightwards along the horizontal lines. We

can indeed trace different routes through a lattice, but along a single line there is clearly only one path.

What I should have said here is (a) that "spiral" is preferred to "circle" since the Pythagorean comma prevents closure, and (b) that it is not the starting from a unison that could result in differences of tuning, but the introduction of non-Pythagorean thirds in triadic sonorities which, when they in turn become the basis for tuning Pythagorean fifths and octaves, will introduce different starting points for those Pygthagorean ratios that are not in unison with the original series.

Walker observes (of Chapter 4 note 9) that "successive sounds *can* be checked quite easily, by plucking the stopped length of string and then the full length. The late medieval interest in polychords, the retention of the name 'monochord' for these devices, and the eventual development of the clavichord would indicate that the trend was towards the more efficient comparison of successive and simultaneous sounds, whether for didactic or musical purposes. If a purely theoretical 'symbolic' monochord was ever desired, the drawing of a line diagram would have sufficed; no purpose would have been served by adding a base, bridges and a string if there was no desire to compare sounds." My point was that the monochord was never an instrument designed for practical up-to-speed accompanying, nor for the simultaneities of polyphony, and that it remained inherently and symbolically monophonic, despite later developments.

Walker points out that "A tuning system *is* a set of relationships." I intended to say that the relationships of the *recta* "scale" can be understood independently of any particular frequency-ratio interpretation, whereas a tuning system must be realised acoustically on a musical instrument, as I suggest in note 11: "it remains clear that, except for such purposes as monochord demonstration in principle, we are indeed dealing with the *recta* 'scale' as a set of relationships rather than as a pre-tuned system."

Aaron

Chapter 5 elaborates the Aaron material first presented briefly within Chapter 4, and anchors some of those ideas more closely in relevant theorists. While Chapters 1 and 4 were quite eclectic in drawing material from a wide chronological range, Chapter 5 considers Aaron alone, and attempts to read his examples, taken in their own musical contexts, in the light of his discussion.[26] I rashly intended it (in note 6) as a complement to a proposed edition and translation, a project I gladly release to others, as there is now no chance that I will undertake it in the near future. I stress that this chapter offers an interpretation, not an edition, designed as a companion to an edition yet to be made. For those without access to the facsimile of the *Toscanello*, a text and translation (complete with contexts drawn from the identified pieces) would greatly facilitate evaluation of my readings and of any divergent views.

I am greatly indebted to Peter Urquhart for setting out his disagreements with this article in a private communication of 29 June 1998. His fundamental charge is that I am interpreting Aaron according to premises with which he disagrees; this is indisputably true. I made no secret of my attempt to second-guess the reasons behind Aaron's statements in accordance with premises I have set out here and elsewhere, and which depend in part upon my close reading of Aaron himself. *Caveat lector*. One of the theses of this article is that Aaron was in some cases demonstrably, but not always, taking his own knowledge of the whole polyphonic texture into account, and that to supply that texture (in my examples) puts us in a better position to see what unstated reasons might lie behind some of his recommendations. I hope that the difference is clear throughout between actual quotations from Aaron (translated or not) and my interpretative comments.

My reading of Aaron's message comes partly from attempting also to observe what he does not say. The inferences that he is, for some but not all of the time, taking the full texture into account, arises from his statement that the singer could not anticipate some collisions. When I found that all cases in this category were simultaneous arrivals, not subject to aural anticipation by singers, it seemed to me that a pattern was forming, that Aaron had performing knowledge of these pieces, was using the partbooks to remind himself, and in order to give reference to his readers. I make no apology for offering interpretative readings in the case of theorists who assume much and tell less, or who tell us the things that we find less rather than more relevant to what we would like to know, or who appear to be internally inconsistent. Aaron may not be the ideal guide for this material; indeed, as Harold Powers (1992) has shown, he can be quite eccentric, not an informant about common assumptions but rather the proposer of an original approach to modal analysis. But he is what we have, the only one who gives a generous number of examples from actual and known music, and, as with the mode examples, invites attempts to come to grips with those specifics.[27] Some of his priorities dovetail neatly with, and therefore tend mutually to corroborate, those given by Tinctoris fifty years earlier.

It has often been alleged that Aaron was in favour of the notation of all accidentals. More precisely, notation was not always needed for accidentals signalling major thirds in final chords or for the correction of melodic tritones, even though Aaron praises composers who clear up ambiguities. Berger reports that Aaron (following Spataro) argued against those who believed that experienced musicians can be expected to recognise the composer's intention during the first reading of a piece. He goes on to say that these texts "should give a pause to those who would want to argue that the problem of implied accidentals has nothing to do with the composer's intentions and that the implied inflections were entirely the province of the performer" (1987: 171). By looking at the full musical contexts of each case he cites, one can perhaps see where Aaron may have been elliptical or even failed to state the obvious. I show how some of his examples may be tediously repetitive, or even unmusical in that they fail to take obvious errors or context into account, and that others may be much more revealing than has been suspected. Above all, although the text could be taken to imply that full notation is needed for simultaneities, Aaron's choice of examples for this category shows that he *did* sometimes know the whole texture, and that his examples are predominantly drawn from cases where the arrival is simultaneous and unexpected, cases where the performer could indeed *not* anticipate without "committing a little dissonance." For Aaron, the notation *should* be such as to permit experienced performers to divine the composer's intention in cases of uncertainty, which is not necessarily a call for full notation of accidentals. Aaron was evidently taking into account all the parts at least for the examples that deal with unexpected simultaneities, but not where he was collecting examples of linear tritones by eye, especially where he was caught out by misprints (notably Ex. 7b).

Guidelines for inflection—a preliminary attempt

Surprisingly few scholars have risked proposing general rules or guidelines for the application of unwritten inflections within a scheme that also takes account of notated accidentals. Even Edward Lowinsky's formulation in the preface to Canti B (Petrucci, 1967) was less specific than we might have hoped for from him, and he never came out with a clear prioritisation of the rules. Berger classified source accidentals in early vocal polyphony, but did not offer prioritised rules to bring his theoretical investigations within practical reach of the modern editor or performer. Urquhart sets aside "harmonic" rules, and Thomas Brothers adopts a literal approach to notated manuscript accidentals. What follows should be understood as an interim statement, not a definitive one, from the perspective presented here.

For most of the fourteenth and fifteenth centuries, theorists' guidance for inflection is simply stated within treatises on counterpoint, applied to dyadic pairs of voices. Earlier scholars who downplayed theoretical testimony *because* it dealt only with two-voice progressions missed the point that it is precisely those underlying progressions that are central, and whose correct inflection takes high priority. The primary rules are:

1) that notated unisons, fifths, and octaves, understood from the context to be those at points of arrival or resolution, are to be intervallically perfect; and

2) that such perfect intervals are to be correctly approached, with a semitone interval in one of the approaching parts (*fa-mi* or *mi-fa*).

Both rules are mutually encapsulated in the prohibition of *mi contra fa* in perfect intervals (see Chapters 1 and 3). Since a progression of two dyads involves a linear movement, the two rules could be said to embody both "harmonic" (i.e., contrapuntal, simultaneous) and melodic considerations.

A separate melodic rule, stated with differing degrees of force at different periods, forbids or discourages the melodic tritone. This is expressed most strongly in treatises on chant; in composed polyphony the rule quite often has to yield to the overriding concern: to maintain the perfection of simultaneous perfect intervals.

In practice, in multi-part music, these principles often come into conflict, and it is not possible to honour all of them, especially when the prohibition is extended to simultaneous or oblique cross or "false" relations between any pair of parts. Some writers have responded to this situation by abandoning any attempt to establish priorities.

· · ·

In Chapter 5 I ventured to set out prioritised rules, inferred from Aaron's *Toscanello*, both the standard contrapuntal rules given in *Toscanello* IV.xiv and their application to actual musical repertory in the *Aggiunta*:

- The melodic tritone should be adjusted to a perfect fourth by means of a b molle on the upper note, whether the interval ascends or descends, or proceeds stepwise or by leap.

- The tritone is to be avoided when the interval returns within itself and does not proceed to the fifth scale degree. But when the tritone does proceed to the fifth degree, it need not be softened because the semitone at the top may be cadential, a leading note, and in any case it will form one of several legitimate species of fifth.

- The melodic tritone may, however, be tolerated (especially if, as in Aaron's main example, mediated) in the interests of achieving a higher priority: perfection in a simultaneous fifth or octave takes precedence over the correction of a melodic tritone.

- The simultaneous sounding of a false consonance is to be avoided; this rule always takes precedence over melodic considerations. Except for some exam-

ples of melodic tritones, and the special cases related to recognition of cadential discant formulae, Aaron's examples overwhelmingly involve the bassus or
the lowest sounding part, and point to particular strength for this rule (a)
when intervals with the lowest voice are involved, often with reference to a fifth
or octave in another part sounding above it, and (b) when they fall on the first
beat of a unit (usually a breve unit). The rule in any case reinforces the proscription of *mi contra* fa in perfect intervals.

- Anticipation of a raised cadential leading note, the upper part of a sixth to
  octave progression, may eliminate the need for a b molle at the top of what
  would be a tritone outline. Having given examples of *b♭ a g f g* under the heading of tritone avoidance, he then allows *b♮ a g f♯ g* to eliminate the tritone if,
  and only if, the cadential intent of the phrase is established. (In such a phrase,
  b♭ a g f♯ g would only be used if two considerations, a perfect simultaneity with
  the *b♭* and a cadence on *g*, were present.) Thus *b♭* is preferred unless there is a
  cadential *f♯*.

- Leading notes are to be raised in, for example, major 6th-8ve progressions
  (but care should be taken with unusual or "deceptive" cadences). This is a
  reinforcement of the standard rule for cadential approaches.

- Thirds in chords at phrase ends should be major, and so indicated.

II. Compositional techniques, written and oral constraints: Chapters 7–11

Notational translation, textual status

In my position paper for a conference at Cremona in 1992 ("The Limits of
Notation in Defining the Musical Text"), I tried to come to terms with a particular problem central in the editing and textual criticism of early music, namely the
textual status of implicit but unwritten elements whose notation is not required
by the old and different notational system but is needed in modern transcriptions. That paper included material that receives a fuller and illustrated statement in Chapter 7. I therefore decided not to include it here; but the Cremona
version also carries a stronger emphasis on stemmatics,[28] which I will represent
here with two extended quotations:

> Most textual and stemmatic endeavours in medieval and renaissance polyphony have
> been directed through the process of transcribing it into some form of modern
> notation in aligned score format, towards establishing the best whole version or the
> best selection of individual readings. The text thus established is then treated as the
> point of departure for further editorial modification or intervention. . . . This
> approach sets up a hierarchy between, on the one hand, the prerogatives of written
> text, transferred into score, and on the other, of subsequent operations upon it by
> editor or performer that in some way change that primary written text. Editors feel ..
> a reluctance to make written "change." There is a tacit understanding that the
> received written text means more or less the same as its modern written transcription
> [i.e., translation]. (Bent 1995: 367)

> I . . . will talk about "original notation" as though a piece comes to us from a single
> viable source, though some form of stemmatic criticism is still fundamental to deal-
> ing with multiple sources, or with multiple versions superimposed in a single source.
> Whether access is from one or more sources, we shall not explore here the idea of the
> work as separable from the text that transmits it, though such a separation is implicit
> in this brief examination of the boundary between authorial intentions and notated
> text. (1995: 368)

I will here take up a question implied above, under "Implicit accidentals."
Can intended, implicit inflections be regarded as belonging to the *text* of the
work? Here, Berger, Cross, and I are in substantial agreement. Berger wrote:
"Most accidental inflections in music of our period, whether notated or implied,
do belong unambiguously to the domain of invariable musical text, but some
clearly do not and are a matter of variable performance" (1987: 168). I wrote:
"More of what is implicit but unwritten in early notation must be regarded as
belonging to prescribed and authorially intended text, especially with regard to
what we understand by editorial accidentals" (1995: 372). I said and meant,
"belonging to," not "the same as," though I should have made the distinction
clearer to avoid misunderstanding. Speaking in the same session, Joshua Rifkin
agreed that accidentals are implicit in the text, but not that they can be called
implicitly textual. Reinhard Strohm agreed with most substantive points in my
paper, but not with the nomenclature "text" for what he would call "work" (1995:
196 n. 9). I have no strong opinion as to whether we call such activity textually
implicit, or even something like hypertext. This problem inhabits a grey area of
translation between two different notational systems, and I would now phrase it

thus: more of what is implicit but unwritten in early notation *would* be regarded as necessarily textual *if* it were being notated according to the norms of modern notation. What we regard as unwritten, therefore not textual, was in some sense textual when the notated text was all that was required. Implicit and partially notated accidentals can be divided (not always neatly, given source variants and scribal accretions) into written and unwritten; but they may not differ from each other in kind with respect to authorial intention.

My Cremona paper and especially the present Chapter 7 were the object of criticism by Maria Caraci Vela (1995: 49-50):

> . . . nella consueta illusione che, di contro all'ipotesi sempre perfettibile della restituzione critica che passa necessariamente attraverso la fase interpretativa della trascrizione, il diretto impatto con un testimone concreto dia maggiori garanzie di lettura della realtà storica. In questa stessa linea è anche la moda diffusissima del cosiddetto "leggere dalle fonti," ossia direttamente dai testimoni antichi . . . [facsimiles]. Considerata da molti un vero uovo di Colombo o addirritura proposta come soluzione innovativa,* questa scelta è stata fatta propria da non pochi esecutori che pensano di possedere in tal modo una sicura garanzia per le loro 'filologiche' interpretazioni. Ma tale soluzione può proporre utili esercitazioni paleografiche e familiarizzare con i singoli testimoni antichi; non può avanzare la pretesa di un corretto approccio al testo, fondata com'è sulla grossolana confusione tra livello del singolo testimone e livello del testo, che in tal modo vengono assunti acriticamente come equivalenti.
>
> *A questa soluzione è approdata—abbandonato il piano del testo e concentrato l'interesse sulla musica come pura prassi—anche una studiosa come Margaret Bent, cui dobbiamo importanti contributi sulla musica inglese e continentale dei secoli XIII–XV. Si osservi il percorso che va da lavori di stemmatica pura come *Some Criteria* . . . al recente *Editing Early Music*, dove il problema del testo non esiste più, sostituito semplicemente da quello della corretta lettura paleografica del singolo testimone.
>
> Col "leggere dalle fonti," viceversa, l'esecutore, solitamente ritenuto incapace di accostare un'edizione critica, si trova improvvisamente proiettato all'estremo opposto, e investito di una fiducia senza limiti, perché al suo solo arbitrio sono lasciati da risolvere problemi delicatissimi e svariati.

The foregoing quotations from "The Limits," and Chapter 7 here, both attest that I still distinguish between text-critical activity and editorial function. I regard my statements as natural evolutions from my earlier article on the adaptation of stemmatic techniques for polyphonic music (Bent 1981). Caraci Vela and I seem to agree that an edition is a translation. But the "dilemma" of my title acknowledges a general assumption that we cannot subject polyphonic music to textual critcism without first making a written translation, even though Judd and Owens have recently presented further compelling evidence to support the practical reality that musicians can handle directly many aspects of notation in parts. Translation into a different notational system occurs merely by putting parts into score, by subjecting them to instant visual control by a single reader and by changing the contextual basis on which the pitches and rhythms of the original notation were read, into a system that is conceptually different, more fixed. Musicians of the late Middle Ages did not use scores for composition; compositional process and the way music is notated are in symbiotic relationship (see Chapter II, pp. 304–05). In verbal textual criticism, it is possible to make text-critical judgments in terms of the orthography and disposition of the original. With polyphonic music, such decisions have to be partly filtered through translation; scoring transforms the spacing and contextual nature of the original notation.

One thing Caraci Vela criticises strongly in the above passage is the practice of singing from facsimiles, which I have been doing for many years with students and colleagues on both sides of the Atlantic. She makes assumptions about what this implies for critical editing, so I should clarify what I do and do not claim for this exercise, what I think it can and cannot achieve.

1) First, the passages she cites reveal a simple misunderstanding. I have never proposed using, or singing from, a single source as a *substitute* for editing or for textual criticism. It should be clear from my own editions and publications on the subject that I am strongly committed to rigorous textual criticism, according to criteria adapted for the particular needs of particular repertories, and using all available evidence (see, here, Chapter 7 pp. 236-37). I regard reading from manuscripts as an additional skill to be acquired, equivalent to gaining competence in speaking a language of which one studies the literature.

2) There has in the past been some scepticism about even the possibility of reading from old notation, or indeed of dealing with repertories that have not been edited in score. Such reading *is* possible; our medieval colleagues could and did perform from their manuscripts, and from the kinds of manuscripts that have come down to us, and so can we. Although the notation may be under-prescriptive by our standards it was sufficiently informative for them to use, in conjunction and complement with the conventions they knew. The *Schriftbild* of any notation profoundly affects

how one reads and performs it. The original notation is the closest thing we have to the thought of the composer, if it is indeed his text we are trying to reconstruct. To use it as he intended it to be used, or as musicians of the time used it, can bring us even closer to those thought processes. To gain fluency, not only in reading an individual part but in the new kind of musicianship that it demands for coordination with others, enables one, when using modern editions, better to keep in mind the language behind the translation. It is also a way for a musicologist to introduce professional singers to aspects of the music, including *ficta* decisions; even slight exposure to the different musical demands of an underprescriptive notation is educative, and can only improve understanding when they return to performing the music from critical editions that may be excessively timid. Of course I deplore the idea that mere notational access has the status of an egg of Columbus; what I and others value are the understanding and insights that can result from acquiring this ability. Some things that can be explained in words or on paper only in a very cumbersome way, like bicycling or cooking, are more easily grasped in the doing. One rarely has to stop singing to debate *ficta*; the habit of adjusting by ear is quickly developed, on the basis of the counterpoint, to what the singer of another part is doing; then the performance can be gradually refined in subsequent readings. Because even "harmonic" problems are usually anticipated by suspensions or overlaps and are not attacked simultaneously, singers can anticipate aurally, and react accordingly. "Harmonic" problems that look difficult often solve themselves when approached aurally, just as errors can often also be diagnosed by ear and solved empirically.

3) Thus to create a "sounding score" is not itself a philological exercise, but the experience gained can inform philological choices and decisions, both directly and indirectly. It is one way of giving each witness literally a fair hearing, testing the integrity and coherence of the version of one manuscript, without the mediation of a translation into modern notation. To read a piece from a unique source may send one back to the published edition in a new critical spirit. But only a limited range of manuscripts is available in legible facsimiles or printouts; the source one would most like to test may be too incomplete or physically damaged to sing from. There is surely a place for giving one's full attention to each individual source, not only when it is unique. To base a performance or a performing edition on such a source, or on an independent and interesting version, may give a hearing to a different version of some interest whose readings have been rejected for purposes of a critical edition. But singing from original notation is not at all the same thing as, nor is it a substitute for, critical editing.

Solus tenor

This section refers to Chapters 8 and 9, both of which deal with the solus tenor. In 1987, Keith Mixter contributed a disappointing article on this term to the *Handwörterbuch der musikalischen Terminologie*. Apart from a simple duplication of his first paragraph, he lists only six compositions with solus tenor (out of the two dozen he mentions), and of those, two are not in any case solus tenors proper but examples of quite different phenomena (a solus contratenor and a tenor *ad longum*); his listing is less complete than that of the earlier articles by Shelley Davis. He writes:

> M. Bent (632) nimmt an, daß der Solus tenor keine Verschmelzung der unteren Stimmen, sondern eher eine ursprüngliche Kompositionsversion war, woraus zwei Stimmen gebildet wurden. Gegen diese Interpretation, die Bukofzer ablehnte (62), spricht der Umstand, daß der Solus tenor als selbständige Tenor-Stimme viel später auftritt (I-IV, nr 1, D-Mbs, nr 107 und F-Sm222, nr 3). D. Fallows Auffassung (111 [Dufay 1982]), daß der Solus tenor die Funktion einer Stimme zur Einstudierung hatte, kann aus demselben Grund fallengelassen werden. Vielmehr läßt sich die Theorie vertreten, daß die Reduzierung auf weniger Stimmen vorgenommen wurde, um ein ästhetisches Bedürfnis nach einem weniger dichten Gefüge zu befriedigen, und daß die Solus-tenor-Stimme daher eine umgekehrte Situation zu der Ausweitung einer dreistimmigen Struktur auf vier Stimmen (3<4) im späten 15. und frühen 16. Jh. durch die Bildung der 'si placet'—Stimme darstellt.

This misrepresents what I said. The solus tenor *is* of course, as I claimed, a conflation of two lower parts (not more), but one that may have been made purposefully, I claim, during the composition process and not after the whole composition had been completed. Leaving aside how Bukofzer in 1950 could have "rejected" my proposal of 1977, Bukofzer in the passage cited by Mixter opposes a generally correct view of the solus tenor (namely, that it contracts tenor and contratenor into a single part) to the anomalous and exceptional situation in the piece there under discussion (Old Hall, no. 28), where the intact chant is presented in the part labelled solus tenor, while the tenor and contratenor, as Collins correctly observed in this case, are indeed simply a broken-up version of that single line, contributing nothing else to it, and are emphatically not a dyadic contrapuntal foundation of the kind normally conflated into a solus tenor (see Bukofzer 1950: 62). Apart from this fundamental misunderstanding, Mixter fails to take into consideration my observation that solus tenor parts are limited to certain compositional types observing particular constraints, and he does not attempt to account for the cases where imperfect conflations challenge the received view. If indeed the solus tenor simply had the function of reducing texture, whether for practical need or aesthetic preference, why is it not matched by a general shrinking of textures from four to three parts (or indeed from five to four in English music) in the repertories for which solus tenor parts were used? Mixter asserts (with Bukofzer) that the solus tenor is a (*post facto*) replacement for a tenor and one or more contratenor parts in some twenty-four compositions between c.1320 and 1460, whose technical affinity he does not specify. He repeats the old view that the practice may have arisen out of need when there were too few singers or when a thinner texture was needed, or as a compositional technique for study purposes, but fails to give other more recent views a fair hearing, or to recognise the anomalies that prompted other hypotheses, including mine.

Cox wrote (1982: 424 n. 27): "While it has been assumed that the solus tenors . . . are reductions of the tenor and contratenor lines, it has been suggested that the opposite is sometimes true." He erroneously cites me for the view "that it is possible the tenor and contratenor can be constructed from the solus tenor." This could only be true in exceptional cases such as Old Hall, no. 28, discussed above.

J. Michael Allsen has kindly sent me a recent paper, as yet unpublished, on the tenor *ad longum*. He correctly reports my proposal "that solus tenors played a role in compositional process, allowing the composer to control the sonority of the lower voices in a single voice, a usage that does not preclude rehearsal or alternative counterpoint." Indeed, I specifically allowed for such use. Allsen rightly recognises what some critics have failed to register, namely that my hypothesis about the *origin* of contratenors in no way precludes their *subsequent use* as *Notbehelfe*, rehearsal aids, or scaffolding to facilitate further arrangements and new counterpoints, any of which, I take for granted, would be among the main reasons for continuing to copy them. An analogy: in a geometric diagram, the arc that had to be drawn to bisect a line or angle may remain visible after its main purpose has been accomplished, and its continuing presence may have positive value to aid further computation or additions to the diagram, as well as demonstrating how the bisection was accomplished. I wrote: "As a basis for further, probably unwritten, compositional growth of these compositions, the solus tenor may have provided a useful or even an essential aid. Given their availability, there is no reason why they should not have been copied for use in rehearsal and, if necessary, for alternative performance or 'Notbehelf.' Fifteenth-century solus tenor parts do in general show more signs [than 14th-century ones] of being intended for use in performance, but the same objections apply to performance being their 'raison d'être.'"

The various hypotheses need not be mutually exclusive alternatives, as some commentators have treated them; mine, rather, by addressing not only subsequent use but also origin, seeks to account for some things that the others do not, notably the occasional deviation of a solus tenor from the parts of which it is supposed to be a *post facto* conflation. Chapter 9 (on Pycard's double-canon Gloria, Old Hall, no. 27) proposes that such discrepancies between the solus tenor, on the one hand, and a conflation of the final versions of the tenor and contratenor, on the other, may be accounted for by the solus tenor being an earlier version of the lower canon, since the discrepancies recur at the five-breve distance of the canon. I have drawn attention to the motet *Inter densas/Imbribus*, [29] whose part marked *solus tenor* is rather, I believe, an *ad longum* part, a performance aid, even though it might have originated in a compositional sketch or as the key to a gnomic notation that, as the composer rightly anticipated, would have been hard to solve without it.

I used Dunstaple's four-part motet *Veni sancte spiritus* (Dunstable no. 32) as an example of a piece which might have had a solus tenor because of the essential nature of its contratenor part, but I was not strictly correct in stating (p. 251) that "no solus tenor survives" for it. Munich, Staatsbibliothek, Mus. MS 3224 preserves fragments from two consecutive openings, with the (untexted) contratenor for the end of the first section on the recto (p. 5) and on the following verso (p. 6) the end of the triplum, and two parts called respectively "solus tenor" and "Residuum tenoris ad longum." Unfortunately, this solus tenor is not a conflation of any kind; it is simply the true tenor of the motet notated in perfect modus and perfect tempus, and indeed cannot be used alone, as in this case the contratenor covers many otherwise exposed fourths. This either represents an eccentric or erroneous use of the word, or perhaps even—and this is the merest speculation—refers back to the presence of a true solus tenor in the scribe's source given that, by the criteria adopted, it could have had one.

My statement (p. 246) that "there are relatively few examples of counterpoint in more than two parts" now needs revision in the light of clearer subsequent formulations of the inherently dyadic nature of counterpoint; additions to that two-part structure are in principle cumulative and successive. The opening two paragraphs of the chapter address the simultaneous/successive issue in relation to absence of written scores; I later addressed these in other chapters.

Daniel Leech-Wilkinson (1989: 61–67) did me the courtesy of a thorough testing of the hypothesis that the solus tenor was a compositional aid, and gave it a generally benign reception, recognising its explanatory power for at least some instances. He likewise clearly understands that this hypothesis for the *origin* of solus tenor parts does not preclude their subsequent *use* for rehearsal, emergency performance, or later compositional activity, all of which I expressly included as reasons for their recopying in sophisticated manuscripts. Hence, features of solus tenor parts that cannot be explained as *post facto* conflations may be accounted for in one way, while their preservation for subsequent use may be a quite separate consideration. In other cases, he and I place a different interpretation on discrepancies between the solus tenor and a combination *basso seguente* made out of the lowest notes of the final versions of tenor and contratenor. I see these discrepancies as possibly reflecting an earlier stage in the composition process, while he sees such solus tenors as newly composed accompaniments to the top parts. He deals with three four-part motets for which solus tenors survive; two are by Vitry, and each has two different solus tenor parts. The interesting case of *Vos quid/Gratissima* apparently marks one of the two contratenors, both in Ivrea, to be discarded (*vacat iste*). He acknowledges that in some places this indeed goes better with the upper parts than does the final version of the tenor and contratenor, but concludes that the rejected solus tenor cannot represent an earlier compositional stage, since it assumes (1) disqualifying changes to the chant-bearing tenor, and (2) changes that fail to reflect identity between each of the isorhythmic taleas. But these objections do not take into account that tenor chant notes might be laterally displaced from their eventual positions, perhaps involving rests, leaving a (now different) contratenor note to be incorporated in the solus tenor conflation; and that such displacement, together with changes in contratenor pitches, might result in a different harmonisation of the tenor, because a different note would be at the bottom of the texture at a given moment. Such changes could mask a perfectly regular, but different, disposition of the notes within each talea without affecting the integrity of the chant tenor, though such dispositions are admittedly hard to second-guess. He does not explain why, according to his view that the solus tenor was composed to the upper voices rather than they to it, it should be this part that is marked for deletion. *Impudenter/Virtutibus* is the other Vitry motet with a solus tenor; this time the two different versions of the contratenor are in different manuscripts, only one of them included in Schrade's edition of the piece. Leech-Wilkinson admits that the solus tenor that deviates more strongly does so at the same place in each talea. His rejection of the possibility that this might represent an earlier version of the tenor-contratenor pair, in accordance with my hypothesis, again overlooks the possibility of lateral displacement, and depends mainly on a presumed rest in both lower voices (but how is that better explained by a later conflation?) and by its failure to take into account the 7/11-breve phrase construction of the tenor, without allowing that phrase construction might have been devised after the first contratenor conflation and before the second. He gives no further examples of "the many cases in which solus tenor anomalies cannot represent earlier states of the lower-voice pair." His only other discussion of a solus tenor motet, *Post missarum/Post misse* (Ivrea no. 11), concedes that its variant solus tenor could indeed represent an earlier compositional stage, and presents this as the explanation that best accounts for the differences. I hope that I have also demon-

strated for Pycard's Gloria, Old Hall no. 27, how an apparently deviant solus tenor
might indeed reflect such revision.

He treats as "more serious a problem" and one of the "weaker points" of my
hypothesis "the necessary inability of the composers to work extensively in four parts,
the apparent contradiction between such an inability and the requirements of the
procedure itself." I should say that when I wrote, "We can surely accept that a 15th-
century composer could handle a three-part song in his head. . . . However achieved,
in the head or in sound, with or without written assistance at each stage, a piece so
composed was both successive in conception and subject to simultaneous aural control of all parts," I had no intention of excluding *four-part* composition from what I
made clear for various levels of musicianship. Experienced composers could
undoubtedly handle four-part textures at least locally; I in no way dispute this, and I
no more placed such limits on their competence than would be argued for the need of
later composers to make sketches or drafts. For longer-range planning involving
complex structuring devices such as canon or proportioned repetition, a crutch of the
kind I suggest could have compensated for some of the visual support not available
from score, without in any way demeaning compositional ability, at least for purposes
of pedagogy. Indeed, I wrote that this "does not of course eliminate the possibility
that composers were able to take into account both parts of the lower duet while composing the upper part to fit it" (pp. 248–49). While Leech-Wilkinson recognised
that to claim compositional procedure as the primary origin of a solus tenor does not
disqualify its subsequent use for other purposes, he did not go on to acknowledge that
pedagogic procedures and theoretical underpinnings can be recognised in such a way
as to suggest that the composer took account of them in composing the piece, without
implying that they imposed any limits on his control of the whole texture. That would
be a better formulation for what I and others have perhaps stated less well in the past.
He ends by agreeing that I provide "a convincing explanation for the survival of solus
tenors in the sources and for their absence from pieces with a grammatically adequate
bass-line in the Tenor" (p. 67).

In a review, Lawrence Earp (1993) somewhat slants the argument to report that
"Leech-Wilkinson has found evidence in support of the view that the solus tenor
served as an aid to rehearsal for the performers of the upper voices, and not [there-
fore] as an aid to composition or as an alternative to four-voice performance. We
should remove the solus tenor from discussion of compositional procedure" (p.
304). This is not quite what Leech-Wilkinson said; Earp accepts too easily his argument from Vitry's motets *Vos quid/Gratissima* and *Impudenter/Virtutibus* whose solus tenor
parts, as I suggest here, can be interpreted in another way. Earp also fails to acknowledge, as I allowed for in my original article and as Leech-Wilkinson accepts, that a

compositional role for the solus tenor does not preclude later use for rehearsal, performance, and recomposition, which indeed would be the only reasons to recopy it. So long as new manifestations of the solus tenor continue to meet the criteria I set out in 1977, and so long as no alternative tenor parts turn up for pieces which by my criteria never needed them, we can assume at least that those who copied them into manuscripts were conscious of the compositional distinction between contratenor parts which are grammatically essential and those which are not.

In an abstract for a paper delivered to the American Musicological Society in Montréal in 1993, Stephen Self reported that I had "suggested instead that the solus tenor was a draft voice" but he subscribed to the common misconception that it was therefore "never intended for performance," which, as indicated above, I never claimed. The various uses, again, are not incompatible as his formulation suggests. He continues: "Since the . . . solus tenor line is often as sophisticated as its corresponding tenor-contratenor pair, it seems likely that some composers wrote the single voice as an alternative harmonic support for upper voices. . . . Moreover, the existence of manuscripts which do not include the tenor-contratenor correspondents supports the conclusion that some composers intended the solus tenor for performance as a viable textural option. Consequently, rather than the product of a redactor or a step in the composing process, the solus tenor voice can now be recognized as a legitimate development in the progress of compositional practice." He is of course perfectly correct in recognising, as I did, that in a very few cases tenor and contratenor seem to have been jettisoned in favour of a solus tenor alone. *O Philippe, Franci qui generis/O bone dux* survives with a solus tenor only, which does not strictly preserve the presumed isorhythm of the missing tenor and contratenor. *O Maria virgo davitica/O Maria, maris stella* is copied as a three-part piece in Bologna Q15 and Munich 3232a, with a solus tenor only, but this time isorhythm has been carefully preserved; its tenor and contratenor survive in the four-voice version in Padua 1106. *Rex Karole/Leticie pacis* is more complex, its problems being compounded by mislabelling of parts. There may well be many other solus tenor parts, not so labelled, which have escaped identification as such, languishing among the corpus of motets with unidentified tenors. We would have little way of knowing that they represented an original contratenor/tenor conflation unless the solus tenor part embodied some but not all notes of a chant or of an otherwise known tenor, or unless the conflation were recognisable in some other way, as embodying notes of a canon, as in the case of *O amicus/Precursoris* and *Blijfs mi doch bi, gheselle goet* (see below).

O Maria virgo davitica/O Maria is exceptional in that isorhythm is preserved; the tenor has not been identified, but if it *is* chant, the integrity of that chant is forfeited. Most solus tenor parts do indeed show "barbarous disregard for such features—isorhythm, canon, notational nicety, plainsong integrity," as in the Pycard Gloria, Old Hall no. 27 discussed in Chapter 9 and the other canonic pieces mentioned below. There is no evidence that such choices were made by composers rather than scribes. When Self suggests that such decisions played a role in compositional practice, he means not in the creation of the composition in the first place but rather in the influence on subsequent composition of pieces so presented; this is undoubtedly true, as it is for the afterlife of compositions affected by the removal and addition of contratenor parts. But he, like Earp, wrongly imputes to me the view of origins stated above to the exclusion of other possibilities. To the contrary, I wrote, "I am not going to dispute that the solus tenor parts may have been used in this way [i.e. for emergency performance], or for rehearsal, or for alternative performance, but there are several objections to this as having been their primary purpose" (p. 247). None of these considerations prevents my original hypothesis from standing alongside these other uses, as I am still persuaded was the case.

At the time of writing my 1977 paper I had little to add to the list published by Shelley Davis in his original article and its supplement (Davis 1967, 1968). NL-Leiden BPL 2515 has on f. II–IIv a copy of the Credo by Sortes with solus tenor. This Credo *de rege*, without solus tenor, is also known from Ivrea no. 60 ff. 47v–48.[30]

Discoveries since then of pieces with solus tenor parts include those listed below. All of them are consonant with my observation made then, that they are provided for pieces with *essential contratenor*, where newly composed upper parts would have to take account not only of the tenor but also of the contratenor, and where omission of the contratenor would result in unacceptable fourths at the bottom of the texture.

1) and 2) Two unique pieces in the Yoxford manuscript, a Credo in void notation (Bent 1990a) and the motet *O amicus/Precursor* in black notation (Bent 1990b), both with solus tenor parts. Both are isorhythmic, the latter also canonic. The two bifolia do not necessarily come from the same original manuscript. Their script, notation, and possible date seem to differ, but the chance of their preservation in the same binding might favour the possibility that despite these differences they originated in the same collection. There has been some confusion about the location of the Yoxford manuscript; some photographs bear an attribution to Keble College, Oxford, where it was on deposit at one time. The manuscript is now at Ipswich, Suffolk Record Office, HA30: 50/22/13.15, ff. i–ii, 159, 162.[31]

3) A motet discovered by Wulf Arlt and Martin Steinmann in Basel (Universitätsbibliothek, Fragments I and II), *Gaudeat et exultet/Papam querentes*, celebrating

the election of the Avignon Pope Clement VII and condemning his rival Urban VI.[32]

4) Oxford, All Souls College, MS 56, which contains binding strips that are partly concealed, very hard to read and almost impossible to photograph. One of the motets preserved (in company with the widely disseminated *Apollinis eclip-satur/Zodiacum signis*) is an anonymous motet apparently on Saint Bernard, with a part labelled "solus tenor."[33]

5) Rob C. Wegman's discovery in Amsterdam, Universiteitsbibliotheek, MS ES 64, f. 1, of the incompletely preserved canonic song *Blijfs mi doch bi, gheselle goet*, provided with a solus tenor. [34] The canonic procedure, based on what could be read of the canon, seems to involve proportional changes resulting in a tenor-contratenor duo of which the solus tenor is apparently a reduction. Other canonic pieces with solus tenor include Pycard's Gloria, Old Hall no. 27 (see Chapter 9), and *O amicus/Precursor* (see above), the last of which involves mensural transformation between the conflated parts.

6) Two incomplete motets in Wolfenbüttel, Herzog-August-Bibliothek, MS 499 (W3), f. 1 (duplum ends 'solis vel syderis cum beatis ceteris coram salvatore') and f. 2 (part of the lower voices of an unnamed motet). See RISM B IV 1, pp. 205–206 and, most recently, Isobel Woods Preece, appendix 1, "W3: Some Fragments of Fourteenth-Century Scottish Polyphony," in Isobel Woods Preece 2000. The author notes discrepancies between the three- and four-part versions of these fragmentary pieces.

Indeed, it was the *departures* from conflation that required an explanation other than *post facto* reduction and provoked my hypothesis. That hypothesis is neither ideal nor complete, but it does account for some things that *post facto* derivation does not; the solus tenor originating in the composition process is just as available to meet subsequent needs in rehearsal and reduced performance as it would be if it had been written afterwards. Those still resistant to a hypothesis about the origins of the solus tenor in compositional technique, after taking into account that other subsequent uses are not incompatible with it and were never excluded, have yet to explain those passages in which the original upper part of the conflated pair clashes with the top parts. As a sole explanation, *post facto* composition for such use offers no better rationale for deviations and alterations from a straightforward lower-voice conflation than my hypothesis; indeed, it is a rather worse one.

I have claimed that late-medieval mensural notation is poorly suited to use in score by a single reader because of the contextual reading it demands of each singer, notwithstanding Ann Besser Scott's attempt to demonstrate that the Old Hall discant settings were so intended (Scott 1970). See also, here, Chapter 11, and Chapter 10 for supporting evidence from texting practices. I also claim that score reading by one person invites notational adaptation towards unit specification of pitch and rhythm for each note, and shuns the contextual determination that is fundamental to mensural notation. The very nature of the changes that were made for keyboard tablatures emphasises the unsuitability of contextual notation for use in aligned score, whether by reader or composer. I have in mind, for example, the notation of lower parts in German organ tablatures, notably the Buxheim organ book (see Chapter 7).

A solus tenor could have been used as the basis for further work on the composition, much as one might keep an architect's blueprints that, although modified in execution, could still serve as a basis for future adaptations. It could certainly have been used for rehearsal, though I would not put that as a primary reason for its preservation. Whatever the reasons for the creation and preservation of solus tenor parts, it remains true that they exist only for pieces that form a distinct compositional category characterised by an essential contratenor and multiple technical constraints. All pieces with a solus tenor have an essential contratenor, but the converse is not true.

Although it deals directly neither with *ficta* nor counterpoint, my essay on text setting (Chapter 10) is included here because it addresses related issues of notated conventions, and the notator's expectations of performers; also partly because the new typesetting used for this volume offers a considerable improvement over the dot matrix printing and limited accessibility of its original publication.

Resfacta and cantare super librum

Some objections have been raised to the interpretation of *resfacta* and *cantare super librum* presented in Chapter 11, principally concerning my challenge to the written-versus-improvised polarity that has attached to Tinctoris's distinction between these terms. I showed that his several definitions of counterpoint and composition, of music mentally conceived, written, and sung, do not correlate consistently (even if those of the later Counterpoint treatise are considered, where different, to supersede those of the earlier Dictionary: cf. Sachs 1983: 182). For Tinctoris, *resfacta* (= composition) is not the same as written counterpoint, though the two were commonly confused (*communiter, vulgariter*). I believe he uses "counterpoint" to mean a successive procedure underlying composition, not composition itself, and that sung counterpoint is the same as singing *super librum*. Written counterpoint cannot correlate with any normal sense of improvisation; writing does not turn counterpoint into composition, but nor is writing the exclusive property of *resfacta*. I proposed to resolve these apparent conflicts by placing unwritten and written activity on a continuum that intersects at certain points with a different spectrum that links the distinct but related entities of counterpoint and composition.

The model of a continuum is encouraged by

a) Tinctoris's description of *resfacta* as characterised by mutually controlled relationships between all the parts, and of counterpoint as laudable when it aspires towards these conditions. Counterpoint can surpass the minimum requirements of relating each part cumulatively to the tenor by relating other parts of the texture to each other and not only to the tenor (explained in terms such as "in the manner of composers");

b) Tinctoris's own written examples, and their accompanying explanations, labels, and part-names, which align the noun "counterpoint" with the verbal phrase *cantare super librum*, and *resfacta* with composition. As well as including writing in the definition of counterpoint "which differs from *resfacta*," he presents written examples of counterpoints that adapt to each other as in mutually adjusted composition, and, conversely, examples of *resfacta* where such mutual adaptation is carried through no more completely than in some of the counterpoint examples. The results of the two processes overlap, as does their written/unwritten status, despite the distinction in principle;

c) recent scholarship, in both Western and non-Western musics, that increasingly blurs sharp dividing lines between composition, performance and improvisation, placing these activities on just the same kind of continuum of practices, linked by common rules and assumptions, by which I sought to resolve the apparent contradictions in Tinctoris's definitions. Few would now assume, for any repertory, that "unwritten" could be simply equated with the traditional view of improvisation as an unprepared or undisciplined process.

Klaus-Jürgen Sachs dismissed the anomaly between Tinctoris's definitions by (surprisingly) accepting an equation of *resfacta* with written counterpoint. He rejected my proposal that Tinctoris was distancing himself from a "common" confusion (Sachs 1983: 182). But Tinctoris did not make counterpoint synonymous with composition, even if the similar-sounding results of each could be distinguished, if at all, only by experts (not "commonly") and only as a matter of degree—hence my continuum, which allows us to maintain Tinctoris's distinction between these different processes.

Bonnie Blackburn has expressed strong disagreement with me: "I believe that by removing a distinction between unwritten and written music and denying the improvisatory nature of singing *super librum*, Margaret Bent succeeds in obscuring rather than clarifying Tinctoris's thought" (1987: 250, referring to the article that in this volume is Chapter II, see pp. 314–15).

Although we differ on several issues of interpretation, more points of accord can be signalled than this formulation suggests. Blackburn agreed with me, against Sachs, that Tinctoris was indeed distancing himself from a common confusion that equated *resfacta* with written counterpoint (pp. 250, 255, 260).[35] She partly addressed the anomaly in Tinctoris's definitions by making a less complete alignment between counterpoint and what is sung (improvised) *super librum* ("Singing *super librum* is a form of counterpoint," p. 255), although acknowledging my observations about Tinctoris's terminology and labelling (in her footnotes 86 and 88). She states that "counterpoint . . . is successive composition" (p. 252), although Tinctoris nowhere equates counterpoint with any kind of composition; and she extends the definition of improvisation to encompass precisely the kind of rehearsal and the role of memory (p. 258) that I proposed and that led me to avoid using the word. Such internal inconsistencies merely move Ferand's anomaly to a different place in Tinctoris, and further confound attempts to make a sharp written/unwritten distinction between these categories, without resolving the conundrum that prompted my enquiry in the first place. In private communication Blackburn now acknowledges a closer equation between singing *super librum* and counterpoint, and no longer equates counterpoint with composition but rather with a successive process; this brings our positions closer together in those particular respects, and I appreciate these clarifications.

I believe that our differences on improvisation can be largely reduced to questions of terminology and definition. Bruno Nettl (1974) argued in a world context that the opposition of composition versus improvisation was unsustainable, and that these concepts denoted, rather, extremes along a continuum. He set out to "demolish the idea of improvisation as a concept separate from composition," but partly reinstated it for purposes of performerly freedom in relation to a model. These models can be as diverse as Indian raga and tala, the blues sequence of chords or the naming of tunes in jazz, the realisation of figured bass, according to whether they depend on pitch, modal, harmonic, or rhythmic models within a particular style and genre. Since all performance involves the realisation of a model of some kind, Nettl concludes that the concept of improvisation is unnecessary in the general sense frequently invoked, reserving it for aspects of a composition where a musician is free to contribute "materials of his own spontaneous making," but that such opportunities vary in inverse proportion to the density of the model. Certainly one factor that would reduce the scope for improvisation in this sense would be ensemble constraints, which are precisely what apply in the case in hand. Nettl writes: "All performers improvise to some extent. What the pianist playing Bach and Beethoven does with his models—the scores and the accumulated tradition of performance practice—is only in degree, not in nature, different from what the Indian playing an alap in rag Yaman and the Persian singing the Dastgah of Shur do with theirs" (p. 19). His question "whether all the things that we now call improvisation are indeed the same thing" leads him to conclude that it is meaningless to consider improvisation as a single phenomenon separate from composed music, but rather that it is a procedure that relates differently to a wide range of models or composed music in diverse musical cultures. The emphasis often placed by ethnomusicologists on the continuum between precomposition and improvisation, in terms of reconstruction rather than of replication, has clear application to fifteenth-century techniques insofar as they are accessible to us through explanations by Tinctoris and others. Mental precomposition may be subject to even stricter disciplines than written composition.

Carl Dahlhaus (1979) likewise placed composition and improvisation on a continuum, as points that can be distinguished but not absolutely separated. He emphasised that all musical interpretation involves improvisatory activity, and that what is commonly called "improvisation," far from being random or arbitrary, depends on models, formulae, or *Gerüsttechnik*. He questioned the association of spontaneity with notions of originality and novelty. His privileging of pitch over other musical parameters as the essence of musical identity can be challenged for much music outside the post-renaissance Western canon; such an assumption has made it unnecessarily hard for some modern commentators to accept notational differences or "shortcomings" in early music.

Older definitions of "improvisation" tended to emphasise spontaneous, unpremeditated music-making. One such was given by Willi Apel under "Improvisation, extemporization," in the old *Harvard Dictionary of Music* (1944): "The art of performing music spontaneously without the aid of manuscript, sketches, or memory." This has become, in the *New Harvard Dictionary* (ed. Don Randel, 1986), "The creation of music in the course of performance." If the one definition had too few constraints, the other is insufficiently distinguished from performance in general. All performance necessarily involves negotiation in real time between composers and performers, performers and listeners; all music might be said to have a greater or lesser component of improvisation, depending on where and how the boundaries are positioned, and in whatever combination of written scores and unwritten conventions. Nettl (1974) identified a further distinction: that Ferand (in *MGG*) treated unnotated musics (mostly non-Western) as improvised, while others (including an unsigned article in Riemann's *Musiklexikon*) "confine the idea of improvisation only to music for which there is basically a notation system from which the improviser departs."

The problem lies in how improvisation is defined for any particular repertory, and even whether it is a useful or separate concept at all. The model proposed by Nettl and Dahlhaus should supersede these older definitions, but at the time I wrote my article it had not yet percolated through to the current debate. First, it is certainly not necessary to translate *mente* as "improvised" in the sense understood by Ferand, Sachs, and many earlier scholars. Tinctoris's statements about mental construction need no recourse to connotations of suddenness, to the lack of disciplined preparation, or the need for concessions, things that are hard to reconcile with his strict regulations for sung counterpoint (Chapter 11, p. 306). Second, if the term "improvisation" is admitted, it should be clearly distanced from the tenacious older view which assigns it a high component of chance, such as Ferand attached to unwritten singing *super librum*, a view shared by Sachs: "the inevitable lack of strictness in improvisation is a concession, not the aim of counterpoint" (*New Grove*, 1980, Sachs, s.v. Counterpoint, vol. 4, p. 838). But as Sachs admits, Tinctoris nowhere makes such concessions, nowhere implies any relaxation of contrapuntal discipline in unwritten practice, but rather the reverse. It is only some modern presumptions about unwritten practice that impose a notion of free improvisation; the notion is absent from Tinctoris, and I endeavoured to remove it from modern definitions: "Assumptions about the nature of early improvisation will need to be re-examined" (Chapter 11, p. 315). Sachs misreads me in suggesting that I propose "a practice of a totally different kind" (p. 183). He rejects my distinctions in favour of maintaining the old composition-improvisation polarity, but it is undisciplined improvisation that in fact would constitute such a "totally different" practice, not documented by or before Tinctoris except as the subject of passing and disapproving reference. I return to Tinctoris's own distinctions, try to make sense of the apparent conflicts, and remove the anachronistic concept that has been imposed on his words. Since then, Blackburn (1987: 250), and Wegman (1996: 431, 442ff), have retained the term "improvisation," but with a more qualified understanding than was applied in the earlier literature. I remain reluctant to introduce a word for which there is no need and which has no licence from Tinctoris, and which may still be open to misunderstanding as an unprepared process, as Blackburn herself shows by opposing, or perhaps simply misconstruing, my attempt to characterise the kind of preparation implied by Tinctoris (p. 256 n. 85), and by inferring from Tinctoris's discussion of the advisability of preparation "that there are some who think singing *super librum* should be completely spontaneous, a kind of musical brinks-manship and absolute improvisation" (p. 256). Wegman endorses my argument: "On the one hand, improvisation, if it was to lead to contrapuntally acceptable results, would necessarily have required such coordination and prior planning as we would associate with the compositional process. A written composition, on the other hand, presupposed such independent initiative and responsibility on the part of singers as we would associate with improvisation" (442–43). He continues: "'Impro-visation' would indeed be an inappropriate term if, as Bent suggested, it 'includes the notion of spontaneous, unpremeditated music-making'" (p. 443). In an associated footnote, he adduces the support of another ethnomusicologist (Bernard Lortat-Jacob) for the dependence of all "improvisation" on models, a view similar to the one cited above from Nettl. In other words, improvisation has had spontaneous connota-tions in older scholarship, but we should remove them from the present issue, what-ever we choose to call the process. Wegman's wide-ranging study sets the relationship between sung counterpoint, composition, and improvisation in a historical and cul-tural context that makes further discussion of that aspect here superfluous.

As to the charge that I have introduced confusion with respect to writing: nei-ther Blackburn nor Sachs accepts my proposal (made on the grounds summarised above) of a continuum between unwritten and written music as different points along a spectrum based on the same principles—in this case the shared language and rules of late-medieval dyadic counterpoint. This is not at all to *remove* a distinction between written and unwritten music, which of course I uphold; the different pro-cedures may however not always result in aurally detectable difference. In that sense, Wegman—I think rightly—considers a distinction between writing and absence of writing "trivial" (p. 444). I place *mente* and *scripto* as points on a spectrum that are neither contrastive nor mutually exclusive, as allowed both by the conjunction *vel* and by common sense: [C]ounterpoint must be carefully thought out; this is not inconsistent with *mente*, a word which cannot be opposed to "written" in such a way as to suggest that lack of forethought is more excusable in unwritten than in written presentation (Chapter II, p. 304).

The same counterpoint can be made in the mind, written, or indeed sung. Tinc-toris not only distinguished written counterpoint from mental (*scripto vel mente*); coun-terpoint subject to the same rules, with the same sounding results, could be mentally conceived and *then* written down. Tinctoris, however, commends those singers who go beyond such minimum requirements for successively constructed counterpoints and strive towards mutually controlled relationships between all parts in a texture, avoid-ing "similarity between each other in the choice and ordering of concords"; in so doing, they would approach the conditions that distinguish composition (*resfacta*) from counterpoint (Chapter II, pp. 304, 306; Blackburn 1987: 252). The more a well-controlled multivoice counterpoint, "sung on the book" by experienced singers, aspires to the mutual relationships between each and all parts that characterise *resfacta*, the less easily might the two be distinguished—whether by the analyst, or indeed by a listener who could not tell if what was being sung, apparently from a book, was written, composed, or improvised: "The difference between *remfactam cantare* and *super remfactam cantare*—singing the music from the book or singing upon the music—might have been imperceptible and insignificant" (Chapter II, p. 315). It is Blackburn who insists that "*res facta* can only be made in writing because the parts have to be 'put together'" (p. 266). "Putting," and mutual adjusting, can be done in the mind and with the voice as well as with the pen. *Resfacta*, composition, could indeed be written and undoubtedly usually was. But Tinctoris did not make writing the defining feature of *resfacta*, as do Blackburn and Sachs, nor is writing its unique preserve, since according to Tinctoris counterpoint can also be written; I am reluctant thus to limit his view of what could be accomplished mentally. Blackburn and I agree (against Sachs) that Tinctoris was addressing a common misperception about written counterpoint. To suggest that both unwritten *and* written processes may play a part in both counterpoint *and* composition is fully in accordance with a literal reading of Tinctoris's words, such as Blackburn herself champions (p. 252). This was how I formulated the matter:

> Our heavy dependence on writing as a means of preserving and transmitting music, serving us as a substitute for both memory and aural control, should not blind us to the possibility of music fully or sufficiently conceived but nevertheless unwritten. This possibility would hold no surprise for musicologists working in earlier or in geographically more remote fields. To remove the presumption of improvisation from this passage in Tinctoris is to present unwritten and written composition or counterpoint as stages in a continuous line of endeavor, based on the same training, rather than as the separate elements implied by our written-versus-improvised antithesis. Tinctoris's *aut scripto aut mente* then emerges as an expression of the possible ways, neither opposed nor mutually exclusive, of preserving music from one performance to another, performance being the end product, the sounding goal, of music, however transmitted. Vocal performance is necessary for counterpoint to happen, either as the realization of what has been written, or as the creation of that which bypasses written storage. Writing is necessary only if transient sounds are to be permanently recorded. (Chapter II, pp. 305–06)

However, while Blackburn agrees that counterpoint can be accomplished in writing or in the mind, and that it is distinct from *resfacta* (p. 252), she elsewhere doubts

that what is sung *super librum* was written (pp. 256, 258), making an exception of Tinctoris's written example(s),[36] but rather equates *mente* with improvised counterpoint.
Yet it remains incontestable that counterpoint, for Tinctoris, could be written, mental, or sung, and that what results from singing *super librum* could have been prepared in
writing or in the mind, or written down later; I think that counterpoint and singing
super librum are synonymous as, now, does she.

She attributes the "confusion over *res facta*" to a failure "to realize that when Tinctoris uses the word *contrapunctus* he does not mean what "counterpoint" signifies to us
today, "the combination into a single musical fabric of lines or parts which have distinctive melodic significance" (Apel's definition, quoted on her p. 251). Blackburn
and I evidently agree in rejecting definitions of counterpoint that depend on combinations of lines, such as that of Sachs: "the combination of simultaneously sounding
musical lines according to a system of rules" (*New Grove* 1980, p. 833). Crocker (1962)
and I are among those who had long recognised that such definitions did not apply to
late-medieval counterpoint; nor did the later usage of Gafurius, who applies the term
to multi-part music, and from whose usage Blackburn also distinguishes Tinctoris.
Our respective interpretations of Tinctoris's view of counterpoint account for our
different theses. I believe that the primary meaning for him is the "moderated and
rational sounding together" of the Counterpoint treatise (see Chapter II, p. 304),
resulting from a two-part combination, a dyadic process constructed over a given
tenor; and that an ancillary meaning is the resulting melody, the "contrapunctus"
added to a tenor (and so labelled in his examples), that results from that process. I
stress the primacy of the dyadic interval successions by which that added melody is
achieved, placing Tinctoris in a direct line of development with other late-medieval
counterpoint teaching. Blackburn treats the resulting *melody* added to a given tenor as
Tinctoris's primary meaning of counterpoint; she decides to render *cantus* as
"melody" in the *Diffinitorium* definition (defended on p. 251 n. 66), making "contrapunctus" in this case refer only to the added part rather than the process or the resulting two-part texture. She translates: "Contrapunctus est cantus per positionem unius
vocis contra aliam punctuatim effectus" as "Counterpoint is a melody brought about
through the placing of one sound punctually against another"). Elsewhere, she translates *cantus* as "composition" (1987: 251 n. 66, and p. 254); these choices for the same
word lie at the heart of our different interpretations. We both assume a preexistent
tenor, a dyadic process of addition, and a resulting melody. But she excludes what I
consider to be the combinational meaning of *cantus*, whereas I would leave *cantus*
untranslated and open to both possibilities: "Counterpoint is a *cantus* brought about
through the placing of one sound note-against-note in relation to another." I am not
sure why she should want to avoid the "implication of fixed composition and over-

tones of polyphony" for the word *cantus*, when it has such connotations in at least some of Tinctoris's own definitions, connotations that she would confine to *cantus compositus* = *resfacta*, leaving Tinctoris without a word for the combination of voices produced by counterpoint. *Cantus* for Tinctoris *can* mean melody, "a counterpoint," but it can also mean song in general, or it can mean any contrapuntal or compositional combination of two or more parts; indeed, it can mean polyphony, as in the fifteenth-century term *liber de cantu* to mean a book of polyphonic compositions. I see no conflict between the *cantus* of the *Diffinitorium*'s definition of counterpoint, and the *rationabilis concentus* of the *Liber de arte contrapuncti*; if the latter is to be reconciled with the former, to translate *cantus* as "melody" simply moves the problem to a different place. The table in Chapter 11, p. 310, tries to reconcile, in a way that Sachs and Blackburn do not, the definitions Tinctoris gave in the Dictionary and the Counterpoint treatise. It is this understanding of counterpoint, and specifically of *cantus*, rather than either the question of writing or improvisation, that underlies the remaining differences of view between Blackburn and myself.

She cites Perkins on "the structural framework of two voices": "It is possible and perhaps even necessary to consider the bass progressions that are fundamental to cadential structures in tonal music as nonstructural and nonessential in the cadence formulas that were contrapuntally conceived." Thus far Perkins is largely correct; it is perhaps necessary to emphasise that to regard the bass as fundamentally nonessential for counterpoint is not to ignore its different and important musical role. But I join Blackburn in disagreeing strongly with Perkins's conclusion that "the basic principles of structural order were *melodic* rather than *harmonic*" (pp. 221–22); they were intervallic and dyadic, as Crocker rightly recognised. Blackburn caricatures Perkins's view of the composer as being led by "where his melodic lines took him" (p. 245), an assumption not needed if one accepts the model of a dyadic intervallic grammar that can underpin composition in more than two parts. But for reasons given in "The Grammar," I agree with Perkins (against Blackburn, p. 223) in objecting to Don Randel's proposal to resurrect Roman numeral chord labels such as V-I; here Blackburn and I do seem to part company; even as descriptive labels they are misleading. That we are "left with only the most circumstantial way to describe fifteenth-century cadences" is, as with many other late-medieval techniques, some indication of how far removed our concepts are from theirs; it is perhaps salutary that we are compelled to strive for new formulations. (A valuable anthology of German writings in translation, on both sides of this debate, has recently been edited, with an extensive introduction, by Kevin Moll, *Counterpoint and Compositional Process*.)

Blackburn asks: "In the definition of *cantus compositus*, what does *multipliciter* mean?" (pp. 250-251, 254). Tinctoris's definition of *resfacta* in the Counterpoint treatise advocates mutual relationships between each and all parts. But his earlier Dictionary definition reads: *Cantus compositus est ille qui per relationum notarum unius partis ad alteram multi-pliciter est aeditus, qui refacta vulgariter appellatur,* which I read as invoking the "multiple relationship of the notes of one part to [those of] another [part]." In fact it is not the word *multipliciter* that is the problem, but that in defining *cantus compositus* here Tinctoris does not say "between each and all parts," but refers only to the relationship between one part and one other. Taken literally, his definition refers to the relationship between two singular parts, and only two. If *multipliciter* is interpreted as extending that two-part relationship to other pairs of parts, a pair at a time, some kind of successive process would be implied. Blackburn says that Ferand and I "translated the definition as if only two voices were involved" (p. 255); I think that is indeed the implication here. It is true that in the Counterpoint treatise Tinctoris is considering mutual relationships between each and all parts; if he can be shown to be doing so here, I would welcome such a reading, and it was only with some reluctance that I resorted, as did Ferand, to reading *multipliciter* as the florid or mensurally enlivened fleshing out of two-part counterpoint, as opposed to *punctuatim* or strict note-against-note counterpoint. I may be wrong, as Blackburn believes; Tinctoris may have had in mind mutual relationships between each and all parts of a texture in three or more parts, as he did more specifically in the later definition, but this is not what he said here. In any case, I saw the two definitions as complementary, not opposed; whether *multipliciter* expresses a mensural relationship complementary to the other definition, or whether it duplicates that definition less precisely, does not affect my more important claims.

Blackburn set out to demonstrate that "the phenomenon called 'simultaneous conception' arose early in the fifteenth century and that it existed side by side with successive composition" (p. 211). She ends up by rejecting the term, as do I. One area where we may agree to differ is her thesis that non-successive composition in more than two parts requires the concept of harmony to explain its "chordal" relationships and also the admixture of controlled dissonance with consonance. I do not think she has shown that counterpoint is insufficient for this purpose; I see no need for a hypothesis that elevates harmony to a status alongside counterpoint. The sources she cites seem to me to use it as a term of approbation, not for a distinct technique; even Spataro is describing a quality such as led Crocker to the memorable line that harmony is "that for which the peoples of the world yearn" (Crocker 1962: 17), a quality that was technically rooted for musicians around 1500 in interval ratios, and only incidentally resulted from compositional techniques. Blackburn distinguishes "harmony" as allowing for the combination of consonance and dissonance, since dissonance had no place in strict or note-against-note counterpoint; but as she admirably demonstrates, dissonance is already allowed for in extended contrapuntal theory from the late fourteenth century onwards. In devoting the whole second book of his *Liber de Arte Contrapuncti* to dissonance, and its treatment in florid counterpoint, Tinctoris had no need to call his treatise "a manual of harmony as well as counterpoint" (p. 246).

The "continuum" model also affects the distinction between successive and so-called simultaneous composition, sharp in principle, more flexible in practice. Counterpoint is successive in principle, though a composer could conceive more than two parts together in such a way that they still reflected an underlying "successive" dyadic grammar (see Bent 1998a). It is a foundation that is in turn both the basis for additions, whether successive or mutually adjusted, and also a detectable skeletal grammar underlying composed music. "Simultaneous," as Blackburn and I agree, is something of a misnomer. My only mention of "simultaneous conception" here (Chapter II, p. 312) was in reference to the passage she invokes from Aaron (p. 215); I would now prefer to translate his "considerano insieme tutte le parti" as "'taking account of the whole complex of parts *together*, i.e., in relation to each other," not as Blackburn's "take all the parts into consideration at once"; she later makes it clear (p. 266) that she means mutual adjustment rather than that they were necessarily simultaneously conceived. But she also writes: "unlike his fifteenth-century predecessors, Aaron does not begin with two-part counterpoint. Instead he starts with chords" (p. 217), but in fact the procedure he describes is successive: he assumes a prior two-part framework of soprano and tenor which constrains the options open to successively added bass and alto (even if handled a "chord" at a time in her terms), and he then proceeds to list those options for adding parts to the existing framework. She says *res-facta* is "harmonic composition." This may describe the end result, but that does not make a term of approbation into a musical technique, any more than does her trans-lation of Aaron's descriptive *concinnior* as "more harmonious," even if "harmony is a principle, not a system of chord analysis" (p. 225). In the case of surviving composi-tion, there are few examples of demonstrably successive composition that do not show a substantial degree of mutual attention between parts, and few examples of mutually adjusted "composition" that lack "successive" elements. In other words, I find Black-burn's "two different compositional processes," "counterpoint and *res facta*," less dif-ferentiated than she implies, though she later makes clear (pp. 234–36) that her concept of "harmonic composition" can be arrived at successively or simultaneously. Wegman (1996) adds further dimensions to the paradox by reminding us that "the notion of successiveness . . . is inherent in the notation, not necessarily in the con-ception. . . . Counterpoint is simultaneous singing; composition is successive writing out" (pp. 451–52).

I had already made a partial case for genre-specific "simultaneous concep-tion," or rather, the taking of more than two parts into account together, in rela-tion to the special case of the solus tenor, in Chapter 8 (pp. 244–46; see above).

That circumstance extends back to motets from early in the fourteenth century, and to the arrangement of two-part discant around a given cantus firmus. Those techniques do not significantly change for the early fifteenth century, the point from which both Blackburn and Lowinsky sought to date the beginnings of "harmonic" thinking. None of these procedures, whether defined as successive, simultaneous, or "harmonic," undermines or is incompatible with the thesis that all fourteenth and fifteenth-century music has a dyadic contrapuntal foundation. In a more recent study I wrote:

> It is not a corollary of dyadic procedure that it limits what can be heard or conceived in the mind. The order of conception is not confined by the grammar. When a native speaker utters a complex and grammatically correct sentence, he surely did not start by thinking of it as a simple subject-verb-object sentence, only then expanding it, even though the sentence can be parsed in an order other than that of its devising. Internalised grammar permits correct articulation of a complex thought, whether in words or music, without violating or necessarily consciously invoking that grammar. As with speech, we need not assume that musical ideas occurred to a composer in grammatical order. While "successive" composition should not necessarily be taken to mean that the piece was composed in that order (although sometimes it almost certainly was), it does mean that the piece was conceived in such a way that the grammatical skeleton was not violated. Exceptions and anomalies can then be isolated, will take on greater interest, and lead to extended formulations of the rules; grammars have irregular verbs or idioms and tolerate exceptions, and advanced accounts of them take account of such experience in usage. "Successive" in music should refer to the procedure uncovered by analysis and inherent in its grammar, and not necessarily to the order of working or compositional process of a native-speaking composer. To talk in terms of triadic harmony no more means that we cannot cope with the five components of a dominant ninth (or the seven or eight of a dominant thirteenth), than dyadic counterpoint means that medieval composers could not conceive sonorities of three, four, five parts as extensions of the underlying dyadic grammar. A dyadic basis doesn't confine composers to hearing only two parts at a time any more than triadic harmony means that its practitioners cannot hear polychords. (1998a: 33)

Blackburn and I agree that the key to understanding Tinctoris's view of *resfacta* lies in a proper understanding of what counterpoint meant to him, and we agree on some essential points of that definition; however, different interpretations and attempts to refine that understanding will no doubt long continue.

NOTES

1. See Hughes and Bent 1969–73.

2. Willi Apel (1953:366) reproduced a monochrome collotype facsimile of the first two staves of the top part of Pycard's Gloria, Old Hall no. 26. The excerpt is supposed to illustrate the use of black void notation: Apel clearly did not realize that all the "black" void notes here, as well as the first "full" breve and two minims, are red.

3. My translation of: "Jedes einzelne historische Stadium müsse anhand damalige Kriterien untersucht werden; die Anwendung moderner Theorien auf ältere Musik sei anachronistisch" (referring to passages appearing in this volume at Chapter 1, p. 63, Chapter 4, p. 119). "Musica ficta sei aus kontrapunktischer Theorie und Praxis der fraglichen Epochen nicht wegzudenken. Deswegen analysiert Bent Einzelwerke und deren regionalen Kontext streng unter dem Gesichtspunkt der zeitgenössischen Theorie" (MGG 2nd edition, s. v. *Musica ficta*).

4. For recent and fruitful studies that proceed from similar premises, see Milsom 2000 and Leach 2000a, b. I would also in general include the premises of Cross 1990: "alteration by either *causa* [*necessitatis* or *pulchritudinis*] depends on counterpoint," though some points of disagreement will emerge in the course of this Introduction.

5. See chapters 1 and 6 of this volume. Thomas Brothers (1997: 43) seems to be in agreement with me here, though he does not say so.

6. Most references in medieval theory to disjunction are to the disjunct tetrachord in the context of classical theory (via Boethius). The word is also used in a mensural context for a separated long, by Gafurius, *Practica musice*, II. In late-medieval usage in hexachordal contexts, Lucy Cross (1990: 53 n. 3) says that the examples in I-Rvat 5129 (ed Seay, Corpus Scriptorum de Musica, 9, p. 27), could suggest that only intervals of a fifth or larger were ever considered *disiunctae*. It is also touched on by the Berkeley (Paris) anonymous (Ellsworth 1984) and very briefly by I-Rvat Capponi 206 (Cross, Appendix, Ital no. 4, p. 432).

7. Brothers writes: "Margaret Bent and Andrew Hughes . . . [suggest] that codes of performance practice favored *musica recta* over *musica ficta*" (1997: 105). See also Berger 1987: 83–84, 216 n.64. See Berger 1987:139–40 for his statement of preference for *mi* over *fa*, and 235 n. 104 for the same point, that cantus g♯ was often preferred to tenor b♭.

8. The *coniuncta* has since been considerably more clearly explained by Ellsworth 1973, Cross (1990: 58 n. 1) and Otaola 1998.

9. See Herlinger 1984: 72, 94.

10. http://www.music.indiana.edu/tml/, reference LAMTRAC MSBCLV30. According to Coussemaker, this treatise was allegedly also to be found in Oxford, Bodley '2265,' the old Summary Catalogue number for MS Bodley 77 (See RISM B III 4, p. 102), but this reference seems to be a ghost.

11. Bragard 1963, Capitulum L, 122–23. My thanks to Leofranc Holford-Strevens for help with the translation.

12. See Palmer 1985, also Guillaume Guerson, *Utilissime musicales regulae* (Paris, 1492); and, as I learn from Leofranc Holford-Strevens 2000, Florentius de Faxolis and Jean le Munerat.

13. La Fage 1864: 308–38, at p. 337. Both *ea* (ablative, through it) and *eam* (accusative) are found, *operari* (the classical deponent infinitive) and *operare* (medieval usage).

14. Scattolin 1985: 239 gives two other concordances (and another edition with "*et ea operari*," paragraph 47). Nigel Wilkins (1964: 99) reports "*et eam operarj*."

15. This correction is now reported in Blackburn 1998:635 and n. 7, where she points out that Brothers is right to say that Tinctoris's comment is not general but confined to the case of b fa♮ mi.

16. Pointed out by Pesce 1987: 189 n. 12; Cross 1990: 205–07, Brothers 1997: 42–43.

17. Cross, 1990: 205–07; Berger 1987: 18.

18. See Ellsworth 1984: 84–85, and the discussion on pp. 2–4.

19. See Rohloff 1943: 60, translated in Seay 1967: 31. See Cross 1990: 122–23.

20. Berger says that Dahlhaus is "incoherent," by which I assume he means "inconsistent."

21. See also Urquhart 1996: 465 and n. 4, and the annotation in this volume to Chapter 4 p.3).

22. See Chapter 4, n. 45 and Chapter 6 ¶ 19 for statements distancing my position from Dahlhaus's.

23. See Chapter 1, pp. 73–76 and Chapter 4, pp. 123–24.

24. Walker observes (personal communication) that measures 1–44 contain nothing to bring about any comma descents (or ascents). There are normally extended passages in early renaissance polyphony during which no conflict will arise between the tuning of perfect and imperfect consonances. Sequences, as in the Josquin example, are particularly likely to cause comma shifting.

25. All references to and citations from Walker refer to personal communications in 1999, for which I am most grateful to him. See also Walker 1996. My notion of the Pythagorean system being shifted successively by syntonic commas is judged misleading: in "Intonational Injustice" he explains how it is a local just default which is shifted by syntonic commas, and incorporates this, and not a Pythagorean default, into his lattice diagrams and plus/minus notation.

26. In recent studies, unpublished at the time of writing (see bibliography), I also attempt to do this for Prosdocimus, relating his Counterpoint teaching to the motets of Ciconia, his contemporary in Padua, and for Tinctoris.

27. On Aaron's other music examples, see Judd 1995.

28. For stemmatic principles adapted for polyphonic music, see Bent 1981.

29. Used as an illustration in Bent 1992.

30. Reaney 1969:310–11, 299.

31. See Wathey 1993: 30-33.

32. See Bent 1998b: 20, n. 42, citing Welker 1993: 77, 101.

33. See Wathey 1993: 80–82.

34. Wegman 1992b, and now available in colour facsimile in Schreurs 1995, pl. 16.

35. I hasten to reassure Blackburn and other readers that I intended no coarse or boorish connotations by the literal rendering of *vulgariter* as "vulgar."

36. *A propos* her statement: "Tinctoris nowhere says that what is sung *super librum* is ever written down (p. 258); in Blackburn, 2000: 109 she writes "I would now view all the two-part examples in Tinctoris's treatise as examples of singing *super librum*, not just the one *a3* so labelled." This brings our positions closer together, in that my fuller equation of counterpoint and singing *super librum* already made that distinction and considered all Tinctoris's treatise examples as examples of written counterpoint = singing *super librum*, unless specified as *resfacta*.

Chapter I

Musica Recta and Musica Ficta[*]

A twofold dilemma faces the editor of early music when he comes to supply accidentals. Firstly, he has insufficient evidence on which to base a definitive solution but
must nevertheless specify what is to be performed; and secondly, such evidence as he
does have appears to embody a conflict between the testimony of theorists and the evidence of manuscript accidentals. The present article attempts to set out a working
hypothesis, presenting the main theoretical evidence relevant to the early fifteenth
century; it arose as a by-product of the task of editing the music of the Old Hall manuscript.[1]

It is axiomatic of this hypothesis that theoretical testimony and manuscript evidence are in fact complementary, and that taken together they point clearly towards a
practical solution. I take it as a precondition of any set of principles for the supplying
of accidentals that it must be reconcilable with both available bodies of evidence.
Some previous investigators in the field of *musica ficta* have tended to reject one in
favour of the other. Those who have favoured the theoretical evidence have drawn up
rules based on harmonic criteria,[2] while those who have favoured manuscript evidence have adopted melodic criteria.[3]

In establishing a set of principles I make one basic assumption: that the fifteenth-
century singer had in front of him the sort of manuscripts that have come down to us
(Old Hall shows clear signs of use by performers), and in particular that the accidentals written in such manuscripts were adequate visual clues for performance. In other
words, the application of unwritten accidentals was essentially part of the medieval
performer's art. Modern performers are no longer able to perceive instinctively the
problems and choices involved: at the present time, the editor must still act for the
performer, suggesting decisions which the medieval performer would have made

himself. His task is [74] to uncover the criteria of musicianship, the methods of teaching singing[4] and the theoretical principles which regulated chromaticism. These he must apply as far as possible to the actual situations he finds in the manuscripts; the main function of manuscript accidentals, in turn, is to guide the detailed application of theoretical principles.*

There are two corollaries to this practical approach. In the first place, if the editor is to simulate a performance practice, then he should formulate practical rules of thumb which a singer could grasp and apply on the spot. Secondly, by its nature as a performing art, there must have been some room for flexible application of the rules, even after full allowance has been made for differing local traditions, and varying degrees of skill, conservatism, and contact with fresh or foreign ideas. We cannot expect, here or in any comparable performing technique, to uncover rules which would yield infallible results at first sight of a new piece, even for experienced singers working within a single tradition. But techniques which evolve practically and, in the final resort, instinctively, rarely lend themselves at any period of musical history to logical formulation in manuals of instruction, partly because contemporary writers take them for granted and have not themselves learned them by rote. There are bound to be equally acceptable alternatives, just as there are for the editor who realises a figured bass; spontaneous realisation is likely to incur discussion and mutual adjustment between players in rehearsal.

The operation of one or other of these two variables in the performance of medieval music is occasionally implied by the presence of conflicting written accidentals in two sources of the same piece, or of incompatible accidentals within a single source, representing two different layers of performing activity. Or in other circumstances, differences in written accidentals may be complementary and do not necessarily conflict. What the editor supplies, therefore, may be only one of several possible interpretations based on a single set of principles.

If the singer was responsible for applying accidentals, he must have done so in the first instance to the single part in front of him, and according to melodic criteria. Cadences and structural harmonic points can normally, in any case, be anticipated by identifying the characteristic cadential figures appropriate to each single line of the polyphony. The simultaneous result, the superimposition of each part upon the others, could then be adjusted in rehearsal to meet any overriding harmonic considerations which individual singers had been unable to anticipate. The fact that many of these additions and adjustments were not added to the manuscripts but retained in the memory need not tax our credulity: medieval singers were subjected to disciplines [75] which must have equipped them for life with enviable musical memories.*

Individual theorists give relatively little help on the subject of *ficta*, and in order to

assemble evidence in reasonable quantity it is tempting to draw it from a wide chronological range. It is hardly surprising when, in these circumstances, some results are at
variance with others and with the musical situations they are applied to. Performance
practices are always closely tied to stylistic and technical changes. Earlier teaching may
be absorbed into later practice: thus, the writings of Jean de Muris are of great value in
dealing with the Old Hall music a century later, when they were still respected and
recopied. The Old Hall composers had been brought up on teachings dating from the
fourteenth century or earlier. But since the teachings of Tinctoris and sixteenth-century theorists, however authoritative for their own period, can hardly have been an
ingredient of their musical training, it is hardly surprising that some of them have been
judged incompatible with music of earlier date. Only by stripping our minds of
anachronistic teachings can we hope to see the problems and solutions through contemporary eyes and tackle them with contemporary tools. The case for adopting a similar restriction geographically is much less strong; I have found no major
contradictions on the subject of *ficta* among theorists of different nationality.

The principles governing *musica ficta* are closely related to general contrapuntal
rules. As the collisions of successive counterpoints, built around a tenor, gave way to
something approaching accompanied melody, so angular chromaticism and false
relations gradually yielded to smoother melodic contours and more euphonious
chromatic inflections.

The Value of Theoretical Evidence

Theoretical evidence has sometimes been set aside on the grounds that it deals primarily with harmonic reasons for chromatic inflection and refers to two-part progressions.* The chief difficulty is to bridge the gap between this and the polyphony of
the fourteenth and fifteenth centuries in three or more parts where each singer had
only his own part in front of him. The answer to this lies, again, in the principle of
successive composition. The author of the *Quatuor principalia* gives rules for three-,
four-, and even five-part writing:

> Qui autem triplum aliquod operari voluerit, respiciendum est ad tenorem. Si dis-
> cantus itaque discordat cum tenore, non discordat [*recte* discordet?] cum triplo, et e
> contrario, ita quod semper habeatur concordantia aliqua ad graviorem vocem, et
> procedat ulterius per concordantias, nunc ascendendo, nunc descendendo cum dis-
> cantu, ita quod non semper cum altero tantum. Qui autem quadruplum vel quintu-
> plum facere voluerit, inspicere debet cantus prius factos, ut si cum uno discordat,
> cum aliis non discordat [discordet?], ut concordantia semper habeatur ad gravio-

||76 -rem vocem, nec ascendere vel descendere debet cum altero ipsorum sed nunc cum tenore nunc cum discantu, etc. (CS IV, p. 295)[5]

He who wishes to fit a third part to something must look to the tenor. If the discant is discordant with the tenor, it should not be discordant with the third part, and vice versa, so that there is always some concordance with the lower voice, and that if it [the lower part] proceeds by concords with the discant, rising and falling, there is not always only [consonance] with the other. He who wishes to compose a fourth or fifth part must look at the parts already written, and see that if it is discordant with one of them it is not discordant with the others, and that there is always consonance with the lower part; neither ought it to ascend or descend with any one part, but now with the tenor, now with the discant, etc.

This tells us that each added voice must always agree with at least one of the others, and that it should not be discordant with more than one other part at any one time. Above all, added parts must adjust to the lowest part; we have no indication that it is ever adjusted to them. To some extent an existing part, especially if it is a plainsong tenor, is regarded as fixed. This is confirmed in a chapter on *musica ficta* by Ugolino of Orvieto, where he determines the tenor progression, including its chromatic notes, before showing how the upper part must be made to fit to it by the rules of permitted consonance, and in these *musica ficta* plays an important part.[6] This means that where a chromatic inflection of the written pitch is demanded by the vertical relationship between the two parts, and where there is an equal choice between inflecting the top part, and inflecting the tenor or lowest voice, it is the upper, added part which should be modified.

In practice, the tenor should take priority for the application of melodic rules; its melodic integrity should be preserved even if other voices have to compromise theirs as a result. The lowest voice takes priority where harmonic considerations are concerned, and the other voices have to conform to it. This usually means the tenor, but another voice may cross below it, particularly in English descant, where the tenor plainsong is usually the middle part. The basic duet between the two lower parts is considered, in this style, before any adjustments are made to the upper part.

With these principles in mind, it is quite possible to apply all that the theorists have to say about *ficta* in two-part progressions to ||77 polyphony in three or more parts, provided always that one is dealing with successively-composed music: the principles will have to be modified somewhat before they can be applied to the more vertically-orientated music of the mid-fifteenth century.

This removes one common objection to the using of theoretical evidence. The other, that theorists deal primarily with harmonic reasons for chromatic inflection, is ultimately not justified. Some of our most valuable evidence is given in purely melodic terms (see p. 77). In most other cases, the evidence of two-part progressions is, from the composer's or choirmaster's point of view, harmonic, but with melodic implications. From the standpoint of the individual singer, it is melodic, with harmonic implications. Most inflections affect cadential figures which are often recognisable melodically. The "harmonic" bias of most theorists must be related to the purpose of the treatise: for it is in manuals of counterpoint that *musica ficta* is usually given separate treatment, as part of the basic training not of singers but of composers. Lowinsky has drawn attention to the fact that "the composer of early music was faced by a problem with regard to accidentals when he was writing, as is the modern scholar when editing."[7] The writers of counterpoint treatises are concerned to prevent would-be composers from building impossible situations into their music. Of course, this does not guarantee that near-impossible situations will never confront the performer, but it does give many apparently difficult situations the stamp of normality. They provide the harmonic guidance we need for our singers' mutual adjustment in rehearsal, as well as incidental melodic hints derived from their chord progressions. Once we have admitted distinct functions in different treatises, we can see that many "contradictory" statements are in fact complementary. Prosdocimus's exhortation to be sparing in the use of *musica ficta* (CS III, p. 198) is often reckoned to be inconsistent with his own music examples, which show angular chromaticism. But if he is encouraging *composers* to avoid situations in which the singer would be forced to apply *ficta* where an alternative solution could be found, or if he is telling them not to *write* too many accidentals but to leave them to the performer, his advice is not relevant to singers, schooled orally in a performing art, nor to the modern editor who acts on the performer's behalf. Prosdocimus does not claim to help singers to solve problems; he tries to eliminate problems before the singer has to tackle them.

The procedure of applying melodic rules and supplementing them with harmonic adjustment has some theoretical support. Anonymous XI and several other theorists give rules for *ficta* in application to plainsong. It is in the plainsong section of the *Quatuor Principalia* that the guidance on *ficta* occurs. But other theorists give strong hints that [178] more *ficta* was needed for polyphony than for plainsong. Vitry, for example, makes the point in a word-play on *vera* and *falsa*:

> non falsa, sed vera et necessaria, quia nullus motetus sive rondellus sine ipsa cantari possunt. (CS III, p.18) <text corrected from CSM 8, p. 23>

not false, but true and necessary, for no motet or rondellus can be sung without it.

John of Garland inserted the following well-known passage in his plainsong treatise, without giving any intimation that *musica falsa* is relevant to *cantus planus*:

> Videndum est de falsa musica, que instrumentis musicalibus multum est necessaria, specialiter in organis. Falsa musica est, quando de tono facimus semitonium, et e converso. Omnis tonus divisibilis est in duo semitonis, et per consequens signa semitonia designantia in omnibus tonis possunt amplificari. (CS I, p. 16)

> It should be observed of *falsa musica* that it is frequently necessary in performance [*musica instrumentalis* has this force in the Boethian classification, which recognises, besides, *musica mundana* and *musica humana*], particularly in *organa*. *Falsa musica* is when we make a tone into a semitone and vice versa. Each tone is divisible into two semitones, and consequently the signs design<at>ed for semitones can be extended to all notes.

Indeed, though it is never explicitly stated, there is a strong tendency to equate *ficta causa necessitatis* with harmonic reasons and *ficta causa pulchritudinis* with melodic reasons for chromatic inflection. The theoretical statement which most nearly supports this claim is from an anonymous Seville treatise:[8]

> Boecius autem invenit fictam musicam propter duas causas, scilicet causa necessitatis et causa pulchritudinis cantus. Causa necessitatis est quia non poteramus habere consonantias in omnibus locis ut supra dictum est. Causa vero pulchritudinis ut patet in cantilenis.

> Boethius contrived *musica ficta* for two reasons: because of necessity and because of beauty of song. It is "of necessity" because we were unable to have consonances in every place as stated above [i.e., harmonic necessity, the correction of vertical perfect intervals]. It is used for beauty as in cantilenas [melodic reasons].

||79 Another possible interpretation of *causa necessitatis* and *causa pulchritudinis* is given by Lowinsky: "Necessity deals with rules pertaining to perfect consonances, beauty with rules pertaining to imperfect consonances."[9] This is apparently true for writers who give us only harmonic or contrapuntal guidance: the perfection of consonances is considered necessary. The two different interpretations of beauty, however, can easily be reconciled: the "colouring" of dissonances (or imperfect consonances: see

p. 86 below) involves a two-chord progression and therefore a melodic consideration.

The Role of Solmisation*

Perhaps the most important guidance we draw from the theorists is insight into the
basic musical equipment of singers—and it was certainly through singing that a
medieval musician acquired his fundamental training, terminology, and musical
thought processes. We need this insight before we can approach the manuscript accidentals through their eyes. For present purposes, the crucial part of this equipment is
the solmisation system, whereby the notes forming the recognised total compass of
music were represented in overlapping hexachords, and came to be shown mnemon-
ically as finger-joints on a hand (the so-called Guidonian hand, although this particular device does not occur in Guido's surviving treatises) which was used throughout
the Middle Ages for teaching singing. Its great value is that it enables the choirmaster
to demonstrate to his pupils, and singers to signal to each other, where semitones
occur, by pointing to the joints of his own fingers. The musical memory of the chorister is reinforced by verbal reminders (the solmisation names for the notes) and by
the physical act of tracing out the steps on his own hand.

 The notes included in this basic system of hexachords are called by the theorists
musica recta or *vera*. They include the ♭♭ below and the ♭♭ above middle *c*, as well as the ♮
adjacent to each, but not the ♭♭ below those.[10] The system caters for the three most
common semitone steps: *b-c*, *e-f*, *a-b♭*. These are always solmised mi-fa, and mi-fa is
always a semitone. Free transition between these hexachords was permitted, and the
point of change was termed a mutation. The note on which the mutation was made
had to have a solmisation name (*vox*) in both the old and the new hexachord. Which of
the two names was actually sung is not always clear; sometimes both may have been
used. In order to preserve the clear demonstration of semitones, mutation was not[180]
permitted between mi and fa. Thus, *a ♭♭ c ♮ c* would be solmised mi fa sol/fa mi fa, with
the mutation on *c*, where sol must yield to fa because of the semitone step which follows it.

 In the course of the fourteenth century the system was extended by theorists to
cater for an increasing amount of chromaticism, so that other chromatic steps could
be indicated by the same mnemonics. This was achieved, according to the theorists, by
the transposition of *recta* hexachords to "alien pitches," "unaccustomed places," where
they were classed as *musica ficta* or *falsa*. All chromatic notes so derived have their basis in
ficta hexachords; the hexachord is created for the sake of the semitone step, mi-fa.

 The term used by some theorists for this transposition process was *coniuncta*, the object of a recent study by Albert Seay.[11] The two main definitions he presents (in the words of Faxolis and Tinctoris) are anticipated almost exactly by an anonymous Paris treatise (of which the earliest known copy, dated 1375, is now at Berkeley):[12]

> Vel aliter: coniuncta est alicuius proprietatis seu deduccionis de loco proprio ad alienum locum secundum sub vel supra intellectualis transposicio.

> Est enim coniuncta quedam acquisita canendi actualis attribucio in qua licet facere de tono semitonum et e converso . . . (p. 6) <text corrected from ed. Ellsworth, pp. 50–52>

In addition to these definitions, we find statements which seem to equate the *coniuncta* with *musica ficta*:

> Coniuncta, secundum vocem hominis vel instrumenti, est facere de tono semitonium et e converso . . .
>
> (Anonymous XI, CS III, p. 426)
> <see now ed. Wingell, p. 28>

> Est ficta musica quando de tono facimus semitonium, et e converso.
>
> (Vitry, CS III, p. 26) <Ars contrapunctus>

> . . . mutatio falsa, sive falsa musica
>
> (Anonymous II, CS I, p. 310)
> <see also ed. Seay, p. 28>

> . . . nisi forsitan intervenerit aliquis inusitatus cantus, quem aliqui sed male falsam musicam appellant, alii fictam musicam, alii vero coniunctas eam nominant et bene . . . Et propterea invente fuerunt ipse coniuncte ut cantus antedictus irregularis per eas ad regularitatem quodammodo duci posset.
>
> (Paris, anonymous, p. 5)
> <corrected from ed. Ellsworth, p. 50>

> <. . . unless by chance some unusual song should turn up, which some call—but wrongly—*musica falsa*, others *musica ficta*; still others name it—and rightly—*coniunctae* . . . And so these *coniunctae* were invented so that a song formerly called irregular could be brought into regularity by them in some manner.>
>
> <trans. Ellsworth, p. 51>

||[81] We must emphasise again that all *b♭*s except the lowest one in the gamut count not as *musica ficta* but as *musica recta*. *It is therefore not correct to equate* musica ficta *with editorial accidentals.*[13] Manuscript accidentals and added accidentals each include both *recta* and *ficta* inflections, and are therefore not different in kind. The editor has to decide how many more of each sort to add to the handful of accidentals he finds in the manuscript. In so doing, he must assess whether the written accidentals were notated because they were in some way abnormal, or whether they constitute an arbitrary sample of normal treatment.

All this may seem unnecessarily cumbersome to the musician schooled in the key system and with reference to a fully chromatic, equally tempered keyboard. If all degrees of the chromatic scale were available (which is almost true by the late fourteenth century: *d♯*, *d♭*, *g♯* and *a♭* appear in Old Hall, *g♭* in Chantilly), would not some system closer to our own have been more convenient, based on a chromatic division of the whole octave? Any idea of a set arrangement of tones and semitones for one composition must be rejected. *B♭*, *b♮*, *f♮*, *f♯*, *c♮*, *c♯* may be used in one voice in fairly close succession, and the system of mutations was undoubtedly the most practical way of keeping in tune. Moreover, a careful distinction was observed in theory (and probably in practice by the meticulous) between major and minor semitones. Mi-fa, the normal semitone step, is always a minor semitone (e.g., *a-b♭*, *f♯-g*).

The solmisation of irregular melodic intervals presents another challenge to the theorists who pitted their ingenuity against an increasingly overburdened solmisation system. Intervals larger than the sixth fall into this category: Jacobus of Liège mentions sevenths and octaves, but excludes ninths and tenths "quia in cantu plano ecclesie nullus ultra dyapason ascendere debet immediate vel descendere."[14] He also includes the "semitritonus" (previously defined, in book II chapter 81, as containing two tones and two minor semitones), e.g. *B♮-F*:

> nec umquam extreme voces semitritoni ad eamdem pertinent solfationem. De hac vocum conjunctione parum aut nihil loquuntur a[u]ctores. (CS II, p. 294) <see also CSM 3/6, p. 188>

The Paris treatise discusses the solmisation of irregular melodic intervals and presents a device (or rather, an excuse) for coping with them: the *disiuncta*.[15*] Major semitones, augmented seconds, tritones (of both kinds) and even minor sixths are among intervals which cannot ||[82] be solmised with regular mutation, as no one hexachord, whether *recta* or *ficta*, can contain both boundary notes of the leap. Yet all these intervals are explicitly used.

Quia ab una deduccione sepe sit transitus ad aliam in cantu, quod absque mutacione
vocum bono modo fieri non potest, licet aliquando fiat per disiunctas. Est enim disiuncta vehemens transitus ab una deduccione in aliam, absque quacumque vocum
mutacione ibi fieri possibile.

(Paris anonymous, p. 4)

<corrected from ed. Ellsworth, p. 48>

The *disiuncta*, then, is a violent transition from one hexachord to another where no
mutation is possible, i.e., when there is no pivotal note in the old and new hexachords.*

Bb–b♮ and *f–f♯* are major semitones, rare in practice, and not susceptible to regular solmisation. When, for harmonic reasons only, it was necessary to use major semitones, the hexachord was changed without mutation on a common note. The
difference between the two semitone steps which fall within any one tone of *musica recta*
(e.g., *eb–d♯*) is the so-called comma of Didymus, or apotome, which Marchettus designated as a fifth of a tone, but which later theorists (including Ugolino) more correctly recognise to be not an aliquot part of a tone. Each tone comprises one major
and one minor semitone. Both semitone pitches are catered for in the sophisticated
monochord tuning systems of Prosdocimus and Ugolino, but would be too unwieldy
for a fixed-pitch performing instrument. The singer is not often concerned with
pitching major semitones. Where he is, he is invariably helped by the vertical sonority
of a perfect interval—the overriding harmonic factor which has forced the use of an
irregular melodic interval. A case in point is the opening of Old Hall, no. 101, where
the *f♯* is in the manuscript:

In general, provided the choirmaster knew his way around the hexachord transpositions, the chorister still needed to bother only about the position of semitone steps,
which he sang when his master pointed to the appropriate knuckle.

The system does indeed have limitations as a vehicle for advanced theoretical
thought, but it was not designed for this. Why, then, should it concern us with music
which must have been sung only by experienced singers? First, because all explanations by contemporary theorists [83] concerning contrapuntal progressions, permitted
intervals, melodic progressions, singing practices, and *musica ficta* are given in terms of

hexachords. An explanation couched in universally understood terminology is more generally useful than one given in more sophisticated but less familiar terms. It is therefore vital to understand how the system worked, and where it was inadequate at any point in time, in order to understand the theorists' statements. Second, if we approach the manuscript situation with the medieval singer's training in mind, we are more likely to reason in his terms and approach his solutions.

Modes have no apparent relevance to *ficta* in the early fifteenth century. So long as the mode of a composition is open to dispute, it is more likely to prejudice than to help arguments based on modal assignations. The modes are fundamentally fixed arrangements of tones and semitones. If chromatic inflection can be superimposed on these arrangements without altering the modal definition, how can assignment to a mode help in the application of editorial accidentals? Theorists before Tinctoris rarely attempt to superimpose the modes onto polyphony. The anonymous treatise from Paris <now at Berkeley> is one of the exceptions; but this short excursion into the modes and polyphony is not worked out in detail, nor is it applied to the exhaustive treatment of hexachords and mutations which precedes it. Without further guidance from contemporary theorists, it is not possible to apply the modes to any but the simplest polyphony. The solmisation system itself does not, of course, solve the problem of added accidentals. If any melody, however angular, can be solmised, we cannot assign accidentals on the basis of what is or is not susceptible of solmisation. By the late fourteenth century the system had, indeed, been extended to cope with all chromatic progressions. The theorists' explanations help us to fix priorities, tentative rules governing choice of hexachords, permitted harmonic and melodic progressions, and thus the accidentals to be applied. Having deduced the rules, the mnemonics are no longer necessary to us in fixing semitone positions: solmisation *ex post facto* is a superfluous chore.

The theorists of the fourteenth century imply *ficta* hexachords. They speak of "false mutation" (Vitry), "mental transposition" (Paris anonymous) and call a *ficta* sharp and its adjacent semitone mi and fa (Muris). But not until Ugolino is the full system of *ficta* hexachords exhaustively tabulated. For normal purposes, this full formulation cannot have been wholly necessary, and the flaws revealed by Ugolino's attempt were probably of no practical hindrance.

The primary rule for applying accidentals is that musica recta *should be used rather than* musica ficta *where possible.** Vitry, for example, writes:

> Et ideo oritur questio ex hoc videlicet que fuit necessitas in musica regulari de falsa
> musica sive de falsa mutatione, cum nullum regulare ^{||}84 debeat accipere falsum sed
> potius verum. (CS III, p. 18) <corrected, but not classicised, from CSM 8, p.22>

And thus there arises the question, namely, why it was necessary in regular music to have false music, or false mutation, since nothing regular ought to accept what is false, but rather what is true.

The anonymous Seville author already quoted (see p. 66) reads:

Et ideo quando non possumus habere consonantias per rectam musicam tunc debe-mus recurrere ad fictam seu inusitatam et eam operari. (f. 97)

And therefore when we cannot have consonances by means of *musica recta*, we ought to resort to *ficta*, or the unusual, and apply that.

Prosdocimus allows the use of *musica ficta* "provided the consonance could not be coloured in any other way than by *musica ficta*" and says that it is never used "except where the context requires."[16] Ugolino tells us not to use *ficta* "except in places of cogent necessity."[17] *Musica ficta*, according to the theorists, is a last resort. However, many theorists were discontented with the terminology, being reluctant to call "false" or "feigned" something which was necessary to musical results. The above reference by the anonymous Seville theorist to the "unusual" is typical. *Recta* preference takes priority over most other rules, including that of plainsong preference, unless the *cantus prius factus* has a very strong melodic claim to use or to incur *ficta*, or if for some reason it is treated as immutable (as might be the case in certain imitative, canonic, isorhythmic or refrain-like repetitions).* It may be impossible to use *musica recta*

1) if the use of a *recta* b♭ incurs the use of other more extreme *ficta* flats than a solution using just one or two *ficta* sharps;

2) if a manuscript accidental (perhaps representing the composer's decision) requires the use of *ficta*;

3) if the music has already been steered into *ficta* channels which it would be aurally perverse to abandon;

4) if it seems musically desirable to preserve exactly a close imitation, voice-exchange, a repeating or sequential figure, or to match one cadence to another in the same piece.

‖85 The Interpretation of Manuscript Accidentals

Most theorists confine their explanations to two symbols: *b mollis* (♭) and *b durum* <♭> (♯

or ♮ usually interchangeable).* Some, however, do observe a distinction between ♯ and ♮, but we can never be sure that this distinction applies to any particular source, which may use both indiscriminately.[18] The modern sharp sign may serve as warning of a major semitone. Marchettus says that this sign is peculiar to mensural music (GS III, p. 89) <*Lucidarium*; see now ed. Herlinger, p. 274>; if he means polyphony, this will accord well with what we have already said about the use of the major semitone, that it is required only on vertical, harmonic considerations. This usage of the ♯ sign cannot be applied consistently, because if it were used for *f-f*♯ in ex. I above, the ensuing minor semitone *f*♯*-g* would then be shown by ♯ instead of the normal *b durum* ♮. Scribes, possibly unaware of this distinction, may use exclusively one or other sign for *b durum*, or a hybrid form not clearly identifiable with either, or an apparently haphazard vacillation between the two forms, perhaps deriving from different layers of activity underlying the exemplars. The distinction may occasionally be meaningful, but we cannot depend upon it, and are forced to regard it as having more theoretical than practical importance. One distinct meaning of ♯ is to designate the hard hexachord on *g*, ♮ <♭> sometimes being used for the natural hexachord on *c*. According to the Paris anonymous:

> Unde cuiuslibet deduccionis cantus habens originem in c cantatur per naturam, in f per ♭, in g per ♯. (p. 4) <corrected from ed. Ellsworth, p. 44>

> Whence, a melody in any hexachord starting on c is sung natural, on f soft, on g hard.

The sign ♭ is sometimes used for the *b* below middle *c*, a double-looped flat sign being reserved for the *b* an octave above. The latter is probably a survival of the use of a double row of letters (♭̵) for higher octaves. This would be a convenient means of distinguishing the only two *b*♭s available by *musica recta*, but here again the manuscript evidence is inconsistent. Often, as in the case of ♯ and ♮, we are faced with the confusion which results when one unthinking scribe has combined different practices. Other signs used in Old Hall, particularly by the second-layer scribes, include the letters c, f, g for the "soft" forms of those note-pitches, ♭ being reserved for *b* in the same pieces.

The universal rule for interpreting the manuscript symbols (here given in Prosdocimus's version) is:

[1186] . . . unde ubicumque ponitur b rotundum sive molle dicere debemus hanc vocem fa, et ubicumque poniturb quadrum sive durum dicere debemus hanc vocem mi, sive tales voces ibidem sint sive non, cuius ratio est quia in hac dictione b fab mi, in qua ponitur utrumque istorum b, immediate ante fa ponitur b rotundum sive rnolle, et tali voci fa famulatur, immediate vero ante mi poniturb quadrum sive durum et tali voci mi famulatur, et ideo ad b rotundum sive molle dicimus fa, et adb quadrum sive durum dicimus mi. (CS III, p. 198) <corrected from ed. Herlinger, pp. 74–76>

Thus, whereverb is placed we should give it the name fa, and whereverb is placed we ought to give it the name mi, whether the *voces* are the same or not [i.e., whether or not they would normally have those solmisation names]. The reason for this is that in b fab mi, where either of these b can be placed, immediately before fab is placed and that note called fa, immediately before mib is placed and that note called mi; therefore we say fa when we seeb and mi when we seeb.

Rarely do we find a direct admission thatb lowers a note or thatb raises it, though it is invariably possible to place that interpretation upon a theorist's statement.* Of the theorists used in the present study, the Paris anonymous states this meaning most clearly:

Item ubicumque ponitur signum b debet deprimi sonus verus illius articuli per unum maius semitonum, et dici fa. Et ubi signum ♯ ponitur, sonus illius articuli debet per maius semitonum elevari, et dici ibidem mi. (p. 6) <corrected from ed. Ellsworth, p.52>

Wherever the sign b is placed, the *recta* sound of that note on the hand should be lowered by a major semitone and called fa.

Wherever the sign ♯ is placed the sound of that note on the hand should be raised by a major semitone and called mi.

But elsewhere he uses the signs simply to show the position of mi and fa. Prosdocimus words his definition with an ambiguity which may be deliberate:

1) in a rising interval b diminishes the ascent and ♯ augments it;

2) these signs can add or subtract no interval other than the diatonic or major semitone (CS III, p. 198) <omit "diatonic": see now ed. Herlinger, p. 76>.*

To explore the ambiguity: the ascending interval is diminished by a ♭ but this may be effected by raising the lower note rather than by lowering the upper note. If the sign adds or subtracts an interval, it will be a major semitone (to place it a minor semitone away from its neighbour), but it may not be necessary to alter the *recta* pitch of the note. For example, the minor semitone between *e* and *f* may be reinforced by ♮ on *e* or by ♭ on *f*; neither pitch will be altered. The minor semitone *f♯*–*g* will normally be shown by ♮ on *f*, which will raise the pitch of that [87] note by a major semitone. Less often, but equally legitimately, the same interval may be shown by ♭ on *g*, indicating fa, making mi a minor semitone below it, on *f♯*. The signs ♭ and ♯ locate the position of the semitone causing inflection only if necessary. Sometimes both may be indicated, as in the examples given on p. 20 of the Paris treatise:

and in B.L., Add. 23220, f.6:

Ugolino indicates *f♯* by placing a ♭ in the space above, on *g*. Thus, some care is needed when handling accidentals which are apparently placed carelessly on the stave. It would be wrong to treat every instance as meaningful, but some undoubtedly are. The context will usually determine whether or not the less usual interpretation of a symbol makes musical sense.

Each letter-name had not three pitches (♮, ♯, ♭) but only two, indicated <theoretically> by ♮ and ♭, and this was bound to lead to some ambiguity. Even where the ♯ sign does have a meaning distinct from the ♮ <in music manuscripts>, it cannot be equated with the modern distinction. *D* is normally the only ambiguous note in practice, but others are encountered in theoretical systems which try to cover all possibilities. These are the normal meanings:

♭	*b*♭	*e*♭	*a*♭	*d*♭/*d*♮	*g*♮	*c*♮	*f*♮
♮	*b*♮	*e*♮	*a*♮	*d*♮/*d*♯	*g*♯	*c*♯	*f*♯

However, when theorists attempt to cover both meanings in a single sequence, confusion arises. For example, when the Paris anonymous constructs a hexachord on *a* with the semitone position shown by *c♯* and *d♭*, is he talking about the hexachord on *a♮* with *c♯*, or the hexachord on *a♭* with *d♭*, or both? Similar problems arise with the hexachords on *b*, *e* and *d*, which are available in ♮ and ♭ forms.

Several theorists tell us that accidentals need not be written in, even though their use is taken for granted.[19] We have already referred to Prosdocimus's admonition against using too much *ficta*, and suggested this as a possible interpretation. More clearly, the Paris anonymous says:

> [188] Circa hec sciendum est quod in cantu inveniuntur duo signa, scilicet signum b mollis et signum b quadrati, demonstrancia ubi fa et mi debeant cantari, et possunt poni in diversis locis manus, ut patebit inferius de coniunctis, sed ipsa frequenter sunt in b fa ♭ mi virtualiter, licet semper non signentur. (p. 3) <corrected from ed. Ellsworth, p. 44 and Holford-Strevens>

> On this matter you should know that two signs are found in song, soft b and square ♮, showing where fa and mi should be sung, and they can be placed in various places on the hand, as we shall show below in dealing with *coniuncte*. But these are, legitimately, virtually never indicated in b fa ♮ mi [i.e., in practice you almost never find them marked in].*

One exception is necessary in practice to the rule that ♭ always means fa and ♮ always means mi. If a more extreme flat or sharp in the same hexachord as an existing flat or sharp is either written in or required in performance, both cannot be called fa (or mi), as they will not both have an adjacent semitone step. Ideally, only the more extreme of these two sharps should be notated. This may, in fact, be one positive reason for the "failure" to notate all accidentals in early music. But in practice it was often more helpful to determine the hexachord by sharpening re if necessary. For a performer familiar with the procedures, there was no more need to mark in every accidental than there is for an accomplished executant to mark in his copy the bowing or fingering of every note—yet every note is played, and its bowing or fingering could be notated if necessary. In either case, there will be a tendency for markings to appear at points of possible ambiguity, irregularity, or changes of "gear," but they will still not necessarily be full markings. It is in this direction, too, that we may seek an explanation for the early placing of accidentals in advance of the notes they affect. In some cases, at least, this practice serves as a warning of hexachord change; in order to solmise correctly, the singer needs to know in advance of the inflection itself. An excessive number of written accidentals may show that a piece has been used for teaching; conflicting accidentals in one piece may reflect the superimposed views of different performers.

This apparently casual attitude to written accidentals only makes sense in the context of performing reminders to the performer. To the singer learning his part without reference to a fixed-pitch keyed instrument, the placing of semitones was much more important than the precise pitch-names of the notes. His problems might be compared to those of the modern singer sight-reading a part in an unfamiliar transposition, clef or key, who locates his semitones as much by aural adjustment to the other parts as by accidentals marked in or absent from his own part. The medieval singer, however, was able to apply a series of rational principles when performing "blind" with others. Once a series of chromatic hexachords has been initiated, in performing[89] a piece, there may be greater need to indicate that an uninflected note is required than to indicate all the inflections of the chromatic hexachords.

Melodic Rules

The next concern is with the melodic rules relevant to *ficta* stated by the theorists. They are few and simple, and in most cases carry the harmonic implications of a cadence figure. The basic rule is stated by Jean de Muris:*

> Quamdocumque [*recte* quandocumque] in simplici cantu est *la sol la*, hoc *sol* debet sustineri et cantari sicut *fa mi fa*, ut:
>
> Whenever in a melody there is la sol la, this sol should be suppressed <*recte* raised> and sung as fa mi fa, thus:

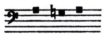

> Quandocumque habetur in simplici cantu *sol fa sol*, hoc *fa* sustineri debet et cantari sicut *fa mi fa*, ut:
>
> Whenever in a melody sol fa sol is found this fa should be suppressed <*recte* raised> and sung as fa mi fa, thus:

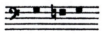

> Quandocumque habetur in simplici cantu *re ut re*, hoc *ut* sustineri debet et cantari sicut *fa mi fa*, ut: (CS III, p. 73)
>
> Whenever in a melody re ut re is found, this ut should be suppressed <*recte* raised> and sung as fa mi fa, thus:

He instructs us to sharpen lower returning notes, and at the time he was writing this was normally applied only where the affected notes were *f*, *c* and *g*. However, in a previous example he uses a *d♯*.

The author of the *Quatuor principalia*, in the course of a section clearly addressed to singers, complains of two debasements of which modern singers were guilty:

> Intervalla etiam vocum perfecte pronuntientur, ut semitonium pro tono pleno non fiat, et e contrario. In hoc autem multi modernis temporibus sunt vitiosi, quoniam cum de *re*, per *fa*, in *sol* ascendunt, vix inter *fa et sol* semitonium ponunt. Insuper cum *sol, fa, sol* aut *re, ut, re* pronuntiant, semitonium pro tono mittunt, et sic genus diatonicum confundunt, ac ^{||90} planum cantum falsificant. Interrogati quidem qua ratione sic semitonium pro tono pronuntiant, pro auctoritate enim atque ratione, cantores de magnatorum capellis allegant. Dicunt etenim eos non sic cantasse sine ratione, cum optimi sint cantores, sicque aliorum vestigiis decepti, et unus post alium omnes sequuntur errores. (CS IV, p. 250)

> Also the intervals of hexachord names should be correctly recited, so that a semitone is not sung instead of a whole tone, and vice versa. In modern times, however, many [singers] are at fault in this matter, for when they ascend from re to sol via fa, they scarcely ever place a semitone between fa and sol [as they should]. Moreover, when they *say* sol fa sol, or re ut re, they *sing* a semitone instead of a tone, and thus they throw the diatonic order into confusion, and falsify the chant. When asked for what reason they recite [the solmisation names for] a semitone instead of a tone, they allege that their reason and authority are the singers in magnates' chapels. And they say that *they* would not do this without reason, since they are the best singers, and thus deceived by the traces of others, they all follow one after the other into errors.

The author is complaining here about singers who fail to sharpen melodic leading notes—they hardly ever sharpen the *f*, in which case it would not be called fa—and thus fail to apply *ficta* where they should. He also objects to singers who correctly sharpen lower returning notes, but use the wrong solmisation names. If they followed the rules of Jean de Muris they would know that these progressions have to be solmised fa mi fa.

Both authors are telling us to sharpen melodic leading notes. The same rule is given in harmonic terms (as "harmonised" leading notes) by Jean de Muris, Prosdocimus, and Ugolino. Jean de Muris is particularly clear. His two-part examples stress the leading-note function of the melodic progression in the top voice (it is, after all, in his *Ars discantus*) as well as the interval progression.

To this rule must be added one provision, that of *recta* preference.* The singer of the top part, in cadencing on *a*, may feel the lower part moving down to cadence on the *a* below, via *b*, and he may have to allow that part to exercise the *recta* preference and sing *b♭*, forgoing his own *ficta g♯*. The justification for this rule, which is surmised rather than stated, is that *ficta* is used only "where necessary," and where a satisfactory result could not be achieved by means of *recta* notes. It is surely possible that singers developed quite refined harmonic senses by learning to anticipate what their companions were about to do. Instead of merely interpreting their own lines regardless of others, and leaving all adjustments until afterwards, they may even have used some form of hand signals to indicate to their fellow singers their own mutations, the direction of their own contrapuntal lines, and the *ficta* they were incurring. It is also possible that this is how singers reading from the same melodic line co-ordinated their efforts in choral performance, and this could [[91]] be the explanation of the slightly raised hands seen in many pictures of medieval choirmen.[20]

Another anonymous Seville treatise gives a further melodic rule, one which is more often taken for granted by modern writers than stated by medieval theorists. The author is talking about the use of *b*, and adds to the *causa necessitatis* and *causa pulchritudinis* the *causa tritoni*:

> Causa tritoni tune est quando cantus ascendit de f grave usque a [*recte* ad?] b acutum, et non ascendit amplius, et descendit in f grave, et tali modo cognoscitur quando b molle habetur causa tritoni, quod debemus vitare in mutationes sane intelligere boecius, quando ubique cantus habetur de f grave usque in b acuto . . . (f. 56)

> The reason of the tritone [for using b♭] is when the melody rises from f to b, ascends no further, and descends to f; and in this way you can tell when you should have b♭ on account of the tritone, which [the tritone] we ought to avoid in our mutations, if we understand Boethius properly, when the melody moves <up> from f to b.

The paragraph which follows is extremely obscure and apparently deficient. However, it deals with the progression *f b c* and appears to indicate that when the *b* serves as a leading note to the *c* it should be a semitone below *c* and therefore natural, the melodic tritone from *f* being permitted in this case. The melodic leading note function, with its harmonic implication, is the strongest melodic reason for inflection, and must be honoured before melodic tritones can be eliminated. The clearest theoretical justification for this is in Prodocimus' two notorious examples in the *Libellus monocordi* (notoriously misprinted in CS III, pp. 254, 256, *recte* below) and the single one in the *Tractatus de contrapuncto* (CS III, p. 199). <See now ed. Herlinger, p. 84.>

N.B.: pairs of semibreves in ligature are shown by joined quavers.

[192] While the melodic tritone was tolerated in the interests of a leading note, it seems that it should be avoided (with or without intervening notes) where the tritone returns within its own confines in the same phrase. This will be overruled in practice only by the need to perfect a strong vertical consonance (see below). The same criterion, of returning within itself, may possibly apply also to certain other melodic intervals, such as the sixth: Prosdocimus, in the examples above, prescribes *bb* where the melodic compass is bounded by *b* and *d*.

The adage *una nota super la semper est canendum fa*, although consistently referred to as a time-honoured statement of medieval theory, cannot be earlier than the abuses of solmisation which set in by the end of the fifteenth century.[21*] It is taken to mean that *a b a* should be performed *a bb a*. Even if sixteenth-century practice admitted la fa la as a proper solmisation of this progression (thus destroying the whole purpose of solmisation (the location of semitones), by the standards of the fifteenth and earlier centuries only mi fa mi could be used. When an upper returning note is flattened, as it frequently is and frequently has to be, the reason is usually either the avoidance of a melodic tritone outline, or the achieving of a correct "adhesion" between an imperfect and a perfect interval by the rules of Jean de Muris, e.g.,

a bb a

f g d

But it may also result from purely aural considerations. What the singer hears happening around him may, in practice, be the strongest influence upon his own solution. In the absence of keyboard anchorage (with its simplification of the chromatic scale and primacy of white notes over black), and of any prejudice that *b* is to be sung natural unless marked flat, the singer is unlikely to persist with *b♮* if the lower parts are constantly using *b♭*.

Rules for Harmonic Adjustment

The speculative reasoning which determined the intervals permitted in counterpoint also lay behind the harmonic reasons for chromatic inflection. These two considerations are, in any case, virtually inseparable. The most perfect intervals are those derived by the simplest ratios—the first few notes of the harmonic series in relation to the fundamental (octave 2:1, twelfth 3:1, fifteenth 4:1) and the fifth (3:2). Most theorists are somewhat reticent on the status of the fourth. Franco writes: *Consonantiarum tres sunt per se, et perfecte, scilicet: unisonus, diapason, et diapente* [93] (CS I, p. 154). Prosdocimus adds to these the third and sixth, calling them *combinationes consonantes sive concordantes*, while his list of *dissonantes, sive discordantes, sive dissonantias auribus humanis resonantes* includes the second, fourth, seventh, and their octaves (CS III, p. 195) <see now ed. Herlinger, p. 38>. While the fourth has some claim to be classed as a perfect interval on mathematical grounds, it is not considered fit to stand on its own harmonically by the fifteenth century. This appears to be the dilemma: however, the fourth is never listed as a perfect interval for purposes of *ficta*.

The nearer an interval can be brought to perfection, the greater its quality becomes (in speculative terms), whether this be achieved by fair means (*recta*, the preferable way) or foul (*ficta*). If the interval cannot itself be made more perfect by chromatic inflection of either or both of the written pitches, then it can acquire some "virtue" from being as close as possible to the interval which follows it, and if that is already perfect, so much the better. In Ugolino's words, it gains *propinquiorem adhaesionem ad suam immediate sequentem consonantiam*. The final cadence of a phrase carried strong philosophical connotations of perfection, as the point to which all the intervals preceding it aspired.

The first essential harmonic rule (given full and lucid expression by Ugolino and Jean de Muris) is that vertical intervals such as unisons, fifths, octaves, and their octaves should be perfect. If such an interval cannot be made perfect by *musica recta*, *ficta* is used. (The question of tenor precedence may then condition the choice of inflection.) The rule is usually stated in the form of a prohibition against sounding *mi contra fa* in perfect consonances:

. . . in combinationibus perfecte consonantibus nunquam ponere debemus *mi* contra *fa*, nec e contrario, quum statim ipsas vocum combinationes perfecte consonantes minores vel maximas constitueremus, que discordantes sunt, ut supra dictum
est (Prosdocimus, CS III, p. 197) <see now ed. Herlinger, pp. 62–64>.

. . . nullibi talibus perfectis concordationibus potest poni *mi* contra *fa*, cum insimul
discordarent . . . Breviter dicendo in contrapunctu, super perfectas species nullibi
contra *mi* potest poni *fa*, nec e contra, in contrapunctu, supra perfectas specias
nullibi contra *fa* potest poni *mi* (from Jean de Muris's statement, CS III, pp. 71–72).

The qualification "in perfect consonances" and the strict application to vertical combinations (i.e., the usual force of *contra*) are of central importance. If *mi contra fa* were to
apply to *im*perfect consonances we should always be forced, for example, to flatten the
b in the progression

$\begin{smallmatrix} a & g & f\sharp & g \\ c & b & a & g \end{smallmatrix}$ so that it could be solmised not $\begin{smallmatrix} \text{sol} & \text{fa} & \text{mi} & \text{fa} \\ \text{fa} & \text{mi} & \text{re} & \text{ut} \end{smallmatrix}$ but $\begin{smallmatrix} \text{sol} & \text{fa} & \text{mi} & \text{fa} \\ \text{sol} & \text{fa} & \text{mi} & \text{re,} \end{smallmatrix}$

avoiding the *mi contra fa* of the sixth, *b g*, which is the only solmisation permitted by the
placing of the semitones if *b♮* is sung. Clearly, a rule which permitted us to approach *g*
only through *b♭* would be untenable against musical evidence, and the theorists do not
call for it.

[94] If mi and fa sound simultaneously in a perfect interval, this may be sympto-
matic of either of two faults. First, and most important, the interval which ought to be
perfect may in fact be augmented or diminished. This must be put right. Second,
even if the perfect interval itself is correct, it may be immediately preceded by an augmented or diminished interval. This could result from two simultaneous applications
of accidentals which are incompatible, and the sounding of *mi contra fa* on the cadence
chord, as Lowinsky pointed out, would serve (to the tone-deaf) as a warning that
something had gone wrong. (The "closer adhesion" prescribed by Ugolino should
thus not be taken too far.) Mi would incidentally sound against fa on the antecedent
chord, but only because each was a semitone away from the final chord. Only the first
of these faults is specifically illustrated by the theorists, but examples of how both arise
include:

*This progression is actually written in Old Hall, no. 16; it must be the result of two incompatible alternatives finding their way onto a single copy. *Recta* names are used above where available. No mutations are used in these examples.

It is clear from the examples given by the theorists that this rule applied to perfect intervals which have a cadence function, although this proviso is never explicitly stated. Simultaneous false relations do occur in the manuscripts in contexts where the conflicting accidentals seem well justified on linear grounds. In Old Hall, these instances invariably occur at weak points in the phrase (that is, not in the last interval of a cadential progression or the first of a phrase). The following examples are selected for their explicit manuscript accidentals:*

Old Hall no. 27, bars 12–16 (Pycard)

[195] no. 36, bars 79–81, 91–95 (Cooke)

The conflict usually occurs between a leading-note function of the upper voice and tritone avoidance in the lower. Unless a melodic tritone is admitted as an adjunct to a leading note (*f b c*) or to avoid a vertical tritone or a false relation on a strong beat (the strength being to some extent a matter of subjective judgment), it should be avoided. Tritones and false relations are admissible as vertical intervals in auxiliary positions, more on the evidence of manuscript accidentals than of theoretical statements, though Tinctoris (CS IV, p. 127) gives later support to this principle. Clashes may be admitted between two voices, each of which has a correct relationship with the lowest part. In the progression

$$
\begin{array}{ccc}
e & f & e \\
c & b & c \\
c & d & c
\end{array}
$$

the imperfect fifth between *f* and *b* is allowable because each upper part behaves correctly with the tenor.

The other harmonic rule given by the theorists requires thirds and sixths preceding fifths and octaves to be major, where the upper note of the first interval rises a single step to the second one. Thirds preceding unisons or fifths should be minor if the top part descends one step. The clearest statement, again, is by Jean de Muris, and is [196] accompanied by exhaustive examples (CS III, pp. 71–73). These can easily be adapted to apply to a lower part where the inflection of the upper is determined by manuscript accidentals, though the tenor is treated as a fixed part to which the others adjust, both in his exposition and in Ugolino's. If the tenor progression is governed by the priority of *recta* over *ficta*, as in

g a

b a

this will be applied instead of inflecting the upper part: in this case the lower part will have b♭ a, instead of g♯ a in the upper. Instead of having a discantus part proceeding by semitone step, we now have a tenor proceeding by semitone step, but the perfect octave is still preceded by a major sixth. The speculative basis of the rule is stated explicitly by Ugolino, who gives two reasons for applying *ficta* to imperfect intervals:

> Sed talem musicam etiam in consonantiis imperfectis sive dissonantiis colorandis fingimus, causa vero fictionis huiusmodi duplex est, scilicet, causa harmoniae dulcioris habendae, et causa propinquioris perfectionis acquirendae . . . (ed. Seay, II, p. 47)

> But we must also feign such music [i.e., use *musica ficta*] to colour imperfect consonances or dissonances. *Ficta* is used here for two reasons: for the sake of achieving sweeter harmony and in order to gain closer proximity to perfection.

Prosdocimus gives a shorter but otherwise similar account of the detailed application of this principle, the main difference being one of terminology. Prosdocimus calls thirds, sixths, tenths, etc. imperfect consonances, major or minor accordingly. Ugolino calls them imperfect consonances or dissonances, and usually refers to them as dissonances.

Chromatic inflection applied to these imperfect consonances or dissonances is often called "coloration" (*coloratio*)—i.e., a musical ornament, like the *chroma* of Marchettus. The notion that this is "ornamental" rather than "necessary" places this kind of inflection in the category of *causa pulchritudinis*. Prosdocimus gives the reason as "for the sake of sweeter harmony." The third preceding a fifth does not need to be made more perfect except for its own good: thus, its perfection classes as ornamental. Some confusion may arise from the constant distinction drawn between major and minor semitones. Ugolino, for example, says in his *Tractatus monochordi*:

Nam potest intelligens organista maiore uti semitonio atque minore, altero quidem
ad perfectionem, altero vero ad colorationem. (ed. Seay, III, p. 252)

For the intelligent *organista* can use major and minor semitones, the one for perfection, the other for coloration.

||97 This might legitimately be interpreted to mean that major semitones are used
to perfect intervals which should be perfect, minor semitones to adjust the size of an
imperfect interval proceeding to a perfect one. In fact, Ugolino makes it clear in the
chapter *de ficta musica* in the *Declaratio* that he means: in order to perfect an interval (e.g.
b-f), a major semitone must be added to one of the notes (i.e., *f-f♯* or *b-b♭*), while
the "coloration" of an imperfect consonance, regarded as an ornament to the ensuing perfect consonance, is achieved by making one outer note of the imperfect interval a mere minor semitone away from the perfect interval (e.g.,

> *f g*
>
> *a g*

requires *f♯*: although *f-f♯* is a major semitone, *f♯-g* is a minor semitone). Major semitones are occasionally required melodically for reasons of vertical perfection (see p.
70 above).

One important rider to the rule that imperfect consonances should be major
when they proceed to perfect consonances concerns the application of the rule to successive part-writing. If each upper voice in the cadence figure shown below is considered only with the lowest voice, and each is made to form a major interval with the
tenor, then the result, in combination, will be the so-called double-leading-note
cadence; not because it is necessary to perfect the fourth between the upper parts but
because *each* of the upper parts has a leading-note function. If the middle part fell
cadentially to *e*, the *f* would be natural:

Prosdocimus extends the principle of "adhesion" to adjacent imperfect intervals.
He justifies the *primam♭ quadrum in cantu inferiori* in the last example quoted on p. 80 thus:

Quum talis sexta in sua minoritate minus distat a loco ad quem immediate accedere
intendit, scilicet ab alia sexta immediate sequenti, quam in sua majoritate. (CS III,
p. 199) <see now ed. Herlinger, p. 86>

Clearly, as in the case of *mi contra fa*, this rule cannot be accorded universal application. To make all consecutive thirds major, or all minor, would incur numerous musical anomalies. But it may sometimes be used in the context in which Prosdocimus himself uses it; the pre-penultimate chord is made closer to the penultimate and thus to the final perfect interval. It could also be regarded as a leading note to a leading note.

Partial Signatures*

The problem of "key"-signatures has formed the starting-point for many recent articles devoted to *ficta*: no survey of *ficta* at this period can [198] overlook them. One of the most far-reaching consequences of the distinction between *recta* and *ficta*, and the prior claims of the former, is its effect on the interpretation of these signatures. All that has been said so far is true for unsignatured parts. Absence of a flat signature would not restrain the application of $b\flat$, since it forms part of the normal scheme for an unsignatured part, and may be sung flat or natural without prior claim by the uninflected form.

The normal solmisation procedure for any piece of music is by *musica recta*, giving a built-in system of priorities for applying editorial accidentals. What difference does a flat signature make? Having rejected a modal basis for early fifteenth-century polyphony, interpretations of signatures based on modal transposition are likewise excluded. There can be no question of applying a modern interpretation: the abiding problem of partial signatures is that a signature sometimes has to be overruled, while an unsignatured part sometimes requires flats. If $b\flat$s can be freely supplied to a part without a signature, what significance can a $b\flat$ signature have? If a $b\flat$ signature were to eliminate $b\natural$ as a *recta* note, only two *recta* hexachords would remain. If a signature of $b\flat$ and $e\flat$ were so interpreted, only one hexachord could be used without incurring *ficta*, and the entire balance of priorities would be upset because a *ficta* note ($e\flat$) would be legitimised by the signature. Yet it is along these lines that the following suggestion is made: a flat signature serves to define the limits of *musica recta*, and the point at which *ficta* takes over.

The set of three hexachords on *c*, *g*, and *f* represents a set of relationships. The terminology of natural, hard, and soft reflects these relationships, for the arrangement of each individual hexachord is identical in terms of tones and semitones. Elimination of one or more of the *recta* hexachords would severely restrict the available mutations and the exercise of priority for *recta*, as well as producing a very different pattern of inflection for a part with a signature. If, however, we see "key signatures" as what might be termed "hexachord signatures," this effect is overcome, and the essential set of relationships preserved. By this reckoning, *flat signatures bring about a transposition of the basic* recta *system of three hexachords one degree flatwards for each note flattened in the signature*. Ficta involves the transposition of isolated hexachords for the purpose of creating chromatic notes, but transposition of *recta* implies that the whole structure is shifted, together with its built-in rules for applying accidentals. This interpretation solves a number of puzzling features. Signatured parts tend to occupy a pitch-range roughly a fifth lower (for one flat) than unsignatured upper parts in the same pieces, yet a bitonal interpretation of the total polyphonic sound is rarely palatable.[22] The hexachord [1199] interpretation removes any need to suggest bitonality. A part with a one-flat signature has two *recta* hexachords in common with an unsignatured part on the one hand, and with a two-flat-signature part on the other, and it therefore shares a high proportion of actual *recta* preferences. Just as $b\flat$ is a legitimate *recta* note in an unsignatured part, $b\natural$ is a legitimate *ficta* note in a part with one flat, corresponding exactly to the status of $f\sharp$ in an unsignatured part. Similarly, $e\flat$ becomes a *recta* note in a part with a one-flat signature; and $a\flat$ is added to the *recta* range in a part with two flats, where $e\natural$ becomes a *ficta* note. (If the lower part of the cadence

$$c \quad d$$
$$e \quad d$$

is governed by a $b\flat$ signature, exercise of *recta* preference will favour $e\flat$ rather than $c\sharp$.)

Double-leading-note cadences are bound to be the normal result in successively composed, unsignatured pieces (see p. 86 above). The same applies to a piece with two unsignatured upper parts and a flat signature in the lowest of three parts. Where both lower parts have a $b\flat$ signature, the middle part may tend more often to forgo cadential patterns incurring extreme *ficta* sharps, and in this case single-leading-note cadences would be the logical result. It must be emphasised that the presence of a signature does not override the sharpening of leading notes.[23] *Recta* transposition is supported by Ugolino's discussion of a "double hand where all the solmisation names of *musica recta* and *musica ficta* are set out" and "another hand of *musica ficta* and *musica recta* starting a fifth below [gamma], on *C*, equivalent to the first hand except for its low pitch."[24]

No satisfactory explanation has yet emerged for the signature of $e\flat$ only, which occurs in Old Hall nos. 21 and 82. However, the clefless flat signatures found in some pieces in Bologna, Civico Museo Bibliografico Musicale, Q 15 and the Escorial *chansonnier* (Madrid, Biblioteca del Monasterio de San Lorenzo el Real de El Escorial, V.III.24) offer some comparison. *Tous deplaisir* (Escorial, ff.7v–8), for example, has a signature of two flats for each of the three parts, in each case on the second and fourth lines of the stave. C-clefs have to be assumed on the bottom line for the top part, on the middle line for the lower two. The flats therefore fall on *e* and *b* in the upper part, *a* and *e* in the lower two. The relationship is that of the signatures ♭ ♭♭ ♭♭, the placing one degree flatter.[25]

The distinction between a signature and an accidental is not always clear in manuscripts, and may not always have been clear to scribes. The flat signature functions as a kind of clef to the use of *musica recta*: ||¹⁰⁰ some accidentals may be treated as temporary signatures in this way. A manuscript accidental may be placed well in advance of the note it affects precisely for this reason or, as suggested above (p. 76), to warn of a single change of hexachord. In either case, early placing of an accidental may give prior warning of the intended solmisation and therefore of the intended inflections.

The principles outlined above provide a basis for practical guidelines. Accordingly, such guidelines are proposed in the introduction to the new edition of Old Hall, to which the present article serves as a background.

Commentary

to passages marked by asterisks in text; see also the Introduction

p. 62   Throughout this article are terms that I no longer accept. These include the adding or "application of accidentals" as something the performer does, "chromatic" notes and "chromaticism," "vertical" (a visual model) rather than simultaneous (a more appropriate aural image). For "harmonic" I would now prefer "contrapuntal," meaning the dyadic successions that underlie the simultaneities of composition. For "successive composition," see below and the Introduction.

p. 62   Thomas Brothers (1997: 43–44, n. 66) criticises the foregoing paragraph: "To assume that the music has been precisely and completely notated facilitates musical analysis. The view that the performer was required to complete the musical text by various conventions of performance practice easily undermines musical analysis." Thus to put ease of modern analysis ahead of tackling the patent problem of undernotation (by our standards) is to stand matters on their head. Brothers also cites Peter Urquhart (1993: 22) against the assumption of rehearsal: "To expect that Renaissance musicians extensively rehearsed problematic passages without signs of congruence . . . is simply unrealistic." Brothers declares, without evidence and apparently on the basis of his own predisposition, that "the procedure imagined by Bent was not a normal part of how polyphony was conceived and disseminated."

p. 63   With clearer understanding of medieval counterpoint than when
this article was written, one could now make a virtue out of the necessity of what I here
called the theorists' two-part limitation; the two-part rules of counterpoint apply to
the underlying dyadic duet that is fundamental to worked-out composition. For
dyadic counterpoint and its implications for revising the notion of "successive composition" see Bent 1998a: 25–35, where I also expand the idea of trained intuition
and internalisation of rules.

pp. 67–71   Some scholars still have the impression—wrongly—that I believe
solmisation to be formative in the choice of inflections, as opposed to being important for understanding their pedagogy and concepts. I hope by now to have removed
any doubt about this; as well as the above, see especially Chapters 3 and 6 here.

p. 69   The same definition of *disiuncta* is reported by Lucy Cross (1990:
432) from I-Rvat Capponi 206. She points out (p. 53) that in chant (I-Rvat.lat.
5129) the *disiuncta* is used for intervals of a fifth (ed. Seay, CSM 9, 27). This is clearly a
different sense, since fifths can be solmised normally within a hexachord, and in any
case, the smaller irregular melodic intervals sometimes required in polyphony (tritone, augmented second, chromatic semitone) have no place in chant, so their
absence in this treatise is not surprising.

p. 72   The notion of *recta* preference now needs even more careful qualification; it should now be considered only partially valid and is certainly not primary.
See the discussion of *recta* preference and tenor priority in the Introduction.

p. 73   Square b (♭) is used by theorists to designate b-mi as part of a system, and is usually distinct from the forms resembling our natural and sharp that are
used in the manuscripts. The signs may not always be as interchangeable between theory and practice and with each other as I implied here.

p. 74 (a)   This claim too, also presented in my article on *Musica ficta* in the *New
Grove*, has given rise to some misunderstandings (noted by Dolores Pesce [1987: 81,
189 n. 12], which become "mis-statements" in Brothers 1997: 42 n. 64). Indeed, I
could have expressed it less elliptically. I intended to draw attention to various circumlocutions used by theorists to define the solmised melodic context of inflections,
stressing the horizontal interval of approach rather than the idea that a note had to be
moved up or down on a vertical axis from its normal position to accomplish this.

p. 74 (b)   Coussemaker (following the Einsiedeln MS) has "semitonium dia-
tonicum sive maius," which makes no sense in terms of Pythagorean tuning. In Herlinger's corrected reading, simply "major semitone," it is clear that (1) refers to
melodic ascent, and that (2) does indeed refer to changing the size of a simultaneously sounding interval; this slightly softens but does not invalidate my claim that
descriptions of the effect of the signs in terms of melodic approach are more common than statements that the individual note is raised or lowered. See Ugolino's similar statement, pp. 85–88.

p. 76   This last sentence ought now to be translated: "But these are frequently present virtually [= effectively] in b fa ♭ mi, even though they are not always
written." [Leofranc Holford-Strevens, cited in Blackburn 1998: 635 n.7). Although
some scholars have accepted my translation of this passage, I now think it to be mistaken, and happily accept the Holford-Strevens reading.

p. 77   Thomas Brothers (1997: 25 n.36) points out that this passage has
since been placed in the third quarter of the fifteenth century by Klaus-Jürgen Sachs
(1974: 180), which makes better sense of the $d\sharp$ in a previous example. But the point is
entirely consistent with similar comments quoted here from the mid-fourteenth-
century *Quatuor Principalia* and sources of earlier date.

p.79   For *recta* preference, see above, pp. 71–72 and 10–12.

p. 80   Andrew Hughes (1972: 63–64 n. 18) reports: "The unfortunate ditty
una nota super la semper est canendum fa is not documented from medieval sources and is surely
the product of a quite different attitude. The earliest version I know, drawn to my attention by Zenoby Lawryshyn, is in Praetorius's *Syntagma Musicum III* (1619), p. 31: *unica notula
ascendente super la, semper canendum esse fa*. Constant quotation of this couplet perpetuates the
perversion of incorrect solmizing, as well as our own rigidity because of the *semper*. La fa
la is not within normal usage. Nevertheless irregular solmizing was certainly known in
the Middle Ages: see Coussemaker II, 293; IV, 223a . . . *aut improprie sumere*; and especially
IV, 376–380 where the second stave of the music example on 380, if the point is to be
trusted, shows precisely A-la B♭-fa A-la instead of A-la-mi B♭-fa A-mi-la."

p. 83   I would now discuss cases such as these in terms of the relationship
of the composed surface to the contrapuntal background, rather than attending to
local clashes resulting from temporal dislocation in that surface.

p. 87   The hypothesis that differentiated signatures may have transposed the relationships of the *recta* hexachords has met with some resistance, despite the abiding possibility of interpreting Ugolino's pair of diagrams in this way. See the Introduction, pp. 10–12.

NOTES

*Originally written (1968) as an Appendix to *The Old Hall Manuscript: A Paleographical Study* (Ph.D. dissertation, Cambridge, 1969), pp. 389–429; revised for publication in *Musica Disciplina* 26 (1972), pp. 73–100. Reprinted in *The Garland Library of the History of Western Music; Medieval Music II: Polyphony*, ed. Ellen Rosand, 1–28. New York: Garland, 1985.

1. *The Old Hall Manuscript*, ed. Andrew Hughes and Margaret Bent, CMM 46 (Rome, 1969<–73>). The spur to the present formulation arose from extended correspondence with Andrew Hughes, after the decision to publish the edition jointly. It owes much to his initial criticism of and subsequent concurrence in its arguments, and he has developed many of the practical ramifications independently (*Manuscript Accidentals. Ficta in Focus, 1350–1450*, Musicological Studies & Documents 27, American Institute of Musicology, 1972). My husband's criticisms <Ian D. Bent> have been invaluable, and two articles, in particular, did much to suggest lines of thought: E. E. Lowinsky, "The Function of Conflicting Signatures in Early Polyphonic Music," *The Musical Quarterly* 31 (1945): 227–60, and R. H. Hoppin, "Partial Signatures and Musica Ficta in Some Early 15th-Century Sources," *Journal of the American Musicological Society* 6 (1953): 197–215.

2. E.g., Hoppin, "Partial Signatures."

3. E.g., W. Apel, "The Partial Signatures in the Sources up to 1450," *Acta Musicologica* 10 (1938): 1–13, and 11 (1939): 40–42.

4. That much depended on teachers is suggested by Anonymous XI. See E. Coussemaker, *Scriptorum de Musica Medii Aevi: novam seriam Gerbertina alteram* (Paris, 1864–76) [henceforward referred to as CS], vol. III, p. 429 <see now ed. Wingell, p. 37>.

5. See also CS III pp. 465–66 for an anonymous 15th-century directive on counterpoint in more than two parts.

6. *Ugolino urbevetani declaratio musicae disciplinae*, ed. A. Seay (Rome, 1959–62), II p. 44.

7. "The Function of Conflicting Signatures," p. 238.

8. Biblioteca Colombina, MS 5.2.25, f. 97. The manuscript is described and inventoried by F. Alberto Gallo, "Alcune Fonti Poco Note di Musica Teorica e Pratica" (Edizioni Centro Studi Sull'Ars Nova Italiana del Trecento), Certaldo, 1966, pp. 11–23. The portions used in this article are short anonymous treatises contained on ff. 56–56v and f. 97. There is no reason to assume any identity of scribe or author between these two items in a miscellaneous compilation. I owe my knowledge of the manuscript to Andrew Hughes.

9. E. E. Lowinsky, Foreword to *Musica Nova accommodata per Cantar et Sonar Organi*, ed. C. Slim (Monuments of Renaissance Music, vol. I; Chicago, 1964), pp. viii–ix.

10. This distinction has, of course, been recognised before, e.g., by Lowinsky ("The Function of Conflicting Signatures," p. 254), but does not yet appear to have been used to support the conclusions drawn below.

11. "The 15th-century Coniuncta: A Preliminary Study," in *Aspects of Medieval and Renaissance Music*, ed. Jan LaRue (New York, 1966), pp. 723–37. The quotations from Faxolis and Tinctoris mentioned below are on p. 730. <See now Oliver Ellsworth, "The Origin of the Coniuncta: A Reappraisal," *Journal of Music Theory* 17 (1973): 86–109.>

12. See R. L. Crocker, "A New Source for Medieval Music Theory," *Acta Musicologica*, 39 (1967): 161–71, and M. Bent, "A Postscript on the Berkeley Theory Manuscript," ibid., 40 (1968): 175. I am grateful to Mr. Oliver Ellsworth for his correction, used on p. 74, of a misreading contained in the latter. <See now Ellsworth 1984.>

13. The misconception is widespread. Hoppin writes: ". . . musica ficta, i.e., editorial accidentals" ("Partial Signatures," p. 197).

14. CS II, p. 294 <see also CSM 3/6, p. 186>.

15. I have not found this term in any other treatise: the word is, however, used in other contexts which invite analogy, e.g.: "ex conjunctione et disjunctione tetracordarum" (Odington, CS I, p. 215) <see now CSM 14, p. 97> and "possibile est perfectiones separari et disiungi, neque continuari" (J. de Muris, GS III, p. 296) <see also CSM 17, p. 84>.

16. In the *Tractatus tertius* of his *Tractatus de contrapuncto*: CS III, pp. 198–99 <see now ed. Herlinger, pp. 70–72>.

17. In chapter 34 of his *Declaratio musicae disciplinae*, ed. Seay, II, p. 45.

18. Prosdocimus, in CS III, p. 258 <see now ed. Herlinger, p. 116>, claims to have elucidated the difference in his counterpoint treatise, but no such passage occurs in the surviving sources; however, only one chapter of the *Tractatus tertius* survives.

19. Later, Tinctoris expresses the same view:

Neque tunc b mollis signum apponi est necessarium, immo si appositum videatur, asininum esse dicitur, ut hic probatur. (CS IV, p. 22) <see also CSM 22/1, p. 74>

The musical example which follows requires b flats but has none written in.

20. For two easily accessible examples that may show such co-ordination see H. Besseler, *Die Musik des Mittelalters und der Renaissance* (Potsdam, 1931), plates I and XIV. Other depictions of singers, where hand signs are in evidence, may be as much concerned with the communication of solmisation as with the beating of time.

21. The sentiment, but not the wording, is widespread among sixteenth-century theorists, e.g., Rhaw, *Enchiridion* (edition of 1518): "Attamen in cantilenis primi & secundi tonorum, ultra la, ad secundam tantum procedendo semper fa canitur. Et hoc, si cantus mox relabitur ad F fa ut. Si vero non, mi cantetur, ut vides in Hymno, Ave maris stella."

22. This problem is discussed at length in Hoppin, "Partial Signatures," Lowinsky, "Conflicting Views on Conflicting Signatures," *Journal of the American Musicological Society* 7 (1954): 118–204, and R. H. Hoppin, "Conflicting Signatures Reviewed," *ibid.*, 9 (1956): 97–117.

23. The signature pattern of ♮♭♭ does, however, appear to supersede ♮♮♭ as traces of successive composition begin to weaken, and as single-leading-note cadences become more satisfactory on musical grounds.

24. Ed. Seay, II, pp. 48–50.

25. A signature involving more flats than conventional notation permitted was achieved by Pycard in a unique way. My solution to the double clefs of Old Hall, no. 76, is incorporated into the edition (see n. 1) and explained in the commentary. <This volume, Chapter 2.>

Chapter 2

Pycard's Credo No. 76[*]

This piece, reproduced from the Old Hall MS (London, British Library, Add 57950), ff. 63v–64 as fig. I, contains a considerable amount of black void coloration within its basically black notation. In effect, such passages shift the mensuration from ₵ to O, neither signature being stated, and cause the imperfect values of black full notes to be halved. Perfection and alteration, used within black void passages in Pycard's Gloria no. 22, are eschewed, black full notes being used where these values are required. That all notes are to be understood as having their minimum, imperfect value before being halved is established in, for example, bar 20, where three breves of black void function exactly as they would if they were an imperfection coloration group of three red semibreves. Red void notation, as used in Pycard's Gloria no. 26, would have shown this more precisely. This is the only first-layer piece which does not use red for normal coloration to show imperfection. In fact, the only red notes are the group of six 3/1 minim triplets on stave 5 of f. 63v. Red notation may have been deliberately avoided so that it could be reserved for the special function which is the main concern of this excursus. Before leaving the matter of black void notes, however, we might question whether the use of black void for diminution may, for some composers and scribes in Old Hall, have been associated with a change from ₵ to O time.[1] The change from full to void notation is usually, and reasonably, associated with the change from parchment to paper as the normal writing surface for music. Both materials span the first quarter of the fifteenth century in England; I believe them to have been contributing factors to the reversal of black and void roles. Had the contratenor of the anonymous Credo Old Hall no. 75 been notated with black void in place of red, the ambivalence of its colorations would have been much more striking to us, and the emergence of some red notes as longer than their black counterparts seemed less unnatural.

The unique feature of no. 76 is that red clefs (see the greyer clefs in fig. 1) are used in conjunction with the black clefs for the central section (ex. 1, bars 72–109). The red clef in each of the four parts is placed a third higher than the black clef of that part, implying a lower reading of the notes. In voice-parts I and III the red clef makes its first appearance at the beginning of a new stave together with the black clef; in II and IV the red clef is stated within the course of a stave. The red clefs appear in fig. 1 as follows, always as the upper of the two clefs: voice I, left-hand page, staves 7–10; voice III (Contratenor), right-hand page, stave 12; voice II, right-hand page, staves 4 (at "Et resurexit") and 5 (beginning); voice IV (Tenor), right-hand page, stave 9 (at "Et resurexit") and 10 (beginning). In voice-parts II and III the clef is discontinued passively, merely by failing to reappear on the next stave. In I and IV it is positively discontinued by a restatement of the black clef without the red clef. (Left-hand page, stave 10 "Qui cum patre," right-hand page, stave 10, below the words "Et resurexit.")

Laborious experiments with canon at various pitch levels and mensurations, prompted by Pycard's known propensity for canon, by the use of a red cipher to indicate canon in no. 123, and by the association of unusual coloration with mensural tricks, failed to produce results.

At no point do directs (*custodes*) indicate that the red clefs affect the pitch at which the music is sung. If we were dealing with a simple case of two alternative readings of this section, a third apart, we might reasonably expect red as well as black directs to be used in conjunction with red and black clefs respectively. But all the directs in this piece are black. Another fact which fails to support the theory of alternative readings is that the use of the lower version according to the red clefs would extend the total pitch range of each part downwards by a third. If read at the pitch of the black clefs, the section which also has red clefs uses the lowest notes of the range of each part, although it uses the top part of each part-range less. A transposition would exaggerate the tessitura of a section which is already slightly bottom-heavy.

Where a red or black clef is placed in the middle of a line, there is no direct to indicate an accompanying change of pitch—and scribe A is normally meticulous about such indications. Where the start or discontinuation of a red clef coincides with a new line, the direct always refers to the pitch of the black-clef note. There can be little doubt that the passage affected takes place at the pitch of the black, not of the red clefs. The possibility of transposition, total or selective, has been extensively explored, but without convincing results.

The hypothesis which follows is the only one to have emerged so far which fits the facts and offers a credible explanation of the red clefs. It has been used in the new edition.[2]

Having pitched his voice according to the black clefs, each singer then reads the intervals between successive notes in his part as if the red clef applied: he thinks the music at the pitch of the red clef, while the black clef functions only as an overall anchor of pitch in relation to the rest of the piece. The technique of transposing at sight, or of setting one's sight differently from one's voice, was familiar to the medieval English singer: the anonymous treatise on faburden in British Library, MS Lansdowne 763 is couched in comparable terms, and Pycard's four-part Gloria, Old Hall no. 26, requires a similar technique. The canon at the fourth is not written out in full; the canonic part is cued to the correct pitch, but reads from the higher part. Nor is it strange to find an ingenious device such as this in a work by Pycard, who seems to have been a technical wizard and notational innovator of no mean talent and musicianship. Indeed, the use of black void diminution in this Credo serves a purpose parallel to the use of red clefs: the avoidance of irregular, unnecessarily complex notation. By writing extensive sections of the top part in void notation, Pycard avoids the use of visually exhausting minims and semiminims. By using the device of red clefs, he avoids incurring extreme written flats, enabling the singer to think in terms of more familiar hexachords.

Indeed, it was the theory of hexachord transposition put forward in the appendix on *musica ficta*[3] which first suggested that a similar device might be in operation here. While applying the range of accidentals available for a part with no signature (or in the tenor, with one flat), the actual sounding pitch of those accidentals will be those produced by a signature of three or four flats respectively. The three extra flats have been supplied editorially as a key-signature in each case. An analogy in modern terms will illustrate the point: a viola part is given to the player of a horn in B♭, who is then instructed to read it as if it were written in the tenor clef.

It remains to account for the accidentals written in the manuscript. Only the B♭s are problematic. Clearly, a singer thinking at the transposed pitch of the red clefs will read them as G♭s, singing fa on G♮ (with mi on F♯, not fa on G♭ with mi on F♮), yet if he is indeed thinking at the pitch of the red clefs it will be irrelevant that they sound as B♭s. The section devoted to *musica ficta* in Ugolino's treatise prompted me to suggest to Andrew Hughes that a manuscript accidental may occasionally indicate chromatic inflection of a neighbouring note and not of the note to which the accidental applies. If a ♯ means mi and a ♭ fa, the use of one or other sign may indicate that the neighbouring note is to be brought to a semitone's distance from it, mi-fa always being a semitone interval. This is sometimes a useful way of handling a difficult accidental, but may create more problems than it solves. Dr. Hughes is a little readier than I am to take this route. In bar 72 of example I, he prefers to naturalise the A in Tr2, as mi of the hexachord in which the manuscript B♭ is fa, and so it appears in the edition. I do not feel that the musical context (cf. bar 73) warrants this interpretation any more than it does the D♭s in bar 8 of this Credo (not illustrated here) which Hughes proposes. Such a violent wrench is surely to be tolerated only in the context of a fully developed secret chromatic art in which it would cease to be a wrench. These are uncharted seas, and I would sail them with caution for the time being. Except where the musical context commends the more adventurous interpretation, B♭ may be considered as a simple restatement of the pitch of that note, or as a soft hexachord signature.

Apparently redundant notated B♭s at the beginnings of bars 86 and 87 of the top part can certainly be treated as implying naturalised A leading-notes in 85 and 86. The red D♭ in the tenor at the same point (bar 86) is the only red accidental in the piece; if its colour associates it with the red clef, it would of course be B♭. The note is certainly flat at either pitch of notation; if the accidental has more significance than merely to confirm this, it must be to show that C (at transcribed pitch) is to be a semitone below it. Thus, the accidentals in both parts at this point establish that the B♭ cadence in 87 is to have a sharpened leading-note (mi-fa) in the upper part, not a fa-mi descent in the lower.

The only other manuscript flat in this section occurs before bar 103 in the top part. The B is flattened, but the part cadences on *c* in 104. While the preceding A may be mi, A♮, the B♭ seems to mark a tenor semitone cadential descent (D♭-C), which is musically acceptable at this point. Two further flats have been erased in the tenor part before bars 101 (B♭) and 103 (E♭). Again, these pitches are called for in any case, and erasure need not be taken as an indication that the natural forms were intended. The E♭ would have implied that the D below it should be mi, a semitone away, therefore D♮. This would have necessitated B♮ in the top part at this point, where B♭ is expressly indicated. The removal of the E♭ therefore confirms a tenor semitone cadential descent.

All the accidentals so far have been interpreted as inflections of the note to which they apply, even where they also affect the pitch of neighbouring notes. The one remaining accidental in the red-clef section cannot be so treated: the C♯ at bar 92. If it is regarded as a signal that C is mi (of the A♭ hexachord), all problems disappear. In bar 93 B♭ and A♭ will be re and ut; in bar 95 D♭ will be fa. Read at the pitch of the red clefs, the C cadence falls on A, and is made "phrygian" by *recta* preference. It makes no sense to regard this ♯ as a misplaced B♮. However, if the C♯ at bar 8 were to be treated as a misplaced B♮, that cadence would become musically acceptable. Assumption of errors must always be a last resort; let us hope that in this case the assumption is merely an interim measure, awaiting surer disclosure of a widespread system of transposition than such isolated accidentals can provide.[4]

My interpretation of the middle section of no. 76 is given in example 1. The exact placing of manuscript accidentals is shown by circled signs for black, square boxes for red accidentals.[5]

NOTES

*This chapter is taken from my dissertation, *The Old Hall Manuscript: A Paleographical Study* (1969), Appendix II to Chapter IV, pp. 266–76. The wording is here lightly revised, but not the substance. Subsequent scholarship has not challenged this solution, or indeed remarked on the circumstances that prompted it. These notes are newly added.

1. This includes semiminims, often flagged under ₵, void under O.
2. *The Old Hall Manuscript*, ed. Andrew Hughes and Margaret Bent, Corpus Mensurabilis Musicae, vol. 46. 3 vols. N. p.: American Institute of Musicology, 1969–73.
3. The *musica ficta* appendix in my dissertation written in 1968 was subsequently revised and published as "Musica Recta and Musica ficta," *Musica Disciplina* (1972), this volume, Chapter I.
4. Various scholars, I among them, have since found isolated instances of this procedure, most recently Pedro Memelsdorff (2000).
5. A further plate in my dissertation shows the music concealed by the pasted patch on f. 64; these notes have been used in the transcription.

FIGURE 1: OLD HALL MANUSCRIPT, FF. 63V–64. COURTESY OF THE BRITISH LIBRARY BOARD.

EXAMPLE 1: PYCARD, CREDO, OH NO. 76, BARS 63–127.

CMM 461

EXAMPLE 1: CONTINUED

CMM 461

EXAMPLE 1: CONTINUED

Chapter 3

Renaissance Counterpoint and *Musica Ficta*[*]

This short paper seeks to make more accessible some of the principles set out in my essays on *musica ficta*, and to take some of them a step further.

Musica ficta is commonly defined in terms such as: "the chromatic alterations that need to be added in performance, or supplied by the editor, in medieval and Renaissance music." Such definitions imply that there is something that needs correction, something faulty, or at least undeveloped, about early notation. They suggest that its composers and notators would have supplied those alterations had they only known how. This, I believe, is to do them less than justice; I have argued that our predecessors' "failure" to give us all the help we need springs not from casualness or incompetence on their part or that of their system, but rather from our failure to grasp the full measure of the difference between their notation and ours, despite superficial similarities and an unbroken evolution of the notation, if not of its interpretation. The common definition is misleading in several ways. The word "chromatic" is widely used in modern discussions of *musica ficta*, but it really has no place in most cases of inflection or even of "accidentalism" (a more neutral, if clumsy, word to denote the use of sharps and flats): the qualification for chromatic status rests on the use of melodic chromatic progressions, or degree inflection (e.g., F—F♯), which occur only exceptionally in late-medieval music. The definition is also unsatisfactory in that it fails to take account of the fact that both notated accidentals and added ones include members of both *ficta* and *recta* categories: *musica ficta* cannot be used as a synonym for added or non-notated accidentals.

The term *musica ficta* is used to distinguish it from *musica recta*; *musica ficta* extends beyond the territory of *musica recta* while enjoying some degree of overlap with it. The *musica recta* system of the gamut, or normal compass of vocal music G—ee, comprises the members of the three overlapping hexachords starting on C, G, and F.[1] Each hexachord is identically constituted (ut-la) with full tones flanking a central semitone mi-fa. Mi-fa is always a diatonic semitone, and a diatonic semitone is always solmised mi-fa. To move from one hexachord to another usually requires a point of overlap or mutation, a note common to the old and the new hexachord. A listener could not necessarily tell, and would not need to know, where the change occurred from one hexachord to another, if there were two or more shared notes, as in:

D	E	F	G	A	B♮	C	or	D	E	F	G	A	B♭	C
re	mi	fa	sol	la				re	mi	fa	sol	la		
		ut	re	mi	fa					ut	re	mi	fa	sol

Hexachords are neither *a priori* nor prescriptive; they are neither keys nor modes. They do not control what sounds are made, but are a mnemonic for dealing with, naming and teaching the sounds that are established by melodic and contrapuntal (i.e., "harmonic") context. Pieces are not written "in" hexachords, nor are hexachords norms from which deviations or inflections require special justification. They are literally a "handy" means of negotiating any given melody, a kind of vocal fingering, and they provide some of the rehearsal-room language we would so love to have. There is no direct route from B♭ to B♮; to approach either note requires a different anticipation, a mutation one or two notes in advance, as shown above.

The hexachords of *musica ficta* are those whose starting points fall on letter names other than F, C, and G. The same rules of mutation on common notes apply; the same latitude of mutation permits notes other than semitone steps to be in either of two hexachords without change of sound, and provides a significant grey area between *recta* and *ficta* status. This is very different from the notion of a note being either normal (*recta*) or inflected (*ficta*). Thus in singing C D E F♯ G the change to a D hexachord (needed to accommodate the F♯—G semitone which is in turn necessitated by a putative cadential arrival on G) can occur on D or E. <u>All</u> of the notes that are sung in the D hexachord (D E F♯ G, or at least E F♯ G), not just the one note that by our standards is inflected, are technically *ficta*. This differs from the standard view that would see only F♯ as the *ficta* note. The E and G are <u>also</u> *ficta*, while the D can be treated as *ficta* or *recta*; because *ficta* is contextual, it is the hexachord segment and not the individual note that has *ficta* status. Contemporaries frequently define *ficta* as occurring when a syllable falls on an unusual letter name, as, for example, re on C; this has nothing to do with inflection, but symptomises a hexachord (on some kind of B) other than the three recta hexachords on G, C, and F. There is no hard dividing line between *recta* and *ficta* as there is between our categories of uninflected and inflected notes.

The conceptual distance between early notation and standard modern notation can be most dramatically demonstrated from a few rather special cases that were set up by their composers so as to stray, in our terms, from the white notes of the modern piano, as a rubato wanders legitimately and intentionally from the ticking metronome. Because our musical culture, or rather our analytic practice, privileges pitch over rhythm, and notates pitch more precisely, we, now, are more troubled by apparent departures from the (modern) notation when they affect pitch than when they affect tempo. An extreme case is the tenor of Willaert's famous so-called chromatic duo.[2] So-called, because it actually is neither chromatic, nor a duo. There are some awkward moments, but all the melodic intervals are diatonic. And although the two parts discussed by theorists form a grammatically self-contained structural duo, Lowinsky's discovery of the altus part-book established that it was a four-part piece that took its place alongside normal repertory, not merely a theoretical curiosity.

Some would say that this, and other pieces requiring similar treatment, are special cases, exceptions, freaks, that take us outside a system that is otherwise comfortably familiar. I would argue, on the contrary, that this extreme case and other special cases lie within, albeit just within, the constraints of the system, and indeed that they deliberately challenge its boundaries, as do other virtuoso feats such as mensuration canons, vocal pyrotechnics or cadenzas. If you take the former view, as in different ways do Edward Lowinsky and Karol Berger, the discussion of their implications for "normal" repertory stops there. If you follow me in the latter, you will see in Willaert's piece an elegant demonstration of a Pythagorean spiral that plays with the notion of retaining the same notation for different sound, rather as a cunning canon plays on the inherent potential of its notation, deriving different rhythms or melodies from a single notated statement. The Willaert "duo" is neither misnotated nor undernotated. Indeed, it even has some redundancies; if we expect to sing melodic leaps of fifths as perfect unless otherwise instructed or compelled, there are more flats than we minimally need. Flats, and what we would call double flats, follow each other by linear logic without being notated. It may not be necessary to refer at all times to exactly where we are in relation to a norm, just as, in later music, we may not refer all tempo shifts to, or seek constant orientation from, the opening measure. But there is no reason for such deviations in pitch to be any less conscious than they are in rhythm, or indeed any less musical or controlled. Few would claim that a mechanically-observed metronomic norm produces results that are more musical or more correct, or even that non-compliance with such a standard indeed involves any deviation at all; I believe that something similar applied to pitch. To observe a rigid standard may itself be misguided or unmusical; better, surely, to recover what we can of those different criteria of timing and tuning that depend on different and more elastic principles of notation, in turn rooted in complementary pedagogical and performing conventions.

What is singular about the tenor of the Willaert is not that it departs from the white notes, but that it describes a forced journey around the "spiral" of fifths, to a point more distant than that necessarily reached by any other known composition; that this spiral is contrapuntally demanded by its unique relation to the discant which does not spiral; and that the constraints of that special (and indeed "forced") counterpoint still require the tenor to lead the way rather than to make mutual adjustments to the top part—at least until after its first arrival on an E two semitones lower, from which point it follows the top part imitatively.

There are certain consequences to accepting that the Willaert is fully and sufficiently notated (never mind, for the moment, over-notated), and that it stretches the principles of the notational system within which it is conceived but does not violate them. This means, for example, that it is not usually necessary to signal what is commonly called chromatic alteration; what we call "accidentals" have become necessary to our notation, but were at that time truly accidental or optional. It means that a note placed on the stave cannot be taken at face value, cannot be assumed to be the corresponding white note, as it would be now, and that no sign is necessary to indicate that it is not. I already went that far in my earlier discussion of *musica recta* and *musica ficta*,[3] in which I argued that a note on b fa ♭ mi has an equal right to be realised as, in our terms, B♭ or B♮, since both have a place in the *musica recta* system; the priority of one over the other is to be determined by melodic and contrapuntal context, not by notation or by white-note supremacy. (It should be noted, too, that the signs and terminology of theorists, as in b fa ♭ mi, are not necessarily the same as the signs used in manuscripts to represent the corresponding sounds.) But for other scale-degrees, too, this overthrows the primacy of "white-note" resolution; *musica recta* only takes priority over *musica ficta* if other considerations are equal.

Those other considerations involve a combination of melodic and contrapuntal factors. The Willaert piece is necessarily constructed so that linear considerations control the counterpoint rather than it controlling them. But in many circumstances, considerations of simultaneity will take precedence even over melodic intervals. According to the two theorists who tell us most about this, Tinctoris in the 1470s and Aaron in the 1520s, simultaneous fifths must be perfect; we probably have to understand this to mean fifths in metrically and therefore contrapuntally strong positions. Once any such fifths have been taken care of, melodic augmented fourths (tritones) and diminished fifths will take the next priority for correction, especially if they are direct rather than mediated leaps and return within their own compass. In other words, it is not the notes themselves but the relationships between them that are thought of as being corrected or altered. Since the notated pitch represents a functional area, a moveable step on the scale (*scala*, or ladder), not a fixed frequency point, there is no question of "altering" one point to another point <u>within</u> that area, but rather of weighing the priorities for one solution over others. A singer would think in terms of reading or construing a phrase, or a passage, not of singing a melody formed of a series of predetermined points, some of which might be subject to unwritten alteration. The monochord could indeed be used as an instrument of reference to pick out pitches, but it has yet to be shown that this was other than a slow and deterringly cumbersome process, not suitable for up-to-speed accompanying. Thus, the pitches it picked out would be the notional ones of the singer reading his own part provisionally before it was tempered by the demands of the surrounding counterpoint. A singer's private reading might already include some progressions which, on purely melodic grounds, lead him to expect cadential formulas and tritone avoidance that would in some but not all cases need added accidentals in modern notation. If he expected to approach a cadence on C from a raised leading note (B♮), he would no less expect to cadence on G with the same formula using F♯.

Having loosened the connection between *musica ficta* and editorial accidentals, *musica ficta* is not "added"; individual notes are not "altered" or inflected; nor is *musica ficta* necessarily chromatic. It is true that what we think of as "F sharp" is a chromatic semitone away from "F natural"; but only if the one directly follows the other does a chromatic progression occur. The tenor of the Willaert duo is completely diatonic in its melodic progressions, and only by the most loose and primitive notions of what is chromatic can it be considered otherwise. Black notes in a C major piece don't necessarily make it chromatic; not only music in C major is diatonic. So the standard often now applied to Renaissance music is even stricter than that for the common practice period from which that standard purports to derive.

Rather, both melodic and contrapuntal (i.e., "harmonic") contexts are what determine the "realisation" or "resolution" of a given notated piece. A simultaneously sounding B and F fifth will usually need to be "corrected" to a perfect fifth, but whether that correction involves, in our terms, altering F to F♯ or B to B♭ would be determined by any overriding (contrapuntal) simultaneities, and by balancing the melodic claims of each contribution to the surrounding musical fabric. If the arrival on a faulty fifth is truly simultaneous, i.e., with neither singer being warned by another's anticipation, the barbarism would have to be corrected the next time through. Such faults can be diagnosed by ear by the experienced, and explained to beginners in the language of hexachordal solmisation; mi *contra* fa is prohibited in perfect intervals, and if the fifth is approached from a major third, C and E, each part will form a semitone to the faulty fifth, fa-mi and mi-fa, resulting in mi sounding *contra* fa. "*Mi contra fa*" occurs where a fifth or octave is incorrect or when it is incorrectly approached by semitones in both approaching voices. (See Chapter I, p. 83, 2nd stave). Its prohibition has nothing to do with oblique or melodic relationships, but embodies both a rule about harmonic simultaneities and about approaches to them. It is not so much a *ficta* rule as a contrapuntal rule, observance of which may or may not involve the use of *musica ficta*.

What the singer heard, the "sounding score" of counterpoint-based polyphony, could modify what he would otherwise expect to do on melodic grounds. It is the expectation, not the white or uninflected form of a note, that is changed. White notes were not at any point his starting assumption; that is not what unqualified notes on the stave necessarily signalled. They would have priority only if there were no overriding (and probably unwritten) other considerations. Our idea of white-note diatonicism largely corresponds to the members of the *musica recta* system, but whereas the white notes of the paradigmatic modern keyboard are notationally specified and individually entitled points, the constituent hexachord segments of early polyphony may bend with the larger structures of which they form part; the pitch content is determined partly by notation and partly by context. To say that the singer adjusted to what he heard is not to say that he proceeded blind. He has a number of sources of help.

First, he will sing in segments that are melodically diatonic, unless for a pressing reason he is forced to adopt a chromatic step as a lesser evil (or "forced" error) in the service of correcting a more serious "harmonic" fault. The diatonicism operates in small, handy hexachordal segments, going off at tangents (i.e., projecting a new hexachord in an "unusual" place) or following sequential patterns, as the Willaert tenor does, without risk of falling off the edge, as it were, of a flat earth. Indeed, in chapter 4, fig. 2, p. 125, by the time we get to stave 3, to sing "fa mi" on the letter names D–C, meaning that there is a semitone between them, that semitone could be, in our terms, D–C♯, D♭–C, D♭♭–C♭, etc.; in any case we have to change hexachord to get down below A to G. Then G A B C, although all are now flats by modern reckoning, and lower than the pitches associated with those notes at their first appearance, can be read on the stave as if they were in the *recta* hexachord on G, even though the sound of that G has side-slipped, because ut on G, whatever the "actual frequency" in relation to any outside standard or to any internal measure, qualifies as *recta*. The standard modern view would qualify this as *ficta* by virtue of requiring flats in its modern rendering, but as we have seen, the correlation between *ficta* and non-notated accidentals does not stand up.

Second, in the absence of overriding melodic or contrapuntal considerations, the singer will normally favour the "background" system of *musica recta*,[4] to which he will be led by the combination of clef and signature. Even that won't necessarily keep him on the white notes, or even at his starting frequency standard, but it will tend to keep him close to the interval information given by the clef and signature, usually within *recta* or at a flatward transposition from it. When invited or forced by the context to venture into the territory of *musica ficta*, the dividing line between the status of the two remains ill defined. Not only the black notes are *ficta*, but also their immediate neighbours. C D E F♯ G; F♯ G must be mi fa in the D hexachord, and C must be in another hexachord, but D or E can be the points of mutation.

Third, he will (or may) be guided by accidentals given on the stave. He might overrule any that don't seem to make sense, just as a pianist may reject a given fingering in favour of his own. The notation of sharps and flats is optional; it may be helpful in resolving ambiguities; some of the ones that do appear may even be subject to interpretative choice, and indeed originate from intermediary performers and scribes rather than from the composer. We try to follow Beethoven's dynamics, but we may cheat with his pedalling, metronome marks, and fingerings, regarding them as more optional, fair game to be overruled if they fail to fit with how we want to play the piece.

Fourth, he will construe his own line, deciding provisionally how it goes melodically, not "what needs changing." He might even learn it ahead of the rehearsal, as a violinist will practise his part without sight of the others, knowing that he will have to rethink some of his provisional interpretations when he rehearses with the other performers.

Fifth, above all, he listens. After thus construing his own line he will allow some provisional decisions to be overruled by compelling situations that emerge in the score as heard. While singing his part he will be aurally guided by that sounding score, adjust and tune his own part within it. Contrapuntal considerations have the power to change what he would otherwise have done. Thus, part of the prescription for pitch determination resides in the sound edifice set up by the composer, rather than in the notated symbols. Here I differ strongly from Carl Dahlhaus's view of counterpoint and composition around 1500, which he presents as an abstract structure separate from its realisation in sound.[5] I believe that the composer had a clear general idea of the intended realisation, or at least of the conventional limits within which a realisation would be acceptable, and some very specific ideas about certain passages, which he will have set up in such a way that his intended rendering was obvious or inevitable, just as Chopin might have had a clear expectation of how rubato would be applied, or Handel of how his continuo parts should be realised. In such matters, the composer might have a strong sense of what readings would be unacceptable or nonsensical, and a fairly broad tolerance of a range of acceptable ones. In various under-notated traditions, some intended solutions would be self-evident beyond discussion; other passages might admit alternatives. The composer's idea was subject to some variation in practice; the performer still has room and opportunity to surprise and delight the listening composer, within limits defined by convention, but the composer's conception, then, as since, doubtless included the possibility of some musical choices that were not explicitly prescribed in the notational system he used. In all the above cases a more explicit notation could have been devised had it been deemed necessary. The fact that it wasn't stands as a reminder that their notation, even when under-informative by our standards, must have served them adequately in conjunction with the expectations they brought to it; it is those expectations that it is our task to reconstruct.

Finally, he remembers, just as performers of later music may remember, without notating, their rehearsed rubato or ornamentation. Only by memory can he take into account future portions of the musical texture, already known from rehearsal, that exercise a retroactive influence on present choices.

What the singer does not do is "change," alter, or inflect individual notes; he does not try to stay in a hexachord beyond the point where other considerations might have encouraged change; nor are there *a priori* modal rules to be obeyed. He does not add accidentals, but "operates *musica ficta,*" operates the system. Theorists' references to the raising or lowering of notes are presented in a horizontal context (e.g., when sol fa sol becomes fa mi fa). The singer may change what he would otherwise have done, but that will involve a contextual understanding, not a distinction between the piece as it stands, as "actually notated," and "as modified," The prescriptive dimension of the notation itself includes the unwritten system of contrapuntal rules shared by the composer and the performer, shared knowledge of which is presumed by both.

Counterpoint is a procedure; it underlies composition, and is concerned with two-part "harmonic" progressions, not with lines. Contrapuntal principles remained fairly constant over a considerable period; compositional practices changed, by adjusting the priorities between the weight with which those principles applied. Composition will normally observe the rules of counterpoint, but some licence is necessary as the number of competing priorities rises. Counterpoint has always been taught fundamentally in two parts, and by extension, in more. The two-part framework of late-medieval counterpoint is also fundamental to late-medieval composition. All the rules that we have for *musica ficta* are rules for the correction of contrapuntal progressions. The two are intimately linked, and it is my view that it only makes sense to consider *ficta* in those terms.

The main and constant rules of counterpoint are few and simple. Perfect intervals are to be perfect, and they are to be approached correctly. This approach has to do with cadences, the main places requiring *ficta* adjustments. Subsidiary to that are rules for melodic progressions. For these purposes, it is essential to maintain a distinction between tritones (=augmented fourths) and diminished or augmented fifths. Fifths and fourths, especially when the leap is direct rather than mediated, should be perfect when they return within themselves and wherever another stronger rule is not thereby violated. One significant chronological shift occurs between the early fifteenth century, when Prosdocimus de Beldemandis boldly allowed melodic tritones (augmented fourths) ancillary to the greater good of a semitone progression at the cadence, and the later fifteenth century, when Tinctoris seems to have preferred to forgo the cadential semitone where it would have to be preceded by a forbidden melodic leap.

Tinctoris's treatise on counterpoint is vivid about the active doing of counterpoint. Counterpoint could also be written, as is clear from a number of references, not to mention Tinctoris's own statement that it can be written or "mental." To equate "mentally accomplished" counterpoint with free-for-all improvisation is to underestimate the careful principles that must underlie it, whether it is written, sung, or thought.

Bonnie Blackburn has recently suggested that "armonia" partly superseded counterpoint as a guiding principle for Renaissance composition.[6] Harmony, however, as Crocker showed, is a term of aesthetic judgment, not a procedure or a technique capable of explanation in a manual.[7] Counterpoint aims to produce *armonia*. There can be no question of adopting the more recent traditional juxtaposition of vertical harmony and linear counterpoint; early counterpoint covers both considerations through the legislation of intervals and the progressions of one to another, which involves a linear progression as well.

What is commonly called successive procedure is in effect when the parts of a composition, or indeed of a counterpoint exercise, are by *post facto* diagnosis hierarchical. It does not necessarily mean that the parts were literally composed in that order, but rather that they could have been, or were composed as if that were the case. There is little evidence of *post facto* adjustment to a primary duet in the light of later added parts, and certainly none that interferes with the integrity of that duet. In fifteenth-century songs, contratenor parts are often unstable, optional, omitted or changed. The discant and tenor are grammatically self-contained—which is not to say that the composer didn't intend there to be, and perhaps even conceive, a contratenor from the outset—just as a sense of what the inner part-writing of a chorale harmonisation is going to be will not affect the treble-bass integrity.

A singer will respond differently, depending on what is or is not going on around him (whether there is a contratenor or not); what he does will be affected by what other singers do, whether in response to visual or aural signals, and how he might be affected by visual signals, such as flats.

We add accidentals in order to change individual notes; they, rather, changed the

melodic interval content in order to achieve correct simultaneities and correct contrapuntal progressions. Reading our notation can be a relatively passive and insular
enterprise; reading theirs is active and interactive. This distinction may seem to be
splitting hairs. But until we think in their terms and approach solutions with their
equipment, we have little chance of coming up with solutions like those that they
might have come up with. We need to abandon some of our visual crutches, to forgo
the easy to-and-fro reference that the visual control of aligned scores gives us.
Because of excessive visual orientation, editors have often accepted intolerable sounds
before they will accept the intolerable appearance, the visual dissonance, of a score
cluttered with accidentals. An anachronistic approach through modern notation will
often produce the same solutions as those produced from the process I have outlined;
what should interest us is not merely the few cases where the results are different, but,
rather, to recreate the habits of musical training and thinking of a historically more
appropriate approach. We will then enjoy the satisfactions not only of the constraints,
but also of active participation in the polyvalence and the elegant economy of their
notational system.

NOTES

*Unpublished paper, first delivered orally in 1983, revised 1987. These notes are new.

1. See Chapter 1 and, for a diagram, *The New Grove Dictionary of Music and Musicians*, s.v. Solmization, 1.2–3.
2. More fully discussed in Chapter 4.
3. The first version of Chapter 1 was written for my dissertation completed in 1968 (degree date, 1969).
4. What I have more recently called a default. I would now treat *recta* preference as a much weaker default
than suggested here and in Chapter 1 (pp. 71–72, 90). See the Introduction, pp.10–12.
5. See Chapter 4 note 45.
6. See Blackburn 1987; previous oral presentations are referred to here.
7. Crocker 1962: 17.

Chapter 4

Diatonic *Ficta**

1. Introduction

This is a preliminary study of how what we call pitch was conceptualised in the four-teenth to sixteenth centuries. Its central concern is with vocally conceived, contra-puntally based polyphony around 1500, and our notational access to it. It does not deal directly with monophony (which only rarely compels a distinction between rela-tive and fixed sounds) or with instrumental music and tablatures (which, for practical reasons, had to work with a preselected repertory of sounds). It attempts to combine some realities of performance with the testimony of contemporary theorists.[1]

Late-medieval and Renaissance musicians had a much richer arsenal of words and concepts for what we, since only the eighteenth century, have subsumed under the umbrella terms pitch and rhythm. When we try to translate *sonus, vox, corda, nota, clavis, littera, punctus, locus, situs, gradus, phthongus, psophos,* and so on, as pitch, step, note, and tone, we lose shadings of difference among the concepts of actual sounds, graphic or mnemonic representations of sound areas or of discrete sounds, sounds defined physically, and fixed or relative points defined in musically functional relationship to each other.

||2 This list avoids making a firm link between each of these terms and a modern definition, because usage varies both between theorists and over the late-medieval period. These distinctions have largely lost their force for us, now that our letter names are inflexibly coupled, at least for most theoretical purposes, to standard fre-quency and equal temperament, even if there are still live traditions of pure intona-tion for voices and strings.[2] A similar point can be made about durational terms: the word "rhythm" is almost totally absent from late-medieval music theory, and its six-teenth-century application is confined to the Greek poetic sense that was still primary

for Mersenne in 1636. What we now gather under this single term was likewise covered by a variety of terms, *mensura, valore, proportio, relatio*—but with the difference that our view of "rhythm" remains more dependent on context than does our view of "pitch." Indeed, the terms "pitch" and "rhythm" are not parallel for the musical dimensions they denote for us; an isolated note has pitch, while without context it cannot have rhythm but only duration. While we deal with pitch relationships on many levels, our notions of pitch *per se* are more inflexibly coupled to physically measurable standards than are our notions of duration; hence the asymmetry of our tendency to treat pitch and rhythm as comparable dimensions of music. For many modern musicians, the isolated sounding of a specific frequency will evoke a pitch-label letter (such as "A") but cannot, without context, be defined as a note value (such as a semibreve). During performances of the older repertory we feel less bound to adhere rigidly to the metronome than to the tuning fork. Our culture reveres the idea of "absolute pitch,"[3] even if we may individually recognise its liabilities, but it has not cultivated a comparable sense of absolute duration. For renaissance vocal polyphony we cannot assume a fixed frequency anchorage as [3] part of a note's definition, its "A-ness"; the selection of frequency for a performance may be subject only to practical constraints. Nor can equal temperament or enharmonic equivalence underlie our presumptions about the equation of letter names with fixed points. While equal temperament may indeed serve to demonstrate examples of Renaissance music without impairing their general sense except with respect to purity of intonation and slight distortion of interval size, this paper presumes that counterpoint was conceived without the notion of enharmonic equivalence between sharps and flats, without the danger of confusion between tritone and diminished fifth, and without the deceptive short cuts of keyboard-based thinking which can impoverish our intellectual understanding of this music.[4*]

For a correct realisation of early vocal polyphony, its staff notation cannot be assumed to have the same connotations as ours, either for conveying the positions of tones and semitones, or for conveying pitch-points that can be transferred mechanically to the keyboard or into modern score. In many senses, we have now isolated and fixed the single note with respect to frequency and prescription; those things formerly depended on context, not only for purposes of construing musical function, as is the case for us, but also for their actual sounding realisation, in much the same way as did durations in mensural notation.

2. Meanings of letters

Alphabetical letters served to represent sounds in two different ways: as labels for separate points on the monochord and as names for moveable steps within adjacent areas of the gamut.

[114] (1) Letters on monochord diagrams mark proportionally derived, non-equidistant points which carry no connotations of scale or musical function. They are like labels on a geometric diagram. The earliest medieval monochord treatises are quite inconsistent in their use of letter labels, and it was only by the time of Odo and Guido that some consistency of labelling began to result from the perceived convenience of aligning gamut letters with monochord points. Many early monochord tunings assign to those points letters which correspond neither to our usage, wherein letters connote fixed semitone positions (B-C, E-F), nor to the late-medieval gamut with its often similar results but different rationale. The choice of letters for monochord points was in principle arbitrary (as Prosdocimus and Ugolino show by their naming of the *ficta* positions: see below) but, because the sounds resulting from the points on the monochord and the norms for steps of the scale did approximately coincide more often than not, late-medieval theory usually brought them into alignment. The convenience of that alignment should not blind us to the fact that they are different in derivation and potentially different in meaning.[5]

Even the points on the monochord are norms that may be deviated from in actual practice: they represent relationships derived from one of several possible starting-points, where the principle of tuning successive adjacent simultaneities would have resulted in frequent shifting of a <syntonic> comma position that is static in any one "demonstration" monochord tuning, and which would therefore yield an often inexact correspondence between an actual sound and its "official" monochord position. This is surely what Prosdocimus meant in his striking passage on the infinity of sounds[6]* and what theorists from [115] Guido to Ornithoparcus meant when they confined to an elementary level the use of the monochord for picking out notes to be sung. It is inadequate beyond that elementary stage, presumably because it cannot supply for the inexperienced singer the component of aural and contrapuntal skill which he must bring to bear upon his reading of the notated pitches, just as, again, the metronome may have a role in rehearsal but will not be adhered to in a "musical" performance.[7] Prosdocimus tuned his monochord first according to *musica recta*, thus acknowledging an alignment between the notional content of monochord and scale, to produce the sounds normally available and normally needed. These were then labelled with the letters of their corresponding steps on the gamut, Gamma, A-G, a-g, aa-ee, with B♭ and B♮ for all except the lowest B. He then gave two methods of deriving the *ficta* pitches interspersed between the *rectas*. First he derived what we would call flats, with the minor semitone preceding the major, labelled H K I L M N O P Q R S T V (i.e., in order of derivation rather than of strictly left-to-right resulting position,

H being the bridge) with no octave repetition of letters. Then he derived what we would call sharps, labelled X Y Z 1–9, ⊙, Φ). After discussing the shortcomings of each method he ended by combining them. These further points were nowhere explained or labelled as [||6] inflections or alterations of their *recta* neighbours.[8] What Prosdocimus produced here (fig. 1) was in no sense an operational scale but rather an arsenal of pitches for demonstration purposes, preselected in the knowledge of musical functions—a selection from which, in practice, singers would need to depart infinitely. His use of the term *fictas musicas* for what we would call "black notes" is further inconsistent with his clarification elsewhere that *musica ficta*, properly defined, embraces the whole "accidental" system (see below) including the notes common to both *recta* and *ficta*. He used it here—as we do more generally—because there was simply no other way for him to designate those sounds that were residual after the *recta* ones had been set up. While this distinction was necessary for his discussion of monochord tuning, it had no place in the conceptualisation of hexachords for their principal purpose, namely as mnenonics for vocal performance.

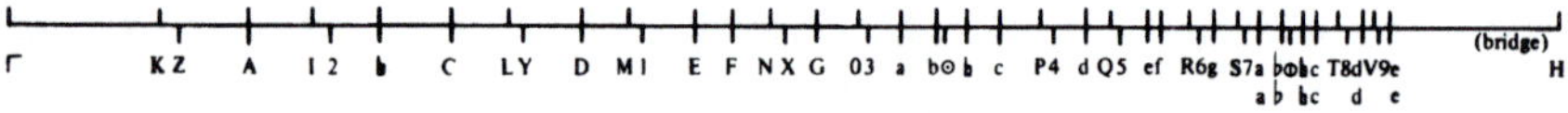

FIGURE 1: PROSDOCIMUS'S MONOCHORD DIVISION SHOWING SUPERIMPOSITIONS OF *RECTA* AND BOTH *FICTA* DIVISIONS (RATIOS ONLY APPROXIMATE HERE)

The monochord is the instrument of reference for medieval theory, and should not be mistaken for being merely a primitive form of our keyboard. It could never have been a practical performance instrument for polyphony.[9] Even if the string of a monochord was often about a yard long, there was no standard for its even approximate tension or frequency. And even if two monochords were tuned with true Pythagorean ratios, their resulting frequencies could be slightly different if those ratios were applied from a unison by a different route through the spiral of fifths.*

[||7] (2) The letters of the gamut, however, stand for steps on a ladder (*scala*), notated as graphically equidistant lines and spaces on the staff—a visual model of the ladder. These, in turn, stand for moveable points in a sound-area to be traversed: B fa and ♭ mi are two different routes between A and C.[10]*

These two uses of the same series of alphabetical letters did roughly coincide in practice for much of the time. Especially in the later Middle Ages, as stated above, theorists tended to align them for most practical purposes, while usually keeping them separate in formal explanations. The similar musical results have blunted our sense of the different origins and function of labels on the monochord and letter-names in the *scala*, and have led us to assume that both can indeed merge into the convenient security of modern letter-names, with their more rigid coupling to frequency and temperament, even though post-Renaissance music theory has of course respected comparable distinctions at many levels. It is for reasons such as this that we should beware of assuming that older concepts and terminology are inadequate to their purpose, and of being too hasty to resort to our own theoretical equipment.[II]

3. Staff, Hexachords, *Clavis*

The lines and spaces of the staff represent points that look more equidistant than they sound; neither formerly nor now are they [II8] spatially differentiated according to whether the steps are to be a tone or a semitone apart. The points on the monochord sound more equidistant than they look. Indeed, one single "place" on the staff serves now for one sound, now for another, of what are two distinct points on the monochord, such as B♭, B♮. That much we have inherited, and the letter-name associated with a staff position may thus stand for different sounds at different times. But we name those differences in relation to letter-norms, F♯ as a modified F, B♭ as a modified B; late-medieval nomenclature, however, could express such differences neither for the monochord, where each point had an independent and indeed arbitrary label, nor on the scale, where the letter B served the whole area between A and C.[12]

A staff position represents a moveable step on the ladder, and the letter-name, *littera*, is a functional label for that moveable step. But the interval relationships among the several rungs on the ladder were articulated only by superimposing on it a network of overlapping hexachords or hexachord segments; hexachordal mutation is a means of negotiating the gamut. Any melodic progression conceivable within or necessitated by the understood rules and limits of late medieval counterpoint could be solmised, by extension of the system. Hexachords provide a functional context for semitone locations which have been predetermined by musical considerations, but they do not in themselves determine what the sounds will be. The hexachordal *voces* are the means by which those sounds become practically accessible in vocal polyphony, just as, by analogy, fingering is the means by which small groups of notes are physically negotiated on instruments.

Hexachords articulate the scale of the letters by means of the *clavis*, often described as *vox* plus *littera*;[13] this clef or key yokes together letter-names of scale-positions and interval-specific hexachords for as long as is appropriate.* The *clavis* functions like a key in a lock, or [II9] like gear-wheels, or indeed like fingered permutations of frets and strings, to make a system operative and to bring two or more different cycles into temporary functioning reconciliation. It has rich parallels with the theory and practice of medieval calendar determination.[14]

It is only when our modern staff lines are labelled by a clef that they take on letter identities and the semitone positions we have assigned to the letter series; similarly, then, it was only when yoked with hexachord syllables that the letters acquired unequivocal tone-semitone definition, even within the norms of *musica recta*. Only when [110] coupled with the superstructure of overlapping hexachords could letters convey the normal, customary relationships in *musica recta*. E-F was a semitone only by virtue of, or by being understood normally to have, the hexachord articulation mi-fa. The C clef, understood as the clef of C sol fa ut, did not even fix the semitone location; since C can be realised either as C fa in the G hexachord (with a semitone below it) or as C sol in the F hexachord (with a whole tone below it), the C clef leaves both possibilities open. C sol fa ut expresses the possible immediate intervallic contexts of a note but is not a label for a predetermined pitch. This is just another way of saying that B fa and B mi are both equally available in the *recta* system, and that neither of them has priority over, or is merely a modification of, the other. If the choice between these options is to be specified, a formula such as Tinctoris's "fa of C sol fa ut" must be used.[15] *Musica recta* is not an arsenal of fixed pitches but denotes a set of relationships to a notional norm of pitch stability that is more like a flotilla at anchor than a Procrustean bed or a pre-tuned keyboard. The "operation of *musica ficta*,"* that is, the substitution at any point, for contrapuntal reasons, of a tone for a semitone (or vice versa), could mean that the absolute frequency of the As, Bs, Cs that follow may not be the same as they were before, although the local interval relationships of small segments will remain intact. The taking of a *coniuncta* (substitution of a tone for a semitone or vice versa) anywhere in the system may change the actual pitches following that point without changing the relationships except at that point. The value of a semibreve may be changed by proportional operation or mensural change; the contextual relationships of that semibreve will continue to be observed after the point of change even if the absolute durations represented by the same symbol in the same context are different from before. Both for mensuration and for pitch, the values are achieved through local context and without reference to long-term absolutes.

It is in order to clarify that the *musica recta* relationships are in effect that medieval theory goes to the seemingly laborious lengths of tagging the hexachordal options onto every letter, even when those [111] normal relationships are meant.* It is not for octave definition,[16] which was effected by lowercase, uppercase or double letters, or by labelling them *graves*, *acutes* or *superacutes*. Some of the letter-plus-*voces* combinations indeed do not efficiently distinguish octaves: D la sol re, E la mi, F fa ut, G sol re ut are all repeated within the normal gamut.

Ramos's revolutionary step was to drop the hexachordal tags which identified the interval structures—even though he needed to use them subsequently in his treatise—and to propose the use of unqualified letters to denote the "white-note" positions on the keyboard. His octave solmisation is in effect a redundant duplication of letter-names as applied to keyboard white notes, and neither he nor anyone else seems to have found it very useful. It is significant that he thus opened up the rift between the underlying concepts of vocal procedures and the practical confines of the keyboard by proposing this system in a chapter entitled "Combining a Voice with an Instrument in a Subtle Way."[17]

For Guido of Arezzo, B♭ was extra, *adiunctum vel molle*;[18] the soft hexachord seems to have taken on its equal status with the natural and hard only after Guido, surely as the first stage in the extension of the solmisation system that became necessary with the growth of polyphony and hence of contrapuntally necessitated consonances that were not called for in chant.* When theorists from Ramos onwards sought, partly under the pressure to accommodate to the exigencies and compromises of the keyboard, to give B♭ accidental status in accordance with its keyboard position, it was back to Guido that they appealed for authority, thus overleaping the period of late gothic counterpoint.

The other important development of the period around 1500 is likewise linked with this keyboard-prompted change in the status of B♭. It was no less than the breakdown of late-medieval solmisation and of the hegemony of the three-hexachord system. Instead of (or at least, in addition to) presenting the full *recta* gamut with F, G, and C hexachords, theorists gave the scalar equivalents as two distinct forms, each representing only two and not three hexachord-types. The *scala ♮ duralis* gave equal access to the members of the hard and natural hexachords but a lower priority to the soft hexachord. In the [112] absence of a signature, B♭ and B♮ thus lost their previously equal status and written B came to express a priority of B♮ over B♭. The *scala ♭ mollis* included the natural and soft but not the hard hexachords. Depending on the absence or presence of a signature, B♭ or B♮ gained a priority over the other alternative if not excluding it. A third scale, the *scala ficta*, with two flats, was predisposed to the F and B♭ hexachords. The full implications of these changes in the status of B♭, of the way in which "black notes" were thought of, and in the meaning of signatures, cannot be explored here, but it is the arguments of the more conservative theorists, with their more purely vocal orientation, that underlie most of the generalisations in this paper. A further important consequence of the breakdown of the three-hexachord system was that full solmisation became impossible, and a "lazy" shortcut solmisation was adopted, allowing 'fa super la' to be sung without mutation.[19] This means, in effect, that the entire rationale of medieval solmisation, namely to identify the semitone (as mi-fa) and give surrounding context to it, was eroded.

4. Linear Operation

Late-medieval notation operates on linear planes, symptomised by the persistent use of notation in separate parts for vocal polyphony, a presentation which is not designed for simultaneous visual control by one musician. This linear quality obviously applies to mensural notation, with its dependence on contextual evaluation, and I now believe it to be equally valid for the notation of pitch. In late-medieval terms, as already stated, a note may be identified in isolation as a semibreve, F, but the actual sounding pitch of the F in relation to other sounding pitches is as dependent on context as is the precise duration of the semibreve. The context dependency operates in two ways: visually, from the individual notated part (i.e., what the singer would do in monophony or expect to do in polyphony unless forced to do otherwise); and aurally, from the process of listening and adjusting to simultaneities that may require the singer to do something other than scrutiny of his own part would have led him to expect. Notation is representative rather than prescriptive and, although it is our only means of direct access to the composer's [13] intentions, is not in itself a complete or unambiguous record of those intentions.

Composing scores do not to my knowledge exist until the sixteenth century, and may not even have been common then; I do not believe that they ever existed in any significant sense for most preceding repertories.[20] We cannot know how composers composed. But it is likely that they conceived actual sounds, some essential or unambiguous, others perhaps open to variation, in some combination of successive and simultaneous thinking, which would then have been dictated or written as representative but incompletely prescriptive notation, to be realised as sounds by skilled performers. The composer could have used performance of successive stages as a memory crutch during the process of refining his aural conceptions.

What singers of the time did instead of depending on visual grasp of the musical entity was to make music by applying their knowledge of contrapuntal simultaneities, acceptable sounds, to the incompletely prescriptive notation.[21]* No notation has ever been fully prescriptive, and the success of a notation depends in different ways on the kind of musical equipment to be presumed for those who realise it. Late-medieval singers were in a very real sense collaborators with the composer in making the music happen—realising it—within the limits of his intentions. Those limits included the possibility of different realisations, of different actual sounds at some but perhaps not all places which are underprescribed by our standards—[14] as indeed they do for many later repertories demanding initiatives from the performer. We do not expect a continuo player to avoid solecisms on a first play-through from a sparsely figured bass which does not include the solo part; we expect him to hear and adjust to what that part does. We expect performers of any repertory to complement the written notation by applying the stylistic assumptions and learned intuitions they share with the composer. I make the same presumptions for the vocal realisation of Renaissance polyphony.

5. Meanings of Signs

The signs we still call accidentals have become essentials of our notational system; a note is presumed "white" on the piano unless it is marked to be "inflected" or "altered." But we should not make the same assumption in a notational system where it was not essential to provide these signs; we cannot regard the non-provision by late-medieval musicians of all the accidentals (now so-called but then in a true sense) that we need as a failure by their standards. In their terms and for their purposes they were not misnotating musical pitch even if, for our purposes and our greater dependence on visual control, they were under-notating it. For us, sharps, flats, and naturals raise, lower, or restore a note from or to its normal or fixed place. Medieval musicians normally operated with only two signs, ♮ and ♭, hard and soft "b," the signs of *musica ficta* or, more properly, the signs of mi and fa (not necessarily fictive); when present, these indicate where a semitone is to be sung. (These statements avoid comparing the different meanings of their and our signatures in relation to "accidentals.")

Signs do not necessarily raise or lower the notes before which they appear, there being no fixed standard but only a relative position for those notes. The signs express a relationship, not absolute pitches within a system. Most theorists explain the signs in a linear-intervallic-hexachordal context, going to considerable lengths of circumlocution to avoid saying that ♮ raises a note or that ♭ lowers it from a fixed place.* Even where there is explicit reference to raising and lowering, this usually occurs either

> (1) in a horizontal melodic context, so that the raising or lowering is explained rather in relation to the neighbours of the signed note than to its removal from a norm; or

> [15](2) in terms of vertical interval size, where the need for correction of the sound is stressed, but expressed rather in terms of adjusting the linear approach to it than of a decision to inflect one of the notes of the offending interval.

In both cases, theorists usually write of increasing or diminishing the <linear> ascent or descent rather than of raising or lowering individual notes.[22] As already mentioned, they refer to the *coniuncta*, the moment of change, at which the singer sings a semitone for a tone, or vice versa. Expressions of concern about the consequences for long-term frequency stability of such substitution are conspicuous only by their absence.

The signs may or may not result in what for us would be an alteration of pitch. If F–G becomes a semitone by the signalling of mi on F or fa on G, this could mean, in our terms, either F♯–G or F–G♭. In context we can usually work out which; but there are cases without context, in treatises, where it is not clear, and where the demonstration is not thereby impaired. Some kind of F goes to some kind of G, proceeding by a semitone. There was no normal terminology to distinguish whether our F–G♭ or F♯–G would occur (or even F♭–G♭♭), certainly nothing, either in terms of the letter labels of the monochord or the scale-steps of the gamut, which conveyed a shifting of one note from its "proper" place, leaving the other unaffected. Both F and G are in this case involved in the placing of a semitone where it does not occur on the hand, *per se*.[23]

[116] Both the F and the G in this case count as *musica ficta*, not just the one which, in our terms, is altered. A *ficta* hexachord starting on some kind of D would be used in either case; the entire hexachord would entail the use of *musica ficta*, not just the F♯ or the G♭. Furthermore, this means that the boundary between *musica recta* and *musica ficta* may not always be wholly clear-cut. The moment at which the singer begins to operate *musica ficta* may have no audible bearing on the resulting sound; for example, when singing from C up to G via "F♯," he may mutate to the *ficta* hexachord either on D or E. (Similarly, the point at which a fingering change occurs in playing such a progression may be neither audible nor musically significant.) The series of letters is rearticulated by the operation of *musica ficta*, but individual pitches are not thought of as being inflected. The resultant sounds exist in their own right and are explained neither on the monochord nor in functional solmisation as modifications of their *recta* "neighbours." There is no absolute pitch G or G fa, even assuming that we know what the frequency of G was at the beginning of the piece. If a new G is established by correct moment-to-moment operation of the contrapuntal rules which are the common property of the composer and the singer, the singer no more needs to keep track of where he was in relation to the original frequency of G than he would need to keep in mind what the original value of a semibreve beat was at the beginning of a piece which has required him to apply a series of proportional relationships.* In terms of both pitch and mensuration, the results of conceptualising in our way and in theirs are often the same, just as was the convenient alignment of two different letter-functions,

but that circumstance removes neither the importance of acknowledging the differences nor the danger of misunderstandings.

6. Willaert Example

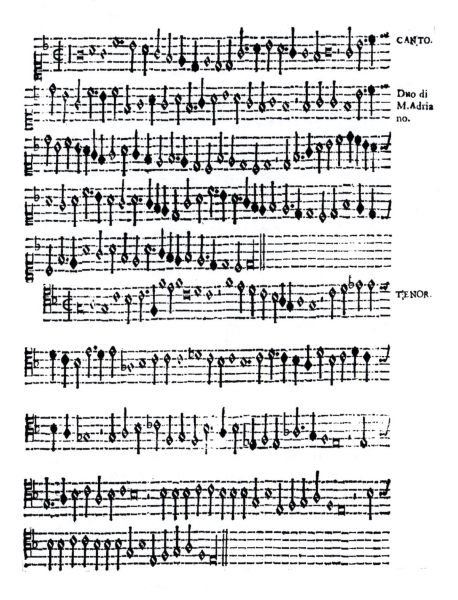

FIGURE 2: WILLAERT "DUO"

Fig. 2 gives the "duo" form of Willaert's famous *Quidnam ebrietas* as presented by Artusi, allegedly in a copy from the composer's autograph.[24]* To sing the first three staves of the tenor will make vivid [18] what their staff notation could do that ours cannot, simply following these rules:

(1) ♭ indicates fa (and therefore has a semitone below it and a whole tone above it) until the sign is superseded;

(2) all melodic leaps of fourths and fifths are to be sung perfect.[25]

The E at the end sounds two semitones below what E would have been at the beginning. The trick of this piece is not that it "modulates" in our sense, but that it ends on a notated seventh which sounds an octave;[26] it thus exercised theorists about its tuning implications. Tuning or temperament only becomes an issue when pre-tuned instruments are involved or have become the focal point for theoretical reference; for unaccompanied singers there is no reason why this, and indeed all late-medieval and Renaissance polyphony, should not have been performed with pure intonation, Pythagorean in principle, but probably with justly tempered thirds in practice. As singing will demonstrate, there is no need either to transcribe it or to rethink it enharmonically in equal temperament in order to achieve the intended result. It uses its notational system completely normally and can be read easily, even though Willaert takes us abnormally far round the spiral of fifths. We know also that this piece exercised the members of the Papal chapel, who had difficulty singing it. It is not the tenor on its own which is difficult but, with two or more voices together, the unavoidable and unusual transition from the point where they are nominally (or "literally") together and then move apart. This moment of the composition sounds much less smooth than does the tenor alone, which indeed has to make a few minor adjustments in response to the superius; singers of both parts would also have been confounded by hearing abnormal combinations of hexachordal *voces*. The aspects of this piece that gave it notoriety had to do with the problems posed by its unique compositional [19] artifice, whether for tuning theories in the abstract or practical questions of coordination between singers, and not the normal notation that guides the tenor securely along its abnormal path.

What Willaert indicates are not "individual inflections" but how to negotiate the points of interlock or conjunction between melodic segments. By our standards the notation is excessively economical; by his standards it is in some ways even overexplicit: the A♭ on stave 2 of the tenor, for example, is reassuring but not necessary if the melodic fifths are sung perfect. There is no need for each note to be related to an absolute pitch; it is not necessary to know exactly where we are in relation to an imagined fixed standard for the piece. To render this piece in modern notation requires either a forest of flats and double flats or enharmonic respelling, both of which would be cumbersome and hard to read, as well as doing violence to the artifice expressed so compactly by the notation in which it was conceived. (A similar point can be made about the awkwardness of rendering mensural syncopations and proportions in modern notation.)

This is an extreme but clear example of the difference between operating *musica ficta*, which we do when reading from Willaert's notation, and adding accidentals, as required by a modern notation which did not lie within the thought processes of composers of Willaert's time; but it is in this context that theorists' pleas for economy in the notation of *musica ficta* should be viewed.[27] Lowinsky has alerted us to several such special pieces;[28] their conceptual possibility, and the more plentiful existence of less extreme applications ||20 of the same principles, should make us hesitate before claiming that "added accidentals" in modern scores are a betrayal of the "actual notes" written by the composer. It is we and not they who add accidentals. What they did was to "operate *musica ficta*" in linear segments on the basis of heard simultaneities, redefining the relationships between the letter-names, untrammelled by our commitment to pitch constancy.

7. Natural and Accidental

The signs of *musica ficta* themselves are almost never called "accidentals."[29] Even as an adjective, "accidental" refers only to the extension of a system, or a dependent or contingent subsystem, such as *musica ficta* is in relation to the "natural" system of the "Guidonian" hand of *musica recta. Musica ficta* cannot stand on its own. What is accidental in this application is the entire subsystem of *ficta* hexachords, not just the notes that are not also available by *musica recta*. Spataro refers to "mi accidentalmente in una naturale positione," meaning that, for example, the letters C, D, F, or G have natural positions on the hand in association with other *voces*, but that mi falling on those letter-names would qualify as accidental; the mi would have its basis in a *ficta* hexachord.[30]

For Zarlino, who drew upon the basis of the Greater Perfect System rather than of the medieval gamut, the tuning of each *genus* in that system, whether diatonic, chromatic, or enharmonic, was "proper and natural." The *genera* exist in their own right, without a hierarchy of dependence. There is no question of the chromatic *genus* being accidental to the diatonic. It is the entire synemmenon tetrachord in each case, not just its trite synemmenon (i.e., B♭ in the diatonic *genus*) that is considered accidental.[31]

These and other uses differ rather sharply from our own; the earlier view of the natural-accidental juxtaposition, rare in music ||21 theory before the sixteenth century, was broader. Among other systems to which the terms are then applied are the ancestors, respectively, of what have become our most common uses, namely that

(1) accidental means outside the key signature, and
(2) accidentals mean black notes.

In the Roman singers' dispute of c.1540, Danckerts deals with the system that by then had more reality than the old *musica recta*: the scale of ♭ *duralis* (no signature) and the scale of ♭ *mollis* (flat signature). Though he avoids calling these systems "natural," he refers to the need to feign "accidentalmente . . . per b molle" when there is no signature.[32]

Theorists around 1500 began to adopt the terms natural and accidental for the systems of white and black ranks on the keyboard.[33] The fact that B♭ had natural status in a vocal hexachordal context and accidental status on the keyboard led to heated discussion by Aron and others, and reflects the erosion of the fully operative three-hexachord system discussed above (Section 3, n. 17), as well as the emergence of the keyboard as an instrument of theoretical reference that would eventually supersede the monochord.

8. Diatonic and Chromatic

The terms "diatonic" and "chromatic" are used by medieval theorists only with reference to melodic entities, the tetrachords of the Greek *genera* which, like hexachords, are segments with identical interval content. Discussion of the *genera* stands somewhat apart from that of practical music where, as many theorists say, nothing good can be accomplished outside the diatonic *genus*. The diatonic semitone mi–fa (e.g., E–F) is distinguished from the chromatic (e.g., F–F♯), which ||[22] is the characteristic and determining interval of the chromatic tetrachord, the chromatic *genus*. Despite theorists' statements about the undesirability of the chromatic, surviving music occasionally demands the chromatic semitone; if used, it has to be solmised disjunctly, i.e., without a pivotal mutation. The distinction between the two semitone types was functional: it was independent of the tuning system in which they were realised.[34]

Early theorists do not find it necessary to classify music as other than diatonic simply because it happens to require use of keyboard black notes. Haar is one of few scholars to have acknowledged the confined and purely melodic definition of "chromatic" in sixteenth-century theory.[35] Others have continued to use the term loosely, thereby creating a misleading and primitive division between white and black notes, and prematurely imposing the concept of chromatic harmony. We do not confine our own use of "diatonic" to white notes alone; not only our major scale is diatonic, let alone not only our C major scale. We use many scales and even modulations we call diatonic, while denying a comparable if different latitude to pretonal music. For Zarlino, only melodic progressions that sound chromatic because they use the chromatic semitone qualified as chromatic.[36] It is not the relationship of sounds to a pre-tuned system, nor even the use of sounds arrived at without reference to such a system, nor yet the way in which they are notated or designated, that allows them to be characterised as diatonic or chromatic, but only their strictly local melodic context. Even Vicentino describes his examples in four flats as transposed diatonic.[37] Diatonicism, in other words, is defined by the interval content of small melodic segments and is not affected by transposition. The famous prologue to Lasso's *Sibylline Prophecies* contains only four truly chromatic progressions.[38] The tenor of the Willaert "duo" is ||23 entirely diatonic in its progressions; it sounds diatonic by Zarlino's standards and was never described as chromatic by the theorists who wrote about it at such length. Hence, diatonic *ficta*.

9. Rules and Priorities

Rules given by theorists for *ficta* and for counterpoint are closely related or complementary. If counterpoint treatises sometimes dwell more on theoretical possibilities than on practical applications, this balance is often redressed by the same theorist's practical hints about *ficta*. Constant throughout the late Middle Ages and early Renaissance is the prohibition of diminished or augmented perfect intervals. Tinctoris illustrates a diminished fifth and an augmented octave, even showing the offending intervals between upper parts supported by a tenor, which might be thought less problematic than having them at the bottom of the texture.[39] The late-medieval formulation of this rule prohibits the sounding of *mi contra fa* in vertical perfect intervals <in counterpoint>, something that can result from either the interval itself or the approach to it being wrong.[40]

Rules for *ficta* and counterpoint respond chronologically to changes in musical style; however, subtle shifts in their formulation and relative weighting are more common than drastic reversals. One rule that did change concerns the melodic tritone: Prosdocimus condones it as a direct leap when it is ancillary to a cadence, in order to maintain the progression to an octave from a major sixth. Melodic tritones came to be proscribed by the time of Tinctoris;[41] indeed, late-fifteenth-century musical style gave much less opportunity to use the progressions demonstrated by Prosdocimus.

For the period around 1500, these are the two primary rules of counterpoint that may require fictive adjustment, and the present illustrations will be confined to them, namely:

(1) the prohibition of imperfect fifths or octaves sounding together;

||24   (2) the discouragement of tritone melodic outlines, especially unmediated ones.[42]*

Armed with proper distinctions, we can approach the theorists for help in establishing priorities; this they give more clearly than is commonly acknowledged. While application of such statements of priority does not solve all problems, it can considerably reduce the number of apparently insoluble situations. For present purposes, two well-known theoretical passages will be used to support the general priority of the first of the above rules over the second. They are from different types of treatises, fifty years apart in date, and neither is even primarily devoted to counterpoint.

The first is from Tinctoris's *De natura et proprietate tonorum*:[43]

De formatione sexti toni.

Sextus autem formatur ex tertia specie diatessaron inferius, hoc est infra ipsum diapente, ut hic probatur:

[example]

Praeterea uterque istorum duorum tonorum [the fifth or sixth] formari potest ex quarta specie diapente quod, nisi exigente necessitate, fieri minime debet. Necessitas autem quae eos ita formari cogit duplex est, videlicet aut ratione concordantiarum perfectarum quae cantui composito incidere possunt, aut ratione tritoni evitandi.

[Passage dealing with ♭ signatures omitted here]

Ut autem evitetur tritoni durities, necessario ex quarta specie diapente isti duo toni formantur. Neque tunc ♭ mollis signum apponi est necessarium, immo si appositum videatur, asininum esse dicitur, ut hic probatur:

[example with unsigned F-B progressions]

Notandum autem quod non solum in hiis duobus tonis tritonus est evitandus, sed etiam in omnis aliis. Unde regula haec generaliter traditur, quod in quolibet tono si post ascensum ad b fa ♭ mi acutum citius in F fa ut gravem descendatur quam ad C sol fa ut ascendatur, indistincte per ♭ molle canetur, ut hic patet;

[examples from all 8 tones]

Non tamen ignorandum est quod in cantu composito ne fa contra mi in concordantia perfecta fiat, interdum tritono uti necessarium sit, et tunc ad ‖25 significandum ubi fa evitandi tritoni gratia cantari deberet ibi mi esse canendum, ♭ duri signum, hoc est ♮ quadrum, ipsi mi censeo praeponendum, ut hic probatur;

[example with notated ♮ confirming tritone outline].

Denique sciendum quod non solum in tonis regularibus et vera musica secundum exempla praemissa tritonum praedictis modis fugere ac eo uti debemus, verum etiam in irregularibus tonis et musica ficta, ut hic patet: [example with tenor avoiding and contrapunctus using melodic tritone].

Sumitur autem hic tritonus ipse, ut clarius quae de eo diximus intelligantur, pro immediato aut mediato progressu, sive per arsin sive per thesin, de una nota ad aliam ab illa tribus tonus distantem. Sed quamvis humana vox tritono mediato possibiliter utatur cam tamen immediate uti, aut est difficile aut impossibile, ut hic probatur:

[example of melodic tritones, direct and mediated].

In defining the sixth tone as using the third species of fourth (C-F) and the third species of fifth (F-C via B♮), Tinctoris feels obliged to introduce examples of two-part counterpoint in order to demonstrate under what circumstances it is necessary to depart from the interval species proper to the mode. He gives two two-part examples, with tenors respectively in the fifth and sixth tone, each provided with a B♭ signature evidently for the sole or principal reason of ensuring that the Fs occurring as fifths with those Bs in the added contrapunctus will sound as perfect fifths. There is not even, here, a question of the modal interval structure being kept intact with B♭ while the contrapunctus adjusts to it. Tinctoris describes this as a situation of "overriding necessity." There are two such necessities: one is the attainment of perfect concords (i.e., simultaneities), and the other is avoidance of the tritone (i.e., as a melodic leap). After his two-part examples of vertical perfections, Tinctoris gives melodic examples to demonstrate tritone avoidance (adding that this applies not only to the fifth and sixth modes but also to all the others). The example includes both direct and filled-in leaps that would be tritones from F to B but for the use of B♭. Finally, in this chapter, Tinctoris deals with conflicts between these two overriding necessities and indicates how the priority between them is to be resolved: "In composed song, so that a fa against a mi not happen in a perfect concord, occasionally it is necessary to use a tritone." In such cases, where B♭ would normally be sung but must be replaced by B♮ in order to achieve a perfect interval, he recommends the notation of the ♭. In his examples, the tritone leaps thus tolerated all have at [26] least one intermediate note. He goes on to say that, while the human voice may possibly use a tritone in a scalewise progression, it is difficult or impossible in a leap. (While he does not directly tell us how to resolve a conflict involving an unmediated tritone, I believe it is implicit that even a direct tritone leap might have to be tolerated in favour of a vertical perfection.) This chapter provides a clear affirmation of the general priority of vertical perfection over both melodic tritones and "modal purity."

The other passage is from Aron's *Aggiunta* to the (Venice) 1529 edition of his 1523 *Toscanello in Musica*: [44]

Si muove fra alcuni de la musica desiderosi, dubbii & disputationi circa la figura del b molle & diesis, utrum se de necessita gli Compositori sono constretti a segnare ne gli canti da loro composti, dette figure, cioe b molle & diesis: overamente se il cantore è tenuto a dovere intendere, & cognoscere lo incognito secreto di tutti gli luoghi dove tal figure o segni bisogneranno. [lengthy discussion and examples of tritone avoidance]

Ma perche io a te ho mostrato che sempre questi tre tuoni continuati luno dapoi laltro, debbono essere mollificati & temperati: pur che non tochino la quinta chorda, per due ragioni la nostra regola bisognera patire. La prima sara per necessita, & commodita: & la seconda per ragione intesa. Volendo adunque procedere da F grave infino a ♮ acuto, & subito dapoi per un salto de uno diapente discendere, sara dibisogno chel cantore alhora commetta & pronuntii quella durezza del nominato tritono per la commodita di quello intervallo, overamente voce posta nel luogo di hypáte mesôn chiamato E la mi: perche volendo satisfare al miglior commodo, è forza a lui preterire la regola. Onde osservando il precetto, accaderebbe grandissima incommodita, con differenti processi: come sarebbe dicendo fa nel ♮ mi acuto: con il qual fa, non mai rettamente discendera al vero suono di quella voce mi: come si vede nel terzo Agnus dei di Clama ne cesses [Josquin, *L'homme armé super voces musicales*]: al fine del controbasso la presente figura da Iosquino composta:

EXAMPLE 1 (A): BASS ONLY, AS GIVEN BY ARON

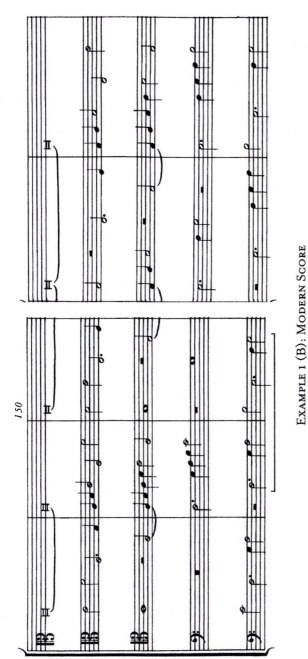

EXAMPLE 1 (B): MODERN SCORE
(SEE ALSO CHAPTER 5, EX. 13.) FOURTH VOICE IS OPTIONAL.

Here Aron specifically addresses the question whether composers should notate the signs of B *molle* and *diesis*, or whether singers should be expected to recognise the "hidden secret of all the places where these figures or signs are needed." His view of signs has shifted [27] significantly from that of Tinctoris and includes a reference to the authority of Guido for the "accidental" status of B♭, alleging that it is "solely for the mitigation and temperament of the tritone," and that musicians understand that it should be used even where it is not notated. Many composers, he says, understood the rule but notated [28] the ♭ out of consideration for the carelessness of the singer. His long list of music examples, mostly from Petrucci prints, show where the composer has helped the singer in this way. Aron states his priority between rules as follows: although the melodic tritone should be avoided when the melody does not rise to the fifth degree (i.e., when F rises to B but not to C), the rule may be overridden for "necessity and convenience" or for "understood reason." His example from the third Agnus of Josquin's Mass *L'homme armé super voces musicales* gives only the bass progression marked by a bracket above, describing it as rising from F to ♮ and immediately afterwards leaping down a fifth to E. It is not clear, without the other voices, why "if he sings fa in the ♮ mi acute he cannot descend correctly to the proper pitch of the note mi," i.e., why all rules cannot be satisfied by singing, in our terms, B♭ and E♭. But as soon as we see the vertical context it becomes clear that both B♮ and E♮ are necessitated by the "greater convenience" of the sustained notes of the *L'homme armé* cantus firmus at this point, and that the melodic tritone outline is the price paid for the greater good of the vertical perfection. In other words, Aron here subscribes to the same priority as Tinctoris: that in order to achieve vertical perfection there must sometimes be a concession with respect to melodic tritones.

Further evidence of the importance Aron attaches to vertical perfection is given a little later in the *Aggiunta*:

> it will now be considered whether the singer should or indeed can recognise at once the intent and secret of a composer, when singing a song he has not seen before. The answer is no, although among those who celebrate music there are some who think the contrary. They give the reason that every composer considers that his songs are to be understood by the learned and experienced, by a quick and perceptive ear, especially when imperfect fifths, octaves, twelfths and fifteenths occur. . . . For it would be impossible for any learned and practised man to be able to sense instantly an imperfect fifth, octave, twelfth or fifteenth without first committing the error of a little dissonance. It is true that it would be sensed more quickly by one than another, but there is not a man who would not be caught.

Therefore, Aron recommends that when such simultaneities occur in situations where correct anticipation and appropriate action would only be possible after an erroneous first attempt, the notes should be appropriately marked. The ensuing examples in his text are all such as would have been difficult or impossible to anticipate aurally [29] without rehearsal. Aron clearly knows the harmonic context of these examples; although he cites individual parts from the part-books, we may have to score them, visibly or audibly, in order to take his point. There can be no doubt that Aron attached the greatest importance to the correction of vertical perfections in the performance of composed polyphony.

10. Josquin Example

EXAMPLE 2: FROM JOSQUIN, *AVE MARIA a4*

With these considerations in mind, let us turn to the passage from Josquin's *Ave Maria* (example 2), given here without the altus.[45] The rising sequence for soprano, tenor, and bass (on the four-syllable units *Coelestia, terrestria, Nova replet laetitia*) is a stock-in-trade of contemporary counterpoint treatises. Hothby, Aron, and others give or explain two-part examples of sequential counterpoint in an alternating chain of \<perfect> fifths and sixths \<example 3>.[46]

EXAMPLE 3: (A) HOTHBY, *DE ARTE CONTRAPUNCTI* SPETIE TENORE DEL CONTRAPUNTO
PRIMA . . . CONTRAPUNTO PER 5 O 6 FUGANDO;
(B) ARON, *LIBRI TRES DE INSTITUTIONE HARMONICA*, III. 52

This is exactly how the soprano and bass, respectively, relate to the tenor of example 2. Any musician of the time would have thought it perverse in bar 3 for the simultaneously sounding B–F fifth between tenor and bass to have been anything but perfect; by singing 'B♭' the bass not only adjusts to the already sounding tenor F but also avoids the linear tritone F–B, which would be tolerated [31] only if it helped to achieve the greater good of a simultaneous perfection. The passage illustrates the satisfaction of both rules, irrespective of priorities between them. It is, moreover, carefully constructed with rhythmic overlaps (notably the soprano B at this point). The almost inevitable result is given in example 4.*

EXAMPLE 4: = EXAMPLE 2 WITH ACCIDENTALS ADDED AS REQUIRED
BY MODERN NOTATION

That the soprano is forced to do something not demanded by that part alone is, far from being a problem, precisely what should happen when a seen expectation is tempered by a heard simultaneity. In the "conventional" white-note reading of this passage, conversely, the bass is asked to perform something (the tritone outline) that he would not do, faced with his own part alone. It has been argued that Josquin's motet may date from the same decade as Tinctoris's dictum quoted above that to notate an obvious case of tritone avoidance (such as this?) was asinine. Any singer of the bass part who brought himself both to sing a diminished fifth with the tenor and, with the very same note, to produce a melodic tritone outline, would have committed a double error.

||32 I believe that this solution can be defended independently of any possible textual or extra-musical significance; the extent to which passages such as this would have been heard as "excursions" by contemporaries remains to be explored, as do many large and important questions of text and music relationship.[47*] To say that the Josquin *Ave Maria* passage is out of place in a C major or Ionian piece and disturbs its tonal stability or betrays its diatonicism is to frame the problem in anachronistic terms. In addition, to recognise manuscript "accidentals" as truly accidental allows the musical case to be built independently of notated signs. The sources of the *Ave Maria* contain very few;[48] since my argument assumes a strong aural initiative in

achieving vertical perfections, it is only "accidentally" touched by the presence or absence of such signs and the reliability of manuscripts containing them.

Example 5 gives all four parts of this passage, also in modern notation with added accidentals. The motet is mainly constructed out of different combinations of paired imitations and with the minimum of true four-part writing, which occurs only at the passages beginning homophonically at bars 40, 94 (tripla), and 143. Each of these punctuating passages is in some way unique within the piece. The first has just served as a *locus classicus* for demonstrating the application of contrapuntal rules.

EXAMPLE 5: = EXAMPLE 4 WITH ALTUS

In this sequential passage, and at this point alone in the piece, the altus part can be diagnosed as a successively conceived addition to the texture, albeit neatly accommodated to the three primary parts of example 2 (4).[49] Even if this [33] view of the status of the altus be contested, the present reading of it can still be defended within fifteenth-century standards by invoking the priority of vertical perfections over mediated linear tritones. To [34] object that I have introduced a linear tritone where there was none before would assume the very correlation between notated pitches and keyboard-definable sounds that has been brought into question here. In the present example, the "essential" piece of three-part counterpoint again takes priority both in its composition and its realisation, and the altus accommodates to this as best it may; there is no "norm" from which this realisation is a departure. Irrespective of voice priority, this is a case of conflict between the claims of vertical perfection and mediated linear tritones; the former takes priority. The last three altus notes of bar 4 and the first four of bar 5 (marked in example 5) then become intervallically identical to the passage quoted by Aron from Josquin's Mass *L'homme armé super voces musicales* (see above) and for similar though not identical reasons.

The example may be considered provocative. I have perpetrated for Josquin something that sounds not unlike what Lowinsky did, to mixed scholarly acclaim, for Clemens and Waelrant, composers about whom we perhaps have less deeply rooted prejudices than we do about Josquin. Despite some surface similarities of result, the reasons underlying my example, and my partial acceptance of Lowinsky's secret chromatic solutions, are patently different from his. The main thing that is wrong with the Secret Chromatic Art is that it is not chromatic; there was therefore no reason why it should have been secret. This reading is fully diatonic in its melodic progressions by any standards known to the sixteenth century.[50]

11. Obrecht Example*

Van Crevel presented the passage from Obrecht's Kyrie *Libenter gloriabor* given here as example 6, pointing out that to follow the sequence through exactly would result in a final cadence on F♭ as in example 6(b).[51] What he actually printed, however, was a version which followed the sequence up to the first beat of bar 93 as in 6(a), but with E♭ and C♮ on the second beat of that bar in order to end on "F♮." As Lowinsky put it, "van Crevel, afraid of his own courage, [35] while holding fast to the possibility of the F♭ ending, proposed a compromise solution [ending in F major]."[52] I agree with Lowinsky that van Crevel's printed version is musically unacceptable. But Lowinsky goes on to reject also van Crevel's (verbally indicated) "spiralling" version, ending on "F♭," on grounds that

(1) singers ending the Kyrie on F♭ would then "have to accomplish the near miracle of beginning the Gloria on F" (which presumes that F is a frequency-determined constant for the performance);

(2) "there is no poetic, emotional, or iconographic conceit that would justify so extreme a departure from the traditional harmonic conception at so early a time";

(3) "there is no theoretical counterpart to such a modulation before 1505 (the year of Obrecht's death) that would conceptualize the use of C♭, F♭, and B♭♭";

(4) the "secret chromatic" modulations proposed by Lowinsky and rejected by van Crevel are musically superior to the latter's Obrecht construction and historically more plausible. In fact, van Crevel admits the possibility of an "F♭" ending which avoids the "unmusical" twist objected to by Lowinsky when van Crevel makes the piece "return home" to F, though Lowinsky, as stated above, objects to the F♭ ending because of its disjunction to the Gloria (which later invites a similar sequential spiral). In other words, Lowinsky objects to a spiral on grounds that are not strictly intramusical, and he objects to a return to the same frequency on grounds of a harmonic wrench that is surely no worse than that which, by default, he seems to accept for bars 87–9, treating the notation as though it were exactly prescriptive, like a tablature. This passage surely must spiral, as in example 6(b); the notated altus E♭ in 87 confirms what must happen, without changing what would have happened without it. Whether F or F♭ is used in bars 89–90 may depend on how the claims of exact sequence are balanced against those of the *recta* interval relationships.

EXAMPLE 6: OBRECHT, KYRIE *LIBENTER GLORIABOR*

Lowinsky objects that the singers would have to start the Gloria on F♭, not that "F♭" at the end of the Kyrie makes that movement tonally incoherent. The objection disappears if we renounce frequency stability. The Gloria would start on the sound that is "F" at that point (lower by one small Pythagorean semitone, and additionally subject to slight frequency difference from the starting point by [136] reason of comma adjustment), and would then make its own spiral. Tenor and bass are in strict canon with a suspended motive which invites a raised leading-note; the musical context allows the tenor to have the subsemitone but not the bass, which would thereby be unable to respect the higher priority of perfect simultaneous fifths. The superius and altus have the first three notes only of the tenor/bass motive, a suspended lower returning note which, other considerations permitting, should be a subsemitone. As in the tenor, there is no reason for the superius not to take the subsemitone, falling as it does on the last beat of the modern bar. In the altus, however, this note always coincides with the superius entry a fifth higher, and produces a diminished fifth if the altus takes a subsemitone at these points. This choice for the altus (i.e., respecting the vertical perfection, even on a weak beat between upper parts, or raising the leading-note in an imitated motive) could be resolved differently in different performances. The bass, however, cannot "raise" its leading notes; this would create not only diminished fifths at the bottom of the texture but also diminished octaves with the altus on all second beats or, if the altus adjusts its octaves to the bass, the effect of the diminished fifth between the lower parts will be worsened by the octave doubling of the bass by the altus. The case at no point depends on the maintenance of intervallically identical sequence laps, but rather on the independent determination, at each moment in the music, of how the priorities of vertical perfection and cadential subsemitones may be balanced.

Further, contemporary singers without commitment to constant frequency, having applied their *coniuncte* in bars 87–88, would then be in a position to read bars 89–96 as if nothing had happened. This would result in F♭ for bass and superius in 89–90, thus preserving the interval relationships proper to *musica recta* (or indeed to the mode), as signalled by the clef and signature. The "minor triad" would be less likely to occur to a modern editor working with a transcription such as this, because it involves "unnecessary" extra inflections of individual notes. I hope to have shown that this is immaterial to the operation of *musica ficta* or indeed, as in this case, to resuming the relationships implied by the clef. For the flats required by modern notation are mostly not even "fictive" any more after the point of change in bar 88, as the nearly white-note transposition of this passage in example 7 shows. This version, included to permit [140] the reader of modern notation to test his prejudices about the sound of the passage without the deterrent of excessive notated accidentals, represents for bar 88 onwards something closer to the thought processes of the Renaissance singer. *Musica ficta* denotes neither the sounds nor the symbols, but a process. The unsightly flats of example 6 are necessitated only by the difference between their relative and our absolute pitch notation.

EXAMPLE 7: OBRECHT, KYRIE *LIBENTER GLORIABOR*

12. Intabulations*

Organ and lute intabulations of vocal polyphony tell the performer where to put his
fingers on an instrument which has been tuned prior to performance and where,
except for the adjustments possible on fretted instruments,[53] a repertory of actual
sounding pitches is established at the outset, in a way that it never was or needed to be
for a-cappella vocal performance.[54] Keyboard tablatures were treated as primary evidence for application of *musica ficta* by Apel[55] while others have questioned the validity
of this evidence on various grounds, including chronological and geographical
applicability. Doubt has been cast upon the testimony of tablatures on grounds of
their inconsistency within and among themselves, and some have wanted to discount
them anyway as going too far, or not going far enough. Despite the note-specificity of
most tablatures, a glaring need for some editorial decisions remains. Admirable work
has been [||42] done on the evidence of tablatures for performance practice of various
kinds, notably embellishment and the "use of accidentals": Howard Mayer Brown has
argued that tablatures for fretted instruments indicate with greater precision and
consistency than do organ tablatures the precise "chromatic inflections"—a "vast and
largely unexplored repertory for the investigation of *musica ficta*."[56] He believes that the
practice of lutenists can be applied to vocal performance, noting that the counterpoint treatises of Gafurius and Burtius state or imply that their teachings can be
applied both to instruments and to voices.[57]

But in subscribing to the much-explored view that intabulations are an important source of information for actual sounding notes in those repertories, we must
remind ourselves that they are not so much transcriptions as arrangements (a point
stressed by Dahlhaus); indeed, the quality that they most often compromise is precisely the contrapuntal voice-leading which invites or even compels a different logic
of step-by-step progression in the vocally conceived original that was not committed
in advance to a finite repertory of pre-tuned sounds. Neither modern notation nor
tablature can provide the only, or the most correct, or even an accurate representation of what singers operating under a totally different set of constraints and options,
i.e., with aurally determined contrapuntal procedures but without keyboard or even
monochord anchorage, would have produced. The view of late-medieval vocal notation offered here is clearly different in principle from a system in which a symbol represents a single predetermined pitch. Renaissance intabulators encountered (perhaps
without conscious rationalisation, because of the very large extent to which the two
systems yield similar results) the same collisions of principle that we as editors do, and
seem to have resolved them on a similarly cowardly and *ad hoc* basis. Modern notation
is a kind of tablature every bit as [||43] confining as those of the sixteenth century. The
keyboard with its fixed places, like modern staff notation with its fixed-point conno-

tations, acted as a limitation upon the aurally determined contrapuntal thinking that is the necessary complement of vocal notation. It rendered Prosdocimus's infinity finite and forced the full notation of what need not, could not and should not be fully notated for voices. Many of the lute and keyboard arrangements fall short of the solutions demanded by the rules of counterpoint and *musica ficta* precisely because those arrangers, despite their different goal, were caught on the horns of the same dilemma that faces modern editors—namely that of finding a compromise between the ideal sound and a notational spelling that would look worryingly different from the vocally conceived original from which each is working. Because the process both of editing and of notated arranging is a written one, it encourages resolutions that avoid the visible anomaly even at the expense of an audible one.

With the important difference that the modern editor is trying to reproduce faithfully and the Renaissance intabulator to arrange, both are trying to reconcile two superficially similar but fundamentally different notational systems possessing a large degree of overlap in practice and effect which masks the extent of their conceptual and potential difference. Keyboard tablatures are as accidental to this argument, and for the same reasons, as is modern notation; my main goal is to show why we must learn to acknowledge that early staff notation differs from both.

The problem of combining voices and instruments exercised theorists extensively from the late fifteenth century onwards, and they make it clear that certain compromises were necessary. Indeed, it is such theoretical testimony that provides almost our only evidence that theorists were aware of the collision of principle that I have here tried to sketch. Vicentino refers to the occasional need for an organist to effect a transposition during the course of a piece: ". . . & perche le voci sono instabili, molte fiate avviene ch'il Choro abassa un semitono, cantando dal suo primo principio, per seguire al fine: & inanzi che i Cantanti aggiungano al fine, qualche volta abbassano un tono; & acciò ch'il Discepolo cognosca il modo di poter sonare le compositioni un tono più basso."[58] *Voci* here surely refer to the results of operating solmisation rather than to poor vocal intonation. [44] If the singers' wanderings were merely careless, Vicentino would surely have counselled them to improve their intonation or to match it to the organ rather than advising the organist to transpose.

Fixed-point instruments engender a different way of thinking from that induced by vocal counterpoint, and this in turn undoubtedly entailed different kinds of musical compromises. Theorists do more consistently present counterpoint as a vocal rather than as an instrumental skill. However, it is not very difficult for aurally alert modern musicians to play, for example on a fretted viol, vocal part-music of the fifteenth or sixteenth century, with appropriate linear adjustments at cadences and, the second time round, to correct or improve simultaneities noticed as unsatisfactory on the first reading. This may or may not involve signals between the performers, but in any case it can be done as simply as in vocal performance in the great majority of pieces. Very few, after all, require the kind of tonal spiralling which involves a change of frequency standard during a piece (which should be easier for renaissance singers not burdened with perfect pitch than for instrumentalists, even those equipped with Vicentino's suggestions). Even instrumentalists may have corrected perfect intervals, balanced priorities, and matched imitative motives by exercising the same aural skills as singers.

An increasing body of evidence is suggesting that *a cappella* performance even of secular music in the fourteenth and fifteenth centuries may have been more common than hitherto thought; the problems that arise from combining voices and instruments may therefore have been avoided, in the same way and for the same reasons that groups of singers fastidious about intonation may prefer to sing unaccompanied.* To combine voices with instruments of fixed tuning, keyboard or otherwise, will always cramp the style of what unaccompanied voices can do. Intabulations of *Fortuna, Ave Maria* and many other pieces which adopt less "bold" versions than those resulting from the application of contrapuntal or other "rules" therefore cannot be used as evidence that Lowinsky's and my readings of these pieces were not applied by sixteenth-century musicians, but rather that the intabulators faced the collision of principles at the point where the nominal and actual sounds, as understood in the different systems, diverged.[59]

||45 13. Tonal Coherence

Our modern overriding concern with "tonal coherence" in analysing music of any period is reflected, for Renaissance music, principally in attempts to reconcile modal theories with musical realities, and in stronger assumptions about the notational prescription of precise pitch content than the evidence will bear.

Early theorists do not discuss long-term tonal coherence in the sense meant by most modern analysts of early music, other than in the context of mode which is obviously subject to at least the thin edge of the wedge of adjustment.[60] The work of Harold Powers has authoritatively disconnected modal assignments from the foreground of realised counterpoint and effectively confined them to background analysis and to precompositional intention in special sets of modally "representative" works. He has essentially discredited the exercise of seeking modal classifications for works in which mode was not such an assumption.[61] Glareanus's exhaustive modal designations, despite their illustration from actual music, take no account of the need to disturb the official modal interval structures for ||46 reasons of contrapuntal necessity. Aron's modal examples in the *Toscanello* are drawn from the same repertory as his *ficta* examples, but without overlap between the pieces chosen for the two purposes. He keeps the discussions separate and displays a totally different kind of musicianship in each. It appears that he too was, in a modal context, unconcerned with the actual intervallic realisation of the written notes. His assignments are abstractly analytical, and show none of the sensitivity to fictive intervallic adjustment that he displays in the *Aggiunta.* Finck assigns the fifth mode to Clemens's *Fremuit spiritus Jesu*, a piece which, in Lowinsky's "secret chromatic" reading, discourages any linkage between modal designation and the prescription of actual sounds.[62]

One recurrent problem in modern discussions of mode and *ficta* in these repertories is the presumption that two such different ways of conceptualising pitch can somehow be reconciled on the common referential ground of the keyboard. Both the structure in principle of the gamut of *musica recta* and the intervallic structure of the modes as theoretical constructs were subject, in practice and when necessary, to adjustments which might create a "departure" from the starting-point, temporary or for the rest of the piece. Analysis of a Romantic piece may reflect the abstract measure of the time signature as a musical reality yet not find it necessary to take account of rubato; the modal analyses of sixteenth-century theorists reflect a similar abstract background structure without taking account of the surface realisation. To alter the scale degree need not change the mode. The "non-returning" sequential spiral at the end of the Obrecht Kyrie may be likened to a ritardando of pitch, the "returning" Josquin to a "repaid" rubato. Was it indeed as unmusical at that time to adhere, as if to a keyboard, to the starting pitch and implied interval structure of the opening of a piece, as it would be today to insist on constant metronomic measure for a performance? Did interpretations that stray from the white-note diatonicism to which we have grown accustomed sound different or special to them? It is hard for us to answer this until we have become used to thinking of sounds in a new way, to doing without the conventional dividing-lines we have applied between diatonic and chromatic, *recta* and *ficta*, not to mention abandoning our inherited faith in a pre-tuned white-note-[47] scalar modal chastity that is open to petty violation up to an ill-defined point. Modal theory does deal with some kind of long-term tonal coherence, but not necessarily such as can be equated with pitch stability—another distinction that has lost its force for us. This does not mean that there were no long-term tonal concerns, but that they were of a different kind from what we have learned to expect.[63] Notated "pitches" await the musical realities of a contrapuntal context before they receive their actual definition in sound.

14. Concluding Remarks

If it is unrealistic to expect in one operation to abolish improper use of the words with which we customarily define *musica ficta*[64]—"chromatic," "inflection," "alteration," "added accidentals"—I hope at least to have injected more self-consciousness into such use. Once the prejudices in both directions have been dealt with, I believe we must learn to feel comfortable both with a different view of how counterpoint operated in practice, and with a more liberal approach to *musica ficta* than is currently considered respectable. If we are going to continue to enjoy the convenience of visual score control of early music, we must at least learn to recognise the nature of the compromises it represents, and learn to read it differently. There is no simple way of embodying choices or "travelling" solutions in conventional modern notation. To put these repertories in score shifts to the editor or performer the onus of responding to aural realities and implementing consequences, even where these are not discernible from the individual parts, as they are not for the Josquin [48] and Obrecht examples. This approach may not solve all problems, but to acknowledge the nature of the notation, to weigh priorities between rules, and sometimes to place the essentials of counterpoint above even notated accidentals does offer possible solutions for cases that have been considered intractable. It cuts through discussion about the duration, redundancy, and cancellation of accidentals as inflections; through the presumption that additions should be kept to a minimum; through the identification of "cautionary" signs that demand a reversal of their normal meaning, or of deliberately unsigned code notes; and indeed through the assumption that signatures are binding in the same way as their modern counterparts. It should disqualify counter-arguments couched in terms of absolute frequency, pitch stability, tonal coherence, modal purity, "diatonic" supremacy, resistance to added accidentals as departing from the "actual written notes," and tablature evidence for such notes as prescriptive for vocal performance. I have had to oversimplify here many issues that will eventually need careful and lengthy working out; but neglect of some primary musical facts has led us to tolerate the aural dissonance of intolerable intervals before we accept the merely graphic dissonance of an intolerable-looking modern score.

Commentary

to passages marked by asterisks in text; for more extended responses and revisions see Chapter 6 and the Introduction.

p. 116   It is quite likely that individual groups of singers developed their own

frequency memories for choices that suited them; it was such convenience of fitting scoring to the range comfort of singing groups that I
intended by "practical constraints." In a valuable series of essays Roger
Bowers has developed a sustained argument relating pitch to ranges; see
Bowers 1999.

Dahlhaus n. 4 see also n. 21. In citing Dahlhaus here with approval of his
distinctions in these categories, I misled Peter Urquhart into thinking
that "Bent borrowed from Dahlhaus the concept of an abstract counterpoint not fully specified as to pitch content by the composer" (1993:
25–26). See also the Introduction for a distinction between the form of
relativism to which I subscribe, and that expressed by Dahlhaus (cited in
my n. 45), from which I strongly dissent, for some but not all of the reasons set out by Berger 1987: 166–70. The present chapter should make
it quite clear that I subscribe neither to Dahlhaus's abstract view of
counterpoint nor indeed to Lowinsky's formulations of "secret" chromaticism; both have been alleged.

p. 117   "Surely" is too strong, but it remains one possible interpretation of
              Prosdocimus's delightful and diverse ways of singing, leading to various
              compositional practices, which cannot be notated on account of their
              diversity.

p. 118 (a)
and n. 9
(p. 153)   For corrections by Jonathan Walker to some of my statements about
              tuning, see the Introduction pp. 27–29.

p. 118 (b)
and n. 11
(p. 153)   Better: "The letters of the gamut, however, stand for variable steps on a
              ladder (*scala*), . . . These, in turn, stand for points (*loca*), that are move-
              able with respect to tones and semitones, and not always equidistant, in a
              sound-area to be traversed . . ."

p. 119   "Hexachords articulate" . . . but they do not determine pitch relation-
              ships. Unlike some readers, Brothers and Cross have understood my
              position correctly: see Chapter 6, ¶ 18, and the Introduction.

pp. 120, 124,
126–27,   For *operare*, see the Introduction, p. 15.
144–45

p. 120   In view of the concern raised by my friend Philip Brett in Brett 1993: 116
                n.12, I should assure him that I intend no heterosexist connotations to
                attach to this use of the word "normal" many years ago.

p. 121   See now, for Guido and these concepts, Pesce 1987.

p. 122, 155   n. 21: Crocker's article deserves even stronger endorsement than I give
                it here. He stresses the nature of counterpoint as a succession of dyads,
                not a combination of lines, and maintains the non-technical applica-
                tion of the term "harmony." I would also now give more prominence to
                the importance of Prosdocimus's revision for overriding other consid-
                erations, such as *recta* preference.

p. 123   See note to Chapter I, p. 74, on p. 90.

pp. 124, 126   This does not mean, and was not intended to imply, that singers would
                not have noticed changes in pitch and found them significant, as Karol
                Berger suggests (1987: 45). I never thought, nor meant to imply, that
                awareness of pitch shifting was not important, only that one did not
                need constantly to measure the results of local operation by the standard
                at which the opening pitch was set (as with tempo). Indeed, their under-
                standing of pitch did depend on a standard established at the beginning
                of the piece, but that does not necessarily mean remaining identical to
                that standard throughout. See also chapter 6, ¶ 8 and 19. Berger puts
                into my mouth words ("she would claim [that] the change of frequency
                would be of no importance") that I neither used nor intended. Indeed,
                I stress throughout the role of careful listening in arriving at contrapun-
                tal solutions (see, *inter alia*, the last paragraph of this chapter). Berger's
                (modern) view of combined frequency stability and frequency standards
                obliges him to assert that to realise the same written G within a piece at
                different frequencies would have been thought of as two different
                "steps," without explaining how this phenomenon would be rationalised
                in the one piece he and I agree must shift, the tenor of the Willaert,
                which gainsays his assertion that the same step could not be expressed by
                different frequencies. Indeed I am well aware of the essentials of solmi-

sation, which he charges me with forgetting; see section 3 above, and
Chapter 6 ¶ 18. See Introduction pp. 6–7.

p. 125   This plate has been "doctored" by obliterating the page join in Artusi's
            print.

pp. 129–30,
134   For more on this point with respect to Aron, see Chapter 5, and to
            Tinctoris, see Bent 2002b, where music examples for the following pas-
            sage from Tinctoris can be found.

p. 137   These statements are now refined and qualified in Chapter 6, which was
            written in response to Roger Wibberley's challenge to this interpreta-
            tion.

p. 139   Karol Berger's critique (1987: 45–46) of the premises of this discussion
            is addressed in the Introduction.

Ex. 6 presents two different continuations from a common beginning of the
sequence, up to bar 88. Ex. 6a (version from bar 89, upper of the bracketed systems)
offers only one of several possibilities for returning to an ending on F♮. Smijers supplied E♭ in soprano, tenor, and bassus in bars 87–92 in response to the notated E♭ in
bar 87, but left all other pitches unmodified, resulting in A♮ in 90, ugly with the E♭
from both harmonic and linear points of view. I have here pushed the inevitable "jolt"
on to bar 93 where, though still ugly, it is a little less offensive. Ex. 4.6b (version from
bar 89, lower of the bracketed systems) maintains the sequence without jolt, ending
on F♭. There are still some options within the general framework of this version:

> a) The suspended leading notes in the altus and bassus could (perhaps
> should) be raised throughout. I have not so marked them here, in order not
> to confuse the issue further by introducing false fifths and octaves on those
> weak beats.
> b) Some will wonder why I have marked the soprano F as ♭ in bar 90; not,
> clearly, to maintain intervallic exactness in the melodic sequence. The
> soprano would be reading of course from an uninflected part and would or
> might read that A-F third as major, on the default basis of a linear reading of
> the staff with its cleffing, rather than thinking (as we might) in terms of
> inflections of individual notes. I believe this is a case of genuine *Terzfreiheit*

(indeterminateness of thirds) which does not affect the spiral of the sequence.

p. 144   In addition to the work of Howard Mayer Brown cited in n. 60 see Robert Toft 1992.

pp. 145–

46   Writings by David Fallows, Roger Bowers, and Christopher Page bring additional evidence to bear in support of this view.

NOTES

*From: *Early Music History* 4 (1984), pp. 1-48. I thank Annie Coeurdevey for her great kindness in making a French translation of this essay, as yet unpublished.

1. I warmly thank Professor Harold Powers for many formative and stimulating conversations while these thoughts were taking shape. Professor Edward Lowinsky graciously engaged in a lively correspondence in which he gave me the benefit of his experience and reactions to a more informal statement of my hypothesis. Many other colleagues, students, and friends have helped and encouraged this enterprise by their comments and criticisms; I beg to defer the pleasant duty of thanking them by name until I have the opportunity to present a more extended and fully documented study. Two summer seminars under the auspices of the National Endowment for the Humanities provided a congenial workshop for performing from original notation and exploring practical *ficta* applications. Earlier versions of this paper were read at New York University in November 1982, subsequently at other institutions, and in 1983 at Oxford and at the Annual Meeting of the American Musicological Society in Louisville.

2. One fairly constant distinction is invoked by Calvin Bower to demonstrate that "The translator has failed to distinguish between Guido's concept of qualitative pitch (*vox*)—sound defined by the intervals surrounding it—and discrete note (*nota*)—sound defined by a point on the system of a monochord and signified by a letter. Thus a subtle, but fundamental dualism of medieval musical thought has been obscured." Review in *Journal of the American Musicological Society* (hereafter *JAMS*) 35 (1982), p. 164.

3. Natasha Spender describes the faculty as a "sensory and aesthetic life-enhancer" whose absence she finds analogous to colour-blindness in an artist—an extreme statement of a common and wholly modern prejudice; the author finds no problem for her "absolutist" acceptance of the modern phenomenon in the fact that "a listener with absolute pitch would now be disoriented to hear a C major work in the pitch of Mozart's day"; s.v. "Absolute pitch," *The New Grove Dictionary of Music and Musicians*, ed. S. Sadie, 20 vols. (London, 1980).

4. Carl Dahlhaus has addressed a number of such questions. The following quotations from his "Tonsystem und Kontrapunkt um 1500," *Jahrbuch des Staatlichen Instituts für Musikforschung preussischer Kulturbesitz 1969*, ed. D. Droysen (Berlin, 1970), pp. 7–17, are offered as samples rather than summaries of his important distinctions between counterpoint, tonal, and tuning systems:

> "Ein System ist . . . ein Inbegriff von Relationen, nicht von bloßen Bestandteilen." ". . . Tonsysteme als Systeme von Tonrelationen [beruhen] auf Prinzipien, die nicht an einen bestimmten, immer gleichen Tonbestand gebunden zu sein brauchen. Form und Material sind nicht selten unabhängig voneinander." "Ein Tonsystem muß andererseits von der Stimmung oder Temperatur unterschieden werden, in der es erscheint oder sich verwirklicht. Eine Stimmung ist gleichsam die akustische Außenseite; und sie kann manchmal, wenn auch nicht immer, mit einer anderen vertauscht werden, ohne daß das Tonsystem, dessen äußere Darstellung sie ist, aufgehoben oder auch nur in seiner musikalischen Bedeutung modifiziert wäre."

5. See C. D. Adkins, "The Theory and Practice of the Monochord," Ph.D. dissertation (Iowa, 1963), especially the table facing p. 94, which documents from a wide range of theorists both before and after Guido the use of letters as monochord labels with the semitones between different letters from our scale.

6. "Reperiuntur etiam tamen alii diversi modi cantandi ab istis et etiam inter se, quos scribere foret valde difficile et forte impossibile, eo quod tales diversimodi cantandi quodammodo infiniti sint, et diversis diversimode delectabiles, qua propter insurgit diversitas componentium, et quia intellectus noster infinita capere non potest, cum non sit infinite capacitatis sed finite, eo quod aliter in hoc intellectui divino adequaretur, quod non est dicendum. Pro tanto huiusmodi modi a scriptura relinquendi sunt, nec adhuc scribi possent propter sui infinitatem . . . Scire autem ubi hec signa [of *musica ficta*] dulcius cadunt auri tue dimitto, quia de hoc regula dari non potest, cum hec loca quodammodo infinita sint" (Prosdocimus, *Contrapunctus*, iv, v; ed. J. Herlinger, who very kindly made his work available to me in advance of publication). <See now Herlinger pp. 66, 68, and 94.> The above quotations embody the revisions of 1425 to the 1413 treatise. See also E. de Coussemaker, *Scriptorum de musica medii aevi nova series* (hereafter CS) (Paris, 1864–76), III, pp. 197–98.

7. Guido recommends use of the monochord in his prologue to the Antiphoner: "Duos enim colores ponimus, crocum scilicet & rubeum, per quos colores valde utilem tibi regulam trado, per quam aptissime cognosces de omni neuma & unaquaque voce, de quali tono sit, & de quali littera monochordi: si tamen, ut valde est opportunum, monochordum & tonorum formulas in frequenti habeas usu" (M. Gerbert, *Scriptores ecclesiastici de musica* [hereafter GS], Saint Blaise, 1784, ii, 36a). But in the *Epistola Michaeli* he qualifies this advice: "Ad inveniendum igitur ignotum cantum, beatissime Frater! prima & vulgaris regula haec est, si litteras, quas quaelibet neuma habuerit, in monochordo sonaveris, atque ab ipso audiens tamquam ab homine magistro dicere poteris. Sed puerulis ista est regula, & bona quidem incipientibus, pessima autem perseverantibus. Vidi enim multos acutissimos philosophos, qui <pro studio huius artis non solum Italos, sed etiam Gallos atque Germanos, ipsoque etiam Graecos quaesivere magistros; > sed quia in hac sola regula confisi sunt, non dico musici, sed neque cantores umquam fieri, vel nostros psalmistas puerulos imitari potuerunt" (GS II, pp. 44b–45a). Translations of both passages in O. Strunk, *Source Readings in Music History* (New York, 1950), pp. 119, 123.

Ornithoparcus writes (in Dowland's English translation): "The Monochord was chiefly invented for this purpose, to be judge of Musical voices and intervals: as also to try whether the song be true or false: furthermore, to shew haire-braind false Musitians their errors, and the way of attaining the truth. Lastly, that children which desire to learne Musicke, may have an easie meanes to it, that it may intice beginners, direct those that be forward, and so make of unlearned learned," *A Compendium of Musical Practice*, ed. G. Reese and S. Ledbetter (New York, 1973), I, 9.

8. *Parvus tractatulus de modo monachordum dividendi*; I again thank Professor Herlinger for access to the typescript of his new edition of this treatise. Ugolino's *Tractatus monochordi* (ed. A. Seay, *Corpus Scriptorum de Musica* (hereafter CSM), 7, III, pp. 227–53) assigns yet a different set of letters to his *recta* and *ficta* divisions. See also A. Hughes, "Ugolino: The Monochord and *musica ficta*," *Musica Disciplina* 23 (1969): 21–39, and M. Lindley, "Pythagorean Intonation and the Rise of the Triad," *R.M.A. Research Chronicle* 16 (1980): 4–61, for the systems of Prosdocimus and Ugolino, and n. 21 below.

9. Adkins ("Monochord") reviews the practical uses of the monochord in his chapter 7, but the pictorial evidence to which he refers does not weaken the general statement made here. It might be suggested that for purposes of theoretical demonstration it was symbolically important that the monochord remain essentially a monophonic instrument (despite later applications of the word to polychordal instruments). It precluded not only the checking of simultaneities, but also the efficient comparison of successive sounds.*

10. They are not, normally, mutually accessible; the only way to travel between two nearby stations may be to ride back to a junction where their lines intersect. A note's presence in the system does not guarantee that it will be accessible from all points.

11. The linking of monochord points by Prosdocimus and others with the corresponding "places" of *musica recta* is a concession much less extreme than that of Johannes Boen's treatise of 1357 (ed. W. Frobenius, *Johannes Boens Musica und seine Konsonanzlehre*, Freiburger Schriften zur Musikwissenschaft, 1971), which fixes, as would be necessary on a keyboard, what would result if the system were restrained from the fluc-

tuations which may occur in *a cappella* vocal practice. Despite a few such attempts to equate actual points with notional *recta* sounds, it remains clear that, except for such purposes as monochord demonstration in principle, we are indeed dealing with the *recta* "scale" as a set of relationships rather than as a pre-tuned system.* Until late-fifteenth-century keyboard-influenced attempts at reconciling the systems, Boen was virtually alone in attempting to expound the monochord and the gamut in a single operation, as distinct from using the gamut letters to label the monochord. He resorted to some unusual vocabulary in so doing, e.g., *mansio* (=lunar mansion?), and *extorquere*, for the removal of sounds from those proper places.

12. See notes 8, 10, and 21. Only for the distinct purposes of tablature did letter-names thus indicate adjacency of keys by attaching genitive endings, as in *fis*; these endings often selected the "wrong" enharmonic spelling of a note, showing that they were less tied to musical function than to keyboard designation.

13. "Clavis est littera localis per voces rectificata" (*clavis* is a letter of a place [on the staff] adjusted to it by means of *voces* [contextual hexachord members]), Adam von Fulda, GS III, p. 344. Du Cange gives *rectificata*=corrected (1332). "A key is a thing compacted of a Letter and a Voyce; . . . A Key is the opening of a Song, because like as a Key opens a dore, so doth it the Song" (Ornithoparcus, *Compendium*, i, 3; see p. xxv for sources of these formulations in Guido and other earlier theorists).

14. F. Reckow, *Handwörterbuch der musikalischen Terminologie* (Wiesbaden, 1972–), s.v. "Clavis," has shown the likely derivation of the musical term from computus terminology, and his brief statement invites amplification of the parallels. The church calendar, with its fixed and moveable feasts, depends on three periodic cycles lacking a common measure: the seven days of the week (A–G); the lunar month (29.<53> days); the solar <Julian> year (365.25 days). The weekday sequence is repeated only every twenty-eight years (not seven, due to the taking up of irregularities in bissextile (leap) years); the lunar month and solar year coincide only every nineteen years (again, with some adjustment of irregularities). The moveable feast of Easter, together with feasts whose dates are dependent upon that of Easter, touches all these cycles: Easter is the first Sunday after the full moon that occurs on or after the vernal equinox (March 21). These calculations were performed with a number of aids, including forms of the wheel diagrams and hands shared with music theory. J. Smits van Waesberghe, *Musikgeschichte in Bildern*, III, *Musikerziehung* (Leipzig, 1969), pll. 57–58, has drawn attention to the existence of calendrical hands from as early as the so-called Guidonian hand (see pll. 55–84 on the musical hand in general) and there are some slightly later ones with even more significant musical analogy in that they link the seven-letter weekly cycle A–G with the permutations of the nineteen-year lunar cycle on which Easter depends and which gives rise to the so-called Golden Number—just as the musical hand links the seven-letter octave A–G with the permutating hexachord superstructures. The nineteen years of the lunar cycle, the nineteen places on the physical hand (knuckles and fingertips), and the decision to confine the usable range of music to those nineteen positions on the Guidonian hand (excluding the later-added place for E la) present a striking analogy. Other calendrical hands show the A–G letters permutated with the so-called tabular or "fnugo" letters, as does the musical hand with the hexachords. See, for an example from a theorist also known to music history, W. E. van Wijk, *Le nombre d'or, . . . massa compoti d'Alexandre de Villedieu* (The Hague, 1936). The *sedes clavium* were fixed dates, the earliest dates on which a feast could occur. The *claves pasche* are a series of nineteen numbers (11–29) which, when added to the *sedes*, provide a ready means of calculating the date of Easter. They are a convenient shorthand, a summary means of regulating the disparate cycles, just as musical *claves* regulate the disparate systems of proportional monochord tuning, the octave cycle, the functional hexachords. In both systems, the respective irregularities of leap years and commas have to be absorbed.

While it is not necessary to bring in the Pythagorean doctrine of the music of the spheres in order to establish a connection between the methods of calendrical and musical calculation and terminology, it is nonetheless worth recalling that the proportionate speeds of planetary revolution were the same set of duple and triple geometric proportions as underlie Pythagorean tuning. Haar (*The New Grove Dictionary*, s.v. "Music of the spheres") has called it a kind of celestial monochord. It is hardly surprising that computists and musicians found common ways and terms for reconciling and illustrating those parts of their subject matter that were explained by geometric proportion, with the nonproportional structures that were to be superimposed on them.

15. E.g., his *De natura et proprietate tonorum* (CSM 22, 1), chapter 2. Indeed, the places on the so-called

Guidonian hand itself embody all those options and do not in themselves assist in making choices between the possible articulations, any more than the unadapted hand copes with *musica ficta*. Such adaptation is only rarely documented, for example by Ugolino; see note 8 above.

16. A myth perpetuated in *The New Grove Dictionary*, s.v. "Pitch."

17. Bartolomeo Ramis de Pareija, *Musica Practica* (Bologna, 1482), [Prima pars] chapter 7, "Copulandi vocem cum instrumento modus subtilis."

18. *Micrologus*, ed. J. Smits van Waesberghe, CSM 4, chapter 8.10, p. 124.

19. Specifically allowed by Listenius, *Musica* (Nuremberg, 1549), chapter 5, discussed and rejected by Aron, *Lucidario in musica* (Venice, 1545), book I, chapters 8, 10.

20. The few repertories that are not obviously for keyboard but for which score is characteristic (including organum and English discant) invite special consideration, but because they are not necessarily designed for or suited to use by one performer, they do not undermine the validity of the generalisation. The assumptions stated here and in what follows are shared with my *"Resfacta* and *Cantare Super Librum,"* JAMS 36 (1983), especially pp. 376–78<=Chapter II>. That article also stresses that, for Tinctoris, the process of composition included not only operation of the rules of counterpoint but the weighing of choices and priorities between them.

21. For examples of theoretical statements documenting the role of the ear in counterpoint see R. L. Crocker, "Discant, Counterpoint and Harmony," *JAMS* 15 (1962): 4; this article presents many important insights about the nature of medieval counterpoint and stresses the importance of trying to conceive it in contemporary terms. To these references may be added a remarkable interpolation near the end of the revised version of Prosdocimus's *Contrapunctus*, ed. Herlinger, in which he says that the signs of *musica ficta* should be placed where they sound sweetly, that a choice between the discant and the tenor should be left to the ear, and that no rule can be given because the possibilities are infinite: "Scire autem ubi hec signa dulcius cadunt auri tuo dimitto, quia de hoc regula dari non potest, cum hec loca quodammodo infinita sint." If the "variatio" sounds equally good in the tenor or the discant, it should be made in the discant. See below, section 9, on rules and priorities: this passage thus expresses a priority for applying *ficta* in a situation not otherwise discussed in this paper.*

22. Typical theoretical statements expressing ideas of raising or lowering in terms of linear context rather than of individual pitch inflection include J. de Muris (CS III, p. 73): "on la sol la (A G A) the sol should be raised and sung as fa mi fa"; Prosdocimus (ed. Herlinger): <♭> augments the ascent and <♭> diminishes it. The two signs do not augment or diminish [intervals] except by a major semitone,' *Contrapunctus* [v. 4]. Contrast the terminology of Johannes Boen (n. 11 above); see also the citation from the 1375 Paris anonymous <now the Berkeley MS, ed. Ellsworth> and other relevant passages cited in Bent, *"Musica Recta* and *Musica Ficta," Musica Disciplina* 26 (1972): 86 and *passim*.

23. These phrases are typical of contemporary *ficta* definitions, e.g., Tinctoris, *Diffinitorium* (1472): "ficta musica est cantus praeter regularem manus traditionem aeditus"; Prosdocimus, *Contrapunctus* [v]: "ficta musica est vocum fictio sive vocum positio in § loco ubi esse non videntur [revised version from §: aliquo loco manus musicalis ubi nullo modo reperiuntur], sicut ponere mi ubi non est mi, et fa ubi non est fa . . ."; Ornithoparcus (*Compendium*, I.10), "a Coniunct is this, to sing a Voyce in a Key which is not in it."

To locate the notes on the monochord would involve a choice, but there is no standard monochord terminology that expresses or identifies any relationship between these notes and their neighbours, just as there are no functional names (such as F♯ and G♭) to distinguish the two possibilities. The two G♭s on the monochord, for example, are labelled by Prosdocimus N, R, by Ugolino O, P; the two F♯s X, 6 and S, 7 respectively. See also Dahlhaus "Zu Costeleys chromatischer Chanson," p. 256: "daß das 16. Jahrhundert für den Ton, das wir 'heses' nennen, weder einen Namen noch ein Zeichen hatte."

24. *L'Artusi overo delle imperfettioni della moderna musica* (Venice, 1600; facsimile, Bologna, 1968), Ragionamento Primo, ff. 21–21ᵛ. See J. S. Levitan, "Adrian Willaert's Famous Duo *Quidnam ebrietas . . .*," *Tijdschrift van de Vereniging voor Nederlandse Muziekgeschiedenis* (hereafter *TVNM*), 15 (1938): 166–233, and E. E. Lowinsky, "Adrian Willaert's Chromatic 'Duo' Re-examined," *TVNM*, 18 (1956): 1–36, where the piece is shown to be a four-part composition. The two parts given here sufficed to demonstrate the problems that engaged theorists.

25. Both principles are widely documented, e.g., Ornithoparcus (*Compendium*, I.10, p. 25 [145]):

"Marking fa in b fa ♮ mi, or in any other place, if the Song from that shall make an immediate rising to a Fourth, a Fift, or an Eight, even there fa must necessarily be marked to eschew a tritone, a Semidiapente, or a Semidiapason, and inusuall, and forbidden Moodes . . ." The example has leaps of those intervals; the principle is the same even where theorists differ in their insistence on what needs to be notated. See n. 27 below.

26. The term modulation is used in contemporary theory only to describe how an interval is filled in melodically. It has no connotations of the kinds of change it has acquired in tonal theory, and must join the ranks of words and concepts that are out of place if applied to early music in a modern sense .

27. Tinctoris's famous statement discouraging as asinine the notation of unnecessary signs is given below, section 9, as is the passage from Aron which, rather than indiscriminately encouraging notated signs, requires them explicitly for cases that could not be anticipated by the singers. Prosdocimus [*Contrapunctus*, v. 2] criticises composers for using *ficta* where it is not necessary, and makes it clear in the revision (see n. 6 above) that it is the unnecessary notating of signs to which he objects.

28. His study of the Willaert composition is cited in n. 24 above. It is hard to single out for mention here anything less than Lowinsky's complete body of writings, so masterfully has he laid out a terrain that must continue to attract further investigation. The reader not already familiar with Lowinsky's writings is referred to the listing under his name in *The New Grove Dictionary* and, even better, to the first few pages of his "Secret Chromatic Art Re-examined," *Perspectives in Musicology*, ed. B. S. Brook, E. O. D. Downes and S. van Solkema (New York, 1972), pp. 91–135, where he reviews not only his own contributions, starting with *Secret Chromatic Art in the Netherlands Motet* (New York, 1946), but also scholarly responses to it and relevant contributions by other scholars. Particularly germane in the present context are his studies of the *Fortuna* settings by Josquin and Greiter, and the study by K. Levy, "Costeley's Chromatic Chanson," *Annales musicologiques*, 3 (1955): 213–63 (see also Dahlhaus, "Zu Costeleys chromatischer Chanson").

29. Marchettus lists them together with stems, dots, rests, and ancillary markings in general in his ostentatiously Aristotelian *Pomerium*, ed. G. Vecchi, CSM 6, book I, part I. Heyden, *De arte canendi* (Nuremberg, 1540), p. 5, gives a different list of "accidentia necessary to the art of singing": *scala, clavis, tactus, nota, punctum, pausa, mensura, tonus.*

30. Letter to Aron, 1531: cited by P. Bergquist, "The Theoretical Writings of Pietro Aaron," Ph.D. dissertation, Columbia (1964), p. 440, from Rome, Biblioteca Apostolica Vaticana, MS Vat. lat. 5318, no. 86, f. 219ᵛ. <See Blackburn 1991.>

31. Zarlino, *Le Institutioni Harmoniche* (Venice, 1558), part III, chapter 72 (same chapter reference in edition of 1573).

32. L. Lockwood, "A Dispute on Accidentals in Sixteenth-Century Rome," *Analecta Musicologica*, 2 (1965): 24–40, especially pp. 28, 32.

33. E.g., Aron, *Toscanello in musica* (Venice, 1529), book II, chapter 40: "Che ne lo instrumento organico secondo il comune ordine, si ritrovano voci naturali di numero xxix, chiamati dal universale uso tasti bianchi: e accidentale di numero xviii, detti tasti negri, overo semituoni: per il qual ordine da noi sará diviso tasto per tasto: dimostrando ciascheduno intervallo del uno al altro cosi accidentali come naturali." Aron's arguments in general for the accidental status of B♭ are to be found in the *Compendiolo* (Milan, post–1545), chapter 10; the *Libri tres de institutione harmonica* (Bologna, 1516), book I, chapter 15; and in the *Toscanello in musica* book II, chapter 5; also in the *Aggiunta* to that work.

34. The relative sizes were reversed in Pythagorean (diatonic smaller than chromatic) and mean-tone (diatonic larger than chromatic) tunings. Dahlhaus has usefully separated consideration of the tuning system from the tonal system: "am Tonsystem . . . änderte der Wechsel der Stimmungen nichts."

35. J. Haar, "False Relations and Chromaticism in Sixteenth-Century Music," *JAMS* 30 (1977): 391–418.

36. Zarlino, *Institutioni*, part III, especially chapters 76, 77.

37. N. Vicentino, *L'antica musica ridotta alla moderna prattica* (Rome, 1555), book III, Chapter 14 (ff. 46ᵛ–47ᵛ).

38. Soprano, bars 4–5, 7–8; altus 18–19, 20–21. For a recent analysis of the prologue and references to earlier studies, see K. Berger, "Tonality and Atonality in the Prologue to Orlando di Lasso's *Prophetiae Sibyllarum*: Some Methodological Problems in Analysis of Sixteenth-Century Music," *The Musical Quarterly* 66 (1980): 484–504.

39. Tinctoris, *Liber de arte contrapuncti*, II. xxxiv: "Concordantiis perfectis que vel imperfecte vel superflue

per semitonium chromaticum."
40. See Bent, "Musica Recta and Musica Ficta," p. 94 <=Chapter 1, p. 82>.
41. Prosdocimus's well-known examples using tritones are given *ibid.*, pp. 91–92 <Chapter 1, p. 80> and in the yet unpublished editions of Herlinger. The late-medieval tolerance of the melodic tritone did of course constitute a departure from earlier abhorrence of it; the reinstatement of this rule in the late fifteenth century is only one of a number of "returns" to earlier positions—another being the reversion of B♭ to accidental status. Tinctoris's statements on the use of the tritone are given in this section.
42. Some statements by modern scholars indicate that the distinctions between these terms are still not clearly understood:

  (1) mi contra fa has sometimes been assumed to include relationships other than simultaneous vertical perfections (e.g., oblique false relations, melodic progressions) and

  (2) implicit assumptions of enharmonic equivalence have led to confusion between the tritone and the diminished fifth. Clearly it is impossible to avoid, all the time, melodic and harmonic tritones and diminished fifths.

43. Dated 1476; chapter 8. Ed. A. Seay, CSM 22, I, q.v. for music examples; translated A. Seay (Colorado Springs, 1976).
44. P. Aaron, *Toscanello in Musica* (English translation, P. Bergquist, Colorado Springs, 1970).
45. Edited in Josquin, *Werken*, ed. A. Smijers, Motets I.1.) Discussed by, amongst others, Carl Dahlhaus in "Tonsystem und Kontrapunkt um 1500," pp. 15–16, with the rather different conclusion that "der Tonsatz abstrakt konzipiert ist und daß sich Josquin über die Unentschiedenheit, wie er zu realisieren sei, hinwegsetzte, da sie ihm gleichgültig war." Dahlhaus thus posits compositional indifference to the actual resulting sounds, and that abstractly conceived counterpoint may have lacked either prior aural imagination of sounds or indeed any musically acceptable realisation. However, the size of an interval (as major or minor) may be determined by the musical context so clearly at crucial points in the contrapuntal fabric that the composer neither needed to specify it nor the contrapuntally experienced singer to be told what to do. Such choices must surely have been a matter of structural if not also aesthetic concern to the composer, even if the conventions of performance did not necessitate, nor the nature of the notation permit, its full prescription. Dahlhaus seems here to approach the notation from a more conventional view based on fixed pitches and alterations although elsewhere ("Zu Costeleys chromatischer Chanson") recognising a principle he felicitously names "relativ Fa-notation." He there presents it as the special property of unusual pieces in which it is applied with extreme results, whereas I seek to bring that relative concept into play as a central and normal feature of Renaissance notation.
46. Hothby, *De arte contrapuncti*, ed. G. Reaney, CSM 26, p. 90; Aron, *Libri tres de institutione harmonica* (Bologna, 1516): this example is there explained only verbally. Similar passages by Vicentino and Lusitano are given by E. T. Ferand, "Improvised Vocal Counterpoint in the Late Renaissance and Early Baroque," *Annales Musicologiques* 4 (1956): 147–51. See also G. Monachus, *De preceptis artis musicae*, ed. A. Seay, CSM 11, p. 53.
47. It may yet be demonstrated that the coincidence of the word *nova* with what we may anachronistically hear as a departure is significant, even though it does not fall within the kind of vocabulary supporting Lowinskian chromaticism. In urging that music must make sense independently of textual considerations that might have helped to shape it, I do not mean to underestimate considerations that cannot receive full treatment here.
48. Munich, Bayerische Staatsbibliothek, Mus. MS 19 marks the uncontroversial bass B♭s shown in bars 1 and 5. Munich, Bayerische Staatsbibliothek Mus. MS 3154 (on which Thomas Noblitt based his dating of the piece in the 1470s) has a B♭ signature in the bass part until beyond this passage. London, Royal College of Music MS 1070 has a B♭ before the bass B in bar 3. (I am grateful to Lawrence Earp for extracting these from the computerised data of the Princeton Josquin project.)
49. Manuscript accidentals in the altus: the late part-books Munich, Universitätsbibliothek MS 8° 322–5 mark the B♭ shown in parentheses in bar 3. Observation of this "fa"-sign might have further consequences quite disruptive for the basic counterpoint of the other parts. A performer studying his part alone might have sung this ♭ (whether or not notated, and whether or not we call it "fa super la") . But on hearing the previously attacked B in the soprano (which also cannot be "changed" without other conse-

quences that are less readily defended than the version I propose), the altus is likely to sing B♮. The linear "rounding-off" of this altus phrase with the ♭ was in any case an incompletely successful attempt to rescue what has to be admitted, here alone in the motet, as a less elegant line, subservient to the tight interlocking of the counterpoint between the other, primary, parts. I would therefore choose to override it, but without insisting that this passage would always have been solved in this way.

50. For those who prefer to define diatonic in terms of segments that can be transposed to piano white notes, this can be done for the last limb of the sequence starting on B♭ if played a minor third lower. See also example 7.

51. M. van Crevel, "Verwante Sequensmodulaties bij Obrecht, Josquin en Coclico." *TVNM*, 16 (1941) pp. 119–21. Modern edition of Kyrie, ed. A. Smijers, *Van Ockeghem tot Sweelink* (Amsterdam, 1939–56), II, 51.

52. Lowinsky, "Secret Chromatic Art *Re-examined,*" n. 63a.

53. See, for example, E. Bottrigari, *Il Desiderio* (Venice, 1594), p. 5: "Gli strumenti stabili, ma alterabili [as distinct from those "al tutto stabili"] sono tutti quelli, che dapoi che sono accordati dal sonator diligente, si possono alterare con l'accrescere, & minuire in qualche parte, mediante il buon giudicio del sonatore toccando i loro tasti un poco più sù, un poco più giù."

54. Most modern writers presume just such a repertory of available pitches, aligning the gamut with the keyboard without recognising that vocal counterpoint and notation did not need to be so anchored. This is true of Karol Berger's excellent study *Theories of Chromatic and Enharmonic Music in Late 16th Century Italy* (Ann Arbor, 1980), from which a quotation will serve to illustrate where his view of tonal materials differs from mine: "Since steps [relatively defined pitches] are defined by means of intervals . . . it is possible to discuss the tonal system entirely in terms of intervals . . . that is, as a set of all intervals available to a composer (that is, the gamut) and its pre-compositional organization. Octave equivalence is basic to the sixteenth-century intervallic system; . . . the gamut consists of all intervals possible within the octave. . . . Certainly more than twelve, and possibly even all twenty-one, different notes are used [notated] in practical sources. Although it can reasonably be assumed that the musicians of the Renaissance were able to notate all the steps and intervals they were using, it does not follow that all differently notated steps and intervals were indeed different" (p. 98). For Prosdocimus on the infinity of sounds, see n. 21 above.

55. *Accidentien und Tonalität in den Musikdenkmälern des 15. und 16. Jahrhunderts* (Berlin, 1936).

56. "Accidentals and Ornamentation in Sixteenth-Century Intabulations of Josquin's Motets," *Josquin des Prez*, ed. E. E. Lowinsky (London, 1976), pp. 475–522. "While the character and extent of disagreement on the practical application of the rules of *musica ficta* on the part of sixteenth-century intabulators differed from that of modern scholars, who do not even agree on the existence and applicability of the rules, there was nevertheless a considerable difference of judgement and taste among the former" (p. 477 and *passim*).

57. F. Gafurius, *Practica musicae* (Milan, 1496), book iii, chapter 2: "Species seu elementa contrapuncti in instrumentorum fidibus atque vocali concentu gravium atque acutorum sonorum commixtionem qua harmonica consurgit melodia proportionabiliter consequantur necesse est." N. Burtius, *Musices opusculum* (Bologna, 1487), *Tractatus secundus*, sig. e. iij, speaks of *cantus*; instrumental reference is not specific at this point.

58. N. Vicentino, *L'antica musica ridotta alla moderna prattica* (Rome, 1555); facsimile ed. E. E. Lowinsky (Kassel, etc., 1959), III. xiv, ff. 46v–47.

59. J. van Benthem, "*Fortuna* in Focus: Concerning "Conflicting" Progressions in Josquin's *Fortuna dun gran tempo,*" *TVNM* 30 (1980): 1–50, argues against Lowinsky's reading of this piece ("The Goddess Fortuna in Music, with a Special Study of Josquin's *Fortuna d'un gran tempo,*" *The Musical Quarterly* 29 (1943): 45–77), on grounds which include the evidence of tablatures, the presence of "mi–fa" false relations in other pieces by Josquin, and the unstated assumption that accidentals are a corruption of the text and should be kept to a minimum. That the result of Lowinsky's version is musically superior seems to me beyond question; the view of tonal materials here proposed helps to legitimate it against some arguments of its critics.

While no attempt has been made to assemble tablature evidence for application to the present examples, it is perhaps worth pointing out that the Kleber tablature arrangement of Josquin's *Ave Maria* avoids the linear contrapuntal approach of the vocal model but does correct the vertical fifth with F♯! The passage in the *L'homme armé* Agnus containing the problem illustrated by Aron is avoided altogether by

Kleber. For modern transcriptions of both pieces see *Keyboard Intabulations of Music by Josquin des Prez,* ed. T. Warburton (Madison, 1980): 32, 27.

60. *Pace* formulations such as "used [*musica ficta*] as a 'peccatum' . . . against the mode"; E♭ as a "violation of the fifth mode": B. Meier, "The Musica Reservata of Adrianus Petit Coclico and its relationship to Josquin," *Musica Disciplina,* 10 (1956): 101, 103. See Howard Mayer Brown (in *Josquin des Prez,* ed. Lowinsky, p. 477): "The idea that musicians of the time were guided by a desire to preserve the purity of the modes must be discarded once and for all. The profusion of accidentals incorporated into intabulations should lead those scholars who still advocate a policy of 'utmost reserve' with respect to *musica ficta* to rethink their positions. Even so well-known a 'radical' in these matters as Edward Lowinsky would never gloss a reading as exuberantly as did some of the sixteenth-century lutenists."

61. H. S. Powers, s.v. "Mode," especially section III, *The New Grove Dictionary;* "Modal Representation in Polyphonic Offertories," *Early Music History* 2 (1982): 43–86; "Tonal Types and Modal Categories," *JAMS* 34 (1980): 428–70.

62. H. Finck, *Practica musica* (Wittenberg, 1556), sig. Rr iii^v.

63. For statements reflecting the primacy that tonal organisation in its modern sense holds for much present-day scholarship, see Berger (*Theories,* p. 2): "There can be little doubt that the organization of a sixteenth-century work is primarily tonal, that it is the organization of various pitches in certain specific ways, whereas organization of other values (temporal, timbral, dynamic) is of secondary importance."

64. See, for example, *Harvard Dictionary of Music,* 2nd rev. ed. (Cambridge, Mass., 1969), s.v. "Musica ficta": "In the music of the 10th to 16th centuries, the theory of the chromatic or, more properly, non-diatonic tones . . ."; "resulted from melodic modifications or from transpositions of the church modes"; ". . . disconcerting to find many long compositions completely lacking in any indication of accidentals"; ". . . the necessity for such emendations cannot be denied"; "Matters were carried much too far in many editions published between 1900 and 1930 . . . no doubt historically accurate view of adding as few as possible." And from *The New Grove Dictionary:* "The term used loosely to describe accidentals added to sources of early music, by either the performer or the modern editor. More correctly it is used for notes that lie outside the predominantly diatonic theoretical gamut of medieval plainchant, whether written into the source or not."

Chapter 5

Accidentals, Counterpoint, and Notation in Aaron's *Aggiunta* to the *Toscanello in Musica*[*1]

The 1529 edition of Pietro Aaron's *Toscanello in Musica*[2] included an appendix, entitled *Aggiunta del toscanello a complacenza de gli amici fatta*,[3] known to us for its advocacy of full notation of accidentals. The special and unique interest of this Appendix is that the accidentals are demonstrated in and authorised by a long series of examples drawn from contemporary polyphonic repertory, mostly in prints by Petrucci. Although he does not name them, we know these are the sources Aaron used. The composer attributions and the grouping or sometimes even the order of pieces also correspond, as do the notated accidentals specified.[4] In addition, for the [II307] *Missarum Josquin Liber Primus*, *Odhecaton*, and *Motetti de la Corona*, he often gives staff locations for the accidental signs; and some of his examples depend on misprints or anomalies peculiar to Petrucci. It seems that Aaron's decision to add the appendix was prompted in large measure by Spataro's response to the 1523 edition of his *Toscanello*, in nine letters of which six survive, as letters 7–12 of the Spataro correspondence. Of 33 surviving letters addressed by Spataro to Aaron, these six form an extended review of the *Toscanello*. Letters 11 and 12 are identified by Spataro as the eighth and ninth of his series; we therefore lack nos. 5–7 of the original nine. The first four of the review-letters deal with mensural issues addressed by Aaron in book I, and the last two with book II, chapters xvii–xx. Aaron chose not to take up in the *Aggiunta* the compositional questions raised by Spataro in letter 11 in response to *Toscanello* II.xvii. *Toscanello* II.xx, *De la natura del diesis*, is the subject of Spataro's final letter of this series, no. 12 in the edition. It prompts an entire section of the *Aggiunta* in which Aaron quotes extensively and almost verbatim from Spataro's letter.[5] Since Spataro seems to have worked through Aaron's treatise in order, and presented his letters as a series, it is likely that the missing three addressed further matters treated by Aaron in the early chapters of book II, and that what Aaron has to say on the tritone, on major and minor thirds and sixths, and on perfect and imperfect consonances, may have been prompted by Spataro's now missing commentaries on those chapters. (Spataro's lengthy commentary on the earlier *Trattato* is also lost.) Aaron's response may in turn embody material directly culled from the missing letters of Spataro, as they do in the case of the surviving letter 12. Spataro's responses to the *Toscanello* indeed appear to have been Aaron's main incentive for writing the *Aggiunta*.*

Book II chapters xiii–xviii of the *Toscanello* deal with counterpoint.[6] In II.xiv, within the traditional context of contrapuntal precepts, Aaron had already given the two standard rules for *musica ficta*. These are, first, the prohibition of *mi contra fa* in perfect consonances, i.e., the complementary statement of the rule that simultaneous octaves and fifths should be perfect; and second, the prescription of correct cadential approaches to perfect intervals, e.g., that an octave should be approached from a major sixth.* Although the *Aggiunta* sets ||308 out to prescribe notational practice, its further implications for interval correction both confirm and supplement those rules. Its particular value in giving examples from actual compositions is to show how choices should be made and priorities set when rules come into conflict.

The first half of the *Aggiunta* falls into the following five sections.[7] In Aaron's usage, and in this article, "tritone" always means the augmented fourth or interval of three tones, and not the diminished fifth, with which it was never at that time considered interchangeable.

> I) Aaron says that the melodic tritone must always be tempered, and advocates the notation of b molle to ensure this (examples 1–12).
>
> II) He shows when the rule against tritones must be broken in favour of respecting the rules already given in *Toscanello* II.xiv:
>
>> (a) honouring the higher priority of simultaneous perfect fifths, and
>>
>> (b) correct cadencing (examples 13–14, and examples A 1–4).
>
> III) He advocates supplying signs to achieve the necessary perfection in simultaneities that the singer cannot easily anticipate by ear (examples 15–36).
>
> IV) He expands on *Toscanello* II.xx, on the diesis (examples B 1–4), in the light of and with extensive quotation from Spataro (*Correspondence*, letter 12).
>
> V) He advocates abandoning the practice of partial signatures.

In a second section of the *Aggiunta*, not dealt with here, Aaron judges the tone or *maniera* of chants for the Mass Ordinary and *Te Deum*.

Aaron makes his purpose clear in the first sentence of the *Aggiunta*:

> Doubts and disputations are circulating among some lovers of music about the signs
> of b molle and diesis, whether composers are constrained to signal them in their
> compositions, or whether the singer ought to understand and recognise the hidden
> secret of all the places where these figures or signs are needed.

‖309 He concludes that the average singer needs the help of signs in order to avoid dissonance, and insists that the [melodic] tritone must always be tempered. "Composers have observed the rule" could mean that they compose in such a way that the tritone can easily be avoided. "But sometimes they show the sign because of the inadvertence of the singer," i.e., inadvertence in not successfully divining the composer's intent; this may mean not so much blameworthy carelessness on the part of the singer as simple misadventure, the singer being literally inadvertent, unwarned; some of Aaron's examples suggest precisely this interpretation, though singers' inexperience is something Aaron explicitly wished to cater to. He approves of giving this help because it alleviates the singers' weakness, because it makes concessions to their inexperience or unpreparedness, not because it corrects incorrect notation. He evidently believes that the printed accidentals in his Petrucci prints were supplied by the composers, though some of the accidentals could derive from Petrucci's editor and not necessarily from the composers themselves.[8] In *De Institutione Harmonica* I.xx (Bologna, 1516) Aaron had defined the tritone as occurring in four places on the hand. Two arise "naturally" within the gamut between F and B♮, two "accidentally" between B♭ and E. He made the distinction, according accidental status to B♭, although his presentation of the hand and of traditional solmisation was otherwise more conservative than in his own later treatises. He stressed the necessity of mollifying the tritone when the phrase does not continue to the fifth degree, e.g., from F beyond B up to C, even in those cases (e.g., from B♭ to E, continuing to F) where the tritone did not arise "naturally." In *Toscanello* II.v he locates two further accidental positions of the tritone starting on E♭,[9] and adds the Greek names for the locations. It is clear that he draws the natural/accidental distinction between intervals confined to what we would call white notes and those that include what we would call a black note.

With redundant thoroughness, the first group of examples (#1-12) shows how composers (or Petrucci's editor) have helped singers by marking the signs of b molle that ensure avoidance of melodic tritones. All these examples involve ♭ signs only and most are direct, ascending unmediated leaps from F to B that return within themselves and are "mitigated" by a notated b molle (#2, <*3,> 4, 5, 6, 7a, *7b, 7c, 7e). Some give a mediated fourth (stepwise ascending, #7d); some ‖³¹⁰ descend through the "tritone," usually after a smaller ascent, but only after the flat has been sounded (##1, *3, 8a, 8b, 9, 12b); only two pieces involve E fa (E♭), both with B♭ signatures: ##11a and 11b in a direct leap, ##10a a mediated leap, *10b a direct leap.

EXAMPLE 1:* MOUTON, *NOS QUI VIVIMUS*, "DOMINUS MEMOR FUIT NOSTRI."
*See note 7, p. 197, for explanation of example numbering.

EXAMPLE 3: MOUTON, *BENEDICTA ES CELORUM REGINA*, "AVE PLENA GRATIA."

Petrucci, *f*

EXAMPLE 7B: JOSQUIN, *MISSA GAUDEAMUS*, CREDO, BARS 41-42.

EXAMPLE 10A: FÉVIN, *BENEDICTUS DOMINUS DEUS MEUS,*
"DEPOSUISTI ADVERSARIOS MEOS."

EXAMPLE 10B: FÉVIN, *BENEDICTUS DOMINUS DEUS MEUS*, SECUNDA PARS ["JUBILATE
DEO IN VOCE EXULTATIONIS"]

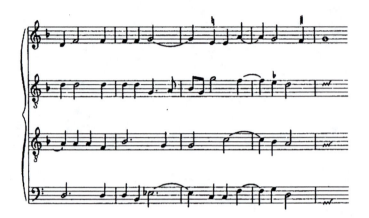

EXAMPLE 11A: LHÉRITIER, *DUM COMPLERENTUR,* "DABAT ELOQUI ILLIS."

EXAMPLE 12A: CARPENTRAS, *BONITATEM FECISTI.*

A few cases deserve to be singled out for comment. In #*1 Aaron's comments, unusually, could apply to any of the four parts. He shows superius and tenor stepwise descents through the fourth from B♭ to F, but he does not say that the B♭ is also required by a simultaneity. Altus and bassus parts descend through the fifth F to B♭, and in both cases pre-place the notated ♭ sign in time to encourage (though not to mandate) an E♭ in the descending scale. In #*3 Aaron refers to the tenor part, which is notated with b molle signs as he wishes. The bass, however, lacks one likely and one essential flat in this passage. #*7b is from the Credo of Josquin's *Missa Gaudeamus* (bars 41–42). Aaron's example locates the flat at the end of the third stave [of the bass part], where in the figure F B♭ A Petrucci has misprinted F for D; the ascending interval to be sung is in fact not a fourth but a minor sixth.[10] The misprinted F occurs in all the editions of Petrucci I have been able to consult, including the first printing of 1502. *Werken* purports to be based on Petrucci 1502, although it correctly gives not F but D in the Bassus at bar 41 and notes no misprint.[11] This interesting mishap is one of many indications that Aaron, in collecting this group of examples, was merely looking through the part-books and spotting by eye where b molle was notated, without mentally reconstructing and taking account of the whole musical texture. That, however, he did in some of the later examples.

#*10a (Févin, *Benedictus dominus deus meus*) has ♭ signatures in all parts, which fits Aaron's disapproval of partial signatures (section V), as do all his chosen examples. It has six E♭ signs in the bassus at the end of the prima pars, some of which (see example) are preplaced by one or several notes. However, Aaron does not comment on this practice of advance warning, but since it occurs in several of his examples (see also example 1) he presumably does not disapprove. Aaron again seems not to have thought through all aspects of this example with care. Several more *fa* signs on E are required by his standards,* at the end of the bass, and in the superius and altus as ||3II marked in the example transcribed here. These signs would be required both for tritone avoidance and by the simultaneous arrivals on fifths and octaves to which Aaron devotes the lion's share of his examples. But he does not point out a problem that this passage shares with #*13. The superius must have E♭ in bar 9 because of the altus, but equally it must have A♮ in bar 8, thus sacrificing the melodic outline, creating a tritone where there was no danger of one on melodic grounds, in the greater interests of achieving a simultaneous consonance between the parts. In #*10b, the secunda pars, three E♭ are marked, although they are aurally prepared by B♭ in other parts, and other unnotated flats must follow from them. Aaron does not single out as errors the failure to notate these other flats, although in his terms they would be "needed." He has not made a full mental transition to the notation he advocates.

In #*12a (Carpentras, *Bonitatem fecisti*) the leap on *ut discant* (*recte "discam"*) from F up to B, though direct, falls between phrases separated by a breve and semibreve rest <*recte*: three breves' rest>, surely sufficient to remove the need for melodic integrity and tritone avoidance, especially given the musical events of the intervening passage. Much more interesting here than the melodic "tritone" is the pattern of four descending imitative entries a fifth apart, on C, F, the B♭ cited by Aaron (which surely is marked more for this imitative entry than for tritone avoidance), and "E", (bar 120). There would clearly be satisfaction in completing the sequence of four entries on descending fifths by sounding E♭ here, against a B♭ in the tenor. But a bass entry on E♭ cannot be prepared in bar 119, soprano (which in turn is not a parallel situation to 118 preceding the tenor entry); and in any case an E♭ would have to be denied immediately by E♮ in the soprano and B♮ in the tenor.[12] Despite the sacrifice of a sequence of entries a perfect fifth apart, I incline to favour E♮ and B♮ throughout bar 120, weighing the importance of local response to what will have been heard in 119 over the awkward progressions that result from completing the cycle of fifths with E♭. But, as Aaron said in another case (#*13) where he addressed the problems posed by considering the entire texture, such things are not easy for the singer.

EXAMPLE 13: JOSQUIN, *MISSA L'HOMME ARMÉ* <SUPER VOCES MUSICALES>, AGNUS. <THE ADDED QUINTA PARS, THE FOURTH PART IN THIS SCORE, SHOULD BE OMITTED.>

EXAMPLE 14A: JOSQUIN, *MISSA LA SOL FA RE MI*, GLORIA, "TU SOLUS ALTISSIMUS."

EXAMPLE 14B: JOSQUIN, *MISSA LA SOL FA RE MI*, CREDO, "ET SEPULTUS EST."

[312]Aaron's second group of examples (##*13–*14, and examples *A 1–4) deals with cases where rules come into conflict. These are much more interesting than the tritone examples, because here he is not merely scanning visually through the part-books (though he uses mostly the bassus), but in some cases recalling or reconstructing passages as entire polyphonic complexes. It is from this group of examples that Aaron draws practical rules for setting contrapuntal priorities, for choosing the lesser among evils. He gives two exceptions to the rule that the tritone must be tempered.

The first is for "necessity and suitability" and is exemplified in ##*13, the Agnus of the Josquin *Missa L'homme armé*, the example that most clearly shows Aaron's approach to cases where rules conflict. If F–B is followed by a descent of a fifth that must, for polyphonic reasons, be from B♮ to E♮, then the fifth is made perfect at the expense of retaining the melodic tritone, even though (says Aaron, apparently contradicting himself) "it is a lesser error to sing an imperfect fifth [melodically] than a tritone." The musical passage Aaron quotes is not self-explanatory, except in that it embodies tolerance of a mediated melodic tritone but not of an unmediated false fifth. Only in context can one see that B♭ and E♭ are impossible and that the real reason for requiring both B♮ and E♮ is their sounding of simultaneous fifths and octaves against the immovable cantus firmus B♮ (it cannot be B♭) sustained throughout this passage, which in turn compels intervallically inexact imitations, F G A B C and E F G A B.[13]

Several illustrations of *musica ficta* in treatises[14] demonstrate rising fourths and falling fifths in a descending spiral. What Aaron means, and what example 13 proves, is that the polyphonic context can prevent the downward spiral by fifths that is deliberately cultivated in some theoretical and practical examples, and can thereby accept the local melodic infelicity of a tritone outline in the interests of rescuing the whole musical framework. Nothing could be clearer than that Aaron had the full context in mind for #*13 but not for #*10 and #*12. The singer (and indeed his reader) cannot decide without the polyphonic context, and that context may temper the tritone rule. #*13 shows that the perfection of simultaneous fifths (and even of direct leaps of melodic fifths) is to take priority over the mitigation of linear tritones, especially if filled in. This is the crux of Aaron's chapter, and provides a touchstone for many principles that can be inferred from [13][13] it. Although he here seems to observe it, Aaron omits to spell out Tinctoris's distinction between the higher priority to be accorded to correction of a direct than of a mediated melodic fifth or tritone; for Tinctoris, to outline a filled-in tritone (augmented fourth) was less bad than to sing one as a direct leap.[15]

#*14a shows a tritone filled in (CBGFGABBE) to protect a leap of a fifth and the "true sound" of the *mi* [with the lower parts]. There is no apparent reason why the tritone outline in this example and the next, #*14b, also involving F G A B E, could not be avoided by F♯, but it seems that Aaron is in the first instance concerned with the use of b molle to avoid tritones:

> I say that you are forced to choose the less unsuitable of the two evils, which will be to utter the proper mi in the said b♭ acute, although it is a lesser error to sing a [linear] imperfect diapente than a tritone. In any case these passages are not easy for the singer.

It would be fascinating to know the content of Spataro's lost letters that corresponds to this section, and whether the apparent discrepancy between Aaron's attention to one part alone (in the tritone examples #1–12) and to simultaneous combinations (in #13–36) reflects a juxtaposition of Spataro's contribution with his own.

As a second class of exceptions to the tritone prohibition (II.b, "understood reason"), Aaron further allows that a melodic infelicity may be tolerated when ancillary to the higher priority of a cadence correctly performed by the rules of counterpoint. The examples for this section are given within the text and not identified as being taken from actual compositions. They follow #*14 and are here numbered A 1–4.

> You will also find in compositions another kind of unmitigated tritone, not tempered by the b, conceded as necessary like the preceding, which in descending changes its nature, and although they appear to be uttered as untempered tritones, by the sounding of the natural syllable mi, they are nonetheless raised because of the lower part, so that what remains is found to be a perfect diatessaron, like this:

> The rule of orderly counterpoint requires that the last semibreve should be raised because of a sixth with the tenor, as in the natural raised <*recte:* suspended> cadences (*naturali cadenze sospese*), and sung accidentally.

||3¹⁴ Because of the cadential descent of the lower part by a whole tone A G, the upper must have a raised (and suspended) leading note on F *mi*. This in turn removes the need for the application of b molle to the preceding B, which otherwise would have outlined a descending tritone to F *fa*. If the B were also sung molle, a diminished fourth would result:

> If it is sung in the same way as other tritones one finds, the result will not be a diatessaron but an interval of a tone and two minor semitones only, thus:

> For that reason I say that in this case the tritone [that would occur from B♮ down to F] is not to be changed into a diatessaron, ditone, or even a semiditone, nor into any other interval in the diatonic genus shown in universal teaching.

Aaron seems here to recommend use of the diminished fourth (for which he has no name). This interval, like the tritone, falls outside the tetrachord of the diatonic *genus*, and hence outside the normal pedagogic examples "in universal teaching" of diatonic progressions. But it is not outlawed; neither it nor the tritone is excluded from diatonic status as an interval, and he is certainly not saying that these intervals are chromatic, as I believe he would if they were. Jeffrey Dean has persuaded me that Aaron indeed means this; moreover, Aaron is not seeking further to shrink the fourth enharmonically.[16] The diatessaron, ditone, and semiditone are intervals with names and with full status as normal members of the diatonic tetrachords, but in this case an interval that falls short of that status is preferred to a fully regular one, for a combination of linear and contrapuntal reasons. It is more important to observe those reasons than to avoid an interval whose status is anomalous but not illegal.

Aaron's convoluted language shows how far he is from being able to describe the signs as causing simple raisings or lowerings of notes from normative positions. This must be because notes are habitually and correctly "raised" without the help of accidentals. He makes rather heavy weather of a situation which could have been more simply explained in terms of anticipating the cadence, but it does enable us to see that he sets high priority by correct cadencing, making a linear tritone ancillary to a cadential decision:

> If you happen to find that the composer has another intention about the last *fa*, then you will do well to change it, especially if the composer wishes to have an octave above his close, thus:

> [11]315 The same is to be understood about the other perfect consonances, and observing this rule, then it will be necessary to sing the dotted semibreve with the sign of *b rotondo*, which progression will be changed into the third species of diatessaron, as the general law commands. But if you find the said tritone in this manner:

I say that without doubt because of the ascending tritone joined to the descending, it will be affected and removed from its order because the first ascending motion opposes it [hence B♭, because the phrase starts on F]. From this, failing to observe the common rule [against the tritone], you will fall into greater error. Concluding then that every kind of tritone, whether natural or accidental, whether or not it returns to its first place, may be in whatever manner it pleases you, I say that the cantor should mollify, temper and annul it every time, whether the sign of b molle is given or not, excepting when prevented by unsuitability, as shown above.

Odhecaton #31

A5

Ex A5 is from *Odhecaton* #31, bars 25–29 of the *si placet* Altus.[17] It is included for comparison with Ex A4. The examples are not rhythmically identical, and they differ by an octave. But it might bear on the question whether the examples not identified by Aaron come from composed music or whether they are made up, by himself or even by Spataro.

Although he has related his comments to the composer's intention, it is not until the third group of examples (#15–36) that Aaron considers whether the singer can be expected to anticipate that intention *at sight*[18] when not openly expressed.

Now it will be considered whether the singer should or indeed can recognise at the first attempt the intent and secret of a composer, when singing a song he has not seen before. The answer is no, although among those who celebrate music there are some who think the contrary. They give the reason that every composer considers that his songs are to be understood by the learned and experienced, by a quick and perceptive ear, especially when imperfect fifths, octaves, twelfths, and fifteenths occur. I say that only God is master of such things, and such silent intelligence belongs to Him ‖316 only and not to a mortal man. For it would be impossible for any learned and practiced man to be able to sense instantly an imperfect fifth, octave, twelfth or fifteenth without first committing the error of a little dissonance. It is true that it would be sensed more quickly by one than another, but there is not a man who would not be caught. For this reason I say that those who do not indicate the sign of b molle where it might naturally appear to be otherwise, commit no little error, because an intention retained in the mind accomplishes nothing.

The examples that come under this third heading all involve cases of a simultaneous or nearly simultaneous arrival on a perfect interval. The singer may have little or no aural warning, and yet be expected to honour the high priority of perfecting that interval rather than performing his part according to purely melodic criteria of tritone avoidance and cadential approach. Here again, Aaron shows that he can recall the entire texture by referring to what is going on in the other parts. The Odhecaton group #30–36 are characterised as *antichi*: "*gli troverai nel libro di cento canti stampati per ordine.*"

A few of these simultaneities involve substantial or slight anticipations, of a unison, fifth, or octave with the affected note, that a singer with a really quick ear should be able to respond to, just as easily as he can decide how to take a suspended discant cadence, rising by whole tone or by *mi fa* according to whether the tenor descends through *fa mi* or by whole tone. Examples *15, *17, 18, 20, 21, 22, *23, *25, 26, 28, 29, 35 permit some such anticipation. But many of Aaron's examples in this category are true surprises, unanticipated simultaneous arrivals, in that the sight-singer could not anticipate the goal of the cadence, and would be caught off guard unless he knew the piece or had looked ahead. The arrivals are more or less unprepared and simultaneous in examples *16, *19a–b, 27, 30, 31, 32, 33, 34, 36.

EXAMPLE 15: JOSQUIN, *MEMOR ESTO*, "SPEM DEDISTI."

EXAMPLE 16: JOSQUIN, *PRAETER RERUM*, "TUA PUERPERIA."

EXAMPLE 17: JOSQUIN, *AVE NOBILISSIMA*, SECUNDA PARS.

EXAMPLE 19A: JOSQUIN, *MISSA L'HOMME ARMÉ*, KYRIE I, BARS 7–8.

EXAMPLE 19B: JOSQUIN, *MISSA L'HOMME ARMÉ*, KYRIE III, BARS 71–72.

EXAMPLE 23: RICHAFORT, *MISEREMINI MEI*, "QUARE ME
PERSEQUEMINI SICUT DEUS."

EXAMPLE 25: LONGUEVAL, *BENEDICAT NOS IMPERIALIS*, "DIVINITAS CUSTODIAT NOS."

The examples speak for themselves. In *15 Aaron gives us no guidance about the
status of the third in the final chord, whether it should be major (as we should expect
him to prefer) despite the roughness thereby occasioned, or whether he objects (as we
probably would not) to the momentary sounding of superius B♮ against the bassus B♭.
In *16 the notated E♭ creates a harmonic "bend" that some editors might be shy of
without that encouragement, though the contrapuntal logic is clear. In *17 the first
bass motion from C to F prevents the superius from raising the cadential leading
note.

##*23 is more problematic. Aaron says that Richafort does not so much consider
the fifths, octaves, twelfths, and fifteenths but the correction of a minor sixth to major
before the octave by means of B♭. This is a surprising choice to illustrate this point,
because the context ‖3¹⁷ of the sixth is not cadential. Also, it is not over the words specified by Aaron but over the preceding phrase, "quare me persequemini," and is fur-

ther complicated by Petrucci's misprint in the bass of C for D. However, it is the only notated B♭ in this area, and Aaron's comments must apply to this, though they cannot increase our confidence in his musicianship. The major sixth and third appear generally to be preferred in simultaneous intervals in counterpoint whether or not they resolve to perfect intervals. For linear leaps returning within themselves the minor sixth would be preferred. The achieving of a major third may also be a reason for the B♭ in #*19b which "deceptively" undercuts a cadence on D. In cadential arrivals where the chord includes a third, Aaron wanted the third or tenth to be shown as major by the diesis (*Toscanello* II.xx, and see below).

When he says, above, that the singer cannot avoid a little dissonance, he may not mean, as is usually assumed, that without any notated accidentals the singer will sing uninflected notes. Aaron never assumes this except to identify it as a fault. Rather, I think he means that in situations that give little or no room for anticipation, the average singer needs help with the process of realisation. As Aaron put it at the end of this section, immediately preceding some lengthy quotations from Spataro's letter 12:

> Just as God has taught us and painted before our eyes the way of salvation and also that of damnation, through which we distinguish the good from the bad, since otherwise without this, we might easily be able to fall into doing evil always, or doing good, or sometimes into good and others into evil; since life is then both good and bad, it was necessary for Him to ordain His precepts and the ways through which we may distinguish the right way to live from its contrary. Further, in travelling one sees places where there are various signs, because there are several roads one might take. By means of these signs those who do not know the country may correctly choose the right road. If there were no sign, they doubtless might choose the wrong road, at the end of which might rise a river by which they might easily become stranded in trying to cross it; or avoiding this misfortune, they at least would have to turn back. Thus the musician or composer is obliged to show his intention so that the singer will not stumble into something the composer did not intend.

Aaron clearly intends that his next section, on the diesis, should supplement *Toscanello* II.xx, where he strongly urges that thirds in chords at phrase ends should be major. He there called the minor tenth an "unpleasant harmony" and recommended notation of the diesis. We are fortunate to have Spataro's lengthy commentary on this subject, and Aaron's incorporation of it into the *Aggiunta*, where he does not retreat from this view.

[318] In *Toscanello* II.xx Aaron wrote that it was necessary to establish the sign ♯ or diesis by whose means the singer could be shown which note should be raised or low-

ered.[19] But he then went on to discuss it in much more convoluted terms, e.g., whether the note was augmented or diminished, whether the interval increased in ascent and decreased in descent. This passage, together with others from this chapter, is quoted by Spataro[20] who points out that it is not the note that is augmented or diminished but the space of the interval. Aaron quotes verbatim three portions of Spataro's reply in his 1529 *Aggiunta*, in and immediately preceding this section, including the following:

> Thus the sign ♯ when it appears in an ascent from a space to a line or line to space, like this:

B1

> will always change the natural space of a semitone into a tone. Since the sign operates like the b quadro, I say that this sign would more rationally be called b quadro than diesis.

Aaron's rather curious denial of mensural value for the diesis, i.e., that it does not augment the length of a note, responds to and directly incorporates Spataro's criticism. ♯ changes an ascending semitone to a tone (IV.13, ex B1). He prefers, with Spataro, to call it B quadro. The composer should show his intention, whereas in II.xx he had said that notation was not necessary for experienced singers. He does not use Spataro's example here, though there is some similarity.

> The obligation then devolves on the composer to remove all danger and cause of the singer falling into error. The composer should show that sign, because of the various intentions and manners occurring in our free counterpoint as shown in Book II, chapter XX above, and in the present example:

B2

In this example the composer does not intend that the last breve, or the last interval, should be raised or diminished, because there is no sign showing any such raising, as is understood in the figure. If it were raised, the last interval would be an imperfect octave with the bass and no unison with the alto. But when such raising is intended, it should be shown, as in the following example:

Here the intent was to change the harmony [of the] first [example], although the progression is the same as in the first. Thus he needs to show the singer his second meaning with the sign, so that one will not [319] think that he means what he did in the first example, as happens if one finds the following example:

Aaron then continues:

> But note now that I should not be accused of being contrary to myself, considering that I said in the above mentioned Chapter 20 that the sign diesis is not needed by learned and experienced singers, since they will easily recognise with their intellect and excellent ear definite progressions where the raised note should properly be used or not used, as the composer intends. They would be so familiar with noticing this through continuous practice of music that they would take the attitude that it does little harm when the sign is not found. This attitude and practice cannot help, let alone give notice to the inexperienced and unintelligent singer, so that for this reason it is necessary for the composer to signify when and where the sign is needed.

This indeed describes well how notation was presented by composers and realised by singers on the basis of the counterpoint that formed their shared training, permitting the composer to expect and the singer to understand what was needed. The "official" or written form of the notation might appear intervallically different from a correct realisation in sound. The written form, undernotated by Aaron's standards and by ours, is neither incorrect nor is it abstract.[21] Aaron implies that even if the singer would be able to get it right the next time, he would first commit some dissonance, and should be saved from this. But there is never any doubt that the correct realisation is always to take priority over any official written form, whether or not it is helped notationally.

Aaron is unquestionably progressive in his view of the meaning of notation, and in this respect he and Spataro take a similar position, following some of the innovations of Spataro's teacher Ramos. Aaron [320] uses the terminology of natural and accidental almost in the modern sense of white and black notes respectively, and invokes the authority of Guido for the two-hexachord basis of this division.[22] Lanfranco, to the contrary, still presented the Guidonian hand as the three-hexachord structure (including B♭) of late-medieval *musica recta*.[23] Aaron points out that for Guido the soft B derived from the F hexachord was not natural (or proper) but accidental (I.6). He thus joins those early sixteenth-century theorists whose nomenclature began to reflect the keyboard as an instrument of reference for theoretical discussion. At one point only (not in the *Aggiunta* but in the *Toscanello* itself, II.xx, on the diesis), Aaron speaks tellingly of the notation "as written": "without the sign the singer would not sing other than what is written unless his ear helps him" while believing that this written form, which served him entirely for the judging of modal classifications on paper, must be overruled in performance by the demands of melody and counterpoint. He advocates abandoning partial signatures in order to ensure consonance between the parts, which shows that he has departed from the predominant late-medieval view in which B♭ from the soft hexachord was equally available by *musica recta* in an unsignatured part. Aaron embraces a "modern" interpretation of the signatures that follows consistently from his allocation of accidental status to B♭. This stance removes from the note B its formerly equal status as *fa* or *mi* according to whether it was approached by the hard or soft hexachord. Above all, he wants notation of the b molle in even very obvious cases that Tinctoris would have considered asinine,[24] as his long first series of examples (#1–12) drawn from Petrucci prints affirms. These, as we have seen, identify examples of melodic tritones where Petrucci gives a sign of b molle, mostly involving direct leaps from F up to B that return within that interval. Aaron assumes that it is the composers rather than Petrucci's editor who have given this help. The language in the *Aggiunta* straddles older and newer ways of thinking and has components of both. Most of the time Aaron retains the circumlocutions habitual to and born of the older tradition in which notation was still considered fully complete and correct without needing to mark consistently what we call accidentals.

That tradition took a long time to decay, and there are still some ways in which he betrays the tenacity of the older view of pitch notation. He largely avoids saying that a flat lowers a note, and speaks instead of increasing or decreasing the interval, or of tempering, annulling or mitigating the tritone. He does not say that [321] notation without this "help" is faulty, although he does once, at the beginning of the *Aggiunta*, imply notational necessity, if only by his new precepts: "places where these figures or signs are needed." But he more often says not that the signs themselves but rather that their help is needed as a concession to the "inadvertenza" of the singer, who, without such help, may commit dissonance, especially at first sight of a piece. This is consistent with their having ancillary, accidental status, such as fingering signs have in our notation. "Without the sign the singer would not sing other than what is written *unless his ear helps him*" (in *Toscanello* II.xiv) implies the necessity of overriding the written form. "Which note should be raised or lowered" (in *Toscanello* II.xx) occurs in context of the interval size being increased in ascent or decreased in descent, rather than referring to the dislocation of an individual note. The [simultaneous] minor tenth is described (in *Toscanello* II.xx) as unpleasant and always to have the diesis applied, which experienced singers do anyway, implying again that its effect is mandatory but its notation is not.

Finally, Aaron objects to the practice of partial signatures, which distort and change the interval species. This is not an objection he has made in the case of the notation of accidentals, and signals a difference in status between signatures and "accidentals." He takes only signatures but not accidentals into account in his discussion of modes in the *Trattato*; these must now be touched on.

Only two sixteenth-century theorists, Aaron and Glareanus, give modal classifications supported by extensive examples from contemporary repertory. Harold Powers has shown how Aaron is not merely an informant about contemporary practice but devises an original and idiosyncratic system, coherent in its own terms, that can be applied universally to a repertory not written in accordance with those precepts.[25] Whether it is useful to us for more than the insight it gives into the workings of Aaron's mind is another matter. But as Powers continued, writing of Aaron: "We can learn nothing from our distinguished predecessors if we take their elegant and novel constructions as mere descriptions of the commonplace." But neither Aaron nor Glareanus allows any fictive colouring to cloud the clear sky [322] of his modal classifications. Both give music examples that display the official modal interval species according to clef and signature, but those intervals cannot be sung consistently because of the demands of the counterpoint. In the modal paradigms in the *Trattato* Aaron is looking only at the tenor part, and he is indeed looking at it, not hearing it or the other parts; all considerations of counterpoint, all the considerations he urges most strenuously in the *Aggiunta*, are ignored. It is these tenor parts, "as written," that yield the criteria for modal classification, and it is those official interval relationships of the background *scala* of the gamut that Aaron means when he refers in the *Toscanello* (not the *Aggiunta*) exceptionally, to singing "as written." At the same time Aaron makes it absolutely clear that the notation "as written" does not condition what must be sung. He seeks to bring the written notation closer to the sounding music, in order to help the singer, but without ever complaining that it is faulty to leave accidentals unnotated, only that it is unhelpful. His language becomes fascinatingly poised between the older and the newer concepts of what notation represents.

Circumlocutions in the *Aggiunta*, as Aaron gropes towards the idea of a notation fixed with respect to the signs of b molle and diesis, show that his training did not fully embrace such fixity, and that he may not have thought through the implications of more explicit notation for, for example, his notation-bound modal theory. That Aaron keeps mode and *ficta* on entirely separate tracks is all the more striking for his full, separate, parallel, and complementary discussion of melodic and contrapuntal correction. He draws his examples for each discussion from a common polyphonic repertory that includes the *Odhecaton*, though <few pieces are shared between> the modal and the accidentals discussion. With a few exceptions, the tenor parts chosen for modal purposes are not copiously provided with accidentals that might confuse that argument, while the pieces from which he draws the *Aggiunta* examples demonstrate the desired notated accidentals. Aaron's purposes for the two demonstrations are very different. The common ground between the modal and the *ficta* discussion is the gamut, which defines the species of fourths and fifths that make up part of Aaron's modal definition. Aaron avoids giving central place, either in the *Trattato* or the *Toscanello*, to the hexachordal structure of the gamut (whether in its two-hexachord or three-hexachord forms) that provides the background system of *musica recta* and the language in which intervallic adjustments can be couched. Aaron uses Greek names in preference to or in addition to hexachord designations wherever he can. Neither in the *Aggiunta* nor in the *Trattato* does he present as a dilemma that the official background species of modal scales (defined by signature and final) undergoes a fictive distortion in ||323 sound, as made necessary by the rules of counterpoint. He accepts it as necessary and not as a distortion.

Aaron's modal designations in the *Trattato* may have little connection with the interval species as heard in performance. He was looking at the tenor parts on paper, not hearing or reconstructing their polyphonic context. For his first group of examples in the *Aggiunta*, he was also looking at the part-books, spotting examples of notated b molle signs to mitigate tritones, and sometimes showing a glaring neglect of other aspects (see above, #*10 and 7), or even being taken in by a misprint of Petrucci (#*7b). Only at the very end of the first half of the *Aggiunta* is there any mention of mode, invoked only in passing, in a polemic against the use of partial signatures. Aaron dislikes especially low B♭ in the "low" part where such signatures are contrary to the species of the soprano, tenor, and contralto:

> When they wish to hold to this ill-conceived notion, they believe themselves excused precisely by the progressions which happen frequently from the note B mi grave, which makes an imperfect fifth with the tenor. This consideration is pointless and vain, since two difficulties result from it.

> The first is that every species becomes changed and varied from its natural order, such as from Gamma ut to D sol re. What is shown as a ditone becomes a minor third or semiditone, so that proceeding also from D sol re to B mi and from B mi to Gamma ut, the syllables become re la, la fa, and fa re, when they were first ut sol, sol mi, and mi ut [i.e., replacing D-B-G with D-B♭-G]. These species are contrary to all those which appear in the soprano, tenor and contralto. They do this especially in songs in the seventh or eighth tone.

> The second difficulty is that the octaves and fifteenths will not sound well [because B♭ will sound against B♮], and that if you want the low B to be flat you should so mark all the others also.[26] Again, he sets the priority on consonance.

Aaron chooses clearly (if still not, for us, quite completely) notated examples, and he sometimes illustrates conflicts between known rules for interval correction. These permit us to extrapolate not only his own contrapuntal priorities, but also point to the more general practice implied by his anthology of examples drawn from Petrucci prints. None of these were expressed in terms of chromatic alteration; all lie within the diatonic genus.

[324] Here is an attempt to set out Aaron's priorities, as described and exemplified by him, in terms of guidance for modern editors and performers, taken together with and to supplement the standard contrapuntal directives given in *Toscanello* IV.xiv. (Rules that are more indirectly inferred than directly indicated are in parentheses.)

- Adjust the melodic tritone to a perfect fourth by means of a b molle on the upper note, whether the interval ascends or descends, or proceeds stepwise or by leap.

- The tritone is to be avoided when the interval returns within itself and does not proceed to the fifth scale degree. But when the tritone does proceed to the fifth degree, it need not be softened because the semitone at the top may be cadential, a leading note, and in any case it will form one of several legitimate species of fifth.

- The melodic tritone may, however, be tolerated (especially if, as in Aaron's main example #*13, also in *14, both mediated) in the interests of achieving a higher priority: perfection in a simultaneous fifth or octave takes precedence over the correction of a melodic tritone.

- The simultaneous sounding of a false consonance is to be avoided; this rule always takes precedence over melodic considerations. Except for some examples of melodic tritones (#4, 5, 6, 7e, 8, 9), and the special cases related to recognition of cadential discant formulae (exx A, B), Aaron's examples overwhelmingly involve the bassus or the lowest sounding part, and point to particular strength for this rule (a) when intervals with the lowest voice are involved, often with reference to a fifth or octave in another part sounding above it, and (b) when they fall on strong beats. The rule is in any case a reinforcement of the proscription of *mi contra fa* in perfect intervals.

- Anticipation of a raised cadential leading note, the upper part of a sixth to octave progression, may eliminate the need for a b molle at the top of what would be a tritone outline. Having given examples of B♭ A G F G under the heading of tritone avoidance, he then allows B♮ A G F♯ G to eliminate the tritone if, and only if, the cadential intent of the phrase is established. (In such a phrase, B♭ A G F♯ G would only be used if two considerations, a perfect simultaneity with the B♭ and a cadence on G, were present.) Thus B♭ is preferred unless there is a cadential F♯.

- Leading notes are to be raised in, e.g., major 6th-8ve progressions (but care should be taken with unusual or deceptive cadences). This is a reinforcement of the standard rule for cadential approaches.

- Thirds in chords at phrase ends should be major, and so indicated (*Toscanello*, II.xx).

[325] Aaron is absolutely clear about contrapuntal priorities and in giving primacy to getting the sound right. He uses the hexachord terminology of *mi contra fa* to

describe collisions and their rectification; but at the same time he is moving strongly towards keyboard-based terminology by using the terms *proprio* or *naturale* and *accidentale* as equivalents not only to *musica recta* versus *ficta*, but also to white and black notes.

Aaron's order for the subjects represented by examples (sections I–III) is quite logical. The singer first construes his own written or printed part, and anticipates certain choices that already override the official modal species of the notated part as defined hexachordally by its clef and signature. Then, when singing with others, he may need to yield to an overriding consideration that arises from the context which he hears. Thus the interval species of the part "as written" that was the basis for Aaron's modal analysis is promptly overruled by several further levels of priority and default. Aaron refers to the need for a quick ear and responsive action, but regards this as something which the average singer cannot do without help. The singer could also, at leisure, as Aaron did in locating his examples, look at the other parts and identify from aural memory where the problems occur, but although he might hear these, he would not see them while actually singing. Then finally Aaron proceeds to simultane-ities that the reading singer could not anticipate without rehearsal, that need to be signed to avoid dissonance at the first attempt. As we have said, Aaron never implies that notation without signs is incorrect, only that the fallible singer should be helped. He thus continues to subscribe to the strictly accidental or ancillary nature of the signs.

Aaron's examples and the precepts drawn from them provide welcome amplifica-tion and corroboration of well-known rules for *musica ficta*. Despite Aaron's inconsis-tent level of vigilance in attention to all the parts, some of his examples provide clear directives on how to exercise priorities between conflicting rules. It is against the background of a changing view of what notation means that Aaron's plea for fuller notation of accidentals needs to be considered. He is himself in active transition. He still uses older circumlocutions that avoid the straightforward claim that a sharp raises a note or a flat lowers it. He still writes of the singer's need to divine the secret intent of the composer, but wishes to bring those intentions into the open, as some worthy composers have done, to his approval.

Table of Examples in the *Aggiunta*

Aaron, citations (in the order of the *Toscanello*, with spellings normalized) composer, work, paraphrase of Aaron's location of the accidental sign and his rationale	voice	Aaron's source (? if not known) Petrucci, *Motetti de la Corona*	Modern edition	Comments * means a music example is included in this article, identified by its number in this table
tritone avoidance:				
1 Mouton: *Nos qui vivimus, tertia pars* over the verse "Dominus memor fuit nostri"	S T A B	Ct S f. 5v T f. 22 A f. 38 B f. 53v	Shine pp. 608–09, bar 317 T/B, then S/A	* S and T have G B♭ A G F G, responding to altus and bassus, both with preplaced ♭ and a simultaneous interval for perfection
2 [Mouton:] *Beata dei genitrici*, bass at the end of the second staff [and beginning of third] over the words "placuisti regina Iesu christo"	B	Ct f. 56v	Shine p. 109, bar 63	F [line end] B♭ A. Name of motet omitted because Aaron failed to notice he was looking at a new piece?
3 Mouton: *Benedicta es celorum regina* [tenor and bass] at the end of the third staff over the words "Ave gratia plena" (*recte* "Ave plena gratia")	[T B]	Ct T f. 28 B f. 59	Shine p. 118, bar 77	* T has A B♭ A G F G twice, the second B♭ together with bass B♭, but then the bass E♭ necessary (in Aaron's terms) to avoid the tritone is not notated!
4 Mouton: *Congregate sunt*, cantus at the end [middle] of the second staff over the word "ignoramus"	S	C2 #16	Shine p. 201, bar 42	G F B♭ A
5 Mouton: *Nos qui vivimus*, contralto in the middle of the third staff in the *prima pars* over the word "retrorsum"	A	Ct f. 37	Shine p. 596, bar 66	F B♭ A G
6 Josquin, *Memor esto*, first staff at the end of the contralto of the *prima pars* over the words "haec me consolata est in humilitate mea", only for the ascent	A	Ct f. 34	*Werken*, Pt 2, V.2, #31	C A F B♭ A

Petrucci, Liber primus Missarum Josquin

7 a	Josquin: *Missa Gaudeamus*, in the *Patrem* in the middle of the second staff of the bass because of the ascending tritone;	B		*Werken*, Pt I, V.1, p. 65 bar 28	F B♭ A	
b	[in the *Patrem*] at the end of the third staff in ascent and descent;	B		p. 65 bar 41–42		*Aaron fails to note a misprint in Petrucci
c	at the beginning of the fourth staff of the second part of the same *Patrem* for the ascent;	B		p. 69 bar 175	G F B♭ A	
d	in the *Pleni sunt celi*;	B		p. 73 bar 40–41	C F E F G A B♭ A B♭	
e	in the first *Kyrie* at the end of the cantus	S		p. 57 bar 13	♭ F B A (B♭ pre-placed)	
8 a	Josquin: *Missa L'homme armé super voces musicales* in the first *Kyrie* in the first staff of the contralto	A		*Werken*, Pt I, V.1, p. 1 bar 10	G A B♭ A F G F	
b	at the beginning of the Sanctus	A		p. 20 bar 7	D A B♭ A F (also with octave B♭ with bass below)	
9	Josquin: *Missa La sol fa re mi*, over the words "et homo factus" in the contralto, b molle signed to the descending tritone	A		*Werken*, Pt I, V.1, p. 43 bar 75	C A B♭ A G F	

Motetti de la Corona

10 a	Févin: *Benedictus dominus deus meus* over the words "deposuisti adversarios meos" signed in six places with respect to the tritone;	[B]	C1 f. 56	Clinkscale II, pp. 322–3		*♭ signature in all parts, as Aaron approves. Some needed E♭ are not signed, and a melodic tritone is forced at bar 8.
b	beginning of the *secunda pars* in two other places	[B]				*E♭ in bass for simultaneous B♭ in tenor, then E♭ in altus.
11 a	Lhéritier: *Dum complerentur* [bass] at the end of the second staff over the words "dabat eloqui illis";	B	C2 # 21	CMM 48. I p. 54. bar 47		*B♭ by signature, in all parts. E♭ signed, enters under sounding B♭; but E♮ probably needed in superius in 48.
b	at the beginning of the fourth staff [over the words] "si feceritis" it is shown because of a leap	[B]		p. 55. bar 90		direct bass leap B♭ – E♭, enters under sounding B♭

12					
a	T	Carpentras: *Bonitatem fecisti* in the *prima pars* for the tenor because of a leap over the words "ut discant" [*recte* "discam"]	C1 f. 19v	CMM 58, V p. 61, bar 118	• F separated from following Bb by rests. The b is needed because of a simultaneous fifth with the altus F. In 120 it must be performed n if the bass enters on Eb below; but if Eb it will be Bb
b	T	stepwise at the end of the *secunda pars*	C1 f. 20	p. 68 bar 289	A Bb A G F G

Exceptions to the tritone rule

Liber primus Missarum Josquin

13	B	Josquin: *Missa Clama ne cesses* [*L'homme armé super voces musicales*], in the third Agnus at the end of the bass	C1 f. 20	Werken, Pt I, V.1, p. 31	• Aaron gives example in text
14					
a	S	Josquin: *Missa La sol fa re mi* in the soprano over the words "Tu solus altissimus" ;		Werken, Pt I, V.1, p. 40	• Aaron gives notated example in text
b	S	in the Patrem omnipotentem [in the soprano] over the words " et sepultus est"		p. 44	• Aaron gives notated example in text

EXAMPLES A 1–4

Can the singer divine the composer's intent?

Motetti de la Corona

15	B T	Josquin: *Memor esto*, at the end of the contrabass over the words "spem dedisti" (for a fifth with the tenor that is naturally imperfect)	C1 f. 50v f.18	*Werken*, Pt 2, V. 2, #31 bar 324	• Bb in bass is anticipated by F in superius
16	B A	Josquin: *Praeter rerum*, contrabass [Bass I] in the sesquialtera section at the end over the words "tua puerperia," b molle on E sounding "over" the contralto for a simultaneity that is unexpected	C3 B I #2	*Werken*, Pt 2, V. 2, #33 bar 112	• Eb signed for simultaneous attack with altus
17	B2 A2	Josquin: *Ave nobilissima* [*secunda pars*] in the second contrabass at the end of the second staff over the words "ab omnibus malis et fraudibus" for an imperfect fifth with the second contralto	C3 B II #3	*Werken*, Pt 2, V. 2, #34 bar 176	• Bass Eb coincides with Bb, somewhat prepared, before unusual cadence with Satzfehler

No.	Description	Voice	Source	Reference	Comment
18	Josquin: *Virgo salutiferi*, bass at the end of the second staff over the words "benigna maris," for an octave with the first contralto	B A1	C3 B #4	Werken, Pt 2, V.2, #35 bar 32	Eb slightly anticipated by altus Eb. Eb in bar 35 is signed although self-evident following Bb (after rest) and entering under Bb

Liber primus Missarum Josquin

No.	Description	Voice	Source	Reference	Comment
19	Josquin: *Missa L'homme armé super voces musicales* in the contrabass in the middle of the first Kyrie because of an imperfect fifth with the tenor	T B		Werken, Pt I, V.1, p. 1 bar 8	* tenor F above bass Bb, no warning
b	in the last Kyrie after 8 breves for a twelfth and fifteenth which were imperfect with the bass	[S] B		p. 3 bar 72. Aaron's "da poi otto tempi" is correct	* Bass Bb enters under D cadence of altus and tenor. Superius F Bb create the 12th and 15th above it.

Motetti de la Corona

No.	Description	Voice	Source	Reference	Comment
20	Mouton: *Gaude Barbara*, [near] beginning of the bass, for a fifth with the tenor	B T	Cı f. 49v f. 18	Shine pp. 303–04 bar 20	Bb sounds below F, with slight anticipation
	bass in the *secunda pars* over the words "et velata nobili," with the tenor	B T		p. 3II bar 147	likewise
21	Mouton: *Nos qui vivimus*, bass over the words "benedicamus domino" [*recte* "benedicimus"] for a 5th with the tenor	B T	Cı f. 53v f.21	Shine, p. 615 bar 433	F G G A C Bb (F sounds ahead of and together with it) A D G
22	Févin: *Benedictus dominus meus secunda pars*, on a dotted breve, bass over the words "in voce exultationis" for a fifth which was imperfect	B [A]	Cı f. 56 f.41	Clinkscale II, p. 324	Simultaneous arrival on notated Eb by alto and bass, easily "divined" following cadence with Eb and slight anticipation by Bb
23	Richafort: *Miseremini mei* contrabass and contralto over the words "quare me persequemini" correction of minor sixth to major preceding the octave by b between bass and alto [see text]	B A	C2 #4	Kabis II, p. 257 bar 38	* NG notes attribution by Glareanus of this *opus dubium*, but not its mention by Aaron. Edited by Kabis as an *opus dubium* of Mouton, reporting two ascriptions to Richafort, two to Mouton, two anon.
24	Constanzo Festa: *Fors seulement* in two places at the beginning of the bass	B	?	?	evidently lost'

25	Longueval: [Benedicat nos imperialis maiestatis] over the words "Divinitas custodiat nos" because of an imperfect fifth between bass and tenor	B T	Corona 1, B f. 56v, T f. 25v	Gehrenbeck p. 1482 bar 31	* on preceding word regalis, E♭ notated in bass with tenor's B♭ by signature. Aaron does not mention the simultaneous E in the altus, which also needs to be ♭ but is not signed
26	Verdelot: Ave virgo gratiosa in the first contrabass part because of an imperfect fifth with the contralto at the beginning	B1 A	?	Willaert CMM 3 IV p. 117, bar 11	Bonnie J. Blackburn identified this as the six-part motet ascribed to Jacquet in Adriani....Motetta VI vocum (RISM 1542^10), where it follows Verdelot's Congregati sunt.[2] bassus B♭ marked for simultaneit y with Quinta pars F
27	Pierre de La Rue: Il est bien near the beginning of the bass part on a breve because of the imperfect diapente with the contralto	B A	?	Picker, p. 208, bar 27	unicum: Brussels 228, ff. 10v-11; attribution to La Rue depends on the Toscanello. Simultaneous arrival on B♭ with F
28	Lhéritier: Miserere mei deus [recte domine] over the words "omni ossa mea" in the contrabass because of an imperfect diapente with the contralto	B A	?	CMM 48, I pp. 173–74	D G B♭ (sounding with F) A G A ample warning from the prior F to encourage B♭
29	Constanzo Festa: Ecce deus salvator meus in the bass over the words "fiducialiter agam"	B	?	CMM 25, III p. 22	F E D C D B♭ (sounding with F) A ample warning from the prior F to encourage B♭
	Odhecaton				
30	Orto: Ave Maria [in the tenor] over the words "dominus tecum" because of the fifth between tenor and contralto	T A	#1, ff. 3v-4	Hewitt, pp. 220–21, bar 46	Tenor E♭, coincident attack with unprepared B♭ in altus; T is lowest sounding voice at that moment
31	Agricola: C'est mal charché at the beginning of the contrabass because of an imperfect fifth with the contralto	B A	#12, ff. 14v-15	Hewitt, p. 244, bar 1	Bass E♭ coincident attack with unprepared B♭ in the si placet altus that is unique to Odhecaton but which alone requires the E♭ that is also unique to this source[3]
32	Pierazzon de La Rue: Pour quoy non in the middle of the first line of the contrabass because of an imperfect fifth with the tenor	B T	#15, ff. 17v-18	Hewitt, p. 253, bar 34	stepwise descent to bass A♭ coincident attack with unprepared E♭ in tenor and superius, both of which are approached by direct leap of a 4th or 5th
33	Japart: [Hélas! qu'il est à mon grel]; in the beginning of the secunda pars in the bass because of a twelfth with the cantus and a fifth with the contralto	B A	#30, ff. 32v-33	Hewitt, p. 285, bar 29	altus and superius F above the notated B♭; superius must be F fa because it then descends a fourth to C

34	Compère: *Nous sommes*; on the second line of the contrabass part because of an imperfect fifth with the tenor	B T	#37, ff. 40v-41	Hewitt, p. 300, bar 34	unprepared attack after a rest, Bb in bass and F in tenor
35	Isaac: *He logeron(s) nous* in the middle of the first line of the contrabass	B [T]	#40, ff. 45v-46	Hewitt, p. 307, bar 15	fifth simultaneously attacked in bass (with Eb) and tenor (Bb). Following the signature this is anticipated by alto Bb
36	Obrecht: *Tandernaken* in the beginning of the second line of the contrabass because of an imperfect fifth with the tenor	B T	#60, ff. 74v-75	Hewitt, p. 366, bar 17	simultaneous unprepared Bass Eb under tenor which must have Bb (as in signature) because of its ensuing descent to F

EXAMPLES B 1-4

The following sources have been consulted, all in photographic copies:

Odhecaton RISM 1504² (Broude facsimile, copy unspecified)
RISM 1501 (I-Bc)

Liber primus missarum Josquin
RISM 1502 (I-Bc (SAB), D-brd B (SATB), I-Mc (TB))
RISM 1516 (US-Wc)
Vivarelli & Gulla facsimile, source unspecified, apparently from one or more late Fossombrone editions

Motetti de la Corona I (C1)
RISM 1514¹ (I-Vnm (SAB), I-Bc (T), A-Wn (T))

Motetti de la Corona II (C2)
RISM 1519 (GB-Lbl, I-Vnm)

Motetti de la Corona III (C3)
RISM 1519² (GB-Lbl)
RISM 1527 (D-Hs)

For help in assembling relevant dissertations and films I am grateful to Bonnie J. Blackburn, Alice Clark, Jeffrey Dean, Paula Morgan, and Jaap Van Benthem. I would be grateful to hear of variants from other states or copies that affect the present readings.

Other bibliographical abbreviations:

Carpentras: *Elziari Geneti (Carpentras) Opera Omnia*, ed. Albert Seay. CMM 58, V (1973).

Clinkscale: Edward H. Clinkscale, *The Complete Works of Antoine de Févin*, Ph.D. dissertation. NYU 1965.

CMM: Corpus Mensurabilis Musicae

Festa: *Constanzo Festa Opera Omnia*, ed. Albert Seay. CMM 25, III (1977).

Gehrenbeck: David M. Gehrenbeck, *Motetti de la Corona: A Study of Ottaviano Petrucci's Four Last-known Motet Prints* (Fossombrone, 1514, 1519), *with 44 transcriptions*. Union Theological Seminary in the City of New York, SMD, 1970.

Hewitt: Helen Hewitt, *Harmonice Musices Odhecaton A*, Cambridge, MA, 1946.

Kabis: Mary Elise Kabis, *The Works of Jean Richafort, Renaissance Composer (1480?–1548)*, Ph.D. dissertation, NYU 1957.

Lhéritier: *Johannes Lhéritier Opera Omnia*, ed. Leeman L. Perkins. CMM 48, I (1969).

Picker: Martin Picker, *The Chanson Albums of Marguerite of Austria*, Berkeley and Los Angeles 1965.

Shine: Josephine M. Shine, *The Motets of Jean Mouton*, Ph.D. dissertation, NYU 1953.

Werken: *Werken van Josquin des Prés*, ed. Smijers.

Willaert: *Willaert Opera Omnia*, ed. Hermann Zenck. CMM 3/IV (1952).

Notes to table

1. The items forming the nearly-consecutive group of 24, 26, 27, 28, 29 have survived in no known sources likely to have been used by Aaron. The Festa *Fors seulement* has not been identified. Nos. 27–29 are all *unica* in manuscript sources, as Bonnie J. Blackburn kindly confirmed. A single printed source containing this group seems unlikely, given the assorted repertory of French songs and Latin motets, as well as the inclusion of motets both in four and in six parts (no. 26, q.v.).

2. Also ascribed to Jacquet in two manuscript sources, and to Vermont Primus (as *Ave virgo gloriosa*) in Attaingnant's third book of motets (RISM 1534[5]).

3. David Fallows informs me that there is no E flat in Seville.

Commentary

to passages marked by asterisks in text; see also the Introduction. Asterisks are also used with "#" to indicate which of Aaron's examples correspond to music examples in this chapter. See note 7.

p. 162   In her magisterial Introduction to *A Correspondence*, pp. III–120, Blackburn sets out how Aaron and Spataro criticised each other for use of diminished fifths in passing contexts. Meter, duration, and harmony are taken into account in a series of examples giving just two parts at a time, providing a fascinating amplification of Aaron's *Aggiunta* comments. In 35.5, Spataro comments of Aaron's *Letatus sum* that it would be more comfortable and regular sung without the B♭ [signature] placed at the beginning, but only to insert the sign wherever it is needed in the course of the work.

p. 162   Peter Urquhart rightly points out (personal communication) that Aaron does not actually call these rules of *musica ficta*. But they are stated within precepts on counterpoint, the prohibition of mi against fa in book II chapter xiv. I have assimilated them to earlier "standard" rules, which are often likewise stated in the context of counterpoint teaching.

p. 169   Urquhart believes that Aaron is considering the single line only, and that therefore the sequencing flats have no consequences, even aurally induced ones, for the other parts.

NOTES

*From: "Accidentals, counterpoint and notation in Aaron's *Aggiunta* to the *Toscanello in Musica,*" *The Journal of Musicology* XII: 1994, pp. 306-44 (Festschrift issue for James Haar: *Aspects of Musical Language and Culture in the Renaissance*).

1. This essay is offered with deep respect and affection for James Haar on the occasion of his 65th birthday, and in recognition of his great contribution to understanding how the notes are illuminated by theory. Jim has maintained a lively and valued dialogue in private with my own work on counterpoint and *ficta*, and it is in the spirit of that ongoing discussion that I offer him this installment as an appendage to some of his larger enterprises.
2. First published in Venice in 1523 as *Thoscanello de la musica* by Bernardino and Mattheo de Vitali, who also published the 1529 edition with the *Aggiunta: TOSCANELLO IN MVSICA DI MESSER PIERO ARON FIORENTINO DEL ORDINE HIEROSOLIMITANO ET CANONICO IN RIMINI NVOVAMENTE STAMPATO CON LAGGIUNTA DA LVI FATTA ET CON DILIGENTIA CORRETTO.* Two later editions appeared from other Venetian publishers in 1539 and 1562.
3. Available in a facsimile of the 1529 edition (Forni, Bologna); in translation by Peter Bergquist, Pietro

Aaron, *Toscanello in Music*, Colorado College Music Press, 1970, and extensive comment in Bergquist's "The Theoretical Writings of Pietro Aaron" (Ph.D. dissertation, Columbia 1964), and other places, most recently in the commentary to the magisterial edition of the Spataro correspondence by Bonnie J. Blackburn, Edward E. Lowinsky, and Clement A. Miller, *A Correspondence of Renaissance Musicians* (Oxford 1991). Examples from Aaron presented here in English incorporate my modifications to Bergquist's translation.

4. Only for #24 and #26–29 are Aaron's sources not known.

5. This was pointed out by Lewis Lockwood in "A Sample Problem of *Musica ficta*: Willaert's *Pater noster*" in *Studies in Music History: Essays for Oliver Strunk*, ed. Harold Powers (Princeton, 1968), 165–66, and judged to be culpable plagiarism. Lowinsky's commentary to this letter in the Spataro correspondence finds Lockwood's judgment in this to be too harsh (*A Correspondence* . . . , pp. 309-10). The Spataro edition italicizes the passages borrowed by Aaron.

6. II.xxii–xxxi deal with the "modo del comporre il controbasso, & alto doppo il tenore & canto," and composition in more than four parts.

7. There is not space here to give texts and translations in full. This article represents my preliminary work for an edition of the texts, translations, and examples. To avoid a separate sequence of numbered examples, music examples in this article are identified by their numbers in the table below, which paraphrases Aaron's own identification of pieces and comments thereon. When pieces are referred to by number (#) in the present text, they are given an asterisk (*) if there is a corresponding example in this article. The examples themselves, preceded by a table, appear at the conclusion of the article. <Here the examples appear in place.>

8. Bonnie J. Blackburn identified Petrucci's editor in a paper read at the Annual Meeting of the American Musicological Society, Pittsburgh, 1992 <now published as "Petrucci's Venetian Editor: Petrus Castellanus and His Musical Garden," *Musica Disciplina* 49 (1995): 15-45>. See s.v. Pietro de Zoannepolo (Petrus Castellanus) in *A Correspondence* . . . , p. 1008.

9. He promises a total of seven tritone locations but—rightly—gives and exemplifies only six.

10. Aaron cannot mean the soprano fourth which, while near the end of its third staff, has no notated flat.

11. Smijers notes this error in Stuttgart, Württembergische Landesbibliothek, Cod. Mus.46, which (as kindly signalled by Jaap van Benthem) is derived from one of the later printings of Petrucci's set.

12. An argument for E♭ that involves maintaining the imitated interval species would itself be vitiated if A♭ in the altus and D♭ in the bassus were allowed to <follow> from a continuation of the E♭; this is clearly not appropriate. This example is further complicated by anomalous text distribution which gives different text to the same point of imitation. Aaron repeats Petrucci's erroneous *ut discant* for *ut discam*; these words (erroneously) appear only in the tenor.

13. This example is discussed at greater length in my "Diatonic *ficta*," *Early Music History* 4 (1984): 26–28 <=chapter 4>.

14. Listenius and Ornithoparcus give melodic examples necessitating such a spiral. Greiter's *Fortuna* spirals by both melodic and "harmonic" consideration; the core duo of Willaert's *Quidnam ebrietas* requires the tenor to spiral.

15. Tinctoris, *De natura et proprietate tonorum*, chapter 8, CSM 22.1, quoted with commentary in "Diatonic *ficta*," 24–26.

16. For James Haar's contribution to diatonic definition see "False Relations and Chromaticism in Sixteenth-Century Music," *Journal of the American Musicological Society* 30 (1977): 391–418; p. 392.

17. Bruce Carvell pointed out to me the similarity of this example, presented on p. 65 of his dissertation, "A Practical Guide to Musica Ficta Based on an Analysis of Sharps Found in the Music Prints of Ottaviano Petrucci (1501–1519)," (Ph.D., Historical Performance Practice, Washington University, 1982).

18. This recalls the innovations of Guido, Aaron's authority for the accidental status of B♭, who had claimed in the prologue to the *Micrologus* that his notation, in conjunction with the monochord, enabled boys within a month to sight-read chants they had not seen or heard, to the amazement of observers.

19. No such simple formulation was used in the *Aggiunta*. See also *Aggiunta* IV.2.

20. *A Correspondence* . . . , letter 12, p. 301.

21. To allow for some alternative solutions, or to speak of performers realising the notation according to

conventions expected by the composer and therefore within limits set by him, is not to say that the sound is abstract. Peter Urquhart has recently attributed to me a view of abstract notation to which I certainly do not subscribe ("Cross-relations by Franco-Flemish Composers after Josquin," TVNM . . . , n. 2). Dahlhaus presented a view of counterpoint as abstract, suggesting that the composer was indifferent to its realisation, or had no intentions therefor, in "Tonsystem und Kontrapunkt um 1500," *Jahrbuch des Staatlichen Instituts für Musikforschung Preussischer Kulturbesitz* (1969): 7-18. The position I take in "*Diatonic ficta*," obliquely documented by Aaron's transitional stance, is that pre-Aaron notation embodied compositional intentions more specific than we can now recover from the notation alone. In Aaron's terms, earlier singers were expected to divine the composer's intent on the basis of their understanding of counterpoint, and so must we. The notation is to be realised in accordance with ability to understand the composer's built-in intentions for that realisation. Aaron sought to relieve the singer of at least part of this responsibility.

22. *De Institutione Harmonica* I xv, and *A Correspondence*, letter 73.

23. "Mano principale di Guido Aretino," in Lanfranco, *Scintille di musica*, 1533.

24. Tinctoris, *Liber de nature et proprietate tonorum*, chapter VIII, De formatione sexti toni. Ed. Albert Seay. *Johannes Tinctoris opera theoretica* I (AIM 1975), 74.

25. "Is Mode Real?" *Basler Jahrbuch für historische Musikpraxis* 16 (1992): 9–52. See p. 43 and n. 30 for the following references. After this paper was completed, I heard a paper by Cristle Collins Judd at a colloquium in honour of Harold Powers <now published as "Reading Aron Reading Petrucci: The Music Examples of the *Trattato della natura et cognitione di tutti gli tuoni (1525),*" *Early Music History* 14 (1995) pp. 121–52>. Professor Judd's handout <tabulated in the published article> assembled Aaron's citations from Petrucci prints, listing the contents of those prints with clefs, system, and final, including the works cited in the *Toscanello*. I regret that it is too late to incorporate her helpful observations on a draft of this paper, but am pleased by the extent to which our articles may be seen as complementary.

26. However, Aaron has here opened a can of worms with respect to his modal categories. Different practice in signatures will affect the species, as he says; but it does seem that he really means to confine the modal categories to the operation of signatures and not of other accidentals.

Chapter 6

Diatonic *Ficta* Revisited: Josquin's *Ave Maria* in Context[*]

ABSTRACT: Roger Wibberley in MTO 2.5 has criticized a version I published of the sequence from Josquin's *Ave Maria*, on grounds that it flouts Glarean's modal classification. Cristle Collins Judd has already challenged Wibberley's construction of mode, and I further deny Glarean's relevance on chronological grounds. The first part of my article restates and revises some of the premises (ignored by Wibberley) which provided the context for my discussion of the Josquin piece; the second part extends my original discussion of that passage, and offers some comments and questions in response to Wibberley's paper.

"A mind is like a parachute. It only works if it is open."

[1] I am grateful to Roger Wibberley and other correspondents following his article in *MTO*[1] for airing some important questions and providing me with an incentive for this reply. I do plan eventually to produce a more fully revised and corrected expansion of the thesis I set out in "Diatonic *ficta*" (henceforth DF<=chapter 4>),[2] incorporating replies to Karol Berger and Peter Urquhart, but this may serve as a partial, interim statement.[3]

[2] Cristle Collins Judd began her posting of July 23 to *mto-talk* ("Wibberley, MTO 2.5," *mto-talk* 23 July 1996) by addressing not so much Wibberley's solution but his modal premises. In order to restore premises rather than symptoms to the centre of the discussion, I shall first set the Josquin aside. Since some readers may not be familiar with DF and the context in which I used that example, and since none will be able to infer it correctly from Wibberley's article, it might be helpful if I now restate and amplify some parts (only) of the thesis particularly germane to this discussion,

and take this opportunity to adjust some areas where my presentation may have proved incomplete or too elliptical.

[3] Since I invoke counterpoint so strongly, I had better explain the specific sense in which I use the term. Counterpoint, as defined in DF from Tinctoris and earlier theorists, is concerned not with lines or vague general attributes but with *two-voice* progressions—what *we* might call two-part or *dyadic harmony*.[4] At least up to the late 15th century, the handling of more than two parts was treated by theorists as an extension of those dyadic principles. It is in respecting and reconciling melodic principles and the rules of counterpoint that *ficta* is necessitated; I have tried to show that *ficta* needs to be viewed in the context of counterpoint as a whole, and not informed just by precepts specifically labelled as *ficta*. The list discussion has referred to the need to set priorities in cases of conflicting principles (Judd, 23 July: "the challenge to Bent's solution of the passage in question comes not from modal theory, but in relation to how one interprets horizontal and vertical priorities in determining *ficta*." Just so.) I did indeed attempt[5] to draw from theorists a set of primary guidelines for applying contrapuntal precepts (melodic and "harmonic") precisely with a view to setting priorities when those precepts come into conflict, though there is still a long way to go in spelling out qualifications, exceptions and licences to those primary considerations, some of which have been addressed by Berger and Urquhart.

[4] A fundamental difference between Renaissance notation and ours is that, then, "not to notate accidentals is not to misnotate the music." Notated accidentals were truly accidental. No more or less importance attaches to their prescriptive power or indeed to their absence than would, say, to that of sporadic fingerings in some early keyboard sources. We may be glad of help, however occasional or eccentric, but notation should not be viewed as incomplete or inaccurate when lacking such accidental indications. When we transcribe old music into a notation in which accidentals have become essential, we tend to read the notation thus transcribed as a stronger default than it ever could have been, one from which "deviations" have to be justified and to which accidentals have to be added, or notes inflected. It is we, *not they*, who "add accidentals," depart from the notation, and make inflections. They had no term to distinguish our F♭ from F: if a note was F according to the clef, it was still "F," even F fa ut, *even if* it had become our "F♭" by local contrapuntal operations. This is what I shall mean by the term "contrapuntal descent" (see [8]), as distinct from a descent caused by tuning.

[5] It is the modern transcription that has traditionally been treated as our default, as when we refer to "the notation as it stands," or at "face value," despite changing standards in editorial practice. After considerable editorial experience, it is now my conviction that so to treat it is a greater disfigurement and source of mispri-

sion than to start from the other end, as I now advocate. It is obvious that *their* starting point for these determinations, *their* access to the music, was not from a modern transcription but rather through singing from their manuscripts and prints. Early notation provided a weak intervallic default organization by clef and signature, but because it was incompletely prescriptive of pitch (hence "weak default"), the performer expected to arrive at actual sounds by some means besides prescriptive notation. Modes and hexachords (see [18] below), while very important for other purposes, run on separate tracks from each other and are at best marginally relevant to the realization of counterpoint and the determination of *ficta*. The most important key to successful realization of weakly prescriptive notation is to complement it as they must have done, armed with an approximation of the elementary training shared by composers and singers, and which composers presumed in their singers when they committed their compositions to notation, namely, for these purposes, practical training in counterpoint. Taken in partnership, notation and counterpoint create a more strongly prescriptive basis for realization. Like them, we should develop the (for us very different) musical skills that are dictated by singing from the original, acquiring an awareness of the constraints and freedoms inherent in the notation, as well as a sense of the violence done by putting weak-default (early) notation (without the complement of a strengthening counterpoint training) into a (modern) form that demands to be read by the standards of modern notation as a "strong" default. DF grew out of a recognition that the answers to many of these questions follow naturally from the experience of reading and singing from original notation instead of from conceptually different modern translations. If this is a counsel of perfection, we need at least to learn (by doing it) to *simulate* that experience so that in using modern scores we can make allowance for their inherent distortions, as one glimpses the original language through the shortcomings of a translation. It is those earlier habits that (echoing Crocker 1962) we need to recover, by reading their books (musical and theoretical) rather than ours, by observing what they don't say as well as what they do.

[6] Armed with the rudiments of mensural and contrapuntal skills (correct realization of perfect simultaneities and cadential approaches in discant-tenor pairs, and perfection of melodic 4ths and 5ths unless prevented), one *reads* one's own part in a state of readiness to reinterpret, of readiness to change one's *expectation* of how to read the under-prescriptive notation (not to *change the notation!*) in prompt reaction to what one *hears*. The "default" of the line you *see*, together with the melodic articulations you expect to apply (perfecting linear fourths, making cadential semitones) is controlled and sometimes overruled by the counterpoint you *hear*. The "default" that is "changed" is not the *notation as transcribed*, but the *expectation* of how the original notation is to be realized.[6] Once the new (i.e., old) habits of listening and adjusting aurally

have been internalized, most solutions follow naturally, and almost never require the lengthy discussions that arise when singing from transcribed score. I fear that I am now as sceptical of the authority of assertions about what is and is not possible in early polyphony, from those who have not acquired fluency in reading in this way, as I would be reluctant to accept literary correction from someone who read a language only in translation. The weak default of under-prescriptive notation becomes a strong default when coupled with contrapuntal training, but it is a different strong default from modern, mostly white-note, notation "as it stands," and the inherent status accorded accidentals by current editorial conventions.

[7] We are still free to treat results so obtained as a default that can or must be departed from, but this default is as different as it could be from that of a modern transcription. We will approach their thinking and musicianship more closely by try-ing to do it their way (the Kon-Tiki principle of testing whether the expedition is possible using the original equipment), even if the results turn out to be very different from what we have grown used to by doing it from the opposite, unquestionably anachronistic direction, and even if we then decided (on grounds *yet to be determined*, since "modal fidelity," *pace* Wibberley, will no longer do) that the new results need further adjustments of a different kind.

[8] Our musical culture has raised the definition of frequency and pitch-class to a high status, for analysis, editing and performance. My reading of a range of early theorists leads me to posit a slightly fuzzier status both for what we would call pitch-class and for frequency, a status that places pitch closer to the more flexible view of durations and tempo that we still have. This reading rests partly on conspicuous cir-cumlocutions and the late arrival of precise language, notation, and measurement, partly on a pervasive Pythagorean mentality expressed in the tuning system, partly on my understanding of counterpoint and the internal evidence of some paradigmatic pieces, *not* the Josquin. We routinely make *rhythmic and durational* analyses on the basis of notated values even though we know that performance fluctuations, some necessary, some elective, expected but elusive to precise definition, are ignored by the analyst. We are not necessarily shocked if an analysis disregards the fact that a piece, any piece, may end slower than it began. A terminal *ritardando* needn't affect certain kinds of analysis; nor need the *ritardando* of pitch caused by a logical downward sequential spiral (Obrecht) shock us. I do not assume, as Wibberley seems to impute [2], that for the "Obrecht piece to begin on F and end on F♭ was of little if any consequence for the singers." By suggesting that if they *knew* they were spiralling for reasons either of tun-ing or counterpoint (if I understand him correctly) they would have found a way not to do so, Wibberley subscribes to a rigid frequency stability which, however well estab-lished it became in the keyboard-reference era, did not, I believe, govern earlier

music (see especially [13] below). Without cumbersome advance planning, I maintain that it is virtually impossible to sing the Obrecht *Libenter gloriabor* Kyrie (and about 30 other pieces) from original notation in any other artful way than to let the sequence, indeed, wind smoothly down in its *contrapuntal* operation (irrespective of the tuning used, even if that were equal temperament). This happened in one of our singing sessions when someone innocent of its notoriety brought a facsimile along. We read it, it descended, as everyone was (and always would have been) well aware as it was happening. The sequence of descending fifths and rising fourths F B E A D G C F is notated only with a few encouraging B and E flats, but its smooth counterpoint locks it into—in our terms, F B♭ E♭ A♭ D♭ G♭ C♭ F♭ (see DF, 34–40 <= pp. 139–43>). Another of us, who had previously been sceptical of "my" solution on paper, exclaimed with surprise that it sounded fine. That is precisely the point. Try it!

[9] Nor need such a spiral impinge on, *pace* Wibberley, a modal analysis. The work by Powers and Judd on Aaron's modal assignations[7] makes it clear that Aaron in the *Trattato* was indeed making those assignations "on paper," in such a way as to permit two startlingly different-sounding pieces (such as *Mon mari m'a diffame* by De Orto and *E la la la* by Ninot le Petit, nos. 12 and 27 in Canti B) to receive the same classification. (How, for example, does Wibberley deal with such witness or advocacy of mode?) This is closer in time to Josquin than Glareanus and should restrain Wibberley's construction of the relevance of (his perception of Glarean's view of) mode to the sound (= contrapuntal realization) of a piece. The relatively higher status we now accord to sounding pitch definition is reflected in the facts that we (not they) have made accidentals essential, and that we fix frequency and pitch class much more sharply than we do metronomic values. Pitch, in short, has a higher status for us than rhythm. Skilled singers *of course* would be aware of changes, both at the micro-level of tuning, shifting commas of intonation, and at the macro-level of occasional contrapuntal spiralling sequences such as I believe to be indisputable in the Willaert and unavoidable in the Obrecht examples.

[10] Berger (in *Musica ficta*) was unwilling to accept the evolution of his "Renaissance" view of a keyboard-like repertory of available pitches from my free-standing, vocally conceived, Pythagorean, pre-keyboard "medieval" view of pitch, tuning, and vocal counterpoint. Indeed, he (like Wibberley) is reluctant to accept any possibility of fluctuation, by tuning or counterpoint, and there we differ. I believe that Berger's view is broadly valid for a later period and with different qualifications from those to which he applies it, and that it can at some point be reconciled with mine, though not as a background to music before 1500, where I judge it to be anachronistic. I wrote: "*Musica recta* is not an arsenal of fixed pitches but denotes a set of relationships to a notional norm of pitch stability that is more like a flotilla at anchor than a Pro-

crustean bed or a pre-tuned keyboard. The 'operation of *musica ficta*,' that is, the substitution at any point, for contrapuntal reasons, of a tone for a semitone (or vice
versa), could mean that the absolute frequency of the As, Bs, Cs that follow may not be
the same as they were before, although the local interval relationships of small segments will remain intact. The taking of a *conjuncta* (substitution of a tone for a semitone or vice versa) anywhere in the system may change the actual pitches following that
point, without changing the relationships except at that point. The value of a semibreve may be changed by proportional operation or mensural change; the contextual
relationships of that semibreve will continue to be observed after the point of change
even if the absolute durations represented by the same symbol in the same context are
different from before. Both for mensuration and for pitch, the values are achieved
through local context and without reference to long-term absolutes." (DF p. 10 <= p.
120>, and *passim*.) Especially since the Powers-Judd illumination of Renaissance views
of mode, it has yet to be shown that there is any basis other than modern prejudice for
claiming such absolutes with respect to sounding pitch, as distinct from notated status, for a musicianship that was not yet, before the sixteenth century, bound by keyboard-like reference. It is the notion of frequency volatility of both these kinds that
has already educed the loudest howls of protest (e.g., from Berger, p. 45). This is a
genuine point of disagreement, much more fundamental than the Josquin example.
That singers were aware of these shifts does not prove (again, *pace* Wibberley and
Berger) that they would have found them undesirable or striven to avoid them. Before
about 1500, and often afterwards, there is nothing to constrain a piece to a fixed frequency or, in certain special circumstances, to a fixed constancy irrespective of tuning, for a letter-name-plus-hexachord syllable point on the gamut; these fixities are
what I see as coming in with the rise of the keyboard as instrument of practical and
theoretical reference. They would have been as ready, I believe (as we are not), to
redefine a frequency or, as in the Willaert, to adopt a changed but logically
approached pitch for E, as to accept (as we can without special pleading) a new value
for a semibreve beat after a proportional shift, whether specified or otherwise necessitated.

[11] Diatonic (and hence also chromatic) status was defined *melodically* in the sixteenth century and earlier.[8] The presence of sharps and flats does not necessarily render music chromatic; diatonic status then, as later, is not confined to "white notes."
F-F♯ is a chromatic, F♯-G a diatonic semitone, *irrespective of the size or tuning of the interval*.
F♯-G-A♭ presents two adjacent *diatonic* semitones. This or any melodic progression
that proceeds by diatonic intervals (e.g., the tenor of the Willaert duo) is diatonic.
Most *ficta* is diatonic, hence "Diatonic *ficta*." I did not intend the apparently paradoxi-
cal title as a label for exotic procedures;[9] rather, I used some unusual pieces to illus-

trate how far diatonicism can go, in order to demonstrate how some modern scholarship has misused the term in relation to early music, and to bring out the different underlying assumptions and the different prescriptive power of old and new notation respectively. I am pleased to note in the recent discussion that most correspondents avoid indiscriminately calling sharps and flats chromatic, and thus tacitly acquiesce in the view that, except for specifically chromatic intervals such as F-F♯, *ficta* was largely diatonic.

[12] I have read with interest the *mto-talk* postings of Nicolaus Meeus on tuning and intonation ("Wibberley, MTO 2.5," *mto-talk* 19 August 1996, *mto-talk* 26 August 1996). He rightly surmises that I believe some kind of just intonation (with pure 5ths and 8ves) applied to *a cappella* vocal counterpoint "with pure intonation, Pythagorean in principle [Meeus and Lindley also use this qualification], but probably with justly tempered thirds in practice" (DF, p. 8 <= p. 119>). However, Meeus's view of tuning is so clearly anchored to a sophisticated keyboard-equivalent that, in setting a standard of reference for a piece or a passage, it comes at the discussion from the opposite direction from mine. As for adjustments on dissonances, the frequent pitch redefinitions that result from a Pythagorean approach (as I understand it; see next para.) result in no bumps, no audible local dislocations.

[13] It is highly significant that there was no standard *starting-point* for tuning the Pythagorean monochord. In DF I presented Pythagorean tuning as the antithesis of keyboard reference: "even if two monochords were tuned with true Pythagorean ratios, their resulting frequencies could be slightly different if those ratios were applied from a unison by a different route through the spiral of fifths." (See DF, especially pp. 3–7 <= pp. 116–19>.) The monochord was unsuitable as an accompanying instrument; apart from very elementary pedagogic use, it was a representation of Pythagorean ratios rather than a proto-keyboard for an individual performance; this of course allows for the kind of disciplined frequency movement I believe to be endemic to their thinking, hence the Pythagorean spiral, not circle, of fifths. The monochord *represented* the proportions that yielded those sounds, but in practice (by pure 5/4 thirds) may have been on a slightly different track from them (separate tracks, yet again). I believe that the view of a constantly redefining Pythagorean application overcomes the rejection (by Meeus, *mto-talk* 26 August, and implicitly by many others) of Pythagorean tuning throughout the very period where it is prevalent, and the point of theoretical reference for proportions of all kinds. Indeed, the better in tune a performance sounds in terms of its local progressions (with pure thirds and fifths), the more likely it is to move down, as several professional performers confirm. It is a short step from here to believe, as I do, that Pythagorean intonation was *constantly redefinable* around new central notes in the course of a piece. The arrival on each new

true fifth sonority would then be the new point of departure for purposes of tuning calculations, thus achieving local perfection and a smooth, gradual descent by comma increments. This rules out a notional keyboard standard for performance; any performance *with* a keyboard necessitated compromises, a fact that exercised several 16th-century theorists. The final sequence of a piece like *Absalom*, in which (I believe) pure (Pythagorean) fifths would, ideally at least, have been mediated by pure 3rds (5/4) which in turn anchor the next pure fifths of the sequence, is almost bound to end at a fractionally lower frequency unless it is (artificially, and irrelevantly for this discussion) disciplined by adherence to a pre-tuned keyboard standard or repertory of available pitches (Berger's view). <See, now, pp. 27–29.>

[14] If you believe, with Lowinsky, that frequency must have been constant, a musical absolute (as if to be accompanied on equal-tempered or fretted instruments), then obviously pieces such as the Willaert duo and Greiter's *Fortuna* can be regarded, as he did, as precocious manifestos for equal temperament.[10] He was prepared to accept *contrapuntal* descent under certain conditions, but not frequency descent. By contrapuntal descent, I mean pieces like the Obrecht and Willaert examples (see DF) and the Greiter where *even with constant frequency* the "F" at the end is, by purely contrapuntal spiralling, one or more semitones lower than the "F" at the beginning. If you believe, with me, that (1) such logical *contrapuntal* and melodic descent through the spiral of fifths in these pieces is inherently Pythagorean in concept and (2) that Pythagorean *tuning* of 5ths in practice, with pure 3rds (5/4), was predisposed to result in comma slippage, pieces which thus descend *contrapuntally* can be construed as (in these cases, late) manifestos of Pythagorean conception and execution, as posited above. Rejection of any degree of frequency volatility obviously makes it harder to overcome resistance to contrapuntal descent, despite the existence of pieces (Willaert, Greiter) where all are agreed that it *must* happen. Otherwise, the tuning consideration need not be an impediment to considering other premises of this argument (notably contrapuntal correction) independently of a specific tuning system.[11]

[15] Now for a confessional review of some miscalculations in DF, and a further unpacking of some ellipses. First, it was misleading to present my examples in modern score. I should never have expected readers to accept, even hypothetically, a paradigm shift that emphasizes the radical difference between old and new notation while at the same time transcribing the examples in such a way as to imply that they are equivalent, and exposing them to all the shock of unfamiliarity, and to conceptually foreign analyses of their tonality and tuning. As I put it, "neglect of some primary musical facts has led us to tolerate the aural dissonance of intolerable intervals before we accept the merely graphic dissonance of an intolerable-looking modern score." (DF p. 48 <= p. 148>.) My examples in DF should, rather, be seen as "phonetic" approxi-

mations, into a different language, of what might be sung from the original, or might be at least the first default so derived. But it is hard to know what else to do. It is unrealistic to assume that readers will have the training or time to get together to sing examples from parts, the counsel of perfection spelled out above, thus simulating the *process* by which contrapuntal training was applied to notated music, but modern scores might at least be read with that awareness.

[16] Since DF I've had the benefit of reading and discussing recent developments in work on mode, especially by Powers and Judd, and I would now reformulate some of what I said about mode in the light of that, though the basic disconnection, on which Judd and I agree, is not much affected. For the moment, I will confine myself to quoting her clear statements to the *mto-talk* discussion: (23 July) "there is simply no need for mode or *ficta* to impinge one upon the other because they occupy different conceptual and theoretical realms," and, after quoting Wibberley's "Only by this means [retaining some diminished fifths in performance] would it have been possible to remain faithful to the mode on account of the actual notes Josquin composed in the particular combination chosen by him," Judd continues: Wibberley's "conclusion is based on a modern understanding of mode as tonal system. Nowhere is such a view articulated by Glarean. Such a view fundamentally misrepresents the very nature of musica *ficta* in seeking to fix pitches in a way that Renaissance musicians clearly did not. Although Bent's solution is not one that I would adopt for this passage, there is nothing in the Glarean passage quoted by Wibberley in [9] to argue against it. Wibberley is imputing to Glarean an 'internal' view of the modes, but nothing in Bent's solution changes the final or range (i.e., the external criteria by which the mode is recognized), hence Bent's view that her solution does not disturb 'modal coherence.'"

[17] While I do not think that I am "mixing up"[12] performance and understanding, I do see that this is something that needs to be addressed, and one way in which I hope to advance the formulations of DF is to make that distinction a bit clearer. I hope I have done so by introducing the "default" element into paras [4–7] above. Having advocated even more separation of tracks than I did in DF, I see that here I have not gone far enough, and that certain rare conundrum passages like the Josquin that are capable of a perfect contrapuntal realization might in practice not receive it. Just as there might be a reading of a piece that was perfectly consonant with the traditional (Wibberley's) modal-scalar ideal, but a reading that one would not choose in practice, so there may be passages like the Josquin sequence where the perfection of the counterpoint would have been tempered in practice. This is where my discussion above of a "default" concept may be helpful. While I in no way withdraw from "my" version of the Josquin as an exercise in contrapuntal perfection, I am perfectly prepared to accept the possibility of a more cautious compromise (see below), if only to

direct attention to the premises by admitting that they need not stand or fall by an "extreme" example. I chose examples that would make vivid the radically different conceptual underpinnings of old and new notation, rather than to illustrate the much subtler consequences that this understanding brings in practice for most "normal" pieces; but if we can now agree to recognise the Josquin as a special case, the way may be open for broader acceptance of what I have outlined above.

[18] In an attempt to set out the main tributaries of a proposed radical shift in *understanding* the basis of notation (not necessarily or always entailing a shift in the sounding *results*), I inevitably overstated or understated some aspects, largely by insufficiently freeing myself of some modern prejudices. In attempting to formulate the complementary nature of notation and counterpoint, I may have overstated the weakness of the default, leading others to impute a less disciplined relativism than I actually intend. I hope that the default element helps here. I seem to have *under*stated my position on the role of hexachords and solmization, and hence misled Daniel Zager and some others about how mastery of solmization relates to *ficta*.[13] I never meant to claim (as Zager implies but does not state) that solmization can resolve counterpoint/*ficta* problems. I do not share his dependence on solmization to determine counterpoint. Rather the converse: contrapuntal decisions, once made, can be expressed in terms of solmization, the nearest they had to a precise language in which to conceptualise and name sounds. But since they stretched the system to cope with all eventualities, so that anything could be solmized by extensions and disjunctions, the criterion of easy solmization is not a valid arbiter of which sounds are or are not possible. To argue a particular solution *from* solmization is to let the tail wag the dog. I wrote: "Hexachords provide a functional context for semitone locations which have been predetermined by musical considerations, but they do not in themselves determine what the sounds will be. The hexachordal *voces* are the means by which those sounds become practically accessible in vocal polyphony, just as, by analogy, fingering is the means by which small groups of notes are physically negotiated on instruments." Hexachordal thinking permeates their terminology. It guides us away from the notion of "inflections" of individual notes and into that of small scalar segments (sometimes projected as tangents from the *scala* of *musica recta*) that accommodate and articulate semitones, the need for which is *predetermined* on contrapuntal principles. It cannot in itself solve individual *ficta* problems just as, conversely, no *ficta* solution can be rejected on grounds that it can't be solmized. Nor, as Judd agrees, can modal theory solve *ficta* questions, whether Aaron's or Glarean's. What I have proposed is the beginnings of a system drawing simple rules and priorities from counterpoint theory, principles whose development, exceptions and qualifications will have to venture beyond the point where theory helps us and be derived in turn from actual composed music; but

they can be projected homeopathically in the direction indicated by that theory (rather than antibiotically from our alien perspective), and fleshed out from a practice stripped of some modern varnish (such as the notion of modal fidelity as an arbiter of tonal stability, and of modern notation "as is"). Some of these precepts are strong and binding. Some are weaker and open to alternatives and competing priorities. All of them can be accepted without the obligation to choke down my Josquin example whole as a prescription for *practice*. That is negotiable.

[19] Having thus slightly rearranged the furniture to permit (I hope) constructive discussion, now to the Josquin. I should add to my list of miscalculations that I ought to have saved that example until a later time, in order not to distract attention from the premises, or at least I should have continued the argument, which I will now try to do. It is an exceptional puzzle, and has been so recognized by several writers, notably by Dahlhaus, with the rather different conclusion that "der Tonsatz abstrakt konzipiert ist und daß sich Josquin über die Unentschiedenheit, wie er zu realisieren sei, hinwegsetzte, da sie ihm gleichgültig war." ("the composition is conceived in the abstract, and that Josquin disregarded the inconclusiveness as to how [the composition] was to be realized, because he was indifferent to [the inconclusiveness].") Dahlhaus thus posits *the composer's indifference to the actual resulting sounds*, and argues that counterpoint thus abstractly conceived may have lacked either prior aural imagination of such sounds or, indeed, any musically acceptable realization.[14] To this view Berger and I join in taking exception, if for different reasons.[15] Josquin's sequence is a conundrum, of a fairly rare type. In the disputed measures, he gives us not just one text-book sequential "cliché" chain of fifths and sixths, but *two* superimposed contrapuntal pairs, discant and tenor, tenor and bass[16] *both* of which (not just the upper pair, *pace* Wibberley [13]), have claims to perfection *and* place constraints on the other. Dahlhaus gave up on the passage. Lowinsky favoured B♭ in bar 48 because it fitted his sense of the piece as being *tonal* as well as (*nearly* pure) Ionian.[17] Urquhart accepts B♭ at bar 48, but avoids my version by accepting the simultaneous false relation of a B *natural* against it in the treble.[18] Wibberley also accepts the B♭, but his compromise has a melodic augmented fourth *and* a simultaneous diminished fifth at 48–50.[19] The conundrum is that, *pace* Dahlhaus, I have shown that Josquin wrote a passage that is capable of contrapuntally perfect realization, whether we like it or not, and this intervallic perfection has been acknowledged by Wibberley (n. 7) and by others in the list discussion. Let us call it "a" solution but not necessarily "the" solution. In the context of DF, I was frankly more interested in its Janus-like status as a theoretical conundrum than in making a binding performance prescription. I would now prefer to call that version a contrapuntally defined default, a *starting-point* for negotiation or compromise. I was exploring the implications of counterpoint, not primarily fixing up a piece for performance—perhaps I did not make this clear enough (in DF, n. 49),

but it is clearer to me now.

[20] The provocation, therefore, is not mine but Josquin's. It remains interesting and inescapable that he set up this sequential passage of two superimposed contrapuntal pairs in such a way that an intervallically flawless reading,[20] if not a perfect solution, is possible. Josquin's conceit deserves better than that we retreat from it on anachronistic grounds based on notions of white-note supremacy or modal chastity. Wibberley has attempted to make the case for doing so on modal grounds, but for reasons given by Judd, and because of the irrelevance to Josquin's personal arsenal of the later testimony of Glarean, let alone Zarlino, it will be clear that I do not think he has succeeded. We have to choose in practice whether to depart from that particular kind of perfection—indeed, whether Josquin was provoking us to do just that, rather than whether to depart from the notational translation of a modern score. That is the nub of the "default" aspect of my hypothesis. Bach chose occasionally to break "rules" about parallels or leading notes; we must be prepared for Josquin to do likewise, and to imply that we need to realize certain passages imperfectly. But we had better have a reason more firmly grounded in what we can discern of the musical practice of Josquin's contemporaries than simply disliking something that differs from what *we* have—perhaps mistakenly—grown used to. Addled by years of hearing and seeing under-inflected performances (of the notation "as it stands") with too many flat leading-notes and proto-tonal diminished fifths, our mistrained ears are not reliable arbiters. That "we haven't tried it because we don't like it" (to quote the old Guinness advertisement) is a self-fulfilling prophecy.

[21] I am pleased to see that there has come to be acceptance of the bass B♭ in bar 48 by Wibberley and Urquhart, despite other disagreements.[21] This note was ubiquitously rendered as B♭ in the Josquin *Werken*, in Miller's edition of Glareanus, by Lowinsky, and in most recorded performances. Good, for that B♭ seems to me the one non-negotiable point, and reflects new acceptance of a strong priority that we can perhaps all agree on. The B♮ was earlier seen as a kind of first-inversion dominant seventh anticipating the leading-note that takes us back to the bright radiance of C major or, if you prefer, Glarean's likewise anachronistic hypoionian. The B♭ in bar 48 *both* avoids a linear tritone *and* a simultaneous diminished 5th in a standard sequential progression, and thus claims priority on two counts. But that B♭ is the thin end of a wedge; that there *can* be an ideal solution but no perfect solution makes it very difficult to define how far is too far, now that we have removed anachronistic tonal harmony, simplistic modal restraints, and, I hope, the misapplication of modern notation as defaults.

[22] Except for the bar 48 B♭, alternative compromise solutions can be entertained in performance, including the different ones of Wibberley and Urquhart (and

see DF, n. 49). Since there is no good solution, the actual performance choice is much less interesting, because to some extent arbitrary. I have summarized the most important rules and priorities, (see above, n. 5) but there are many caveats, and a much longer discussion is necessary, especially of the circumstances where diminished fifths may be permitted, and where there is some common ground between my views and those of Berger and Urquhart. I could, for example, more readily tolerate an—albeit unnecessary, and denied by a notated B♭—diminished 5th in the different context of bar 43 (with B♮ below F contracting to a third on C and E between the lower parts) before Wibberley's example begins:

[discantus]	D		C	B
[tenor]	F		E	D
[bassus]	D	B*	C	G

The fifth at bar 48 on the other hand does not contract but forms part of an ongoing sequence and must, as we seem to agree, be perfect. But how do the following limbs of the sequence differ in the constraints that are placed on consonance and contrapuntal perfection? Wibberley cites Aaron in support of his claim [15] that "None of this means, however, that diminished fifths were to be completely banned from composed music; it simply means that perfect consonances did not admit them, and that where perfect consonances were *to be attained* [my emphasis] such intervals had to be eliminated." If *this* chain of fifths is not a prime, and literally text-book, candidate for "where perfect consonances were to be attained," I don't know what is. Having accepted the B♭ in 48 by the rules of consonance [4], his version presents both a linear tritone and a simultaneous diminished 5th in a standard sequential progression, and thus merely pushes further on the crisis that was avoided at bar 48. He invokes a lower status for the relationship between the upper parts, which might be acceptable when the main contrapuntal relationship was between the lower two. Indeed, diminished fifths sometimes occur either, as Wibberley puts it, between upper parts that are supported from below, or, as I would more often prefer to put it, when the primary contrapuntal cadence, the 6th to 8ve between the lower parts, has an added part above, e.g.:

[discantus]	F	E
[2nd discantus]	B	C
[tenor]	D	C

But he fails to recognize that the Josquin passage does not meet those criteria, because its unique feature is that *two* primary and non-cadential contrapuntal progressions are superimposed, and that the upper part therefore cannot be treated as subsidiary.

[23] In light of Judd's postings to *mto-talk* it is almost superfluous for me at this point to deny the relevance of Glarean's twelve-mode system (or for that matter Zarlino's counterpoint theory)[22] to discussion of constraints and freedoms that might have applied in Josquin's mind and his expectations of performance. Glareanus says nothing relevant to counterpoint and *ficta*. His 12-mode system is no more germane to how *Josquin* might have classified the *Ave Maria* than would be a roman numeral analysis to his harmony. Wibberley would be mistaken to assume that my silence on Glareanus was for any other reason (see DF, p. 45 <= pp. 146–47>). Judd published a modally based analysis of the motet, not mentioned by Wibberley;[23] in principle, her and my statements can co-exist without disagreements affecting our different approaches: "there is simply no need for mode or *ficta* to impinge one upon the other because they occupy different conceptual and theoretical realms" ("Wibberley, MTO 2.5," *mto-talk* 23 July 1996).[24] Judd further commented in the same posting: "Wibberley's straightforward mapping from composer to theorist (and *vice versa*) highlights an even more problematic issue. I find his view of theorists as "witnesses" difficult to sustain. Aron, Glarean, and Zarlino are, after all, advocates of their own agendas as well as witnesses." Then Wibberley ("Wibberley, MTO 2.5," *mto-talk* 19 August 1996): "The presumption underlying my article was that the Josquin motet WAS [Ionian tonality], especially since Glareanus said so" and ("Wibberley, MTO 2.5," *mto-talk* 5 August 1996): "What is clear to me is that Glareanus is telling us something quite definitely about the way the COMPOSER has composed the music, rather than about the way others might have performed it." Does Wibberley not distinguish between subsequent comment and classification on the one hand, and what could have been in the composer's mind, on the other? It is indeed a big leap to go from a subsequent theorist (especially Glarean) with his own axe to grind to make the assumption that because this was in his mind it must have been in Josquin's more than 50 years earlier.

[24] Finally, some further comments and questions for Wibberley. Why is it acceptable for *Absalom* to "modulate" (a modern term and concept) and, as Wibberley would have it, to "remove the harmony from its base," but not (by his standards) for the Josquin or indeed the Obrecht? By what standards does he judge such "removal" not only permissible but "very successful" while other comparable pieces are not similarly favoured?[25] Indeed, we cannot be sure exactly what Glareanus means by his "without removing the harmony from its base,"[26] invoked by Wibberley against excessive fictive adjustments. Glarean's language and context *may* suggest some connection with Aaron's *distonata via* and Tinctoris's *distonatio*, neither of which easily lends itself to the construction Wibberley would wish to place on it. This is a difficult area, yet to be explained; Wibberley jumps too readily to the conclusion that it must mean removal

from defaults of modern, not of Renaissance, imposition.

[25] That Wibberley accepts *some* "*ficta* additions" (I would prefer to call them contrapuntal adjustments) is clear in his posting of 8 August ("Wibberley, MTO 2.5," *mto-talk* 8 August 1996). Are all of these consonant with his view of mode in pieces classified by Glareanus (or indeed Aaron), or with the way that these theorists *would have* classified them? Up to what point does he accept "inflections," and which ones, on what criteria and authority, and why no further? How does he reconcile the constraint he draws from Glareanus with explicit and incontrovertible text-book examples of *ficta* from the early sixteenth century, such as offered by Ornithoparcus and Listenius?[27] Are works classified by Glareanus to be given different treatment in order that they can conform with Wibberley's sense of what Glarean means, irrespective of any musical characteristics that may suggest otherwise? He also accepts ([13]) that my example is consonant. He sometimes invokes the rules of consonance, though he does not make it clear where he departs from the notational-contrapuntal premises of DF—where indeed? It is on (albeit anachronistic) modal grounds that he determines that the rules of consonance may here be broken. Wibberley adopts the B♭ in the bass at bar 48 "by the accepted rules of consonance," but it was not widely accepted before I spelled out those rules (see above, n. 5). Wibberley and others think that my Josquin example takes the application of the rules too far for practical purposes, and I might even agree with them, but they (and I) have yet to define precisely at what point and why the "accepted rules of consonance" become unacceptable. Does Wibberley have a view on this?

[26] Wibberley ([21] and n. 11) is unclear about the status of the fourth. When the fourth appears in composition treated *not* as a dissonance, it is because it is not part of the primary contrapuntal pair. In this case there will be a fifth or a third below it:

[discant]	F♯	G
[contratenor]	C♯	D
[tenor]	A	G

Another and more medieval way of explaining this would be that *each* of the upper parts formed a contrapuntal pair, cadencing on a 5th and 8ve respectively, with the lowest part, when that part is functionally the tenor at that moment. When the fourth occurs between the primary dyadic pair—that is what Tinctoris means by "in counterpoint"—it must be treated as a dissonance, i.e., prepared and resolved. Wibberley's citation of Tinctoris's "Hence it is rejected [as a consonance] by counterpoint" (n. 11) means just that. He misinterprets Tinctoris's statement as meaning generally in the musical texture, but counterpoint clearly must be understood specifically here, or it doesn't make sense, and Wibberley has to labour to do so. He confuses the issue by bringing in acoustics ([15] and n. 15). Acoustic perfection is on a separate track (again!) from contrapuntal perfection. Later instructions for the behaviour of a third or fourth voice are also ancillary to the primary dyadic counterpoint.

[27] A substantial portion of Wibberley's article [14–19] is devoted to the examples in Aaron's *Aggiunta* to his *Toscanello*. I have discussed these examples and rules,[28] and invite interested readers to compare my explanations with Wibberley's for some of the features he observes. He fails to point out [14] that Aaron's discussion of partial signatures relates them to mode; see ACN, p. 321. See ACN, p. 324 <= pp. 183, 185–86> for a discussion of Aaron's bias to the lowest voice. In [18] Wibberley raises Orto's *Ave Maria*, used as an example in Aaron's *Aggiunta*, and says that the only reason for the diminished 5th in the preceding bar is that there is a G in the bass beneath it. Not so. The B♭ above E contracts to a third, but this E is making a discant-tenor 6–8 cadence with the bass. This is one case for possible exemption for diminished fifths (see [22] above). Indeed, a fifth contracting to a third might sometimes be regarded as "exempt" when it is not part of the primary discant-tenor contrapuntal relationship, and it does not always have to have bass support. Aaron's weighing of priorities in the Agnus of Josquin's Missa *L'homme armé super voces musicales* is discussed in DF pp. 26–28 and ACN p. 312 <= pp. 132–34, 171–72>; he allows a mediated melodic augmented fourth (but not in a sequence) in order to avoid a simultaneous diminished fifth, *and* to concord with the cantus firmus. The melodic augmented fourth is here mediated, and is tolerated in the interests of perfecting a simultaneous fifth; Wibberley's solution achieves neither.

[28] No one these days can deny the importance of language, and the way the terms we use permeate our thought-processes and prejudices. Thus it is surely also important, for our purposes, to flag dangerous short-circuits or shortcuts that may symptomise inappropriate matching of concepts and terms, so that, when we have to use modern terms, we can at least be aware that the *absence* of an early term may be eloquent.[29] I pointed out at the beginning of DF that medieval theory had no single word for pitch or for rhythm, but rather *congeries* of differently shaded words, a powerful symptom of the separate tracks on which, for example, mode, counterpoint, solmization and tuning operate. These tracks are interdependent, but not in the way we imagine when we prioritize not only pitch, but a frequency-biased notion of pitch.

[29] In conclusion: there is still a widespread and under-supported belief that Renaissance composers must have stuck largely to "white-note diatonicism" except where we are forced to believe otherwise. This has been supported from modern misprisions of mode (such as Wibberley's), now being unpicked, that were in turn introduced to counter what we now see as the excessively harmonic-tonal approaches to

early music by previous generations of scholars. The unpicking of all related assumptions still has a long way to go. The recent repudiation of artificial shackles of "modal purity" (or whatever we call it) invites us to start afresh with open minds about the sound of early vocal polyphony. (The question of tuning is separable, but obviously important, since it is loaded with many of the same modern assumptions. The contrapuntal arguments are not affected by precisely what tuning system they are realized in, but can be made on their own track.) The urgent question remains: if Judd's view that "modal fidelity" poses no constraints on *ficta* prevails over Wibberley's view that it does, i.e., if it is true that "paper" modal assignations may be disconnected from realized sounds; and if my premises outlined above find even partial acceptance, are we not further overlaying modern prejudices on early music by assuming that in order to be "coherent" it must conform to *our* standards of long-range tonality (and frequency)? Some of the same questions arising from our imposition of value-laden terms have been raised by Richard Taruskin and others for "authenticity," a term of approbation which admits no alternative; I believe we must do the same for "stability" and "coherence."

NOTES

*Originally published in: *Music Theory Online* 2.6, 1996 (http://www.societymusictheory.org/mto/), as a response to Roger Wibberley, "Josquin's *Ave Maria*: Musica Ficta versus Mode," *ibid.* 2.5, 1996; see Wibberley's response, "'Mode versus Ficta' in context," *ibid.* 2.7, 1996. It is reprinted with the agreement of Dr. Wibberley not to reprint his contributions here as well.

1. Roger Wibberley, "Josquin's *Ave Maria*: Musica Ficta versus Mode," *Music Theory Online* 2.5 (1996).
2. Margaret Bent, "Diatonic *ficta*," *Early Music History* 4 (1984): 1–48 <= chapter 4>.
3. Karol Berger, *Musica ficta: Theories of Accidental Inflections in Vocal Polyphony from Marchetto da Padova to Gioseffo Zarlino* (Cambridge: Cambridge University Press, 1987), especially 43–48; Peter Urquhart, "Canon, Partial Signatures, and '*Musica Ficta*' in Works by Josquin DesPrez and His Contemporaries," Ph.D. dissertation, Harvard, 1988; Urquhart, "Cross-Relations by Franco-Flemish Composers after Josquin," *Tijdschrift van de Vereniging voor Nederlandse Muziekgeschiedenis* 43 (1993): 3–41. Their paraphrases have been invaluable in showing where my formulations need to be strengthened.
4. Richard Crocker, "Discant, Counterpoint, and Harmony," *Journal of the American Musicological Society* 15 (1962): 1–21.
5. In DF, pp. 23–29 <= pp. 129–35>; also in my "Accidentals, Counterpoint, and Notation in Aaron's *Aggiunta* to the 'Toscanello in Musica,'" *The Journal of Musicology* 12 (1994): 306–44 (Festschrift issue for James Haar: Aspects of Musical Language and Culture in the Renaissance), henceforth ACN. See especially pp. 324–25 <= pp.185–86>.
6. See also my "*Resfacta* and *Cantare super librum*," *Journal of the American Musicological Society* 36 (1983): 371–91, and "Editing Early Music: The Dilemma of Translation," *Early Music* 22 (August 1994): 373–94 <= Chapters 11 and 7>.
7. Harold Powers, "Is Mode Real? Pietro Aron, The Octenary System, and Polyphony," *Basler Jahrbuch für historische Musikpraxis* 16 (1992): 9–52; Cristle Collins Judd, "Reading Aron reading Petrucci," *Early Music History* 14 (1995): 121–52.
8. James Haar, "False Relations and Chromaticism in Sixteenth-Century Music," *Journal of the American Musicological Society* 30 (1977): 391–418.

9. As Wibberley, [2] and [10].

10. E. E. Lowinsky, "Matthaeus Greiter's *Fortuna*: an Experiment in Chromaticism and in Musical Iconography," *Musical Quarterly* 42 (1956): 500–19; 43 (1957): 68–85.

11. Of course, transcriptions of these or any pieces *can* be sung in equal temperament, but I disagree with Lowinsky that they *must* be; indeed their spiralling and fifth-based conception makes it most unlikely that this would have happened in a locally well-tuned vocal performance.

12. As Berger alleges, *Musica ficta*, 46. He also rebukes me for not keeping in mind letter-plus-solmization designations, a charge directly contradicted by DF, 7–12 <= pp. 119–22>.

13. Daniel Zager, "From the Singer's Point of View: A Case Study in Hexachordal Solmization as a Guide to *Musica Recta* and *Musica Ficta* in Fifteenth-Century Vocal Music," *Current Musicology* 43 (1987): 7–21, referred to by Wibberley. Urquhart (p. 368) invokes awkwardness of solmization against my version of the Josquin.

14. Carl Dahlhaus, "Tonsystem und Kontrapunkt um 1500," *Jahrbuch des Staatlichen Instituts für Musikforschung preussischer Kulturbesitz* 1969, ed. D. Droysen (Berlin, 1970), pp. 7–17, especially pp. 15–16.

15. Berger, *Musica Ficta*, 166–70.

16. I give "text-book" sources for this sequence from Hothby and Aaron in DF pp. 29–30 <= p. 136>.

17. E. E. Lowinsky, *Tonality and Atonality in Sixteenth-Century Music* (Berkeley and Los Angeles, 1961): 20.

18. Urquhart discusses the *Ave Maria* example on pp. 368–69 of his dissertation. His solution, couched in an often seriously misleading report of my premises, is given in his article cited in n. 3, especially pp. 25–28, and also in a paper to the American Musicological Society, November 1995.

19. Wibberley states [13]: "Since it is impossible to render the Josquin passage in any way other than that proposed by Bent without failing to eliminate all diminished fifths otherwise occurring between notes of the upper voices (such an elimination being her prime motive)." I invite him to reread the way I set up the Josquin example. If any fifths, by Wibberley's criteria, are to be regarded as "where perfect consonances were to be attained," they are surely these. See [22] below on diminished fifths, and [27] on Aaron.

20. Before someone raises it on the *mto-talk* discussion list, I explain in DF (pp. 29–34 <= pp. 135–39>) why the altus part, for internal and diagnosable reasons, takes a low priority in this passage, and why the sequence, as "pure" counterpoint, can be contemplated separately. But the altus may yet be the best way into arguments as to how one might depart from a contrapuntally pure default.

21. See DF, n. 48, where I comment on the source status of the bass B♭. Wibberley, however, places it in parentheses in "my" version, while stating: "By the accepted rules of consonance, the bass b must be flattened to b♭ in order to provide a perfect consonance with the tenor" (Wibberley [4]).

22. Wibberley [29] "Josquin would seem, in the example under consideration, to have arrived at Zarlino's "impasse," but Bent has not followed Zarlino's advice in finding a suitable way around it." Why should I have taken the advice of a theorist 100 years later whose theoretical world, including his use of terms like diatonic, is entirely different from Josquin's?

23. "Some Problems of Pre-Baroque Analysis: An Examination of Josquin's *Ave Maria . . . Virgo Serena*," *Music Analysis* 4.3 (1985): 201–39.

24. Why, incidentally, does Wibberley so dislike Zager's term "modal purity," and how does it differ from his own "modal fidelity" [13, 26]? He complains "If, by 'modal purity,' [Zager] has in mind a succession of notes and harmonies that arise only from the pure diatonic notes of a particular scale," but in his own n. 8 Wibberley refers to "the use of notes outside the diatonic notes of that mode."

25. Wibberley, *mto-talk* 5 August. His reference to this as a "powerful rhetorical device" suggests that he might be following Lowinsky in demanding extra-musical reasons for what they both call "modulations," a position that can lead to great inconsistencies of treatment between musically similar constructions. Consider the arcane lengths to which Lowinsky went to defend his Secret Chromatic sheep against the musically similar goats who did not qualify by virtue of their texts. See also DF, n. 47. (NB the *Absalom* "modulation" is not *dependent* on notated accidentals and would have to occur, even without them, as in the Willaert and Obrecht pieces.)

26. I plead innocent to the mind-boggling charges packed into sentences such as Wibberley's [10]: "The whole point of Margaret Bent's solution is that the harmony is, via the 'necessary' application of diatonic *ficta*, 'removed from its base.'" And I don't know what Wibberley means by claiming [7] that I see "modal

coherence as a close relative of pitch stability," citing DF 45–47 <= pp. 146–48>, where I wrote: "Modal theory does deal with some kind of long-term tonal coherence, but not necessarily such as can be equated with pitch stability—another distinction that has lost its force for us." There are numerous examples in Wibberley of discourteously careless reporting, not only of my alleged views but also Bonnie Blackburn's, astoundingly misrepresented.

27. These and others are cited in E. E. Lowinsky, "Secret Chromatic Art Re-examined," *Perspectives in Musicology*, ed. B. Brook *et al.*, (New York, 1972), pp. 91–135.

28. DF 19 <= pp. 132–35 and Chapter 5>, ACN (see n. 5); for Aaron see also Judd's article in n. 7.

29. In view of his reproaches to me for anachronism, I'm surprised to see Wibberley use terms such as root (n. 16), tonicization (n. 7), and modulation [10].

Chapter 7

Editing Early Music: The Dilemma of Translation*

A sobering message is reaching us: we don't always try to re-create authentic sound even when we have access to it. Richard Taruskin has shown how we remake music, whether Mozart or Machaut, according to our own taste, and that that taste changes by genera-tion or even faster.[1] Robert Philip's new book on historical recordings shows how little we aspire to re-create the sounds and techniques of pre-war works (Elgar, Puccini) even when we have recordings made under the direction of the composer or to his sat-isfaction.[2] Is it an accident that our efforts of reconstruction are concentrated on what we can't know? That we apply them with the greatest conviction to repertories where the performing tradition has been broken and there are no recordings?

This message can be transferred to musical editions. Just as we may choose to avoid some authentic aspects of performance when we could do so, so we avoid fidelity in the written presentation of music as a basis for performance, while surrounding it with scholarly apparatus that appears to confer authenticity. Nothing goes out of fash-ion as fast as authenticity. We should abandon use of the word and its false advertising.

It has been assumed until quite recently that early music is not accessible until it has been edited, or at least transcribed in score, enabling a single musician to read it. There has been a deep reluctance to assume that the near-absence of early scores might mean that its first creators and performers managed quite well without them, and hence that we had better do so too if we are to master their musical language and the essentials of their musical thinking processes.[3] To assume that they must have depended on visual control through aligned score imposes our canons of musician-ship on them. There is little evidence that fifteenth-century musicians did so depend. Also, the discovery that it is not difficult to read and sing from facsimiles makes us more willing to believe that they might have been able to read their own manuscripts. Claims that modern editions represent the original in some authentic way hardly stand the test of time; even our preferred appearance (in reduction of note values and so on), has proven subject to just the same swings as our tastes in performance.

[1374] Now, of course, we can't do without scores. They provide an indispensable shortcut that enables one person to read the music, silently or digitally, whereas the process of mental re-creation from parts by a single reader, or in sound with singers, as we know they sometimes did, and as we can if we wish, is too time-consuming for most of our purposes. But it will be a short-circuit, not a shortcut, unless we learn to use a score, any score, with allowance for what it distorts and what it doesn't tell us, and to read it with allowance for what we are missing. Verbal translations are read with such awareness. A reader familiar with the original language knows that puns and verbal flavours are being missed, and may make a partial attempt to restore that original while reading the translation. Musical translations offer the same challenge.

For different reasons, neither the Old Hall edition of 60 years ago nor the Old Hall edition of 20 years ago (examples 1, 2) may now feel quite right with respect to note values and presentation; they measure change in cosmetic fashion and, more significantly, a changing aesthetic of notational appearance that parallels changing aesthetic tastes in sound. The only constant is, of course, the original notational representation of the piece (ex. 3).

EXAMPLE 1: BYTTERING, GLORIA, TRANSCRIPTION FROM *THE OLD HALL MANUSCRIPT*, I, ED. A. RAMSBOTHAM (LONDON, 1933), P. 47

EXAMPLE 2: BYTTERING, GLORIA, TRANSCRIPTION FROM
THE OLD HALL MANUSCRIPT, ED. A. HUGHES AND M. BENT,
CORPUS MENSURABILIS MUSICAE, XLVI
(AMERICAN INSTITUTE OF MUSICOLOGY, 1969), I, P. 29

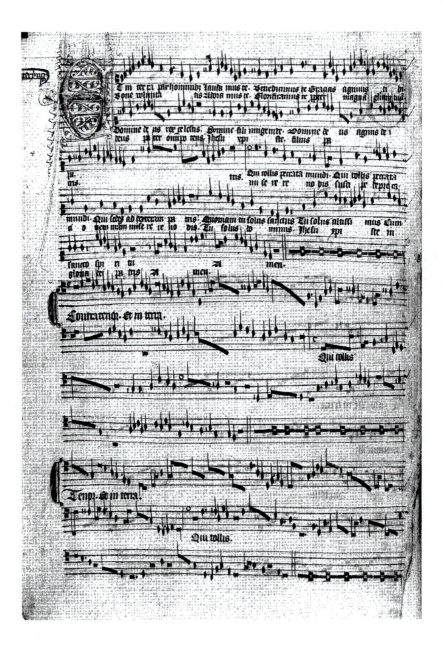

EXAMPLE 3: BYTTERING, GLORIA, AS IT APPEARS IN THE OLD HALL
MANUSCRIPT (LONDON, BRITISH LIBRARY ADD.57950, F.14V)

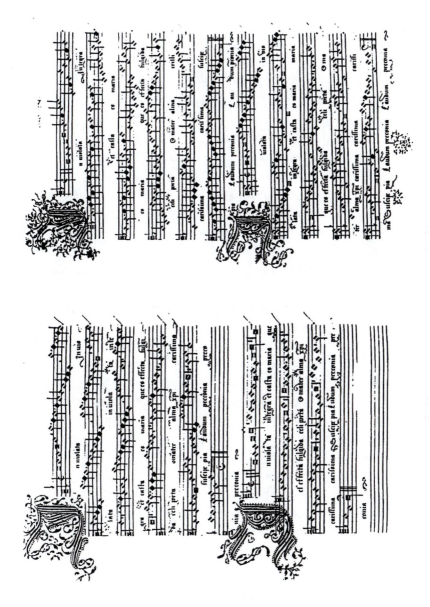

EXAMPLE 4: JOSQUIN, *INVIOLATA* (FLORENCE, BIBLIOTECA MEDICEA-LAUREN-
ZIANA, ACQUISTI E DONI 666 [MEDICI CODEX], FF.89V–90)]

Another lesson to be learned from this example is that there is a compactly notated canon unsignalled in OH [1378] except by the double line of text. This was not noticed by the older editors but pointed out years later by Strunk. It is possible for musicians to deal with such a piece for some decades without noticing that it contains an unrealised canon. Look at how the notation may affect our perception of another better-known canonic piece, Josquin's *Inviolata*. As presented here in the Medici codex, it looks [1379] on the page like a four-part piece, and the canonic indication is no more than a fragile signum (ex. 4).

If that sign were absent, one could imagine singers knowing and enjoying the four-part version before (if ever) noticing the missing canon. In transcription, however, the opposite might be true (ex. 5).

Because of the imitative [1381] opening and the way the canon is buried in the texture, it could take inattentive singers some time to realise that, in this five-part piece, the second tenor and altus parts are in strict canon. Such canons and their notation provide one illustration of how radically different one's perception of a piece might be, depending on whether the starting point was the original notation or the modern edition.

If it were a mensuration canon requiring different modern transcriptions of the same original, they [singers] might never notice. Such an example measures the distance between what old notation can and new notation must mean, and should be enough to alert us to the fact that we are dealing with different conceptual bases for canonic derivation. The single notated triplum part on the left-hand page (ex. 6) yields three [1382] canonic voices that read the notation (black, red, and blue) according to different mensural rules that are stated in the Latin instructions at the bottom of the page. (The beginning is disfigured by the removal of the initial together with the opening notes, clumsily replaced in the nineteenth century.) This is a piece that could not be conceived in modern notation, and yet in a real sense it is a strict canon. Very few scholars would be able to reconstruct the single notated part from which were derived the canonic parts that look to us more like rhythmically free imitation than strict canon; see the opening transcribed in example 7.

EXAMPLE 5: JOSQUIN, *INVIOLATA*, FROM *THE MEDICI CODEX OF 1518: A CHOIRBOOK OF MOTETS DEDICATED TO LORENZO DE' MEDICI, DUKE OF URBINO*, TRANSCRIBED BY E. E. LOWINSKY, MONUMENTS OF RENAISSANCE MUSIC, IV (CHICAGO, 1968), PP. 231–32

EXAMPLE 5: CONTINUED

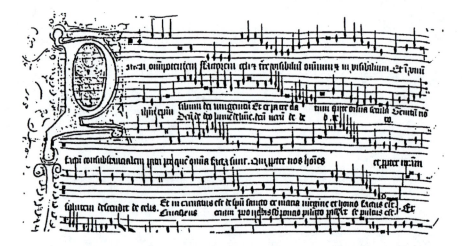

EXAMPLE 6: CREDO, NO.75 IN THE OLD HALL MANUSCRIPT
(LONDON, BRITISH LIBRARY ADD.57950, F.63R)

EXAMPLE 7: CREDO (NO.75), TRANSCRIPTION FROM *THE OLD HALL MANUSCRIPT*,
ED. HUGHES AND BENT, 1969: 201

The original notation is the only *Urtext*. Its relative freedom from auxiliary signs
coincides with our taste for an uncluttered score. Modern editions now often avoid
realising figured bass and providing ornamentation, on grounds that performers who
in other respects are competent to play those repertories can do it themselves; that
our taste in continuo realisation may have changed—and may yet change further—
from versions fixed in print; and that we prefer the uncluttered appearance of what is
often (perhaps misleadingly) called an *Urtext*. We may reasonably hope that the next
generation of early-music singers will advance on the present in not needing full
instructions on the operation of *ficta*, as the present generation of continuo players
has advanced on their predecessors in preferring to make their own realisations. But

our taste for a clean-looking score is precisely where the problems begin. We cannot transfer a clean original text to modern notation, with its very different connotations, and assume that it means the same thing, any more than we can translate a sentence from a foreign language simply by substituting individual words without regard to different grammatical and semantic structures. So we produce a clean modern score that, while retaining something like equivalents of the original symbols, means something different from the original notation, and then we agonise about what to add to it or what to change in it. We want to make this different thing, our modern score, correspond in sound to the notation from which it is adapted, without appearing to be too interventive, but we take more note of its modern visual impact than of its original visual appearance. So we are sometimes more swayed by its modern appearance than by what it will sound like, more by keeping it notationally clean than by what is really ||384 required to reflect the original sound in modern notation. We would like the modern score to look as uncluttered as the original. We avoid adding accidentals where possible, in order not to have too many. We make a radical change to the basis of the notation, then we try not to compensate for having done so.

Any act of copying changes the musical text. Music copying is of course more dependent on spacing and other intangibles than is the copying of words, and these intangible aspects are vulnerable to suppression or interpretation by scribes ancient or modern. One big change comes at the moment of putting the parts in score. It is at this point that a transition is made from context-dependent notation to the implied unit reference of our modern notation. By unit reference I mean that each symbol, as in modern notation, has a precise value with respect to pitch and rhythm, e.g., F♯, dotted minim; whereas an original minim F might await contextual determination of those more precise qualifiers. Where else in the process of transcription the shift can occur, and with what apparently merely graphic changes—with changes of clef, note values, barring—may vary with individual perception; but first of all the fact of a shift has to be acknowledged, and it barely is in most discussions of editorial practice.

Editors feel a strong sense of fidelity to the written or authorial text, and a reluctance to make written change. Here's the problem. What exactly, if anything, is being changed? A tacit understanding, but I think a mistaken one, lurks behind most of the editorial statements that preface our editions, namely, that the modern transcription means more or less the same as the original notated text, and that it has neither lost nor gained in the process. We leave the balance of activity to transient interpretative decisions by performers, or by editors cautiously, even timidly, inscribing some of those decisions. This attitude is of course not new. The coyness and circumlocution of medieval and Renaissance musicians in writing about the status of *musica ficta*, and avoiding its notation, is ||385 exceeded only by our own, with the important difference that our notation requires the results to be notated and theirs did not.

To talk with reference to the transcription of "singing what is written" or of "modifying the text" implies that the notational symbols have undergone a fairly simple transliteration when transferred from old to new notation. It assumes that the one means more or less what the other means, and that the notation has in the process of being aligned in score taken on the meanings of modern notation. Superficially similar notational symbols are transplanted into modern dress. Once there, they are assumed to behave as if they had been conceived in modern notation; they are presumed to mean what their nearest modern equivalents mean. We cannot do this safely with language or its pronunciation, and we certainly cannot do it with mensural notation and its corresponding sounds. What has been insufficiently challenged is the silent short-circuit here. A translation has taken place, not a mere transliteration. The conceptual shift may be larger than the—often slight—symptoms of that shift, but it is crucial to be aware of it, especially if we edit the translation and not the original text. For it is a translated text that usually forms the point of departure for further editorial modification or intervention to fix it up for performance. What in original notation was a matter for realisation becomes, in terms of modern notation, one of change or intervention with respect to the imposition of metrical and rhythmic groupings, beamings and spacings, choice of note values and mensural relationships, the refinement or correction of text underlay, and the addition of editorial accidentals. A modern edition may be said to represent a set of performance options selected from those available, whereas the original notation is material awaiting realisation in performance. Our notation tends to confine the options for realisation in ways that have more to do with modern notation than with the inherent potential of the original.

The differences between old and modern notation operate at many levels. Here are some of the most obvious ones.

(1) Text underlay.

Here we are perhaps readiest to admit that modern conventions fail to apply and that different standards are in force. The physical alignment of note and syllable is so often blatantly casual by modern standards, or different from them, that we cannot rest on a literal approach, or talk meaningfully of an edition "deviating" from a given alignment. Deviation implies a norm from which there is deviation. Scholars have formulated a variety of principles for applying verbal repetition, for splitting notes to accommodate syllables, for matching imitations, for accepting the singer's responsibility to associate in detail the syllables and notes of a given phrase of text and music. It is clear enough in the case of texting and underlay that we are dealing with realisation rather than correction.

(2) Pitch level: transposition and frequency.

To place notes on the staff of a modern score gives them a more specific pitch identity now than did earlier staff notation. The modern clef serves to identify a precise pitch within a system whose internal relationships are fixed. At the same time, it implies an approximate or exact frequency anchorage for that structure. The old clef, rather, had the function of defining default semitone locations within the staff. That staff conveyed neither precise positions relative to each other within a system, nor absolute frequencies for them, but corresponded approximately to the vocal range of the singer.[4] Insofar as notation communicated frequency, it was by association of habit, convenience, comfort, practical limitations, physiology, memory, and in some circumstances accommodation to an instrument that was cumbersome to tune. In such a context, transposition is not an appropriate term, because, again, it implies a norm from which the "transposition" counts as a departure. It is more appropriate to talk of selecting a pitch (or frequency) at which to realise the notated music, and it is therefore misleading to equate with transposition the choice of a frequency which happens to lie outside the range of ||386 modern standard tunings. I prefer to reserve the word transposition for re-notation, either in their notation or ours, at differently named pitches. Frequency selection is not the same as transposition, even when it involves a different frequency from that implied by modern notation. The pitch notation of late-medieval music is tied loosely, if at all, to any standards of frequency, and we as scholars and singers should learn to read it with open minds and open ears.

(3) Note values.

The choice of note values, reduced or unreduced, is an issue for the modern editor in conveying appropriate groupings and motion of rhythm and tempo to a modern performer. Fashions and conventions have fluctuated widely in the matter of preferred note values for singers and instrumentalists.

Much discussion of complex or proportional notations has centred round the concept of *integer valor*, projected from 16th-century theory back to 14th-century practice. This is sharply focussed in those instances when simultaneous voice-parts are notated in different values, and prompts the definition of one normative level from which the others then deviate. But in fact it is only necessary to define this norm—which part is in augmentation or diminution in relation to which other—for purposes of meeting modern guidelines of editing and transcription, and of establishing consistent ||387 practices of presentation within and between pieces. Singers singing directly from original notation do not need to decide which of them is the norm from which the others deviate. "Your semibreve equals my minim" is sufficient for performing purposes, if not for all theoretical arguments, and need accord the normative status of *integer valor* to neither part.

EXAMPLE 8: OCKEGHEM, *MISSA L'HOMME ARMÉ*, (a,b) opening of cantus and tenor as they appear in the Chigi Codex (Vatican City, Biblioteca Apostolica Vaticana Chigi C.VIII.234, f.33v); (c) cantus and tenor in their original notation put into score; (d) cantus and tenor as they would be customarily transcribed in a modern edition.

(4) Rhythm.

Mensural notation operates contextually. The singer construes his own part by linear context; and then when he hears what others do, he, or they, may need to modify what would have happened, to resolve ambiguities. This is not the same as change or correction of what is notated. The dimension of realisation is sacrificed (or clarified, depending on your point of view) when the pitches and rhythms are transferred to aligned score format where they can be read by a single performer. The very act of putting music in visually aligned score signals and requires a shift from contextual linear reading to the modern principle of unit reference, whereby we can know from a notated symbol what its duration is within the mensural scheme, and what its notated pitch status and actual frequency are. Convenient in some ways but impoverishing in others, this fixity is not yet in place, practically or conceptually, for the early Renaissance. (There are many parallels in music history. Think, for example, of the complaints about rhythmic decline that followed, and were attributed to, the IIth-century invention of the stave facilitating the reading of pitch.) Perhaps modern notation fixes too much. Scholars and performers need to come to a clearer recognition of the perils as well as the convenience of transcription, in order to make and use editions in ways that bring us closer to the recoverable conventions of their original creators and performers.

When medieval notations were adapted, in the fourteenth and fifteenth centuries, for use by a single performer reading from some kind of aligned score, notational adjustments were made, with respect both to pitch and to rhythm. These adjustments produced something closer to a system with unit reference, enabling the performer to know the duration and pitch of any symbol at sight, without ambiguity and without consideration of context. In German organ tablatures, for example, notational values for the lower parts are counted out in units, so that an imperfect breve or an altered semibreve each gets two dots, regardless of its context and status (Ex. 9, no. III, bars 13–14). Similar adjustments are found in other keyboard notations, and in tablature-like notational features for singers. These concessions violated, to different degrees, the elegant grammar of the mensural system, but did not widely invade vocal notations until the sixteenth century, when they eventually overtook and gradually superseded those habits of thought that made mensural notation, in its heyday, so radically differ-ent from ours.

(5) Pitch, individual "inflections," *musica ficta*.

The notation of pitch also operates contextually. The singer, again, construes his own part by linear context and makes provisional decisions about its realisation. When he hears what the other parts are doing, he or they may need to modify those provisional decisions, which is not the same thing as changing the notated music.

EXAMPLE 9: BUXHEIM ORGAN BOOK (MUNICH, BAYERISCHE
STAATSBIBLIOTHEK, CIM.352B), NOS. 110, 111.

Notes on the modern staff are presumed to be the corresponding "uninflected" or white notes of that pitch unless marked to be otherwise, or unless the system has by means of a signature determined that their default value is other. I use the term default to mean the value (in pitch or rhythm) that a note will assume if there are no other circumstances to define it at another value; it is emphatically not a norm against which to measure change, inflection, or deviation. Medieval pitch notation is more neutral than this. Our fifteenth-century colleagues were not misnotating music when they did not notate accidentals. We should do them the credit of recognising that their notation is complete and correct for their purposes, and only deficient and incomplete for ours. They could and did write signs of *musica ficta* when these would be helpful, but the notation of these signs was rarely necessary. Our ‖389 notation requires them all the time. Theirs did not. This indicates a major conceptual difference between the two systems. Our mistake is to read either their notation or ours without awareness of the magnitude of that difference, even if the differences that force its recognition are infrequent or small.

Once a singer (even a modern singer) becomes accustomed to the process of listening and adjusting, it is easier to read early notation unencumbered with written signs of inflection, more of which appear superfluous the more experienced he is. The same is true for a modern score cluttered with "accidental" fingering or dynamic signs that seem irritating, unnecessary or even wrong to an experienced performer. It may be even more true where superfluous symbols on the staff visually disturb the process of contextual construing that is essential to the reading of early notation. Of course, we cannot be immune from bringing other anachronistic biases to our realisation of their grammar, but those dangers are no greater than those for any modern performer or editor.

The reading process itself involves several levels of default, and they are different from ours. The first is the *scala* of *musica recta* presented in elementary diagrams and embodied in the mnemonic of the Guidonian hand. This scale would be operated as a default in reading single notes free of anything recognisable as musical context. The default values for notes would then be quickly overruled by linear considerations in the singer's individual line, a line which he then construes visually, recognising unmediated leaps of fourths and fifths, and cadential formulae, and adjusting the intervals accordingly. (By analogy with the distinction between transposition and frequency selection, this is a case not of changing notes but of adjusting intervals.) If the line is to be fitted into a yet unknown polyphonic context, the singer will treat those decisions as provisional until the texture is assembled, much as a modern string quartet player may learn his part knowing that many passages will have to be rethought—with respect to bowing, articulation, tempo, and dynamics—when the whole texture is known and has been subjected to group rehearsal. Thus prepared, our medieval singer likewise tempers his "default decisions" by what he hears others doing and by whatever mutual adjustments are decided in rehearsal. His apparent cadence may turn out to be "interrupted" (=deceptive) or "phrygian" and prevent the raised leading note he expected to sing. A linear fourth may have to be augmented in order to avert the—usually—worse case of a false simultaneity. None of this involves changing or inflecting what is, in our terms, the force of the written notes, because they are not precisely prescribed in the old written notation. Put another way, a note has a much weaker claim to "uninflected" status than its notation alone, and the assumptions we bring to it, would suggest. Instead, successive layers of default decisions are overruled by the more special needs and contexts of the case in hand, and the art is to learn within what range one can balance priorities.

In German organ tablatures, again, there are more indicated inflections than in most vocal sources. Allowing for incomplete notational transliterations (for that is what they are), the objective was to define the physical position of a note on a keyboard, allowing the organist to find simultaneously sounding keys with his fingers; they could even be spelled enharmonically, as in the Buxheim organ book, where E flat is usually spelled D sharp (ex. 9, no. 110, bar 3). In lute tablatures the commitment to specific semitone positions is even more far-reaching. Tablature is at least in part instrument-specific and is intended to show the performer where his fingers should go, though in practice it may fall short of this goal and itself reveal a translation process. In vocal notation, on the other hand, the singer finds the definition of his individual notes, in their own linear context, in relation to others sounding simultaneously, by applying his knowledge of interval combinations, i.e. what we would call harmony and what they called counterpoint. Inflection signs may have held subtly different meanings in vocal and in keyboard notations.

||39° Considerations such as these are preliminary to considering what the text is, which may, in turn, be preliminaries to knowing what the work is, and where it stands between what is seen, heard, and technically or intellectually understood. It is probably impossible to present in modern form a text that retains the range of these dimensions. We have been in the habit of refracting the text through a distorting translation. If we pursue the unattainable ideal of presenting the music in terms as close as possible to its own, we may at least learn not to regard as eccentric those pieces that, rhythmically or tonally, strain at the limits of modern notation. By looking extreme and awkward in modern dress (e.g. the mensuration canon in ex. 6), they may expose the conceptual gap between the notation in which they were conceived and a modern form that ill fits them, but what they represent may be far from extreme in its own

terms. The very nature of the editorial process can all too easily subordinate what is heard to what is seen, the sound to its representation. Something is wrong when we are readier to accept the dissonance of (to them) intolerable musical intervals than the visual dissonance of a (to us) intolerable-looking score.

Many questions arise. To what extent may the work be separable from the text that transmits it? Where does the boundary lie between authorial intention in sound and in notated text? Can the work have a life of its own apart from its written form, even where the written form may be essential to the substance or aesthetics of its conception? The goal of textual criticism is to establish the original notated form, that of editing to produce a prescriptive sound map for the piece. These goals may be incompatible and not easily met by the same transcription. The former is an exercise in intellectual, stemmatic and graphic reconstruction within the framework shared by composer and singers; the latter is more like a phonetic transcript for non-native speakers. We have tried to make our editions do double duty, accessible to performers but provided with scholarly apparatus; perhaps we need to be more aware of these different goals.

At the same time as we try to present the edited original texts with as little graphic or conceptual distortion as possible, we may—I think legitimately—seek to enhance the graphic element of the presentation by making some compensating virtue out of the necessity of modern score. Some analytic information or overlay may be conveyed in our transcriptions that is rarely apparent in the original layout in parts, and which few modern-notation editions attempt. An obvious example is to align isorhythmic or other repeats in parallel, or otherwise to signal correspondences that receive no graphic signals in the original. Tenor parts signalled for repetition in the original must be written out *ad longum* in modern score; more attention to the placing of line-ends and alignment will greatly aid the silent reader to grasp the main structural shape of the piece.

For whom do we edit? The expressed goal of editions has usually been to bring music to performers and secondarily to scholars, who are expected to provide and to use critical commentaries of often forbidding appearance and indigestible compression that, at worst, may be merely uncritical dumps of unmodulated data. Any conclusions we might reach about how to edit for future scholars and performers ought, I think, to recognise as their starting point that all transcription translates; that a transcribed and scored version is no longer the original text; and that the uncomfortable implications of that gap for our hygienic visual tastes in musical notation must be faced. Some aspects of the written text may be essential to the conception of the piece but impossible to retain in translated transcription. More of what is implicit but unwritten in early notation must be regarded as belonging to authorially intended sound prescribed by training and convention, especially with regard to what we understand by editorial accidentals or *musica ficta*. In other words, more of the sound of the musical work may be recovered as explicitly prescribed than the bare notation suggests. This is slippery territory, and hard to apply in making a responsible edition of a written text. Conversely, [391] and perhaps easier to implement: more of what we treat as fixed written text must be loosened from its moorings and given neutral status, taking on its intended definition from contextual considerations grounded in the musical language shared by composer and performers (e.g., notated F is not necessarily "F natural until proved otherwise"). We shall have taken a large step forward when, as editors, we recognise that we are translating, not merely transcribing, into modern notation, and that what we present is subject to all the hazards of interpretation and loss that beset a linguistic translation. We shall have taken a second large step when we recognise that, in adopting the convenience of aligning music in score, necessary for purposes of most modern readers, we have stripped it of the contextual reading it would have received from a contemporary with respect both to pitch and rhythmic realisation.

Scholars and performers need to learn the language(s). This means learning to read fluently directly from, and in the first instance to sing from, original notation in facsimile. The most legible source for singing, however, is often not the best text for editing. In producing an edition in score, the available versions of a piece should be edited in terms of the original notation, and a stemmatically informed version of the written text of the piece arrived at, re-notated as non-interventively as possible and provided with a truly critical commentary, not a mere pseudo-scientific amassing of data. Access to films and facsimiles, at least of major sources, can now be assumed for serious scholars and performers who want to know the basis of an editor's decisions, and who will consult those rather than deciphering and trusting someone else's telegraphic account of what they contain. The reporting of variants between sources, or between them and the printed text, should weigh the merits of readings, and make it clear when the source is judged to be in error and when it presents a legitimate alternative reading that deserves separate consideration.[5]

We've had the early-music equivalents of the old Bach- and Mozart-*Ausgaben*. Now we have to work towards ways of presentation that more frankly recognise the difficulties of reconciling critical texts with performing translations. Scholars and performers need to remain more firmly attached to the polyvalence of early notation as they learn to deal with it directly, reducing the need to spell out performance options. Our "*Neue Bach Ausgabe*" will be textually edited diplomatic scores with a layout that makes analytic sense, and beautiful computer-assisted typography from which parts can be extracted for further editing for performance. There should be no objection to fully edited prescriptive "phonetic" performance copies, in modern notation and in score, that will save expensive rehearsal and recording time, provided they are recognised for what they are.

The original notation is the only textual representation of the work, and may have its own polyphony of graphic, abstract intellectual, and sound-specific dimensions. To some extent it *is* the work, in that it is the only authority to which new editions [392] and performances can turn for the notes and rhythms. The modern transcription, in providing a sound-map of a piece that is more prescriptive for modern users, may sacrifice some of the dimensions present in the original, as any translation represents loss. The extent of the sacrifice can be measured when the sounding results differ as in the foregoing examples; but even when there is little or no difference in sound between versions arrived at by these different routes, the graphic and conceptual sacrifice should still not be underestimated. There are even some cases where this sacrifice was made by contemporaries, as in notational translations from English to continental notation which dispensed with the proportional colour-coding of English practice, or from Italian to French notation in which differences in the practice of alteration had to be clumsily added as a verbal rider; and most strikingly in cases such as the piece presented in the shape of a harp in the Newberry theory manuscript and transcribed onto normal staves in the Chantilly manuscript. We need to be as much aware then as now of the possibility and nature of such change.

In one sense, music exists only in sound, but paradoxically, sound is its least stable element. But also, visual presentation may be an important or essential ingredient, even to the extent of constituting part of the structure or at least of the aesthetic. And there are other senses in which the music exists in dimensions (e.g., numerical) that are not immediately audible. Access to a work could be through sound, through sight, and through understanding of form and structure, then as now. There is obviously a special relationship between the work and its physical presentation both in sound and in notation. The appearance of the notation affects the way one reads the music; students have often observed that extended work from original notation is like learning a new kind of musicianship. We should try to read old notation approaching as closely as possible the ideal of becoming native speakers of its language, rather than giving in, before we start, to the distorting filter of modern transcription. Only then will we learn to understand what the notation conveys beyond its written symbols in a rich context of grammar, syntax, metre, contrapuntal simultaneities, and combination with verbal text. The composer could close off certain solutions and invite, indeed compel others by the way he arranged the musical fabric, rather than by notational prescription alone. He could set up, compositionally, with different degrees of constraint, a self-correcting structure that depended on active realisation by skilled performers who would recognise how those constraints were to operate. Scribal errors needed correction. In other respects, composer and singer were concerned not to correct error but to avoid it; not to compensate for incompleteness but to realise the notated text.

NOTES

* From: *Early Music* 22/3 (August 1994), pp. 373–94. This article was first presented as a paper at a Royal Musical Association meeting on 6 February 1993. Thanks for their role in forming these ideas go to all those with whom I have sung and played early music over many years, and for their specific responses to David Fallows, James Haar, and the *musicorum collegium oxoniense*.

1. In a series of articles in the *New York Times* and in *Authenticity and Early Music*, ed. N. Kenyon, Oxford 1988, and in *Early Music* 20, 1992.
2. *Early Recordings and Musical Style: Changing Tastes in Instrumental Performance, 1900–1950*. Cambridge, 1992.
3. This is not the place to go into the history of early scores. There is no evidence before the sixteenth century of anything like a composing score, especially for the more complex music that would, in our terms, be most helped by visual control. Aligned scores do exist in some forms of tablature that represent adaptations of notation not originally designed to be so used, and later examples, including most of those adduced by Lowinsky, put music into score for study purposes *post facto*.
4. Roger Bowers and I have long shared this view; see his classic statement of it in "The Performing Pitch of English 15th-Century Church Polyphony," *Early Music* 8 (1980): 21–28, and subsequent correspondence 1980–81.
5. Similar issues are addressed in sympathetic fashion by Bruno Turner and others in *Companion to Medieval and Renaissance Music*, ed. Tess Knighton and David Fallows (London, 1992). See also Bojan Bujic, "Notation and Realization: Musical Performance in Historical Perspective," in *The Interpretation of Music: Philosophical Essays*, ed. Michael Krausz (Oxford, 1993), 129–40.

Chapter 8

Some Factors in the Control of Consonance and Sonority: Successive Composition and the *Solus Tenor**

Discussions of consonance and dissonance in medieval music sometimes imply that the composer must have worked in some kind of score, and that he was in a position to manipulate his part-writing on the same basis and with the same visual control as we are. I believe that this was not the case, and that it is a necessary preliminary to considerations of euphony in the finished product to explore the technical and practical problems which faced the composer in combining more than two contrapuntal voices. The rules of two-part counterpoint have been extensively treated both by medieval theorists and modern scholars: my concern in this short paper is more with how, in practical terms, such rules could be applied in composition, and by what means they were applied to composition in more than two parts.

Score notation does indeed exist, but I know of no cases from the 14th or 15th centuries that can be considered as composing scores. (Their absence does not constitute an argument, for we likewise lack performing parts: I simply wish to establish that none of the surviving scores are of this kind.) Only in the case of keyboard notations is there any evidence that a single musician was expected to read a score. In all keyboard music of this period, special adaptations to mensural notation are made, ||626 eliminating the need to operate imperfection and alteration on more than one horizontal plane. The values of notes may be "counted out" as in the Buxheim organ book, or made dependent by alignment on a single rhythmically explicit line as in the Robertsbridge MS. Even the need to read two staves simultaneously, in Faenza, does not surpass these rhythmic limitations. The English repertory for which "score" notation was used is largely homophonic and much of it could be visually grasped in the same way. However, when rhythmic complexities do occur and when alignment of parts is careful, as in Old Hall, the alignment very clearly follows the demands of the single row of verbal text rather than those of musical simultaneity. Mensural notation, in short, is inherently unsuited to use in score. Had it been habitually so used, by performers or composers, it would surely have given way much sooner to a system in which the value of a note was independent of its linear context, as it did in response to the special requirements of keyboard music, and as it did in the 16th century when scores—at least study scores, whether or not for composition and performance—do exist.

Some composition may have taken place in some form of written score, but I doubt whether this was either necessary or normal. The handling of a two-part texture without the visual assistance of a score requires no ambitious assumptions about musicianship. The extension of such a two-part texture to three or four parts by means of successive addition does however require a little more explanation. Two distinct situations exist:

(1) where the technique is clearly successive in that the third voice to be added, the contratenor, is detectable as such, and is grammatically inessential even where it goes below the tenor (example 1), and

(2) where there is no self-contained discant-tenor duet: where the addition of two upper voices depends on a framework of two lower parts, tenor and contratenor (example 2: ignore the fifth staff at this stage). In both examples 1 and 2 the contratenor crosses below the tenor. In 1 it enriches the harmony but does not support it. In 2 it shares the essential harmonic foundation with the tenor. These two situations presuppose different compositional techniques.

EXAMPLE 1: DUFAY, *ADIEU CES BONS VINS*

EXAMPLE 2: DUNSTABLE, *VENI SANCTE SPIRITUS*

EXAMPLE 2: CONTINUED

The first category presents few problems. We can surely accept that a 15th-century composer could handle a three-part song in his head. The discant-tenor duet can be invented, and then notated in separate parts. The contratenor can be thought out in knowledge of this duet and in turn written down. For longer compositions, weaker memories or weaker musicians, we can put it in terms of the composer-singer—most 15th-century composers being employed as singers. He invents and writes down his melody, handing it or teaching it to a colleague who sings it while he improvises and empirically refines a tenor, which he then writes down. Another colleague then sings the tenor with the discant while he improvises, refines and writes down a contratenor. This is the normal order in which parts appear in the sources for compositions of this kind. The instability of contratenor parts in 15th-century chansons—and indeed 14th-century motets—might suggest that it was this last stage which was most commonly left to the test of a "sounding" rather than a written score, or to the mercies of an alien hand. However achieved, in the head or in sound, with or without written assistance at each stage, a piece so composed was both successive in conception and subject to simultaneous aural control of all parts.*

That is the technique in its simplest form. It can easily be extended to cover longer compositions (mass movements using song technique) or compositions in four or five parts where each extra part [627-8] can be shown to have been added in successive fashion—the test being that the music makes sense without it. Many isorhythmic motets of the 14th and 15th centuries are also wholly or partially successive.

Most compositions which depend on the combination of tenor and contratenor are motet-types with at least two upper parts: no pair out of the four can be taken as the backbone of the piece as can the discant-tenor duet in a composition using *chanson* technique. My second category comprises compositions where some such degree of simultaneous conception for three or more parts seems to be a necessary assumption. The simplest examples act as a bridge between the first and second categories.

In writing a two-part canon which is going to have a third, free, accompanying voice, licences such as vertical fourths may be permitted between the two canonic voices if it is known that these can be rectified when the free tenor is added.

EXAMPLE 3: ANON., *Fuit homo* (KYRIE)

Example 3 (from the English mass *Fuit homo missus*, c. 1425) shows the two upper parts forming a self-contained, grammatically complete duet of the discant-tenor type. The tenor cantus firmus moves in even notes, much like the tenor of a cantus-firmus *basse danse*, and it can be thought of as some kind of simultaneous conception. The composer simply steers his duet through a predetermined scheme of harmonies compatible with his tenor, which might therefore be allowed to supply the occasional essential note.

EXAMPLE 4: DUNSTABLE, *Albanus roseo rutilat*

Example 4 takes us a little further. It is from a three-part isorhythmic motet without contratenor by Dunstable (*Albanus roseo rutilat*) and was surely managed in a similar way. The upper duet has a very strong musical impulse of its own, and was apparently conceived simultaneously with the slow-moving tenor, which is sometimes grammatically superfluous to the duet (bar 11) and sometimes furnishes an essential harmony note (bar 1).

Before coming finally to the most difficult and interesting class of composition, comprising mostly four-part isorhythmic motets with a fairly high level of apparently simultaneous conception, I should point out that there are four-part isorhythmic motets that do not require such explanation. An example is Dufay's *Vasilissa ergo gaude* in which the contratenor is not essential, even though it is often below the tenor, or sounds when the tenor rests. At times the duet between the two top parts is self-contained, and at times it requires the completion of the tenor. The composition can be explained successively, at least as far as the contratenor is concerned; the upper duet may have been written simultaneously to the tenor. At all events, the contratenor was added last to that three-part texture. Not so in example 2, where tenor and contratenor together provide the harmonic support.

||629 In suggesting one of several possible methods composers may have used in handling such situations without written scores, I offer two kinds of evidence, theoretical and musical. There are relatively few references to counterpoint in more than two parts before the late 15th century.* One which is significant for the present argument is given by the author of the *Quatuor Principalia*, dated 1351:

> Qui autem triplum aliquod operari voluerit, respiciendum semper est ad tenorem. Si discantus itaque discordat cum tenore, non discordat cum triplo, et e contrario, ita quod semper habeatur concordantia aliqua ad graviorem vocem . . .

> Qui autem quatruplum vel quintuplum facere voluerit, inspicere debet cantus prius factos, ut si cum uno discordat, cum aliis non discordabit, sed ut concordantia semper ad graviorem vocem habeatur . . . (IV.2, chapter xliii, British Library, Add.8866, f. 61v; cf. Coussemaker, *Scriptorum* . . . IV, 295.)

||630 This reference to the lowest voice, or rather the lower of the bottom two, is not isolated. A later reference from Anon XI (c. 1450) reads:

> Et est sciendum quod contratenor, in quantum est gravior tenore, dicitur tenor. (Coussemaker, *Scriptorum* . . . III, 466.)

Clearly, we do not need to apply this when the contratenor is added last, and is inessential, even where it is lower and even where it changes the harmony. But where it is both lower and essential, it is reassuring to find theoretical support for this important function of the bass note.

The musical evidence is largely self-evident, from the essential nature of many such contratenor parts. But important further testimony is found in the provision of solus tenor parts for some twenty compositions of the 14th and 15th centuries, all motets or mass movements in four or five parts, all isorhythmic except for two which undertake the comparable technical challenge, respectively, of a double canon, and of an essay in mensural permutations, and all of the non-successive type. This is a significant proportion of the repertory which meets those conditions. Indeed, if we discount the four relevant motets of Machaut, three-quarters of the 14th-century motets to which this discussion relates have a solus tenor. A solus tenor can be roughly defined as a kind of *basso seguente* conflation of the tenor and contratenor and has been regarded by, I think, all writers on the subject as a "Notbehelf für kleine Besetzung,"[1] enabling a four- or five-part composition to be performed with one line fewer. I am not going to dispute that the solus tenor parts may have been used in this way, or for rehearsal, or for alternative performance, but there are several objections to this as having been their primary purpose.*

These parts are associated with only a handful of manuscripts containing highly sophisticated repertory: principally Ivrea, Modena 568, Chantilly, Old Hall, Canonici misc. 213, Bologna Q15. If the calibre of repertory in these sources is any indication of the flourishing state of the establishments at which they were used, here of all places would these simplified arrangements have been least necessary. Nor is it likely that singers who had taken the trouble to seek out or compose music of the highest erudition and artifice would have taken pleasure in the barbarous disregard for such features—isorhythm, canon, notational nicety, plainsong integrity—which solus tenor parts often display. Moreover, these manuscripts are often particularly authoritative and in some cases thought to have been compiled in the orbit of the composers prominently represented.

Only in a minority of cases are solus tenor parts strict tenor-contratenor conflations throughout. For the rest, they deviate to a greater or lesser degree and are often not explicable as conflations at all. If they were normally made in the manner and for the purpose generally claimed, they show a level of incompetence hard to reconcile with the authoritative character of their sources. As far as I can ascertain they are always copied integrally with the composition and never as later additions.

If we admit this abnormally high level of error or incompetence as an objection to the received definition of a solus tenor, what then is it? It remains generally true

that the solus tenor goes at least as well with the upper parts as do the tenor and contratenor of which it is supposed to be a conflation. And yet, if it is regarded as a freely
composed "new" tenor to fit the upper parts, it is hard to explain why so much of it is
indeed a conflation. Sometimes the solus tenor does not give the lower note of the
tenor-contratenor duet, or even a note compatible with those parts; although some
such cases provide a full triad where the lowest note would not, there are equally
numerous instances where no such reason for the deviation can be adduced. Sometimes the solus tenor does give the lower note at a certain point but nevertheless fits
the upper parts better than does the tenor-contratenor pair. In these cases, the
offending element is often the upper voice of the tenor-contratenor duet, the note
which was not embodied in the conflation (example 5, Dufay, *Rite majorem*, bar 28).

EXAMPLE 5: DUFAY, *RITE MAJOREM*

I believe this can be explained as follows. The composer made a conflation of his
first draft of the contratenor-tenor duet—a solus tenor—which then served as tenor,
or *gravior vox*, upon which he constructed the upper parts in the manner proposed for
examples 3 and 4. Since he was not at that stage taking close account of the upper part
of the lower duet, anomalies between it and the upper [631] parts are explained. They
usually result from *ficta* problems or from the conflict between a 6-3 and a 5-3 chord:
the solus tenor was not a figured bass, but the rough general rule seems to have been to
use or imply 5-3 chords most of the time, reserving 6-3 for cadential approaches.
The upper part of the lower duet could be the one existing voice, but not the lowest,
with which the 14th-century *Quatuor Principalia* permitted dissonance; 15th-century
composers usually avoid even one such dissonance, but not always, as this Dufay
example shows. Increasing fastidiousness about total consonance would have brought
about the demise of a technique which lacked total control, as did the reinstatement
of the tenor and contratenor in place of the solus tenor at this stage in the composition process, at just the time which marks the end of the solus tenor's traceable career.
The procedure suggested here does not of course eliminate the possibility that composers were able to take into account both parts of the lower duet while composing the

upper parts to fit it. In some cases, solus tenor parts were written *ad longum* or in a sim-plified rhythm which matched that of the upper parts. This could of course be explained along the lines of a "Notbehelf," but I am tempted to suggest that it would also be useful in a compositional draft, the "difficult" and more elegant notation being reserved for the definitive notated form of the tenor.

One way, not of course the only one, of accounting for differences between the solus tenor and the tenor-contratenor, is that the process of composing the top parts led the composer to make some revisions in the final form of his tenor-contratenor duet. Where the tenor is a *cantus prius factus* the changes between the solus tenor and the final form of the tenor are often confined to rhythmic displacements. An obvious example of this is the motet *O Maria virgo davitica*, where the discrepancies between the solus tenor and the tenor-contratenor can be accounted for by simple adjustments in durations. Example 6 can probably be explained, though less simply, in similar fash-ion. There are occasionally octave displacements between tenor and solus tenor which may obscure operation and detection of the *basso seguente* principle: see example 7. The contratenor usually has more freedom of movement than the tenor, not being a pre-existent melody, and it may venture in its final form to pitches lower than those embodied in the solus tenor, as in example 8. These adjustments may involve changes of harmony which are compatible with the top parts though no longer compatible with the solus tenor, such as those in example 6.

EXAMPLE 6: M. DE PERUSIO? *GLORIA*

Ct.
T.

S.t.

EXAMPLE 7: ANON., *HUMANE LINGUA*

T.
Ct.

S.t.

EXAMPLE 8: DUFAY, *RITE MAJOREM*

||632 I am suggesting, therefore, that the solus tenor may have been primarily a stage in the composition process, one of several possible methods of handling three or more parts without the aid of a written score. The surviving solus tenor parts may provide unique and valuable evidence of the genesis of a composition, comparable to sketches and drafts from later periods. (Where more than one solus tenor survives for a single composition, these may reflect different compositional stages.) Sometimes the solus tenor is indeed given alone, taking on the status of a new tenor. In such cases it is usually made isorhythmic, and reflects the 15th-century taste for the greater control of consonance which three-part writing provided. Some compositions on "free" tenors may in fact preserve solus tenor parts in which traces of plainsong are embedded. It is possible that the kind of process described may account for those 14th-century motets that have labelled but unidentified tenors. In one case where a four-part composition has been reduced to three parts, *O Maria virgo davitica* in Bologna Q15, the tenor has not been identified as a plainsong, and the solus tenor is isorhythmic. There is thus no obvious barbarity in ||633 this three-part version, which might there-

fore be considered an alternative. It does, however, show no significant increase in consonance over the four-part version and offers no basis for a claim that it was composed for this reason. Any argument that solus tenor parts were composed for alternative performance is weakened by the fact that no solus tenor parts survive for compositions which, in the terms I have defined, would not have needed them. (The only exception to that statement is the unique case of a solus contratenor for Binchois's *Dueil Angoisseus,* which is simply an alternative additive part to a grammatically complete discant-tenor duet.) If solus tenor parts were commonly written *post facto,* some of the factors which underlie pitch discrepancies between the surviving examples and their tenor-contratenor pairs would surely have encouraged the composition of new solus tenor parts for successively composed pieces also. Harmonic change in such pieces was achieved instead by the use of alternative contratenor parts; the techniques seem quite distinct. The inevitable question "why were these parts preserved?" is no more readily answerable in terms of their compositional function than of their use as "Notbehelfe." Given the objections raised above, why should either be preserved in the manuscripts which do, after all, preserve them? Modena 568 and Old Hall both contain palimpsest revisions of a compositional nature, suggesting ongoing compositional activity at least in those sources. As a basis for further, probably unwritten, compositional growth of these compositions, the solus tenor may have provided a useful or even an essential aid. Given their availability, there is no reason why they should not have been copied for use in rehearsal and, if necessary, for alternative performance or "Notbehelf." Fifteenth-century solus tenor parts do in general show more signs of being intended for use in performance, but the same objections apply to performance being their "raison d'être."

I am also suggesting that compositions which meet the same requirements but for which no solus tenor survives, such as example 2 again, may have been composed with the aid of a conflation such as that suggested on the fifth staff, below it. Compare the projected solus tenor version of Dunstable's *Veni sancte spiritus* with the four-part version to see two features which make the latter look more archaic: the ungainly line of the contratenor with its leaps of sevenths (bar 14–15) and the necessity to make sudden rests to avoid dissonance (bar 21) where the corresponding place in the solus tenor is a moving bass line.

While much of this is merely informed guessing about how composers might have set about composing, it does fit many of the musical facts. It accounts for the absence of composition scores, while offering an explanation of solus tenor survivals. It implies a new approach to the analysis of an important sector of 14th- and 15th-century music and, I believe, amplifies the notion of successive composition by attempting to define the nature and extent of its simultaneous controls.

Discussion:

Perkins: You invoke in the course of your discussion the quality of the repertories involved and the quality of the musical establishments reflected in those repertories. One might add that the manuscripts preserving the repertories also often seem to reflect the same kind of quality, if we think of manuscripts such as Chantilly and Old Hall with their illuminations and decorations. I wonder if you could explain why these solus tenor parts that you suggest might have been simply sketches for compositions were included in such elegant sources from such high-level institutions.

Margaret Bent: I offer the possibility that if the manuscripts continued to be used by the composers and if the written form of a composition was not regarded as the only form that the composition was ever going to take, but rather that further impromptu and improvised refinements were intended, then the composer or performers may have wished to return to the solus tenor as the basis for this later embellishment.

William Mahrt: I have found the solus tenor very useful in rehearsing the other parts without requiring the tenors to be present.

Margaret Bent: Yes, even when this involves rehearsing to notes that are different from those that will be heard at the final performance.

Alejandro Planchart: I would like to offer a bit of paleographic evidence that I believe supports what Prof. Bent has just said. These manuscripts are indeed very elegant and carefully done, but scribes sometimes did make mistakes. One of the most interesting of these appears in Dufay's motet *Rite majorem* in manuscript Bologna Q 15, where the solus tenor supports an introductory duet and thus acts as a contratenor to the upper two voices. Invariably this part is connected with the [first] note of the later contratenor. So clearly this voice had been composed to accompany the introductory material and then lead on into the contratenor in the four-voice sections. The scribe of Bologna Q 15 seems to have ignored these introductory trios.

Mixter: I am wondering how you account for a certain problem in chronology. For example, I think that Shelley Davis mentions two versions of solus tenors for motets by de Vitry that appear in rather late manuscripts, from the end of the 14th and beginning of the 15th centuries. In contradistinction, there are some very early sources for the solus tenor, for[634] example, in the manuscript that Frank Harrison discovered, Oxford, New College, 362. Does this apparent problem of chronology disturb your thesis?

Margaret Bent: I don't think that the lateness of the de Vitry examples is necessarily an objection. There are, incidentally, instances of two different contratenors surviving for the same piece. One is marked "vacat" in Ivrea, indicating that it was perhaps too far afield even to be used for rehearsal. It is possible that these may reflect different stages in the compositional process. New College, 362, is, as you say, the earliest example, and the Dufay pieces the latest. Thus the solus tenors do span more or less the complete history from New College through Dufay, and it is remarkable that they coincide with the life span of that particular four-part repertory.

Commentary

to passages marked by asterisks in text; see also the Introduction pp. 39–48, and Chapter 9.

p. 244   I would now qualify "successive in conception" to make clearer, as I have tried to do in "The Grammar of Early Music" (Bent 1998a) that while composers *could* have worked in this order, and although the music lends itself to analysis in this way, it is no more necessary to assume that this always reflected their order of working than that a native speaker who utters a complex, grammatically correct sentence needed to build it up from a simple sentence. Likewise, I believe that while the successive stages may have been pedagogically useful, experienced composers no more needed to go through them than they did to solmise what they wrote.

p. 246   This now needs revision in the light of clearer subsequent formulations of the inherently dyadic nature of counterpoint; additions to that two-part structure are in principle cumulative and successive. The opening two paragraphs of this chapter address the simultaneous/successive issue in relation to absence of written scores; I have since addressed these in other essays, including Bent 1998a.

p. 247   Since some have assumed that I am proposing an alternative hypothesis for the use of solus tenors, as apart from the origin of at least some of them, I wish to stress that I do indeed think that rehearsal or even reduced performance may be among the reasons that they were still copied into manuscripts. I would also emphasise that solus tenors exist *only* for pieces with essential contratenors, never for those with inessential contratenors; this attests awareness on the part of those who made or copied them of fundamental differences between these two motet types.

NOTES

* From: *Report of the Twelfth Congress, Berkeley 1977*, ed. Daniel Heartz and Bonnie Wade (Kassel: Bärenreiter 1981, 625–34.

1. H. Besseler, *Bourdon und Fauxbourdon* (Leipzig, 1950), p. 94. For the only study devoted entirely to the subject see Shelley Davis, "The Solus Tenor in the 14th and 15th Centuries," *Acta Musicologica* 39 (1967): 44–64, and Addendum in 40 (1968): 176–78. I plan to prepare a fuller presentation of the ideas put forward in the present, necessarily brief, paper. <See now the Introduction to this volume.>

Chapter 9

Pycard's Double Canon: Evidence of Revision?[*]

The Old Hall Manuscript, known since its acquisition by the British Library in 1973 as Additional MS. 57950, contains on fols. 22v–23 a Gloria by Pycard (fig. Ia,b) which is a rare and early example of double canon, published as no. 27 in the edition.[1] Its only clear antecedent in that respect is the—likewise English—'Sumer' canon in B L, Harley MS. 978, technically a very different piece, involving that special form of canon we know as round, over a simple two-voice rondellus ostinato.[2]

Notwithstanding the origins implied by his name and in documents, Pycard was in English service in the 1390s; his musical style shows him to have been thoroughly assimilated as an English composer.[3] His ascribed compositions are preserved mainly in the Old Hall manuscript. They include the Gloria no. 26 a4, with canon 2 in 1 at the fourth; the present double canonic Gloria no. 27; the isorhythmic Gloria no. 28 a5, also with solus tenor; the Gloria no. 35 a5 with canon 2 in 1;[4] the Credo no. 76 a4 (non-canonic, but with an interesting transposed section); and the Sanctus no. 123, with canon 2 in 1 and tenor, probably lacking on the missing facing page a contratenor and fifth free voice. In addition, an incomplete and largely illegible Credo in Stratford is ascribed to Picart.[5] The conspicuous presence of canon among these works raises the possibility that two anonymous Credos with treble canons three in one, no. 71 and the tour de force no. 75, might also be his work. I have suggested elsewhere, very tentatively, that Pycard might be the author of a cycle of five-part Ordinary movements, unified by the shared technique of canon, by number of voices and general style, of which we have the Gloria no. 35, Credo no. 75 (anonymous), and Sanctus no. 123 (incomplete).[6] The Gloria under discussion, no. 27, is also in a total of five parts; as a canon four in two, each comes follows its dux at the unison and at five breves' distance, with an additional, free fifth voice in the same clef and range as the upper canonic voices. The first half is given as ex. 1. The procedure of the lower voices, that they called *fuga* and we call canon, is specified by the "canon" *Tenor et contratenor in uno unus post alium fugando quinque temporibus.* The upper-voice canon is signalled only by portions of double text underlay to the single notated top part. Oliver Strunk observed this as a symptom of canon in ᴵᴵᴵᴵ several Old Hall compositions and was the first to identify this Gloria as a double canon.[7] It is a piece of full sonorities, including thirds above the bass line. It makes the most of its full five-voice texture which, together with its "major" tonality and lilting metre (6/8 in transcription), contributes to a characteristically English sound quite different from Machaut and his successors, despite the significant extent to which English composers had absorbed French mensural techniques by this time.[8] The upper parts are managed with considerable skill, including gentle proportional enlivenment and hockets. Although the opening presents a widely spaced imitative introitus, similar to that in Italianate motets of this period, the remainder of the canon is achieved without such extensive resort to echo and rests to facilitate exactness.

The question to be pursued here is how the double canon was constructed, and is prompted by some observations about its solus tenor. This is one of some two dozen pieces surviving with a solus tenor part. All such parts more or less strictly conflate tenor and contratenor in such a way as to present the essential foundation of what we would call the harmony and they the counterpoint—usually but not always the lowest note of the lower-voice pair. In compositions where the tenor consistently provides that support, even where a subsequently composed contratenor goes below it, the contratenor can be counted grammatically *in*essential. No such pieces have solus tenor parts; reduced performance could simply be accomplished by omitting the contratenor. The texture would be thinner, but unsupported fourths in strong positions would be avoided. A solus tenor would neither serve nor be needed, either for reduced performance or to facilitate composition.

All the solus tenor parts so far discovered are only for compositions where the contratenor fills an essential role, that is, where it partly assumes the contrapuntal role of the tenor. Sharing of roles may be necessary when the tenor is simultaneously obeying other constraints such as the presentation of a structural cantus firmus or, in this case, canon. Such pieces could therefore not be reduced to fewer voices simply by omitting the contratenor, because the contratenor at certain points underpins the tenor and averts unsupported fourths with the upper parts. This is the principal criterion of essential contratenor function, not whether it goes lower than the tenor.

Besseler, whose *Harmonieträger* theory did not permit him to recognise this criterion of essential function, diagnosed the solus tenor as a *Notbehelf für kleine Besetzung*,[9] an emergency device enabling the piece to be performed with fewer singers. This view has been generally accepted in the form usefully compiled by Shelley Davis.[10] However, several puzzles remain if reduced performance was the primary function of the solus tenor. It is hard to believe that the composers and collectors of these highly clever and specialised pieces, using canon, proportioned or mensural tenor transformation and the range of techniques commonly gathered under the umbrella of isorhythm, would have chosen to violate in performance a prized art that they laboured to produce and reproduce, particularly in these, some of the most technically demanding pieces.

EXAMPLE 1: PYCARD, GLORIA OH 27 FIRST HALF ONLY. Reproduced, with permission, from A. Hughes and M. Bent (eds.), *THE OLD HALL MANUSCRIPT*, Corpus Mensurabilis Musicae, xlvi.

EXAMPLE I: CONTINUED

EXAMPLE I: CONTINUED

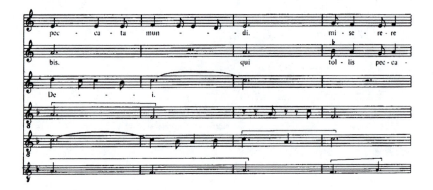

EXAMPLE I: CONTINUED

EXAMPLE I: CONTINUED

FIGURE 1: PYCARD'S GLORIA, FROM THE OLD HALL MANUSCRIPT
(ADD.MS.57950, FOLS. 22V–23).

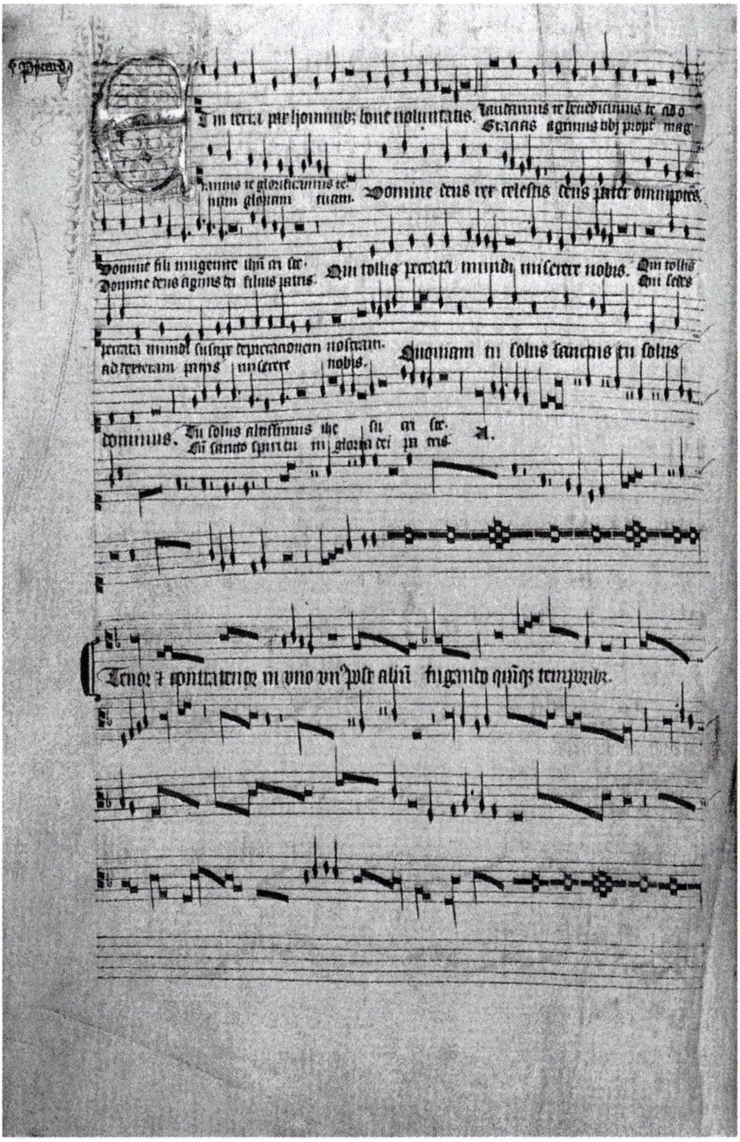

FIGURE 1: CONTINUED

‖12 Pieces with solus tenor usually meet at least two different technical constraints at the same time (e.g., isorhythm of upper parts, tenor isorhythm, cantus firmus). Usually the primary discipline was isorhythmic. Another English example, involving an elaborate lower-voice mensuration canon reduced to a solus tenor, is the recently found motet *O amicus/Precursor*, a rare combination of isorhythm and canon.[11] In Pycard's ‖13 Gloria no. 27 the operation of a double canon clearly poses a set of constraints for which special treatment by him requires no special pleading by us. How might its composer have gone about satisfying these constraints in the process of composition?

That process must normally have been possible without visual dependence on aligned score. There are of course some examples of roughly aligned score notation, ‖14 but it cannot be argued that these are composing scores or that their primary purpose was visual control of the texture by a single reader. The English repertory notated in score is aligned rather for three singers to apply the same text than for one musician to read the score, as one can tell from divergent line-ends where the settings depart from strict homophony. Late-medieval mensural notation is poorly suited to use in score by a single reader because of the contextual reading it demands of each singer. The notation of vocal polyphony did not yet undergo adaptation for use in score, as it surely would have had it been commonly so used, and as it did as score-reading became more common. Demonstrable changes towards unit reference both of pitch and rhythm were made in those cases when music was scored for a single performer to read. By unit reference I mean the context-free notation of a specific pitch or note value that bypasses the need to be construed by the performer. This happens in keyboard tablatures that notate "black" notes by physical adjacence to their white neighbours (where G sharp may be treated as synonymous with A flat), and where a note may be counted out as two units regardless of whether it originated by alteration or imperfection. Score-reading by one person invites notational adaptation towards unit specification of pitch and rhythm for each note, and shuns the contextual determination that is fundamental to mensural notation. The very nature of the changes that were made for keyboard tablatures emphasises the unsuitability of contextual notation for use in aligned score, whether by reader or composer. In addition, the complexities of textual and musical structure and cross-reference undertaken in the simultaneous strands of *Ars nova* motets, for example, are such that physical alignment would hinder as many aspects of such control as it helped.

In view of these considerations, I have suggested that the solus tenor was not only or even primarily a performance expedient, but that it may have been in the first instance a compositional aid, one of the closest things we have from this period to a sketch or draft.[12] In composing a piece with essential contratenor, the composer would make a bass (or *basso seguente*) conflation of the tenor and contratenor, using that line for the contrapuntal projection of the upper parts, and then reinstating the lower pair. In this way, he could project two (or in some cases three) voices at a time, observing various combinations of the fundamentally dyadic relationships of counterpoint, while allowing for there to be further voices in the texture. And he could do this by combining a successive procedure with an aural image of the whole, without ever having visual control of that whole in aligned score, a control I do not believe to have been available to or sought by composers at this time.

In answer to the question "Why were solus tenor parts preserved?" only guesses can [20] be hazarded. They *are* preserved, an indisputable fact no less puzzling if explained by emergency performance than as compositional support. A solus tenor originating in the process of composition could have been retained for the private delight of initiates (and solus tenor parts are indeed conspicuously preserved in connoisseur manuscripts such as Modena A, Chantilly, and Old Hall). It could have been used in rehearsal, while putting the piece back together in sound by a process parallel to, and perhaps in the same order as, that by which it was originally composed (put together) in the mind of its inventor, probably with the support of performance at each stage. It could have been used as the basis for further work on the composition, much as one might keep an architect's blueprints that, although modified in execution, could still serve as a basis for future adaptations. Such further work on a composition might result in discrepancies with the solus tenor's origin as a conflation. The crutch was not thrown away, perhaps because fellow-craftsmen might use it again for further extension or refinement of the piece. And use in rehearsal, or pragmatic emergency or didactic use in accordance with Besseler's hypothesis, would still not be excluded as secondary functions. Whatever the reasons for the creation and preservation of solus tenor parts, it remains true that they exist only for pieces that form a distinct compositional category characterised by an essential contratenor and multiple technical constraints. This encourages one to identify with some confidence (a confidence vindicated by the most recent new discoveries of solus tenor parts) which pieces might once have had such parts. All pieces with a solus tenor have an essential contratenor, but the converse is not true. A number of motets and motet-like mass movements do have essential contratenors but no surviving solus tenors. In these cases, solus tenor conflations might have existed, whether as part of the compositional process or for reduced performance, but happen not to have been preserved.[13]

During the entire period of discant-tenor hegemony, no subsequent revision of tenor parts ever seems to have been undertaken in such a way as to violate their status as bearers of a discant-tenor duet. If tenor parts were revised in the light of subsequent contratenor composition, they have left us little evidence of such a process, just as canonic revisions are not betrayed by canonic deformation. The disciplined relationship was central.

||22 Most solus tenor parts form a reasonably strict *basso seguente* conflation of tenor and contratenor parts; the Pycard Gloria attracts attention by its numerous deviations from that model. What could possibly account for such divergences in a *post facto* conflation? If it was simply an incompetent conflation, why does it go so well with the upper-voice canon? Moreover, the points of deviation tend to repeat at a distance of five breves, that is, at the temporal interval of the canon. Does the solus tenor vary from a bass conflation simply because it was intended as a free and partly new accompaniment to the upper canon, and if so, how is it able to show a periodicity in its deviation that goes beyond what would result from a free accompaniment to the upper canon? It is the regularity and nature of its departures from the *basso seguente* principle that invite a different hypothesis. The variation must, I think, represent a different, probably earlier, version of the canon. Only thus can the regularity of the differences be explained. Ex. 2 shows the points of divergence between solus tenor and lower-voice canon in the first half of the Gloria (*cf.* ex. 1). The five-breve groups of the canonic interval can be compared with the tabulation in ex. 3. The solus tenor is only given where it differs from what that conflation would be. Its notes are marked with a triangle (▲: 21, 26, 35, 40, 45, 50, 54) where they correspond neither to the tenor nor the contratenor, and with a diamond (◇: 9, 15, 39) where they are incompatible with them. In the canon, upstems indicate the *dux* and downstems the *comes*.

EXAMPLE 2: PYCARD, GLORIA OH 27, FIRST HALF ONLY. ST=Solus Tenor;
T/Ct=Tenor and Contratenor; Upstems=dux, downstems=comes; Lower staff of
each pair gives ST where different from T/Ct; ▲ marks points where ST=neither T
nor Ct; ◇ marks points where ST and T/Ct are incompatible.

Ex. 3 tabulates the lightly varied ostinato structure of the piece, showing both the solus tenor and the tenor-contratenor forms of the ostinato. It demonstrates how the ostinato shifts position by one breve, exactly at the middle of the 108 breves. The tenor rhythm is also reversed at bar 54, the mid-point of the piece, with two iambic instead of trochaic pairs.[14] Also between breves 51 and 56 the ostinato pattern changes to extend its penultimate (usually G) to two breves before each arrival on F. The second half of the piece proceeds with only superficial variants to this ostinato, and equally minor variants between the solus tenor and the lower voice of the canon.

The first half of the Gloria presents a rather more complex picture, as the alternatives noted on ex. 3 indicate. The form of the ostinato embodied in the solus tenor is more varied, signifying a more ambitious canon. The penultimate note of each group of five is never more than a single breve on G or B. The first two are and were on G, the next four on B. But if the solus tenor represents an earlier version, the next four were originally on G, whereas they are all on B in the final version. Thus six out of the ten penultimates were originally on G in the first half of the Gloria, whereas now eight out of ten are on B. This shift away from penultimate G to B in the first half of the piece sharpens the contrast between the ostinato pattern in the first half (with B penultimate predominant) and in the second half (with predominant and prolonged G), and thus sharpens the overall harmonic contrast between the two halves, an articulation reinforced by the ostinato shift.

Did Pycard start with the upper or the lower canon? Was the solus tenor devised as [||23] an accompaniment to the upper canon, then to be teased out into two canonic strands (hard to do *post facto*), with the changes representing revisions required for the canon? Or does it indeed embody an earlier version of the lower canon that was modified in the light of the upper one? Leaving aside a growing number of cases in which verbal and other extra-musical building blocks must have preceded musical ones or been coeval with them, many of the purely musical disciplines dictate that the lower voices were often the compositional starting point. This is true for borrowed chant tenors and for isorhythmic statements in successive diminution, and remains, I think, the likelier order here. There would be no real need for an upper-voice continuous canon to observe any ostinato discipline. If he started with a bass ostinato and constructed the canon as a free variation upon it, the ostinato might be expected to be even more repetitive at the cadencing notes between each five-breve cycle and the next (see ex. 3). Any such canon will tend to produce ostinato-like repetitions at the canonic time interval; the freely shifting pattern revealed here suggests that the ostinato character was a by-product of the canon, not the canon of the ostinato. Pycard's canonic Sanctus no. 123 is an upper-voice canon on a plainsong that is cunningly rhythmicised so as to form a free ostinato; the composer makes compatible notes fall at the beginning of each ostinato period, and he manages the present canon in a similar way.

Presuming that he started with the lower-voice canon, its single-line reduction, a *basso seguente*, could serve as a foundation upon which to erect the upper voices. Using a technique that must have been very common in the composition of cantus-firmus masses,[15] the composer invents a new self-contained duet (in this case, the upper canon) that follows the predetermined harmonic movement of his cantus firmus (in this case, the solus tenor derived from the lower canon). When he had done this, the lower-part canonic duet could be reinstated, copied, and performed. Possible moments of awkwardness would arise between the upper voices and the upper part of the lower-voice duet that had not been taken <directly> into account when composing the upper pair. This solus tenor goes well with the upper parts. So, equally, does a lower-voice conflation of the canon as we have it, in what is presumably its final form. The upper of the present lower canonic parts also goes well with the upper voices. Was this achieved through revision of the reinstated lower canon to remove roughnesses with the upper canon? There are a few simultaneous false relations, notably a B flat and a B natural notated in the canonic *dux* that coincide with inexorable logic at bar 15; this can stand or be softened at discretion. The repetitions of notes at five-breve intervals in the solus tenor, sometimes identical (cf. 21-26, and 35-40-45-50), sometimes merely compatible, are insufficient to reconstruct more than occasional notes of the canon with certainty, but permit suggestions for a few passages. That Pycard then no longer needed to change the solus tenor to reflect those revisions helps to confirm that its primary role was rather as a compositional crutch than as a performance expedient post-dating the final version of the canon. The solus tenor, of course, destroys the canon. If one of the five [||24] required singers was absent it would have made more sense to choose a different, four-part Gloria, or to omit the other, technically inessential, upper part, than to deform the primary technical strategy of the piece. The free fifth (middle) part goes equally well with the solus tenor *or* with the tenor-contratenor pair. Procedurally last, it could have been added to the solus tenor plus canon, or after the revised and reinstated lower canon. It adds motion and texture, but is grammatically expendable.

The opening ten breves of the piece may indicate that the solus tenor lies somewhere on a spectrum between an earlier and revised version of the lower canon. The G and A at breves 3 and 4 correspond to the final version, whereas the *longa* D is compatible (albeit not the lower note) at 8, and incompatible at 9. This D, however, goes equally well with the *comes* of the upper canon at 8-9 as it would have with the corresponding point in the *dux* at 3-4. Did the composer originally plan the lower canonic voice to be C, D (longs), G, F (breves), followed by rests? If so, he may have rejected it as being too thin and static after deciding on the introitus-like upper-voice opening with rests. The revision represented by the final version gives more motion, and was incorporated in the solus tenor at 3-4 but not at 8-9. Such reasoning could be continued for many points in the canon, but that is enough speculation for now.

In sum, the nature of the solus tenor's differences from the expected tenor-contratenor bass conflation suggests that it represents an earlier draft of the canon. This analysis, particularly in ex. 3, attempts to show how the revisions, insofar as they can be recovered, were part not only of a refinement of the lower canon and of its relationship to the upper canon, but of a plan to sharpen the formal profile of the Gloria in two distinctive and balanced halves.

EXAMPLE 3: TABLE OF FIVE-BREVE OSTINATO FORMS

The primary pitch given in each column is that of the solus tenor's first note in each breve. Superscript + indicates that there are other notes in the bar. All annotations in parentheses indicate where and how the lowest note of the final tenor-contratenor pair differs from the solus tenor, and whether it too has other notes in the bar. Where there are no annotations, the two agree. This does not of course mean that the upper canonic part was also the same at those points. B is usually flat, in accordance with the signature.

bar (breve)

I	c	c	g	a	g	
6	f	c	d(g)	d(a)	g	
II	f	$a^{(+)}$	g	c(a)	$b^{+(+)}$	
16	f	a^+	g	a	$b^{(+)}$	
21	a(f)	d^+	a	-(c)	$b^{(+)}$	
26	a(f)	f^+	a	c	b^+	
31	f	$f^{+(+)}$	a	c	$g^+(b^+)$	
36	a	f	a+	d(f)	$g^+(b)$	
41	a	f	a	f^+	$g^+(b^+)$	
46	a	f	a	a	$g^+(b)$	
51	a	f	c(a)	$f^+(a)$	g	d
57		a	a^+	c	g	b
62		a	$f'(a^+)$	c	g^+	g^+
67		f	f	c	g	g
72		f	c^+	c(a)	b	b
77		a	a	a	g	g
82		f	a	a(c)	g	-(g)
87		f	c	f	g	g
92		f	a	a	-(g)	g
97		f	c	a	g	g
102		f	f	a	g	g	f

Notes

* From: *Sundry Sorts of Music Books. Essays on The British Library Collections. Presented to O. W. Neighbour on His 70th Birthday*, ed. Chris Banks, Arthur Searle and Malcolm Turner. (London: The British Library, 1993), pp. 10–26.

1. Andrew Hughes and Margaret Bent, eds., *The Old Hall Manuscript*, Corpus Mensurabilis Musicae xlvi, 3 vols. (n. p.: American Institute of Musicology, 1969–73).

2. Although Odington exemplifies rondellus by a three-voice example of voice-exchange, I see no reason to follow Sanders ("Rondellus" in *The New Grove Dictionary of Music and Musicians* (London, 1980), vol. xvi, pp. 170–71), in confining the term to examples in more than two parts.

3. The latest work on Pycard's biography is Andrew Wathey, "John of Gaunt, John Picard, and the Negotiations at Amiens, 1392," in *England and the Low Countries in the Fifteenth Century*, ed. N. Saul and C. M. Barron (Gloucester, 1993).

4. Rather than 3 in 1, as proposed by Frank L. Harrison, "English Church Music in the Fourteenth Century" in *The New Oxford History of Music*, ed. Dom A. Hughes and G. Abraham, vol. iii, p. 103.

5. Shakespeare Birthplace Library, MS. Willoughby de Broke 1744, f. Bv. <Now MS. DR 98/1744/1. See www.diamm.ac.uk.>

6. In my unpublished Ph.D. dissertation, *The Old Hall Manuscript: A Paleographical Study*, University of Cambridge, 1969, p. 95.

7. "The Music of the Old Hall Manuscript—A Postscript," *The Musical Quarterly* 35 (1949): 244ff, reprinted with additions in M. F. Bukofzer, *Studies in Medieval and Renaissance Music* (New York, 1950), pp. 80–85.

8. The lovely recording by Christopher Page's Gothic Voices (*The Service of Venus and Mars*, Hyperion CDA 66238), track 6, emphasises the gentler end of the piece's interpretative spectrum. It could also be performed higher and faster.

9. H. Besseler, *Bourdon und Fauxbourdon* (Leipzig, 1950), p. 94.

10. Shelley Davis, "The Solus Tenor in the 14th and 15th Centuries," *Acta Musicologica* 39 (1967): 44–64.

11. Margaret Bent, with David Howlett, "*Subtiliter alternare*: The Yoxford Motet *O amicus/Precursoris*," in *Studies in Medieval Music: Festschrift for Ernest Sanders*, ed. Peter M. Lefferts and Brian Seirup (New York, 1990), *Current Musicology* xlv–xlvii: 43–84.

12. "Some Factors in the Control of Consonance and Sonority: Successive Composition and the *Solus tenor*," in *International Musicological Society: Report of the Twelfth Congress, Berkeley 1977*, ed. Daniel Heartz and Bonnie Wade (Kassel: Bärenreiter, 1981), pp. 625–34 <= Chapter 8>.

13. This is a possibility for some of Dunstaple's motets, notably his well-known *Veni Creator/Veni Sancte Spiritus*, a later addition to Old Hall, Manfred Bukofzer (ed.), *John Dunstable Complete Works*, Musica Britannica, viii (London, 2nd, rev. ed. prepared by Margaret Bent, Ian Bent, and Brian Trowell, 1970), no. 32. See also *The Old Hall Manuscript . . .* , no. 66. and ex. 2 in M. Bent, op. cit. n. 12 above.

14. Jeffrey Dean observes that the other "reverse" rhythm in the tenor falls for the *dux* at the Golden Section of the music.

15. See ex. 3 in M. Bent, op. cit. n. 12 above, "Some Factors . . .", from the anonymous Mass "Fuit homo" (published in *Early English Church Music*, xxii), where the contrapuntally self-contained moving parts move at each new breve to notes compatible with the chant presented in breves.

Chapter 10

Text Setting in Sacred Music of the Early 15th Century: Evidence and Implications[*]

This paper deals with a number of different points which have arisen in the course of studying certain early-fifteenth-century repertories and composers with a view to uncovering both scribal and compositional texting procedures. The principal manuscripts mentioned here are the Old Hall MS and Bologna Q 15; the principal composers, Dunstaple and Ciconia.[1] I have cast my net rather wide, in place if not in time, in order to be able to include mention of both contrasts and similarities between approximately contemporary manifestations. The following observations will be [||292] concerned first with questions of the detailed fitting of notes and syllables, based mainly on a study of the Old Hall MS, and then with some larger-scale issues connected with the isorhythmic motet.

That the study of word-tone relationships is at a more primitive stage for the 14th–15th centuries than for the 16th is due in no small measure to the lack of any significant and detailed body of theoretical or aesthetic guidance as to what was considered acceptable in our period. Underlay, moreover, is perhaps the most fragile ingredient of the transmission process. Because it involves graphic presentation of two separate languages, neither of which can be incorporated into the other, it is the hardest to convey objectively—witness the failure of modern editions and commentaries to deal with it other than mechanically or subjectively. Even less than with *musica ficta* can we be sure that what we are presented with in the manuscripts is the exactly transmitted intention of the composer without the intermediate initiative of an editor-scribe, whether or not the composer expected such editing.

While it is indisputably true that some scribes and some manuscripts (including, for example, Wiser's work in the Trent codices) give us no detailed guidance, contributing to the overall picture of negligence and inconsistency, I think we can do better than to assume that any scribe's testimony can be lightly overruled by application of our own anachronistic aesthetic. It is all too easy to follow modern, or at least 16th-century preconceptions when making arbitrary decisions about questions such as the following: Which syllables of a word or verse line should fall in a metrically strong position? What is vocally most grateful? Should we avoid the repetition of a note without a new syllable? Is there a minimum note-value that may carry its own syllable? Should extended melisma be "rescued" by prescribing text repetition? May ligatures never be broken? Should plainsong-bearing parts in polyphony have their underlay adjusted to that of the original chant? Should underlay be adjusted so that words are not broken by rests? Should declamation be simultaneous where possible and the texting of imitations matched? And should the mensural unit or the musical patterning receive the further emphasis of syllable placement? For these and other questions we have, as yet, no consistent answers. In some cases we can predict with some confidence what a given scribe or composer would have done. Each of these prejudices needs to be tested against the available evidence of the sources.

||293 One of the issues central to my argument is how far we can determine the composer's role and to what degree it is separable from that of the scribe; but for practical reasons I shall start with the scribe since it is he who transmits both. When I speak of "scribal intention" this may include the composer's intention, but unless the "intention" is composed organically into the music and cannot be separated from it, we can only safely assume that we are receiving the scribe's interpretation. Composers, performers, and scribes may be good, bad, or indifferent in various respects, and all may have exercised their varying degrees of competence upon the transmission of any of the music surviving. We cannot always extricate scribal competence from other elements in an individual transmission, but we can identify a scribe's sensitivity and care with respect to certain aspects of the copying process, and fortunately text underlay is one of these. A scribe who is "good" for our purposes may be able to show what one musically literate and performance-conscious contemporary of the composer would have done with a passage that is open to more than one solution. (A similar statement might be made about *ficta* solutions; in both cases, neither the composer nor the scribe may have felt obliged to spoon-feed the performer. Failure to give us all the help that we at this distance would like does not necessarily mean that they were negligent.) Where a scribal intention is clear, it could be transmitting faithfully what was clear in the exemplar; it could be a resolution of what was ambiguous; or it could represent a deliberate change in accordance with personal taste. The cumulative effect of clearly expressed solutions may be to provide us with some tentative criteria that may, with due caution, be applied to certain other situations for which a specific solution is lacking. Initially, such data should be reapplied only within

the repertory which provided them; they may help us to interpret places where the scribe has passed on an anomaly, such as mismatched textual and musical line ends, or the unclear placing of fewer syllables under more notes (In ex. I, stave 2, *glorificamus*, everything is clear except on which of the small notes -*mus* should fall). I have found the scribe of OH to be extraordinarily clear in nearly all cases. However, similar studies of other suitable manuscripts will have to be undertaken before we can speak of a more general application. Without yet having made as exhaustive a study of the texting habits of the Q15 scribe as for OH, I have found him, in the cases I have examined, to be equally meticulous. This encourages the expectation that a more complete study of this manuscript would produce results that have some ||294 common ground with those from OH, providing by their different underlying traditions and by the taste of a different individual a consensus or range of tolerance for underlay principles at this period.

The picture of how deliberately a scribe has achieved his mutual placing of music and text must be built up painstakingly from a complex pattern of evidence. The most overt symptoms of deliberate rather than casual placement include (1) the drawing of occasional guide-lines to improve note-syllable alignment (e.g. BU f. 50ᵛ, Kras f. 174ᵛ); (2) a consistently accurate matching (where verifiable) of text and music across the breaks from line to line (OH is excellent in this respect, and Q15 good) and (3)—most fundamental but least easily detectable—the erasure of notes or syllables to effect often very slight adjustments, where the erasure cannot be accounted for in any other way. There are numerous examples of the last two symptoms of concern in both OH and Q15. But even where such care has been taken, we cannot always assume that the result will be an exact vertical alignment of note and syllable, and we must learn to interpret the signals given by individual scribes. All too often, modern editors observe the actual physical alignment without adequate consideration of the practical constraints which produced it. If we attempt rather to follow the spirit than the letter of a scribe's work, we may find that indications are susceptible of precise interpretation, even where they depart from an exact physical alignment. An extreme example of this would be a syllabic melody where the music was written with too much lateral compression, and the words were then of necessity placed increasingly far from their associated pitches, although the intention remained clear. In order to interpret such evidence it may be important to know whether the words or the music were copied first, or whether there is evidence of both being entered in tandem. Only in this context can one judge in which direction imperfect alignment should be accounted for and corrected.

There is occasionally very clear evidence of one process having preceded the other. On the one hand, there are many examples of music preserved without text within repertories where one would have expected text to be provided. On the other, there are a few examples of complete text with ruled staves but no musical notes. Ox is

very tightly planned by text and the music unevenly spaced to it, with cramped melismas and spaced-out syllabic passages. Freehand stave-extensions and some misalign-
ments were necessitated by the fact that the text was already in place and too little space
||295 had been allowed.[2] Much of OH was also written in this order, including all syl-
labic passages, but in some cases (e.g., ff. 25^V–26) in writing the text, too much space
had been left for ligatures that are consequently elongated. OH f. 57^V contains an
addition by a later scribe of a piece he never completed. The first four staves are complete with text and music; the next 2 $^1/_2$, where the copy breaks off, lack not only text
but also the semiminims, which remained to be filled in in red, as a separate operation, showing that it is not necessary to assume that one operation will be completed
before another is begun. (Sometimes it is evident from the even spacing of the musical notes that they were written first. The text was then supplied, with phrase corresponding to phrase, but with no attempt to convey syllable placement in more detail.
Such a copy cannot be expected to provide more information than it set out to. An
example from a manuscript comparable in neatness and calligraphic care to OH may
be found in Br 5557, f. 30^V, the triplum of Frye's Gloria *Flos regalis*.)

Syllabic text occupies more lateral space than the symbols that go with it, as anyone who has tried to copy syllabic monophony the other way round knows to his cost.
A more accurate placing of nearly syllabic text is possible when the text is written first
and the musical notes are placed above it. Our most precise evidence comes from passages or whole manuscripts that have been copied largely in this way. In copying the
text, the scribe would keep his eye on the music of his exemplar to enable him to assess
how much space to leave for a melisma. When he came to enter the musical notes
above the words, he might find that he had left too much or too little space at some
points, as in the examples given above.

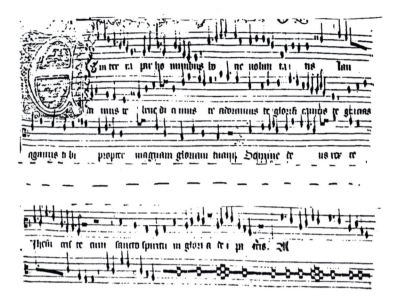

EXAMPLE I: OH, F. 12V, ROY HENRY, GLORIA

||296 Example I shows the OH scribe writing the text first, and allowing a little more space than necessary for the short melismas (*voluntatis*, lau*damus*, *tibi propter*), perhaps because he was thinking along with the music and equating musical time, rather than the number of symbols, with horizontal space. This was probably the first of the Glorias in *cantus collateralis* to be copied, and we can detect more finely calculated spacing in some of his presumably later work. A scribe who worked in this way for a fairly heavily texted Gloria might temporarily change his method when he came to a longer melisma. The OH scribe routinely did this for a melismatic Amen, leaving the syllable -*men* to be added after the music was copied, in order to be able to place it precisely. In some cases, including this, he forgot that he had not completed the texting, and the syllable was never entered. (Virginia Newes draws attention in her paper to *En ce gracieux tamps* by Senleches, in one source of which the "cocu" motive has been musically spaced in anticipation of text that was never entered; this was to have been the only texted passage in the triplum. It represents a further possibility for spatial organisation, but would not have been practical for entire texted voices.) When copying a melismatic Sanctus, where the music occupied more lateral space than the text, the OH scribe would ||297 write the music first in order to achieve a more accurate placing of the widely spaced syllables, changing either his order of work or his spacing to accommodate any more syllabic passages.*

One symbol or spacing device cannot serve two conflicting functions: modal notation cannot indicate both rhythm and syllabification by ligatures, hence the use of separate *cum* and *sine-littera* notations. Sometimes a slight space or a line end may serve as an intangible dot of division to indicate rhythmic groupings.[3] This often happens in passages where music was copied first, including melismas. On the other hand, if musical groups are broken at line ends while words are left intact, this may be a symptom that music was copied to fit previously copied text. There are many examples of this in OH, including ex. 2, where the line end falls at the end of the word *domine* but not at the end of the rhythmic group.

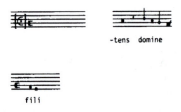

EXAMPLE 2: OH, F. 24V

Keeping his eye on the music of his exemplar while copying text may lead a scribe to leave a small space between syllables where a melisma, even of only two notes, occurs. If this happens with any consistency, showing that he was thinking the music while copying the text, we may have independent corroboration, in his text spacing, of his intended underlay, which may also be independently indicated by the musical spacing. Similarly, notes are placed closer together where [1298] they are to share a syllable.

EXAMPLE 3: OH, FF. 30V, 23V

Ex. 3 shows some examples of both. In *tu solus, domine,* and the first *spiritu,* there is no real obstacle to using alignment as a third means (in addition to textual and musical spacing) of indicating precise syllable distribution. But in cases like *unigenite* and the second *spiritu,* the musical gap signifying syllable change will fall sooner than the text gap signifying melisma. Underlay indicated by two separate acts of spacing may be even clearer than exact vertical alignment, and the two may indeed not be mutually compatible, as we see in this example. By involving two scribal acts, such evidence also has the advantage of being demonstrably purposeful.

Cum   sancto

EXAMPLE 4: OH, F. 21V

The underlay of example 4 is clearly indicated by musical spacing, as shown. It is one of a number of cases where the underlay could have been adjusted to avoid the sounding of a repeated note without a new syllable, but was not so adjusted. The inevitability of this feature in melismas as well as a significant incidence of examples such as this surely indicates that at least some musicians then did not object to it. Avoidance of untexted repeated notes cannot therefore be assumed as a primary criterion in editorial underlay.

With regard to syllable stress, the casual observer sees at once that there is a wide range of tolerance for how a word is construed musically. An examination of all settings in OH of the words *benedicimus* and *omnipotens* yields the unhelpful result that each syllable appears in a rhythmically strong position (i.e., on a first beat, and with a total note-value longer than that of its neighbours) in at least one setting. While macaronic carol texts may lead us to the ||299 general surmise that medieval Latin in England was pronounced with some of the characteristics of the vernacular (and similarly for other countries), there is clearly no consistent evidence in these musical settings for normal spoken Latin stress at this period. William Beare points out that medieval Latin was an artificial language, primarily for written communication, and that it cannot be expected to show consistent stress patterns because it was nobody's vernacular, also that "ancient theory knew no terminology but that of metric for describing the rhythmic value of words."[4] There is a strong danger that any attempts we may make to improve declamation, or even to identify the claims of word and verse accent, may be misguided. Elders seeks to demonstrate that Ciconia balances conflicts of word-ictus and verse-ictus, or that he makes conflicting metres correspond isorhythmically. He claims that, in addition to using rhythmic means to cancel out or compensate for accents that would otherwise offend against good declamation, Ciconia also makes such adjustments by means of high or low pitch, or of leading or subordinate voices.[5] Given the uncertainty and controversy that surround the nature of word-accent and metric stress, compounded by unknown regional and chronological variation, we should perhaps beware of assuming that such stresses were stronger than their authors perceived them to be. Our imperfect understanding of how Ciconia or the composers of OH perceived verbal stress may lead us all too easily to judge their declamation good or offensive in accordance with criteria to which we have given too strong a profile.

The OH scribe tends to place syllables on rather than between beats; ex. 7 (in O time) includes some rather rare exceptions (-*mus* of *adoramus*, *agimus*, the syncopated *magnam gloriam tuam*). In the next generation of English music there is a greatly increased use of O time with cross-beat sequential patterning, but the sources of that repertory are poor with respect to underlay.

||300

a) Gra - ti - as__ a - gi - mus__ ti - bi
b) Gra - ti - as____ a - gi - mus____ ti - bi

EXAMPLE 5: GLORIA, *QUEM MALIGNUS SPIRITUS*

Whether for ex. 5 one should follow the normal practice of OH, implemented as ex. 5a, or the rather solitary precedent provided by ex. 7 as the model for ex. 5b, is hard to say.

There seems to be no general rule, as there was in the sixteenth century, about how short a note may carry a syllable. The notational variety of OH, and the range of musical motion between pieces, are very considerable, and offer us examples of syllables on all note values, including the semiminim, as shown in ex. 6.[6] Syllables on minims are too common to warrant special comment.

EXAMPLE 6: OH, F. 63V

EXAMPLE 7: OH, F.13V, BYTTERING, GLORIA

One of the most difficult details for the editor is the handling of upbeats. Normally, when two syllables are available for the upbeat and its downbeat, one will be given to each (e.g. ex. 7, [301] _bone, domine deus rex, deus pater_; see also ex. I). Occasionally, however, an upbeat is left untexted, even when two syllables are available.[7] This usually happens when the preceding word ended with a vowel whose sound could be continued on the upbeat without awkwardness. When only one syllable is available at such a point, usually in melismatic passages, the OH scribe rather consistently places it under the upbeat if it is a new word, and under the downbeat if it is a syllable other than the first of a word.

EXAMPLE 8: OH, F. 95V, LEONEL, SANCTUS

Ex. 8 -_tus_ of the third _Sanctus_ and -_ri_- of _gloria_ <fall> on [302] the downbeat, while the new word _in_ after _Osanna_ is placed under the upbeat. (The same principle can be observed on OH f. 93[V].) There are of course exceptions, such as the _lau_- of _laudamus_ in ex. I, stave I, but these are in the minority.

Ex. 8 also shows the interruption of a number of words by rests, and not only
short rests. It would in fact be quite simple to rearrange the texting of this Sanctus in
such a way that no rests broke up a word, and had we less reason to trust this scribe,
such editorial adjustment would be tempting.[8] That the version we see here represents
not only the scribal but also the compositional intention is confirmed by the fact that
this part bears the plainsong whose intonation appears as Sanctus I. The underlay of
the polyphonic voice closely follows that of the slightly ornamented plainsong. Morley
complained in 1597:

> We must also take heed of seperating any part of a word from another by a rest, as som
> dunces have not slackt to do, yea one whose name is Iohannes Dunstaple (an ancient
> English author) hath not onlie devided the sentence, but in the verie middle of a
> word hath made two long rests . . .[9]

Dunstaple indeed permits himself such interruptions, though the Sanctus of ex.
8 is by Leonel. Also by Leonel is the *Ave regina* of which [1303] ex. 9 is the beginning of the
plainsong-bearing tenor (the middle part of an English discant setting). In this case,
the ligaturing and note-values of the polyphonic line, associated with the upper row
of underlay, prevent restoration of the plainsong underlay in this setting, given as the
lower row of text.

EXAMPLE 9: OH, F. 36, LEONEL, *Ave regina*

In both this Sanctus and antiphon by Leonel, the decision to follow or not to follow the plainsong underlay is a compositional one, and we should be alert to such
symptoms before making an editorial decision to restore plainsong underlay.[10]

In individual, texted voice-parts the main scribe of OH never forces us to break
the one-syllable-per-ligature rule.[11] The question whether untexted lower parts were
performed with text is too lengthy for consideration in this paper, but I will touch on
it briefly.[12] Several largely untexted lower parts in [1304] OH have small portions of precisely underlaid text, usually in shorter notes than are normal for that part, and often
while the uppermost voice is resting. Such passages often occur at points where that
text would otherwise be omitted (during a rest of the top part), or where the texted

fragment participates in an imitation. In a sense, the text they have is obvious, and an editor would be tempted to provide it anyway.[13] I am inclined to see these passages as supporting Harrison's case for vocal performance of tenor and contratenor parts in this repertory, but to what extent the parts might have been texted remains uncertain. For fully texted performance, ligatures and single notes would have to be split up into smaller rhythmic units—a task in which we, and perhaps also the medieval singer, could have used more guidance from the scribe or composer. The selection of obvious passages of special musical or textual importance for specific indications suggests to me that the composer (or scribe) wished to ensure that these would be properly texted, but was prepared to leave the remainder to the risk of mumbling, or at least very indeterminate texting, if any at all. Zacar's ubiquitous Gloria[14] appears in OH with a normally ligatured slow-moving contra. In all other sources the contra is split up into individual symbols and repeated notes to accommodate the trope *Gloria laus*. The high incidence $^{||305}$ of repeated notes strongly suggests that this trope was an afterthought to the original composition, but it may provide a pattern for the addition of full text to other lower parts. Reaney has discussed this problem, and cautiously raised the possibility that full texting of lower parts may be an Italian custom. A new Zacar fragment, which I have discussed elsewhere, adds some support to this suggestion.[15]

Text repetition is something which OH, like most manuscripts of sacred music until the late fifteenth century, gives us no encouragement whatsoever to attempt. The practice is of course common in Italian secular music, especially of the late trecento.[16] One example of "composed-in" intention to repeat a word in sacred music in the same voice is so unusual and striking that it deserves special mention. It concerns the word "pax" (see ex. 15) in Ciconia's well-known Gloria. This word is heard six or seven times; each individual part sings it two or three times. *Pax* was an inflammatory word in early fifteenth-century Italy. Marsilius of Padua's treatise *Defensor Pacis* (1324) has been likened to a Marxist manifesto of its time. It argued that the ruler is merely the delegate of the people, not the source of power, an idea already current in scholastic philosophy. Marsilius applied this also to the church, urging conciliar governance. This provided important arguments for conciliar action to end the schism. Ciconia's patron Zabarella was one of the main architects of the solution finally achieved at Constance; his *De Schismate* was completed by 1409. (Ciconia also composed a Gloria troped with a prayer for the end of the schism, *Suscipe trinitas*.) In the same year severe riots took place in Milan, with starving and oppressed mobs beseeching the despot Giovanni Maria Visconti for "pace." In quelling the riots, he ordered that the words *pace* and *guerra* not be uttered, on pain of the gallows, and required that the word *pax* in the Mass be replaced by *tranquillitas* (*dona nobis tranquillitatem!*). Given the well-founded and recently provoked Paduan hatred of the Visconti just prior to the Venetian conquest in 1405, is it going too $^{\parallel 306}$ far to see in Ciconia's unique insistence on this word something of the climate it stirred during his decade in Padua, connotations such as the word "freedom" had for Beethoven and Verdi 400 years later?[17]

We have observed already that we cannot hope to find consistent stress patterns in different settings of the $^{\parallel 307}$ same text within the same repertory, or even in different voices of the same composition. But a special case of applying different music to the same text is that of music notated in score, and the OH scribe here provides us with a very interesting piece of performance testimony. Much of the English discant repertory so notated is unrelievedly homophonic, with most non-syllabic underlay closely circumscribed by ligatures. The musical alignment of these copies is often not perfect, sometimes because of the exigencies of ligatures to be aligned with separate symbols or of a more space-consuming figured upper part. Most cases of "bad" alignment that defy such practical explanation occur where the syllables do not fall simultaneously in the three parts; the notes do, however, appear above the correct syllables. In other words, staggered alignment occurs, too often for coincidence, in passages where the music itself is not strictly homophonic. This method of texting was designed for three singers, each applying a single line of text to his own musical line; the score alignment was never intended for a visual acrobat to play at the keyboard, and I believe that this evidence overrides Ann Besser Scott's hypothesis of organ performance.[18]

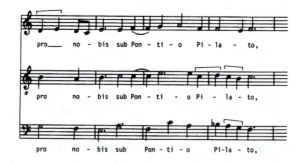

EXAMPLE 10: OH, F. 50V

[1308] Ex. 10 shows a short passage in facsimile and transcription in which *Pontio Pi-* do not coincide musically, though the MS aligns notes with text. Even more signifi- cant is [1309] ex. 11, the only instance in this scribe's work where a line end (marked by a dotted line in the transcription) does not fall at the same point musically in the three parts. It is, however, correct for the text. Even without this help, it would be impossi- ble to set the text in such a way that more words sounded simultaneously. The choice is still circumscribed, but the graphic [1310] presentation gives us very clear evidence of its vocal purpose. The alignment of notes with syllables, which I have marked on the fac- simile, is still not perfect, but it is much closer than the musical alignment, it can be explained by the extra space required by the middle part, and the intention is clear.

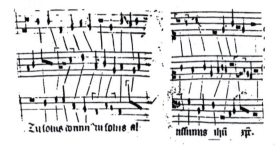

EXAMPLE 11: OH, F. 4

If this evidence was drawn from an example involving different music set to the same text, the converse, different text set to the same music, has much to teach us and offers even more opportunity than we have had so far for distinguishing compositional from scribal decisions. Musical repetition to a different text is of course a feature of secular *formes fixes* and is less common in sacred repertory. Examples within the latter include a Ciconia Gloria (ex. 12), containing a large-scale musical repeat. The repeat of the lower parts is not written out but indicated by a double text incipit. The top part is rhythmically adapted to the second half of the Gloria text which, being prose, lacks exact symmetries that could be duplicated to identical music. The different syllable count and word divisions result in different ligaturing and splitting up of unisons, requiring the repeat to be written out in full. Ciconia likes not to split words, and he or his editor here gives priority to keeping both words and musical sequences locally intact, rather than maintaining an exact long-range musical identity.

Do - mi - ne   De - us,   rex ce-le-stis,   De - us Pa-ter   om - ni po-tens

Quo - ni - am   tu   so-lus san - ctus   tu   so - lus   Do - mi - nus

EXAMPLE 12: CICONIA, GLORIA, *PMFC* XXIV NO. 8

Imitations are not always as exact textually as they are musically. Even where both parts have the same text, the musical impulse for the imitation frequently overrides that of textual exactness, even in free composition where the composer could easily have arranged it otherwise.

Ox : Nunc plau - dat cor - de*
Q15: Nunc plau-dat cor** - de   sup - pli - ci

Nunc plau-dat** cor - de sup-pli - ci

(* LINE END IN Ox, ** LINE END IN Q15)
EXAMPLE 13: CICONIA, *O FELIX TEMPLUM*, *PMFC* XXIV NO. 12

||311 Ex. 13, from Ciconia's *O felix templum*, with its exact imitation of music but not of text, could be matched many times over from a wide range of early-15th-century repertory; in this case, the underlay is confirmed by manuscript line ends. Some of the canonic Glorias and Credos in OH include passages of telescoped text, with a double row of underlay to the same music. In these cases, enough notes are always

provided for the longer of the two texts. Bi-textual motets may also include imitation of differently texted passages; Ciconia does not seem to engage in imitation to any lesser degree in such pieces. This suggests that textual matching took rather low priority in imitation, where rhythm, and then melody, usually rated much higher.

The case of different text to the same rhythm of course embraces isorhythm, and most of the remainder of my paper will be concerned with some observations about isorhythmic motets. Because of their inherent constraints, they afford a unique opportunity for isolating deliberate compositional intent, difficult otherwise to distinguish from scribal editing. Pieces for which we could confidently match separately transmitted text and music are exceedingly rare at this period. The English repertory of the 14th century does have some such cases, including the topmost part of *Patrie pacis,* given complete as ex. 14.

EXAMPLE 14: CGC 512/543 (TRIPLUM; SEE RISM B IV[1] P. 468)

‖312 The determining constraint here is not isorhythm, but the discipline of strict alternation of groups of two and three notes in a strictly syllabic setting of an irregular poem. Four 16-syllable units, separated by rests, are followed by a textually irregular (and perhaps textually corrupt) coda. The entire text fits the music like a hand in a glove, and the purposefulness of the melodic and rhythmic shaping leaves no doubt that it is a compositional rather than an editorial act. This piece could certainly stand the test of re-uniting text and music, hypothetically separated in transmission. Such a high level of syllabic correspondence is characteristic of the English 14th-century repertory. But not all such pieces can be so explained. Another example might at first sight appear to the Ciconia Gloria already cited (ex. 15: where music differs, Q15 has stems up, Tr stems down).

EXAMPLE 15: CICONIA, GLORIA, *PMFC* XXIV NO. 1

||313 Had we only one of the two sources, it would be tempting to see its texting as compositionally determined, even though it lacks the decisive discipline of ex. 14. The fact that we have two sources which differ not only in text placement but in the associated rhythms suggests that each scribe has given his own realisation of a much less explicit blueprint, and that Ciconia himself may not have prescribed every detail of rhythmicisation at the points of variance.

A different case of scribal interpretation is offered by the group of pieces added later to OH which, I have argued elsewhere, are as close to autographs as we can hope to find in this period. Although they lack the ||314 polish and regularity of professional scribal work, they convey musical intelligence. The intention for underlay can usually be inferred, but its expression is unclear graphically. In addition, we have professional copies of three of these pieces, which were evidently made from the OH autographs. These professional copies realise, much more precisely, the textual intentions of the autographs, and introduce some clarifications at the initiative of the later scribe.[19]

Syllabic text-setting can often be assumed to be compositional, but is open to some question when there is no corroborative constraint. I suspect that similar scribal editing may sometimes account for strings of declamatory repeated notes such as we often find near the beginning of Gloria settings (e.g., ex. 7, *benedicimus*).[20] Whether the composer or the scribe arranged such details, it seems fairly apparent that they were among the last to be attended to in the process of composition and writing down, perhaps leaving room for initiatives by scribes or performers that were required to a much greater extent in the case of lower parts. The consistent evidence of detailed and careful prescription in upper parts, on the one hand, and the absence of detailed provision for lower parts, on the other, constitute such a glaring discrepancy that it is hard to believe that composers and scribes expected these parts to be texted in performance with the same detailed focus as upper parts. This does not preclude either vocal performance or some *ad hoc* application of text.

Most Latin-texted isorhythmic motets use texts that are regularly patterned, either in respect of syllable count or of metre, usually arranged in couplets or in stanzas. Important observations about such texts in Machaut's motets and those of the Chantilly repertory have been made by Reichert, Ziino, and Günther.[21] The [|315] act of combining isorhythm and text form forces the composer to make certain choices; to identify these may offer us valuable insights into how he balanced the claims of music and text.

Our only specific theoretical authority for the role of text in motet composition comes from Egidius, who tells us that, after picking the tenor according to the proposed subject matter, the music is composed, apparently without consideration of the text. Finally, the words are to be divided into four, the music likewise, and the words fitted as well as may be. He gives no hint that the composer is expected to tailor the structural divisions of the one to the other, nor that the choice of text or of musical specifics should take the other component into consideration. Many motets with a low ratio of syllables to notes fail to show such close linkage, and remind one of Egidius's "aliquando est necesse extendere multas notas super pauca verba"—which is not much help to the modern editor.[22]

The converse of this procedure is that demonstrated very convincingly by Günther.[23] In some cases it can be shown that the composer took the text into account in writing the music. A striking example is *Sub Arturo plebs*, where the statement of the diminution and the composer's name are built into the duplum text, and where considerations of accent and rhyme together with extensive syllabic treatment lead her to argue that the text was written by the composer, before the music, and [|316] was in his consciousness as he composed.[24] Sometimes it is possible to demonstrate that the text strongly conditioned the musical planning, whether the text was newly written or pre-existent. I shall try to show how some larger concerns are implicit in detailed symptoms.

Motets or motet sections with syllabic or nearly syllabic treatment help to establish for that composer or repertory the range of tolerance with regard to declamation, placing of rests within words or phrases, handling of upbeats, etc. We have already made a distinction between "composed-in" syllabic writing (e.g., ex. 14, *Patrie pacis*) and pieces where such details may have been arranged *post facto* (ex. 15, Ciconia Gloria, Byttering Gloria). The presence of isorhythm in the upper parts usually provides strong evidence of compositional control of such syllabic writing. Ziino has discussed some examples from Machaut, and I would cite his example of M 18 as a good instance of even more detailed compositional planning than he discusses, with regard to the placing of rests.[25] The third and fourth colores differ from the preceding in being fully isorhythmic (except for minor irregularities in the triplum) and in coinciding with a change of stanza structure in the texts of both upper parts (triplum, v. 5, motetus, v. 3). As Ziino points out, the verse structures of both texted parts match the talee of the music. In addition, the triplum has rests at poetic line ends, and also to mark off the two monosyllables which fall at the same point in the second line of each half-stanza (*vis ut*, *que est*, *et cum*, *huic rex*); nowhere else. This surely indicates even more strongly than the near-syllabic nature of the setting that Machaut fashioned this part with close awareness of the text. Similar treatment is given to the monosyllables in the first line of each half-stanza of the motetus; in this case, however, the position of [317] the monosyllable in the line is not quite regular, even though there are sometimes two monosyllables. It would not have been possible to arrange for a monosyllable to be set off by rests *and* for the underlay to be identical for each talea.[26] I think we have here an explanation for the syllable displacement pointed out by Ziino, which Machaut also took advantage of in setting *Elegit* at the beginning of the talea, not as an upbeat to it. *Elegit* could not start earlier without disturbing the pattern, previously established, of providing musical rhyme for stanza ends up to that point.

Similar testimony, from the relationship between rests and word breaks, comes from the isolated surviving triplum part of a motet in OH, *Carbunculus ignitus lilie*, for Thomas of Canterbury.

EXAMPLE 16: OH, NO. 143

```
I

Car-bun-cu-lus ig-ni-tus li-li-e /   flam-mas vi-brans lu-cis      ex-i-mi-e / no-ctis la-te-bris
gem-ma ra-di-ans Can-tu-a-ri-e /    or-bis ju-bar ju-gis        me-mo-ri-e / Tho-mas ce-li-ce
cla-ri-ta-tis cu-ius e-gre-gi-e /    splen-dor ve-ra   nor-ma   jus-ti-ci-e / se-det spe-cu-lum

    ful-gor An-gli-e / lu-cer-na      de-co-ris ec-cle-si-e /
    si-dus pa-tri-e / vir-tu-te       ru-ti-lans con-stan-ci-e /
    con-sci-en-ci-e / sed his  qui    cle-ro pre-sunt ho-di-e /
```

II

En	pro-pter Chri-sti te -	sti-mo - ni - um /	ec - cle-si - e quo-que ze -	lum pi-um/du - rum	fa-sti-gi-um
tam coq - na - ci -	o - nis quam pro-pri-um /	fert e - qua-ni-mi - ter ex -	i - li-um/pre - cum	pro-hi-bi-tum
pro-pter in - ju - ri - a -	rum te - di - um /	do - nec in - ge-ni - tri-cis gre-mi-um/sper-sum	dans ce-re-brum

ob - pro-bri-um /	ar - chi pre - sul men-tis ab - sin-thi - um /
suf-fra-gi - um /	nus-quam a - ni - mum red-dens va - ri - um /
per gla-di - um /	sic com - ples-set mar-tir mar - ti - ri - um /

III

Sed hec re - pro-bo - rum ne - qui-ci-a /	co-mi-tans san-cti	de - si-de - ri-a /	men-su-ra	pro-pter
e - ya mul - ti-pli-cant ce - le-sti-a /	ma-gni-fi - ca - tur	quo le-ti-ci-a /	qui di-gna	me - ri -
re - por-tans in san-cto-rum glo-ri-a /for-tis a - go - nis	pro vi-cto-ri-a /	ce - li-ca	co - ro -

| tem-po-ra - li - a / |
| to-rum pre-mi - a / |
| na-tur cu - ri - a / |

EXAMPLE 16: CONTINUED

[11318] Ex. 16 shows the rhythm and text of the entire piece in diagrammatic form. In colores 1 and 2 each of the three talea statements has 4 x 10-syllable lines with no regular accentual pattern and no regular caesura. In color 3 each of the three statements has only 3 x 10-syllable lines. The resulting 33-line poem lends itself to analysis neither in stanzas nor in couplets. A change of rhyming disyllable coincides only with the beginning of each color: 12 lines end -ie, 12 -ium, 9 -ia. Even without more detailed examination, this can be claimed as a text written or adapted for the specific purposes of this musical composition.

The musical structure is 3 x 12 breves for each color, the three colores being respectively in ⊙, ₵, and C, i.e., reducing in a ratio of 9:6:4. The musical setting is completely syllabic and completely regular in its coincidence of syllables and isorhythm. The decasyllabic text lines have no regularly placed caesura. Two text lines in each of the first two colores and one in the third are run on without a rest, despite the word break between lines (/). Two coincident word breaks in the first color <shown by arrows> are also not marked by a musical rest, apparently to permit the rhythmic sequences. Otherwise, not a single opportunity has been missed to observe a coincident word break by supplying a musical rest. No words are broken by rests; this is carefully and deliberately arranged, and can by no standards be claimed as accidental. It shows careful [11319] planning of rhythms and rests by the composer on a custom-made text (whether written by him or for him). At the same time, he was tailoring the pitches of these same rhythms to the harmonic scheme imposed by his pre-selected (and alas unknown) plainsong tenor, and by the isorhythmic layout he had set for it, each color with a number of notes divisible by three. Such control of all details could only have been achieved by attention to their claims at all stages of the composition, and shows an approach very different from the *laissez-faire* of Egidius.[27]

Another piece from a different repertory raises entirely different questions of concern and planning. In Ciconia's *Albane misse celitus,* as in all his motets, the tenor appears to be freely composed to fit the other parts, so that the additional tonal discipline of a pre-existent tenor does not come into play. Like all of Ciconia's isorhythmic motets, this falls into two symmetrical, rhythmically identical halves. There is no diminution. Each of the upper voices has a different text but of equal length and syllable count. It is an occasional piece written presumably for the installation of Albane Michiel as bishop of Padua in 1406. Both parts begin with *Albane.* The second text incorporates Ciconia's name in such a way as to affect the rhyme scheme and syllable count. For all these reasons the text can be assumed to have been written by or expressly for him. Each text consists of four sextains (887 887) with some trochaic-iambic variation. If the verse-lines are to show "in principle" (as Elders puts it) "an equal number of syllables," some lines have to be treated as corrupt, while other metrical irregularities can be explained by elision. Each text is divided equally ||320 between the rhythmically identical halves of the piece, two of the four sextains each, for each voice. The details of the text setting, however, show striking variation between passages which should correspond metrically and isorhythmically, very different from the faithful matching of my previous example. They indicate that Ciconia set the text without observing the elisions necessary for a correct syllable count, and that he, or an editor realising his intentions in detail, was working with the further irregularities of the received text, given here without emendation of any kind, either metrical, syntactic, or for sense. (The handling of supernumerary syllables in other pieces has been discussed in the papers of Professors Baumann and Von Fischer.) If the corruption is blamed on the transmission, and the adjustments explained as editorial, then they intrude far into the compositional domain and, because of the isorhythm, cannot be dismissed as merely local adjustments.

a

1.4-5	cu - i de - so-la-te pe-ni - tus /	con-fer me - del - lam pro-ti - nus /
3.4-5	con - stans le-ni do-mi-na - ris /	ve - ra lau-de___ pre - di - ca - ris /

b

2.4-5	auf-fer quit-quid est a - ni-ma - rum /	ni-chil si-nas es-se ma-ni - tum /
4.4-5	Mi - cha - el, o stir - pe cla - rus /	ti-bi an-ti - stes da-ti-um ana-rus /

EXAMPLE 17: CICONIA, *ALBANE MISSE CELITUS*, PMFC XXIV NO. 16

Ex. 17 a shows lines 4 and 5 of sextains I and 3, respectively, with their corresponding isorhythmic settings. Note that the prevailing metre in stanza I is iambic, in stanza 3 trochaic. *Cui* is treated metrically as a monosyllable, musically as two syllables.[28]

||321 Possibly in order to stress the penultimate of the line (*dominaris*), and certainly in order to keep words intact (note the placing of rests for *medellam protinus, laude predicaris*), the corresponding passages of text are differently distributed at the isorhythmic repeat. Ciconia always provides enough notes, in the correct relationship to rests, to allow for such rearrangements, and must to some extent have anticipated them, since not all can be explained as last-minute adjustments of surface detail, as might *desolate, dominaris*. Ex. 17b, also from *Albane*, includes apparently corrupt hypersyllabic lines which require some emendation both on grounds of metre and sense. But the careful manuscript underlay of the unique source, the number of notes provided, the ligature on *stirpe*, the placing of rests so as not to interrupt words, leave little doubt that this "corrupt" text was indeed the one Ciconia was working with.

Before we dismiss this as barbarism, we should consider certain points. Ciconia gave his name to a learned if derivatory treatise* and had close contact with an important circle of early humanism. The poet was at least a close associate, if not Ciconia himself, who was sufficiently surrounded by highly educated men to be saved from making, not just one but many times over, anything they would have considered to be crass, elementary blunders. We may have to assume that the concerns of the composer did not at all points coincide with those of the poet, and that he was free to impose musical patterning on a text quite independently of its verse form. In any text there may be strong conflicts between the word accent (where definable) and the metric accent (if any). Instead of committing itself to [322] and resolving this conflict by underscoring one or the other, might a musical setting not elect to follow quite different criteria? Ciconia seems deliberately to reject word accent <and> metric accent as determinants of musical rhythm by choosing to set lines of opposite accent to the same musical rhythm in *Albane* and *Petrum Marcello*. Lines which are metrically equal are, conversely, not given equal music; once this licence has been taken, and musical shaping given priority over that of poetic metre, a few extra syllables will make little difference to how the poem is perceived through the musical clothing. If Ciconia was indeed as rhetoric-conscious as Elders suggests, he would surely have sought his *varietas* by means precisely such as those just enumerated.

We do have occasional glimpses of his other concerns. In *Ut te per omnes*, he so arranges things that *Franciscus* and *Francisce* coincide in the two differently texted parts so as to form a string of imitations featuring the name, quite as emphatic as the *pax* of his Gloria. In the other Gloria I have referred to (ex. 12), where not merely rhythms but notes are duplicated in the second half, he so arranges the prose text that the words *Jesu Christe* occur at corresponding places, i.e., with the same music. In *Petrum Marcello* he goes against the isorhythmic symmetry by setting the text to the music in such a way that the word *Marcello* (again, a proper name) is given emphasis by falling at the rhythmically corresponding place, even though it does not occur at the same point in the text line.

| Pe | - | - | - | - | trum | Mar-cel-lo | Ve | - | ne - | tum |
| Stirps | lit | - | - | te | - | ris | Mar - | cel - li | - | na |

EXAMPLE 18: CICONIA, *PETRUM MARCELLO VENETUM*, PMFC XXIV NO. 18

Observations such as these permit some very imperfect and tentative gropings towards the concerns that determined Ciconia's priorities in setting up patterns or deviating from them.

Ciconia's motets stand apart from the tradition represented by Machaut-Dunstaple in that they have equal amounts of equal-metred text (equal but for some iambic-trochaic reversals, as we have seen) for each of [323] two equal-ranged cantus voices. The transition from the 14th to the 15th century brought with it important changes in the relative weighting of triplum and motetus parts in the mainstream French-English tradition. The indexes of Trémoïlle and Machaut A list pieces by motetus, as do most fourteenth-century theorists. Carapetyan's Florentine vernacular treatise of c. 1400, English chronicles relating to the early 15th century and the index of ModB list them by tripla: this symptomises a change in thinking. The "less important" but higher-ranged 14th-century triplum usually had more text than the motetus which gave its name to the composition (and in the case of *Sub Arturo plebs*, more trivial text, listing names of contemporaries, than the motetus with its timeless worthies). In Dunstaple's motets, only one has an equal amount of text in the two parts, and most adopt the 14th-century balance. Like Machaut's usual practice and unlike Ciconia's, Dunstaple prefers, but does not confine himself to, different metres for the two voices.[29] Also unlike Ciconia, Dunstaple uses a diminution pattern over three sections for all his regular isorhythmic motets, which makes Ciconia's procedure of matching corresponding text to corresponding music (albeit with "strophic" variation) inapplicable. Dunstaple's more complex musical structure would lead us to expect that it is given higher priority than the detailed considerations of text setting that engaged Ciconia, and indeed this seems to be so. There are, however, some points of interest which sharpen the comparison between the two composers.

Also unlike Ciconia, Dunstaple makes some use of known texts. In all such cases, he uses the text complete, a discipline which is not necessarily compatible with arranging stanza divisions to coincide with the main divisions of a musical isorhythmic structure subject to diminution. The triplum of *Veni sancte spiritus a* 4 uses all five of the double stanzas of the sequence. A text so structured does not readily lend itself to proportioned distribution with synchronised joins over ||324 an isorhythmic scheme of any of the normal ratios. Dunstaple here uses a 3:2:1 reduction, with two talee to each color statement. He distributes the triplum text so that the first color takes five, the second three, and the third two half-stanzas. While the main color statements therefore coincide with half-stanza divisions, only in the final color do the half-stanzas coincide with the talea divisions. This shows more careful planning than we sometimes find in situations where, in accordance with Egidius, the text distribution has been left until last; however, it cannot be claimed here that the text exerted any organic shaping influence upon the rhythmic or structural organisation of the motet.[30]

That Dunstaple did not simply distribute a given text over a composition as Egidius recommends is shown by two cases where a text, although used in its entirety, was too short for his needs; *Gaude felix Anna* (no. 27) uses the known sequence text complete, and then continues with an unknown text which differs in both metre and rhyme scheme. In *Ave regina celorum* (no. 24) the sequence text is used in both upper parts. The triplum has double stanzas 1-3 until halfway through the final color, while the duplum has stanza 4—one half-stanza for each of the first two color statements. The remaining text of both upper parts is taken from stanzas 1 and 8 of the sequence *Ave mundi spes Maria*, whose melody forms the tenor of the motet. Dunstaple does not seem to have used this opportunity to bring about a tidier alignment of textual and musical divisions: indeed, he seems studiedly to have papered over the joins.[31]

[325] Exceptional is *Salve scema sanctitatis* (no. 30), Dunstaple's only motet with the same amount of text in both upper parts. The texts are alike in metre and rhyme scheme; however, unless some text has been omitted, they are not cut from a single poem, because the chain-rhyme is not continuous between them. The text is distributed in the proportion 3:2:1 over the three colores, which are also thus musically proportioned. *Dies dignus decorari* (no. 26) and *Preco preheminencie* (no. 29) also have a proportioned distribution of text: 6:4:2 couplets in voice I and 3:2:1 in voice II. Their texts are likewise not known from elsewhere, and the pairs in each case match in alliterative technique and in metre. While *Preco preheminencie* is composed musically in the proportions 3:2:1, Dunstaple chose, perhaps perversely, to compose *Dies dignus* in the proportions 6:4:3. Thus, while the sectional joins coincide, he fails in the latter case to exploit the opportunity to match textual and musical proportions.[32]

He thus shows a considerable range from indifference to commitment in his matching of textual and musical structure and in proportioning texts to each other and to the music. His care for local detail and local effect is less developed than Ciconia's. Like some but not all OH composers he sometimes tolerates the interruption of words by rests. At least in his motets, Dunstaple gives us less syllabic writing and less imitation than Ciconia, and does not exploit textual coincidence or proper names. He had, however, undertaken a much more disciplined musical structure, with pre-existent cantus firmus, restatement of colores in diminution, talea repetition in all parts within each color, and occasional additional refinements, all of which place the musical priorities higher in relation to the text than in Ciconia's motets, in all [326] of which the second half is an undiminished rhythmic duplicate of the first. Both composers allow different aspects of their texts to shape their musical decisions and at different levels of detail.

We can observe certain deliberate acts, by composer or scribe, at large-scale or at detailed levels. To draw other than tentative or local conclusions from these is premature at the present stage of work. Some of the few I have offered are iconoclastic, negative, or cautionary. But I submit that it is enquiries along such lines that we need, and I believe that, if we are prepared to put aside our ingrained preconceptions about how text and music should fit together, there is some room for optimism that such study can be placed on a more secure basis in future. I hope it is clear that I see this as a necessary preliminary to any attempt to evaluate in detail the aesthetic, rhetorical, or other significance of the composer's approach to his text.

Commentary

to passages marked by asterisks in text; see also the Introduction.

p. 277   The implications of discerning the order of copying text and music are subsequently developed in Lawrence M. Earp 1983 and in Jonathan King 1996.

p. 293   This characterisation of course needs revision now that the treatise has been published, ed. Oliver B. Ellsworth 1993.

NOTES

* From *Musik und Text in der Mehrstimmigkeit des 14. und 15. Jahrhunderts: Vorträge des Gastsymposions in der Herzog August Bibliothek Wolfenbüttel, 8. bis 12. September 1980*, ed. Ursula Günther and Ludwig Finscher. Göttinger Musikwissenschaftliche Arbeiten 10 (Kassel: Bärenreiter, 1984), 291–326.

1. Manuscript *sigla* used in this paper are as follows:
     OH: The Old Hall Manuscript, now British Library, Add. 57950.
     Q 15: Bologna, Civico Museo Bibliografico Musicale, MS Q 15.
     Tr: Trento, Museo Provinciale d'Arte (ex Museo Nazionale), MS 87.
     Ox: Oxford, Bodleian Library, MS Canonici misc. 213.
     BU: Bologna, Biblioteca Universitaria MS 2216.
     CGC: Cambridge, Gonville and Caius College, MS 512/543, see RISM B IV 1, pp. 468–71.
     Kras: Warsaw, National Library, MS III. 8054, olim Krasinski 52.
     Br 5557: Brussels, Bibliothèque royale, MS 5557.
     Machaut A: Paris, Bibliothèque nationale, f. fr. 1584.
     ModB: Modena, Biblioteca Estense, MS alpha X.1.11.
     Trémoïlle: see RISM B IV 2, p. 205; now Paris, Bibliothèque nationale, n. a. f. 23190.
Much of the ensuing discussion of texting procedures in OH is adapted from my unpublished dissertation, *The Old Hall Manuscript: A Paleographical Study* (Cambridge University, Ph.D. 1969), pp. 111–28, q.v. for further details.
2. See, for example, f. 17. Facsimile in J. F. R. and C. Stainer, *Dufay and His Contemporaries* (London, 1898), plate 1.
3. For an example, see Machaut A, facsimiles in W. Apel, *The Notation of Polyphonic Music 900–1600* (Cambridge, Mass, 4/1953), plates 68, 69.
4. *Latin Verse and European Song* (London, 1957), pp. 194, 289, and *passim*.
5. Willem Elders, "Humanism and Early-Renaissance Music," in: *TVNM* 27 (1977): 65–101.
6. Technically, and possibly for this reason, these are void minims rather than semiminims. Void notation is applied in this piece to various note-levels to encode duple proportion.
7. There are two possibilities for the interpretation of *benedicimus* in ex. 1. Either it is an exception to this principle, as the alignment would suggest, and *be-* takes the downbeat, or alternatively, the slight space in the text after *bene-* might be taken as indicative of a melisma of two notes, leaving *be-* for the upbeat.
8. It appears that in this piece the scribe wrote words or music first according to whether the passage was melismatic or syllabic, thus ensuring good alignment.
     Extensive treatment of this subject is now to be found in Lawrence M. Earp, *Scribal Practice, Manuscript Production and the Transmission of Music in Late Medieval France: The Manuscripts of Guillaume de Machaut* (Princeton University, Ph.D. dissertation, 1983), chapter 3.

9. Thomas Morley, *A Plaine and Easie Introduction to Practicall Musicke* (London, 1597),p. 178.

10. I think we have too little evidence as yet to justify the restoration of original text to the tenors of English cyclic masses and isorhythmic motets. Many of these are so obscure that it is doubtful if contemporaries could have been expected to supply them, and the process often involves disturbing the ligatures. For the texting of lower parts in masses by Dufay see Alejandro Enrique Planchart, "Guillaume Dufay's Masses: A View of the Manuscript Traditions," in: *Papers Read at the Dufay Quincentenary Conference*, ed. Allan W. Atlas (New York 1976), pp. 26–60, and an expanded statement of the same point by Gareth R. K. Curtis, "Brussels, Bibliothèque Royale MS. 5557, and the Texting of Dufay's *Ecce ancilla Domini* and *Ave regina coelorum* Masses," in: *AMl* 51 (1979): 73–86.

11. Only three of his ligatures have to be split between two syllables; all occur in homophonic-syllabic compositions notated in score, with the text under the lowest voice. All are by one composer, Chirbury, and may reflect some anomaly of his personal usage.

12. In addition to the articles cited in n. 10, the following have dealt with this problem: Gilbert Reaney, "Text Underlay in Early Fifteenth-Century Musical Manuscripts," in *Essays in Musicology in Honor of Dragan Plamenac*, ed. Gustave Reese and Robert J. Snow (Pittsburgh 1969), pp. 245–51; Frank Ll. Harrison, "Tradition and Innovation in Instrumental Usage 1100–1450," in: *Aspects of Medieval and Renaissance Music: A Birthday Offering to Gustave Reese*, ed. Jan LaRue (New York 1966), pp. 319–35.

For important recent contributions to the question of vocal versus instrumental performance of lower parts, see D. Fallows, "Specific Information on the Ensembles for Composed Polyphony 1400–1474," in *Studies in the Performance of Late Medieval Music*, ed. S. Boorman (Cambridge 1983), pp. 109–59, and C. Page, "The Performance of Songs in Medieval France," in *Early Music* 10 (1982): 441–50.

13. A later example may be found in the Offertory, *Domine Jesu Christe*, of Ockeghem's Requiem, where the duet of the lower voices, vividly symbolic of the words *de poenis inferni et de profundo lacu*, is untexted in the only source. See *Johannes Ockeghem, Collected Works*, vol. II, ed. Dragan Plamenac (n.p., American Musicological Society 2/1966), p. 94 and pl. XIII.

14. Published in *The Old Hall Manuscript*, ed. A. Hughes and M. Bent (n.p., American Institute of Musicology, 1969–73), vol. I, no. 33, and in *Early Fifteenth-Century Music*, CMM 11, vol. VI, ed. G. Reaney (n.p., American Institute of Musicology 1977), no. 16.

15. Trento, Biblioteca Comunale, MS 1563; "New Sacred Polyphonic Fragments of the Early Quattrocento," in: *Studi Musicali* 9 (1980): 171–89. Reaney's discussion is in the article cited in note 12 (1980).

16. There are striking examples in Ciconia's ballate *O rosa bella*, *Ligiadra donna*, and the setting of *Merce o morte* in BU (p. 101) which may also be by him.

17. This suggestion is based on reading in secondary sources, including Denys Hay, *The Church in Italy in the Fifteenth Century* (Cambridge 1977), p. 82 and notes; R. N. Swanson, *Universities, Academics, and the Great Schism* (Cambridge 1979), p. 51 (for bibliography on Marsilius); S. Clercx, *Johannes Ciconia: Un musicien liégeois et son temps* (Brussels 1960) vol. I, for some basic bibliography on Paduan history in the first decade of the 15th century.

The presence in the Padua fragments of two admittedly much older motets for Luchino Visconti, both with acrostics and both possibly by Jacopo da Bologna, might weaken the case for reading the Ciconia setting as an anti-Visconti gesture; the dating of these fragments is still uncertain.

See vol. II, no. 21 (pp. 98–101) for Clercx's edition of this Gloria, of which my version appears as no. 1 in *The Works of Johannes Ciconia*, ed. Margaret Bent and Anne Hallmark, PMFC XXIV (Monaco, Editions de l'Oiseau-Lyre 1984). The only comparable treatment of the word *pax* is in Zacar's Gloria Anglicana (no. 20 in Reaney's edition *CMM* 11, VI). Here, however, no voice utters *pax* more than once, though the word is heard three times if text is applied to all voices. Rather more common in mass settings of the period is the setting of *pax* to a long note. Ursula Günther has pointed out an instance in Ciconia's above-mentioned Gloria *Suscipe trinitas* the word "pax" in the trope text is set to a longa with fermata, in: *Quelques remarques sur des feuillets récemment découverts à Grottaferrata*, in *L'Ars Nova Italiana del Trecento* III (Certaldo 1970), p. 349. She presents identification, dating and parallel transcriptions of three sources of this Gloria on pp. 342–49, 383–97, with facsimiles of I-GR 197 as plates VI–VIII. Mirosław Perz has also published this Gloria in facsimile and transcription from PL-Wn 373 in *Antiquitates Musicae in Polonia: Sources of Polyphony Up to c. 1500*, vol. XIII pp. 152–55, and vol. XIV, pp. 449–57 (Warsaw: Warsaw University Press [1973, 1976]). It <is> no. 7 in the edition of Ciconia's works PMFC XXIV.

18. "The Performance of the Old Hall Descant Settings," *MQ* 56 (1970): 14–26.

19. Margaret Bent, "Sources of the Old Hall Music," in *Proceedings of the Royal Musical Association* 94 (1967–68): 19–35, and "A Lost English Choirbook of the 15th Century," in *International Musicological Society: Report of the Eleventh Congress, Copenhagen 1972* (Copenhagen 1974), pp. 257–62.

20. See also Dunstaple's Credo, no. 5 in *John Dunstable, Complete Works*, ed. M. F. Bukofzer, Musica Britannica VIII (London 1953, rev. 1970).

21. G. Reichert, "Das Verhältnis zwischen musikalischer und textlicher Struktur in den Motetten Machauts," *AfMw* 13 (1956): 197–216; A. Ziino, "Isoritmia musicale e tradizione metrica mediolatina nei motetti di Guillaume de Machaut," in *Medioevo Romanzo* 5 (1978): 438–65; U. Günther, "Das Wort-Ton-Problem bei Motetten des späten 14. Jahrhunderts," in *Festschrift Heinrich Besseler*, (Leipzig 1962), pp. 163–78.

22. Coussemaker, *Scriptores* III, pp. 124–28.

23. Günther, *op. cit.*, note 21. She observes (p. 164) that the diminution section of *Pictagore* is "offenbar wegen seiner hoquetierenden Stimmführung—untextiert überliefert und zweifellos instrumental auszuführen". Other motets, including her next example *Rex Karole*, and Machaut's motet 18 cited below, show that hocket sections did not deter all composers from supplying text. The final section of motetus text is omitted from Dunstaple's *Gaude felix Anna* (*Complete Works*, no. 27) in its sole source, but being a known text it can easily be supplied and was clearly intended.

24. Günther, *op. cit.*, pp. 167–74. See also her edition and commentary in *The Motets of the Manuscripts Chantilly, Musée Condé 564 (olim 1047) and Modena, Biblioteca estense, alpha M.5.24 (olim lat. 568)*, CMM 39 (n. p., American Institute of Musicology 1965), no. 12. (No. 6 of this edition, *Alpha vibrans*, also has untexted hocket.) For another edition with an arguably preferable solution to the final color see ed. Frank Ll. Harrison, *PMFC*, vol. V (Monaco, Editions de L'Oiseau-Lyre 1968), no. 31.

25. Ziino, *op. cit.*, note 21; see also *Guillaume de Machaut, Musikalische Werke*, vol. II, ed. Friedrich Ludwig (Leipzig 1929/1954), pp. 65–67.

26. The texts of both voices are given by Ziino, *loc. cit.* Stanzas 3 and 4 of the motetus are as follows (/ marks the beginning of a talea; the monosyllable which is set off by rests is underlined):

3a.	/Elegit <u>te</u>, vas honestum,	3b.	De/quo nichil <u>sit</u> egestum
	Vas insigne,		Nisi digne.
4a.	De/dit te, <u>vas</u> speciale	4b.	De/dit te <u>vas</u> generale
	Sibi regi;		Suo gregi.

27. This motet is no. 143 in *The Old Hall Manuscript*, CMM 46, ed. A. Hughes and M. Bent. OH no. 146, *Are post libamina* by Mayshuet, on the other hand, shows no signs of such planning. There is no correspondence between poetic lines and musical structure, and its few rests are placed without regard to splitting words. OH no. 112, *Alma proles* by Cooke, a second-layer addition, is a motet constructed with a 9:6:4 reduction. The two texts have different metrical schemes (lines of 7, 6 and 7, 7, 7 syllables); the lines are proportioned as nearly as possible to the isorhythm and to each other, voice I 10:6:4, voice II 5:3:2. The details of MS underlay do not exactly coincide but could be made to do so.

28. See the editions by M. J. Connolly of Ciconia's Latin texts in *PMFC* 24. His suggested emendations, on grounds of sense and poetic metre, are as follows for the passages used in ex. 17:

constans lenis dominaris;

auffer quidquid est avarum, nichil sinas esse amarum;

antistes dantium gnarus.

Acceptance of these affects this example only for *animarum/ avarum*, where it can still be maintained that at least the Q 15 scribe was working with the corrupt text. If *amarum* is accepted for *manitum*, the syllable count is not affected because the rest prevents musical implementation of the poetic elision made possible by the vowel. Elders, *loc. cit.*, (note 5), pp. 86–88 cites part of this passage to make a slightly different point. In discussing *Ut te per omnes* he assumes that the two texts are a single unit that has been cut in half. In view of the coordination of *Albane-Albane*, *Marcello-Marcellino* and *Franciscus-Francisce*, we should consider the possibility that these texts were written as pairs.

29. The two texted voices have the same metre in no. 23 (hexameters), nos. 26 and 29 (alliterative), no. 30 (chain-rhymed) as well as in no. 32 where voice II is a "trope" upon the well-known sequence text of voice I. Nos. 24, 25, 27, 28, including most of the already-known texts, all have different poetic metres in the two voices. A more detailed review of voice-designation practices in the 14th-century motet has

since been given by Earp, *op. cit.*, (n. 649), pp. 65–67.

30. This motet is not to be confused with Dunstaple's three-part motet on a tenor which is to be read also in inversion and cancrizans, which distributes the *Veni sancte spiritus* text in telescoped fashion between the two upper voices: no. 33 in the *Complete Works*. The four-part motet discussed here is subject to a further discipline self-imposed by the composer, in that the triplum paraphrases the *Veni creator* hymn of the tenor whenever the tenor is silent. This and other aspects of the motets are discussed in my monograph *Dunstaple* (London 1981), chapter IV.

31. Some local tidying up can be effected editorially, but in cases where there is no detectable, purposeful plan to adjust to, extensive rearrangement seems unjustified. The classic French-English isorhythmic motet, as represented by Machaut to Dunstaple, lends itself more naturally to musically and textually overlapped seams than does Ciconia's non-reducing strophic form. *Petrum Marcello* is Ciconia's only motet with reduction, but the reduction occurs within each of the two rhythmically identical halves of the motet and does not therefore require the composer to combine equal verses with an overall diminishing musical structure.

32. In no. 23, *Albanus roseo rutilat*, written in hexameters that are possibly an adaptation by Wheathampstead from a rhymed office by Bede. The poetic lines are neither synchronised with the colores nor proportioned as the music.

Chapter II

Resfacta and *Cantare Super Librum**

These terms were first used by Tinctoris and are paired only by him. To judge by scholarly reiteration from Coussemaker to the present day, it seems that few have found cause to question the definition of *resfacta* as written composition and of *cantare super librum* as improvisation on a given tenor.[1] Ernest T. Ferand, the scholar who has investigated this area more exhaustively than anyone else, pointed out apparent self-contradictions in Tinctoris that led him to propose two irreconcilable and contrasting pairs of definitions:

> [*Resfacta*] may mean either a written contrapuntal composition, plain or florid, as distinguished from improvised counterpoint, again either simple or florid; or it may mean florid, in contradistinction to simple, counterpoint, whether written or improvised—depending on which Tinctoris we believe, the author of the *Ars contrapuncti* or that of the *Diffinitorium*.[2]

||372 Ferand sought to explain this undoubtedly thorny matter by invoking theorists writing around 1500 and later;[3] while illuminating both the subsequent career of the term *resfacta* and of the procedures he had with some hindsight applied to the pair of terms, these explanations do little to explain what Tinctoris meant by them. This paper seeks to demonstrate that the riddle can be solved on Tinctoris's own ground, and that while Ferand rightly recognized that a problem exists, his own presumptions kept him from making the right diagnosis and solution. Definitions published since his article have continued to promulgate the older written-versus-improvised distinction, often without mentioning, let alone resolving, those statements of Tinctoris that led Ferand to his secondary, conflicting definition.

The passage central to any interpretation is the following, offered here with a parallel translation that is intended to be as neutral and literal as possible:[4]

Tinctoris, *Liber de arte contrapuncti* (1477), II.xx

1. Quod tam simplex quam diminutus contrapunctus dupliciter fit, hoc est scripto vel mente, et in quo resfacta a contrapuncto differt.

1. [Chapter heading:] That counterpoint, both simple and diminished, is made in two ways, that is, in writing or in the mind, and how *resfacta* differs from counterpoint.

2. Porro tam simplex quam diminutus contrapunctus dupliciter fit, hoc est aut scripto aut mente.

2. Furthermore, counterpoint, both simple and diminished, is made in two ways, that is, either in writing or in the mind.

3. Contrapunctus qui scripto fit communiter resfacta nominatur.

3. Counterpoint that is written is commonly called *resfacta.*

4. At istum quem mentaliter conficimus absolute contrapunctum |373 vocamus, et hunc qui faciunt super librum cantare vulgariter dicuntur.

4. But that which we make together mentally we call counterpoint in |373 the absolute [sense], and they who do this are vulgarly said to sing upon the book.

5. In hoc autem resfacta a contrapuncto potissimum differt, quod omnes partes reifacte sive tres sive quatuor sive plures sint, sibi mutuo obligentur, ita quod ordo lexque concordantiarum cuiuslibet partis erga singulas et omnes observari debeat, ut satis patet in hoc exemplo quinque partium existenti, quarumquidem partium tres primo, deinde quatuor ac postremo omnes quinque concinunt:

5. However, *resfacta* differs importantly from counterpoint in this [respect], that all the parts [= voices] of a *resfacta,* be they three, four, or more, are mutually obliged to each other, so that the order and law of concords of any part may be observed with respect to one and all [others], as is amply evident in this example in five parts, of which first three sound [= sing] together, then four, then finally all five:

[example omitted here]

6. Sed duobus aut tribus, quatuor aut pluribus super librum concinentibus alter alteri non subiicitur.

6. But with two or three, four or more singing together upon the book, one is not subject to the other.

7. Enimvero cuilibet eorum circa ea, que ad legem ordinationemque concordantiarum pertinent, tenori consonare sufficit.

7. For indeed, it suffices that any of them [each?] be consonant with the tenor in those [matters] that pertain to the law and ordering of concords.

8. Non tamen vituperabile immo plurimum laudabile censeo si concinentes similitudinem assumptionis ordinationisque concordantiarum inter se prudenter evitaverint.

8. I do not however judge it blameworthy but rather very laudable if those singing together should prudently avoid similarity between each other in the choice and ordering of concords.

9. Sic enim concentum eorum multo repletiorem suavioremque efficient.

9. Thus indeed they shall make their singing together much more full and suave.

It is this chapter that has led to the written-versus-improvised distinction subscribed to by all writers including Ferand. While he expressed concern that the evidence of the *Diffinitorium* (which we shall consider shortly) failed to support it, he did not question the imposition of that distinction upon the passage just quoted.[5] My first [374] and most important claim is that this chapter, taken alone, does not require us to assume that improvisation is being discussed; on the contrary, in the context of the treatise as a whole, as well as of the evidence from the *Diffinitorium,* it forces us to assume that Tinctoris meant something rather different. We shall have occasion to qualify the received definition of *resfacta* as *written* composition, but it is the equation of *cantare super librum* with improvisation that forces upon the pair of terms a contrast that is in turn at the root of the problem of reconciling the apparent conflicts between Tinctoris's statements.

Our understanding of "improvisation" includes the notion of spontaneous, unpremeditated music-making: "The art of performing music spontaneously without the aid of manuscript, sketches, or memory."[6] However we might wish to qualify this widely accepted definition, and for all the careful distinctions made by Ferand himself,[7] few of those who have echoed the "improvisatory" definition of *cantare super librum* seem to have felt any discomfort about implying a spontaneous process. One who has is Klaus-Jürgen Sachs, who acknowledges the problem but does not solve it:

> [Counterpoint] can be extemporized (*mente*) or written down (*scripto*). But Tinctoris
> called the improvised form "straightforward" (*absolute*) counterpoint (or *super librum*
> *cantare*), and the written form *res facta* or *cantus compositus*. . . . This terminology—unknown
> before Tinctoris and used afterwards only with reference to him—should not be taken to
> imply that the aim of the theory of counterpoint was improvisation. Tinctoris seems to
> have wanted to emphasize something else: that, particularly in composition for more
> than two voices, the result of all improvisation relating several parts contrapuntally to a
> given tenor . . . differs from carefully planned composition; the inevitable lack of strict-
> ness in improvisation is a concession, not the aim of counterpoint.[8]

[375] As Sachs says, and as Tinctoris clearly states, counterpoint must be carefully thought out; this is not inconsistent with *mente*, a word which cannot be opposed to "written" in such a way as to suggest that lack of forethought is more excusable in unwritten than in written presentation. This is a presumption more readily made in our writing-dependent culture than in that of the fifteenth century.

Indeed, there is little in the vocabulary of music theory before 1500 to encourage "improvisatory" interpretations of words such as "mental" and "singing." Even the word "improvisus" is rarely used, and does not in all instances denote desirably spontaneous performance.[9]

We shall see that Tinctoris's rules for sung counterpoint (*cantare super librum*) require careful forethought and, moreover, that there are no signs of "concession" to an "inevitable lack of strictness" in those rules, but rather the reverse. It is hard to imagine that Tinctoris would have dignified as "counterpoint in the absolute sense" a haphazard procedure that would mock the very principles his treatise is devoted to setting out. Tinctoris defines counterpoint thus:

> Contrapunctus itaque est moderatus ac rationabilis concentus per positionem unius
> vocis contra aliam effectus, diciturque contrapunctus a contra et punctus (*C* I.i.3).

> Counterpoint, therefore, is a moderated and rational sounding together, effected by
> the placing of one sound against another, and it is called counterpoint from "con-
> tra" and "punctus."

[376] To understand singing, or at least sounding together, as an essential stage both in the making of counterpoint and also in the realization of polyphonic music, carries with it two linked presumptions, neither of which is widely recognized:

1.   There is no evidence that fifteenth-century composers used scores in the process of composition. A composer could work out his ideas, and/or realize his mental conceptions, by communicating the successively conceived parts, either orally or in writing, to singers who then substituted for the function of a written score by providing aural, not visual, control over the simultaneities. I develop elsewhere the claim that late-medieval notation, with respect to both pitch and rhythm, was conceptually unsuited for use in score; that where it was used in score (as in keyboard notations) it had to be adapted for the use of a single reader; and that, had late-medieval notation been habitually used in score as a vehicle for composition, it would have changed sooner than it did to a system of unit rather than contextual reference, for both mensuration and pitch.[10] In other words, composers neither had ‖377 nor needed the visual control of simultaneities that modern scores give us.

2.   The singer's task was to apply his contrapuntal training to producing sounds that correctly realized the intentions of the written notation. Sharps and flats have become essentials of our notational system, even though we continue to call the symbols accidentals. It is clear from practice and theory that we cannot regard late-medieval "failure" to notate all the accidentals we need as a failure by *their* standards; not to notate them was not to misnotate musical pitch. The signs of *musica ficta* were truly "accidental" in late-medieval notation. The singer did not add accidentals omitted by the composer or scribe to notes presumed "white" unless otherwise indicated; rather, he had to apply the rules of counterpoint (often, as with Tinctoris, directed explicitly to both composers and singers) to the achieving of correct progressions and correct intervals, "operating *musica ficta*" where necessary. To sing music from written notation required knowledge of the same rules of measure and consonance that would have governed music devised in the singer's own head. In both cases, he had to listen to what was going on and to use his knowledge of counterpoint in order to respond and adjust to what he heard. The singer thus neither merely sang the written notes nor departed from them, but, using them as a starting point, he applied his knowledge of counterpoint and *musica ficta*, familiarity with the piece gained in rehearsal, experience of the style, and aural judgment, to the end of making the music sound correctly.[11] His role was not only vocal but mental; he was an active partner with ‖378 the composer in the realization of a written composition and an active participant in the creation of new counterpoint. Both activities required the same background of skills and experience, and similar planning and rehearsal.

Our heavy dependence on writing as a means of preserving and transmitting music, serving us as a substitute for both memory and aural control, should not blind us to the possibility of music fully or sufficiently conceived but nevertheless unwritten. This possibility would hold no surprise for musicologists working in earlier or in geographically more remote fields. To remove the presumption of improvisation from this passage in Tinctoris is to present unwritten and written composition or counterpoint as stages in a continuous line of endeavor, based on the same training, rather than as the separate elements implied by our written-versus-improvised antithesis. Tinctoris's *aut scripto aut mente* then emerges as an expression of the possible ways, neither opposed nor mutually exclusive, of preserving music from one performance to another, performance being the end product, the sounding goal, of music, however transmitted. Vocal performance is necessary for counterpoint to happen, either as the realization of what has been written, or as the creation of that which bypasses written storage. Writing is necessary only if transient sounds are to be permanently recorded.

Tinctoris tells us in *C* II.xx (p. 302 above):

  (a) that *resfacta* differs from counterpoint (.1) in the way the parts are mutually related (.5);

  (b) that counterpoint may be written or mental (.1, .2);

  (c) that written counterpoint is commonly called *resfacta* (.3).

Here lies the apparent conflict: if *resfacta* differs from counterpoint, which may be written or mental, how can written or indeed any kind of counterpoint be equated with *resfacta*? Clearly, it is not the fact of being written that distinguishes *resfacta* from counterpoint, since counterpoint can also be written! Rather, it is common usage that (improperly) applies to written counterpoint the term *resfacta,* which, properly used, distinguishes the way the parts relate with respect to mutual consonance. "Counterpoint which is made in writing is *commonly called resfacta*" (.3) stands in evident distinction to "that which *we* make together mentally *we* call counterpoint absolutely" [379] (.4), which in turn is distanced from its immediate continuation, "and those who do it are *vulgarly* said to sing upon the book." The first and last statements are third person passive, qualified by *communiter* or *vulgariter,* while the second has the authority of the first person and no qualification about common usage. Since Tinctoris uses both terms elsewhere in *C* he cannot have objected to them altogether; he is merely insisting on precise usage and fine distinctions.

Here now are the relevant terms in the *Diffinitorium:*

CANTUS est multitudo ex unisonis constituta qui aut simplex aut compositus est.

CANTUS SIMPLEX est ille qui sine ulla relatione simpliciter constituitur, et hic est planus aut figuratus.

CANTUS SIMPLEX PLANUS est qui simplicibus notis incerti valoris simpliciter est constitutus, cuius modi est gregorianus.

CANTUS SIMPLEX FIGURATUS est qui figuris notarum certi valoris simpliciter efficitur.

CANTUS COMPOSITUS est ille qui per relationem notarum unius partis ad alteram multipliciter est editus qui resfacta vulgariter appellatur.

COMPOSITOR est alicuius novi cantus editor.

CONTRAPUNCTUS est cantus per positionem unius vocis contra aliam punctuatim effectus; et hic est duplex: scilicet simplex et diminutus.

CONTRAPUNCTUS SIMPLEX est dum nota vocis, que contra aliam ponitur, est eiusdem valoris cum illa.

CONTRAPUNCTUS DIMINUTUS est dum plures note contra unam per proportionem equalitatis aut inequalitatis ponuntur, qui a quibusdam floridus nominatur.

CONTRATENOR est pars illa cantus compositi que principaliter contra tenorem facta inferior est supremo, altior autem aut equalis aut etiam ipso tenore inferior.

RESFACTA idem est quod cantus compositus.

TENOR est cuiusque cantus compositi fundamentum relationis.

(The definitions will not be translated here but paraphrased as appropriate in what follows.)

Anyone looking up *resfacta* in Tinctoris's dictionary is simply referred to *cantus compositus*, which in turn is said to be characterized by a "multiple relationship of the notes of one part to another" ("counterpoint" does not appear). The *resfacta* entry is in effect a cross-reference. In defining the standard term *cantus compositus*, Tinctoris adds *vulgariter* when offering its informal equivalent *resfacta*. Moreover his use of *resfacta* in *C* indicates that he finds it a serviceable ||380 synonym for *cantus compositus* (albeit "vulgar"), just as he likewise uses *cantare super librum* despite the "vulgar" qualification given it in II.xx.4. On the other hand, *communiter* is applied to a definition from which Tinctoris distances himself and which he does not use: that of *resfacta* as written counterpoint (II.xx.3).[12]

The distinction lies not between written and unwritten music but between composition and counterpoint. Writing does not figure in the definition of *cantus compositus* or of what a *compositor* does (*D*); though we might presume that it is a normal if not necessary feature of composition, it is not one that Tinctoris chooses to bring into his pedantic distinction, and it will not help our understanding of it if we do so. We have argued above, following Tinctoris, that music may be "put together mentally" without being written down. *Resfacta* is neither necessarily written, nor is it the same as counterpoint, though both confusions are "common." We may therefore redefine it minimally as composition, usually but not necessarily written. Thus to lose both "written" and "improvised" as the essential distinguishing features of *resfacta* and *cantare super librum* removes the opposition that has been imposed upon them and leaves us free to examine the minimum qualifications of each, how they may depart from those, and how the apparent contradictions may be reconciled.

Let us now consider the definitions offered by Tinctoris (in *D*) that led Ferand to propose an alternative pair of meanings aligned respectively with florid and simple counterpoint. Tinctoris observes a distinction between counterpoint and composition: *resfacta* is equated with *cantus compositus*, not with *contrapunctus diminutus*, and there is no common ground of definition between these latter terms. "*Cantus compositus* is that which has been produced by the relating of the notes of one part to [those of] another in multiple ways, vulgarly called *resfacta*." (Use elsewhere by Tinctoris of the terminology of multiple note relationships strongly suggests that mensural relationships are meant here.) "*Contrapunctus diminutus* is when several notes are placed against one in equal or unequal proportion, called by some florid." In neither of these definitions is there any explicit reference to the arrangement, or law and order, of consonances, which forms the basis [138] of Tinctoris's distinction between *resfacta* and counterpoint in *C* II.xx.5. It seems that, in order to have a more complete definition of both terms, we should add the primarily concord-based distinctions of *C* to the apparently mensural ones of *D*. Composition is characterized by mutual relationships between the parts with respect to consonance (*C*) and by multiple relationships between the parts with respect to mensuration (*D*), and is commonly known as *resfacta*. Singers of counterpoint are (minimally) required to adjust only to the tenor with respect to consonance (*C* II.xx.6–7), and counterpoint is concerned with a mensural relationship of two voices at a time (*D*). (This does not necessarily mean that the rules for counterpoint are less rigorous than those for composition, as will appear below.) The distinction may seem fine to us but was sufficiently meaningful for Tinctoris to evoke his "important distinction" between *resfacta* (= *cantus compositus*) and counterpoint. Thus Ferand's equation of *resfacta* with florid *counterpoint* has no basis, and especially not his assumption of a complementary negative definition of *cantare super librum* as simple counterpoint.

Further support for the present interpretation of Tinctoris's use of *resfacta* and *cantare super librum* can be drawn from their occurrence at several points throughout the Counterpoint treatise. The terms are usually paired, and when there is a substitution it is clearly intended as a close synonym. Thus for *resfacta* we also find *cantus compositus* (as in *D*), and hence *compositio, compositor, componere*; for *super librum cantare* or *cantare super librum* we find *concinere, canere* substituted for the verb, also *cantatio, cantantes, concinentes, concentus*; *contrapunctus* is substituted for the whole phrase or rather as the noun expressing the result of that singing (e.g., "when many sing upon the book in order to diversify the counterpoint" [III.iv.4], or the fourth and its octaves "are not used in counterpoint unless many are singing upon the book" [I.v.6, I.x.10, I.xv.6]).[13]

As we have seen, Tinctoris's definition of counterpoint gives prominence to the singing or sounding together of parts.[14] This is the end product of counterpoint, whether simple or florid, and whether [382] made and stored in writing or in the mind. It seems fitting, therefore, that "singing on the book" should be associated with the definition of counterpoint in the absolute sense. But while, as we have also seen, there are several synonyms for *cantare*, the only related nouns are *cantatio* and *concentus, cantantes*, or *concinentes*, never "*cantus*"—i.e., the singers or the act of singing, not the resulting song. *D* is devoted to nouns, such as *resfacta, cantus*, and *contrapunctus*. *C* is devoted to the technique that forms the basis both for sung counterpoint and for composition (III.ix; see n. 20), but the actual doing of counterpoint (*cantare super librum*) did not evoke a dictionary entry from Tinctoris.[15]

According to the *Diffinitorium*, *cantus* may be *simplex* (*planus* or *figuratus*) or *compositus*. The definition of *cantus compositus* in terms of its multiple relationships leaves us with the suspicion that the hierarchy of *cantus* subsets here is incomplete. In *C* I.v.8 we find *cantus quem faubourdon vocant*, and yet the relationships of fauxbourdon do not seem to qualify as multiple either in terms of mensuration or of consonances. *Contrapunctus est cantus . . .* (*D*): this cannot be *cantus simplex*, whose definitions are patently monophonic, and it cannot be *cantus compositus = resfacta* because that differs from counterpoint, and because at least *contrapunctus simplex* excludes the "multiple relationships" of *cantus compositus*. Counterpoint is a kind of *cantus* that is neither *simplex* nor *compositus* but has its own subdivisions (*simplex* or *diminutus*). The study of counterpoint is the foundation both for singing *super librum* (counterpoint in the absolute sense) and for composition (*C* III.viii, III.ix; see n. 22, n. 20). While those singing *super librum* are minimally required to adjust only to one other voice at a time (the tenor), the results are judged better if they do take account of more than one other part, either in avoiding similar successions or in adding counterpoint to two or more existing parts (*C* II.xx.5–9, II.xxii.4–6 [see n. 27], I.vii, xii, xvii [see n. 16]). In this respect, counterpoint is considered more laudable the more closely it approaches the mutual adjustments of composition. No wonder Tinctoris had trouble expressing this in his hierarchy of definitions and avoided doing so. Figure I attempts to conflate the complementary testimony of *D* and *C*.

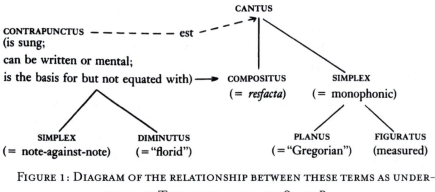

FIGURE 1: DIAGRAM OF THE RELATIONSHIP BETWEEN THESE TERMS AS UNDER-
STOOD BY TINCTORIS; BASED ON *C* AND *D*

Even though counterpoint may be put together mentally, the definition in *C*
II.xx.1–2 allows it to be written down. We have [383] already argued that *resfacta* is not
distinguished from *cantare super librum* = counterpoint by being written as opposed to
unwritten. Further support for this comes from the written examples, in the treatise,
of counterpoint and *cantare super librum,* as well as of *resfacta.*

EXAMPLE I: TINCTORIS, *LIBER DE ARTE CONTRAPUNCTI,* I.X.11

Many of the music examples are undesignated and lack voice labels; but in construing them we can rely on Tinctoris's general statement (*C* I.ii.38) that void notes
represent the tenor, filled notes the *contrapunctus.* These examples are unmeasured, and
are intended as a neutral basis for either simple (measured but equal notes) or diminished (florid) counterpoint. They are an abstraction, corresponding to no kind of
counterpoint recognized by Tinctoris: unmeasured counterpoint is not a possibility.
Some of the examples are referred to in the surrounding text as *contrapunctus* (e.g., I.x;
see Ex. I and n. 18), or as what happens when singing *super librum.* When Tinctoris is
specifically illustrating *contrapunctus simplex* or *diminutus,* the examples are given in appropriately measured form (II.xix, xxi–xxii). Many of the longer examples of counterpoint have the voice labels tenor and *contrapunctus.* Most examples that are either
specified as illustrating *contrapunctus,* or can be so construed from the distinction
between void and filled notes, are *a* 2. Exceptions are the tenor with two *contrapuncti*

(III.iv) and the examples of a *contrapunctus* added to a tenor-contratenor pair (to be discussed below).

All examples described in *C* as *resfacta* are measured. Most are *a* 3; the only exceptions are two-voiced excerpts from pieces known or suspected to have been in three or more parts,[16] and the one five-part [I384] piece in II.xx. Voice-labeling, where present, is so consistently differentiated for counterpoint and *resfacta*—counterpoint having a tenor and *contrapunctus* (two *contrapunctus* parts in III.iv), *resfacta* having supremum (in one case discantus and in some, no label), tenor, and contratenor (three contratenors for the five-part piece in II.xx)—that undesignated music examples can confidently be diagnosed as counterpoint or *resfacta* by their voice names, if they have them.[17] (III.v, for instance, has one example of each.) All measured examples of *resfacta* and counterpoint are in a constant number of parts throughout. They are descriptive of choices that have been made between alternatives. Abstract possibilities for interval successions have been realized. They differ in that respect from the unmeasured examples, but it is not possible to draw Tinctoris's line between composition and counterpoint on grounds of written or unwritten, measured or florid. Many of the unmeasured counterpoint examples are written for a changing number of parts. They are prescriptive of possibilities, choices between some of which may have been left open.

That does not mean, however, that all options are available interchangeably. In some cases, notably the clear and thorough demonstrations of the use of the interval of the fourth and its octaves, it is shown that the vertical fourth (the altus part in the penultimate, fermata-marked chord in Example I) can only be used when it is the last, fourth part to be added to these progressions.[18] The singer must [I385] already know the existing three-part structure before he can determine whether a fourth above the tenor on the penultimate note will be made possible by the sounding of a fifth below it. The example does not introduce this altus-function part until the penultimate note; we have just argued that it is not an alternative to any of the other parts. In the final, five-part chord, the *a* and *f* might be regarded as alternatives to each other, but neither is interchangeable with any of the other voices. In other words, this example and the similar ones in I.v and I.xv begin in three parts, expanding at the end to either four or five; in that sense they are abstract with respect to their pitches as well as to their unmeasured presentation. However, the unlabeled, unmeasured examples are extremely varied in what they illustrate. In the examples discussed above, all four parts of the penultimate "chord" are essential to the illustration. In other cases, often apparently involving a progression from a two- to a three-part chord, only one at a time of the latter (black) notes should sound with the tenor (void); see examples 2a–c. The same applies to the five- and six-part combinations in III.i, which show the impossibility of combining, for example, both a fifth and a sixth above the same tenor note, or the corresponding notes below it; see example 2d.[19]

(a) I.iii.18   (b) I.vii.11   (c) I.xii.16   (d) III.i

EXAMPLE 2: TINCTORIS, *LIBER DE ARTE CONTRAPUNCTI*

[||386] Tinctoris urges diligent application to and an early start in the study of counterpoint.[20] Several statements call for art and practice in order to achieve the more "laudable" counterpoint already alluded to in II.xx.8–9 (see above) and further described as *tanto laudabilior quanto difficilior* in II.xxii.6 (see n. 27). At no point is there any suggestion that singing *super librum* may be any less rigorous than composition, except in the distinguishing feature that allows *contrapuncti* to accord only with the tenor and not necessarily with each other. More licenses are granted to *resfacta* than to counterpoint.[21] A famous passage lists devices (proportions, syncopations, imitations) that apply both to composition and to singing on the book; it also prescribes that more such means of diversification should be used in a mass than in a motet, and more in a motet than in a cantilena, with the clear implication that there is no distinction between *cantare super librum* and *resfacta* in these respects.[22] Tinctoris goes on to list [||387] compositions by well-known composers as examples of *resfacta* that show the desired variety and as additional illustrations of the rules he had demonstrated through models of his own devising.[23]

All of these observations point clearly to the conclusion that singing *super librum* is a carefully structured procedure in which only one part at a time can be added to what is already worked out, whether written or not. It is a far cry from the unpremeditated, collective improvisation we have been led to understand by modern writers. The "mutual obligation" of the parts in *resfacta* almost suggests that we might find here a statement about simultaneous conception, fifty years earlier than the first unequivocal testimony to this way of composing in Aron's *Toscanello*;[24] however, none of Tinctoris's examples of *resfacta* gives us a good justification for claiming that they have broken with the successive principles that so clearly apply to his "pure" counterpoint.

Because of the successive nature of counterpoint, it follows that the references to "many" singing *super librum* (e.g., I.v.6, I.x.10 [see n. 18], I.xv.6, III.i.7 [see n. 19]) must be interpreted modestly. Because account must always be taken of what has already been decided, the addition of a new strand presumes the agreement of singers among themselves if there are more than one to a part. The distinction between *resfacta* and *cantare super librum* seems at no point to depend on the total number of parts.[25]

Many of the examples in the treatise show a wide vertical spacing between parts, especially in discussion of the larger intervals, such as [||388] we rarely find in surviving compositions. It is clear from their context, however, that we cannot treat these as features of counterpoint as distinct from composition.[26] Having established that *cantare super librum* alias counterpoint requires advance planning and preparation of a kind that disqualifies it from being improvised in the normal sense, and having eliminated questions of genre, range, and number of voices as differentiating features, it remains to explore how much closer we can get to defining it and its relationship to *resfacta*.

Although "we put together mentally" counterpoint that may be "either written or mental," the presence of a book is central to *cantare super librum*. Clearly the book contained written music, but of what kind? Tinctoris mentions counterpoint *super planum cantum* (III.vii.2) and says elsewhere that the tenor may be *planus aut figuratus* (II.xxi.7–8).

Although in *D* "Tenor" is only defined as the foundation of *cantus compositus*, it is clear from many passages in *C* that the tenor that provides the basis for counterpoint may or may not be derived from *resfacta*. That the book upon which the singers sang might contain not merely chant, not only tenors taken from polyphony, but complete polyphonic compositions is suggested at several points in *C*. "And there are some, albeit rarely, who sing together not only upon the tenor but also upon any other part of the *resfacta*."[27] Here is confirmation that counterpoint was sometimes made upon tenors of *resfacta* of which other parts were also available. If Tinctoris meant that another part was used *instead* of the tenor, it is hard to understand why he should consider it "more laudable and difficult," and if only [1389] one voice was used, there would have been little reason to note that it was derived from *resfacta*. We have seen confirmation elsewhere that counterpoint could be constructed over the two-part framework of tenor and contratenor of *resfacta*.[28]

The present discussion has been deliberately confined to Tinctoris's own testimony, with few glances over the shoulder at arguments based by others upon the foundations here questioned. It does, however, seem appropriate to introduce the highly interesting documentation assembled by Craig Wright for the practice of singing *super librum* at Cambrai Cathedral, where Tinctoris had been a vicar for four months in 1460 under Dufay's administration.[29] Of Wright's three pre-1500 references, the first, from 1485, mentions that the *magister cantus*—a post filled at that time by none other than Jacob Obrecht—was to teach the art of singing on the book; Wright speculates whether "the musical style of this improvised polyphony had an influence on his written counterpoint." A provision of 1493 that a vicar "assist [singing] on the book in descant" confirms that, at least in this instance, polyphony is intended. Wright wonders whether "the phrase *cantare super librum* might be construed to mean to sight-sing out of a music book in a general sense" in addition to its "specific import" at this time, the improvisatory interpretation of Tinctoris. In fact, none of Wright's documents appears to require the assumption that new counterpoint was being made: the singers might well have been reading from the music. It is only Tinctoris who forces us to assume that, at least sometimes, singing on the book lies towards the creative rather than the reproductive end of what I here propose was a continuum.

Counterpoint was put together successively, as the instructions for the use of vertical fourths show (I.v, x, xv; see above). It might therefore make little difference whether a fourth successive part was added to a newly conceived three-part structure or to an older *resfacta*. It is presumably at this very time that three-part songs of the Franco-Burgundian repertory were being provided with the added altus parts [39] with which Petrucci printed them. The singers who worked out such added parts must have known and performed the compositions as written in their book as well as, and indeed as preparation for, making their added counterpoint. Since counterpoint could be written they presumably, on occasion, wrote down their additions to existing pieces, or their new pieces, thus creating new *resfacta*—whether in the proper or common sense might be very hard to judge. Surely it is precisely in such a manner that families of compositions arose, based on the tenor, or on the original tenor and descant, or even on a combinative *quodlibet,* for pieces such as "Fors seulement" and "De tous biens plaine."

The "important difference" between *resfacta* and *cantare super librum* is that the parts of *resfacta* are "mutually obliged" with respect to the law and ordering of consonances, while the minimum requirement for *cantare super librum* is that each voice be consonant with the tenor, not needing to be subject to other voices. Having made the distinction of principle, Tinctoris goes on to say that it is better if singers upon the book do in fact arrange among themselves to avoid similar successions of consonances, that their singing may be sweeter (II.xx.8).

Since he only gives one example of florid *counterpoint* in more than two parts (III.iv), and since this seems to meet his highest standards of mutual obligation, his own works do not provide us with ready material to illustrate how the difference might be detected. Indeed, that example employs a leap *instar quodammodo compositorum* (as used by composers). The result of constructing a *contrapunctus* over a composed tenor and contratenor would probably defy classification as either counterpoint or composition, further suggesting that the difference is more important in principle and procedure than in the result. When counterpoint exceeds its minimum requirements and takes account of parts other than the tenor, it clearly approaches the definition of composition, and in so doing "requires more science and practice, is more difficult and more laudable."[30] It is in this sense that the study and practice of counterpoint may be seen as approaches to composition, in which the practice of *cantare super librum* aspires to the achievement of *resfacta.*

If the singers were seen to be reading from a book containing polyphony—possibly the very book from which they had just performed a *cantus compositus*, a *resfacta*; if they were heard to be obeying [||391] the laws of counterpoint in their adjustments at least to the tenor; and if, moreover, they were mutually adjusting by Tinctoris's highest standards and were well prepared, how would even the most discerning listener have been able to tell whether they were realizing a written composition by someone else or performing a new piece of their own invention and preparation? Small wonder that written counterpoint was commonly confused with *cantus compositus*. The difference between *remfactam cantare* and *super remfactam cantare*—singing the music from the book or singing upon the music—might have been imperceptible and insignificant, even in Cambrai.

In sum, *resfacta* is composition, usually but not necessarily written, a completed piece resulting from application of, and choices between, the rules of counterpoint. The successive construction of those parts will still usually be perceptible in the finished product. *Cantare super librum* is the singing of counterpoint, following strict rules of interval combinations in relation to a tenor and, with experience and skill, to other pre-existing parts as well. It requires careful, successive preparation. *Resfacta* and singing *super librum* therefore differ but do not contrast in principle, and indeed their results may be so close together as to defy diagnosis. Tinctoris can no longer be regarded as an authority for improvisatory practices, and several assumptions about the nature of early improvisation will need to be re-examined. As is often the case, the revision of an accepted view involves not its reversal but a recognition of the subtler dimensions of the problem.

Notes

* From: *Journal of the American Musicological Society* 36 (1983), pp. 371-91. This paper is dedicated to Kurt von Fischer; a shorter version was read to the Schweizerische Musikforschende Gesellschaft in May 1983 at a colloquium honoring his 70th birthday, and published as "*Resfacta und Cantare super librum,*" in *Schweizer Jahrbuch für Musikwissenschaft/Annales Suisses de Musicologie*, n. s. 3 (1983), 47–52.

1. This article adopts the single-word form *resfacta* found for most occurrences in the Tinctoris manuscripts at Brussels, Bibliothèque Royale II 4147, and Valencia, Biblioteca Universitaria 835. All citations from Tinctoris are here corrected to agree with the Brussels manuscript; I have not consulted MS Bologna, Biblioteca Universitaria 2573, but am grateful to Professor F. Alberto Gallo for checking the reading mentioned in n. 4. I would like to thank Professor Leeman Perkins for the loan of his film of the Valencia manuscript, and Professors Paul Brainard, Harold Powers, and Edward Roesner for their helpful comments on an earlier draft of this paper.

2. Ernest T. Ferand, "What Is *Res Facta*?" *JAMS* 10 (1957): 143. Ferand's article, pp. 141–50, summarizes the history of the term in scholarly literature from the mid-nineteenth to the mid-twentieth century. See especially his n. 1. He also pursued sixteenth-century uses of the terms connoting spontaneous music-making, notably *sortisatio* (see also n. 9, [4] below). See, inter alia, his "'Sodaine and Unexpected' Music in the Renaissance," *The Musical Quarterly* 27 (1951): 10–27; "Guillaume Guerson's Rules of Impro-

vised Counterpoint (c. 1500)," in *Miscelánea en homenaje a Monseñor Higinio Anglés* (Barcelona, 1958–61), pp. 252–63; "Improvised Vocal Counterpoint in the Late Renaissance and Early Baroque," *Annales musicologiques* 4 (1956): 129–74. He documents the increasing (or, as he thought, continuing) alignment of the term counterpoint with improvisation. Abbé Jean Prim, *"Chant sur le livre* in French Churches in the 18th Century," *JAMS* 14 (1961): 37–49, provides a link between the late use of *cantare super librum* to mean improvisatory practices and nineteenth-century assumptions that Tinctoris meant the same. All these later usages lie outside the scope of the present paper.

3. E.g., Johannes Tinctoris, *The Art of Counterpoint*, trans. Albert Seay, Musicological Studies and Documents, V (1961), *passim*; David Fallows, "Res facta," *The New Grove Dictionary* (London, 1980), XV, 755.

4. All citations from, and references to the *Liber de arte contrapuncti* (hereafter *C*) will be identified here by book, chapter, and sentence numbers in Johannes Tinctoris, *Opera theoretica*, ed. Albert Seay, 2 vols., Corpus scriptorum de musica, XXII (n.p., 1975), II. The other Tinctoris source for this question is the *Diffinitorium* (hereafter *D*); see Edmond de Coussemaker, ed., *Scriptorum de musica medii aevi nova series* (hereafter *CS*) (Paris, 1864–76), IV, 177–91. Several small corrections have been made, the most important of which is *evitaverint* instead of *cantaverint* in *C* II.xx.8, in accordance with all three manuscripts (see n. 1).

5. The only things that seem to have puzzled him here were: (1) that popular usage was claimed for terms that lacked earlier documentation (he went on to trace them in the later writings of Guerson, Wollick, Cannuzzi, and others [Ferand, "What Is Res Facta?" *passim*]; see also pp. 297–98 below and n. 2); and (2) that "What strikes us in these definitions of *res facta* (or *cantus compositus*) is the absence of any allusion to its supposedly characteristic feature, stressed in the *Liber de arte contrapuncti,* that it is a written, not improvised counterpoint. The situation becomes even more obscure when we discover that there is no entry in the *Diffinitorium* for *super librum cantare* (or *cantus super librum*), nor can any hint be found, in the various definitions for *contrapunctus* and its species, of its allegedly improvisatory character" (*ibid.*, p. 142). See below, p. 297, for *D*.

6. Willi Apel, "Improvisation, extemporization," *Harvard Dictionary of Music*, 2nd rev. ed. (Cambridge, Mass., 1969), p. 404.

7. Ernest T. Ferand, *Die Improvisation in der Musik* (Zurich, 1938), pp. 6–15; the discussion of *res facta* on pp. 146–63, however, subscribes to the familiar opposition of the terms.

8. Klaus-Jürgen Sachs, "Counterpoint," *The New Grove Dictionary*, IV, 837–38. Tinctoris's distinction between composition and counterpoint is not observed in this article, at least in its English translation, p. 837: "Counterpoint is here described [by Tinctoris] as 'restrained and thought-out polyphonic composition'" (see I.i.3, cited above, on this page). Sachs minimizes Tinctoris's emphasis on singing and follows the "improvisation" school. His excellent study *Der Contrapunctus im 14. und 15. Jahrhundert*, Beihefte zum Archiv für Musikwissenschaft, XIII (Wiesbaden, 1974) is fundamental to further pursuit of many of the issues mentioned here, including the distinction between composition and counterpoint, which however he does not address directly in connection with Tinctoris's use of the terms here discussed.

9.

(1)   "Ex negligentia male cantatur ab ebriis, & ab illis, qui pigritantur, vel contemnunt cantum diligentius usitare, & etiam ab illis excusant, qui totum a parte iudicant improvise; & isti autem vix excusantur, aut omnino venia non sunt digni" (Martin Gerbert, *Scriptores ecclesiastici de musica* [Saint Blaise, 1784], III, 233); on this anonymous treatise, datable 1274–1312, see Ulrich Michels, *Die Musiktraktate des Johannes de Muris*, Beihefte zum Archiv für Musikwissenschaft, VIII (Wiesbaden, 1970), pp. 16–17.

(2)   "Quae sunt praevidenda in musica: Si quis igitur ex improviso dicere qualitates diversorum cantuum, ac quantitates, differentiasque proportiones, similitudines, tempora, et mensuras, nec non et diffinitiones longarum, brevium, semibrevium, minimarum, atque figurarum discernere voluerit, principia huius scientiae cognoscat et eorum certitudinem experietur" (*Quatuor principalia musicae*, I.iv, CS IV, 202, colophon date 1351).

(3)   ". . . cantus specialiter ecclesiasticos invisos et inauditos, quasi ex improviso et sine magistro, secure decantare sciat ut sit musicus practicus vel cantor dici mereatur"

(Jacobi Leodiensis Speculum musicae, Corpus scriptorum de musica, III [n.p., 1955-73], VI, 199). (I owe the above references to the opportunity to consult the files of the *Handwörterbuch der musikalischen Terminologie,* Musikwissenschaftliches Institut der Universität Freiburg, by courtesy of Dr. Wolf Frobenius.)

Ferand produced the only occurrence that could mean spontaneous polyphonic creation or unprepared performance but is not otherwise supported by the ensuing exposition:

(4)   ". . . artem sciendi componere et proferre discantum ex improviso . . ." (Anon. II, CS I, 311; "What Is Res Facta?" n. 13; MS Saint-Dié, Bibliothèque Municipale 42, fol. 39r). While the author of this Franconian compendium is clearly late thirteenth century, the accretions are hard to date. The most recent dating of the manuscript itself is "15th century" (Gilbert Reaney, ed. of CS III, Anon. VII, with inventory of this so-called Blankenborch manuscript in the anonymous *De valore notularum . . .* , Corpus scriptorum de musica, XXX [Neuhausen, 1982], pp. 46–49).

(5)   "Sortisare est aliquem cantum diversis melodiis inprovise ornare" (cited by Klaus-Jürgen Sachs, s.v. "Sortisatio," *Riemann Musik-Lexikon* [Mainz, 1967], Sachteil, p. 887, after Regensburg, Proskesche Mus.-Bibl., 98 th.4°, copied in 1476); this antedates the sources for these and related procedures discussed by Ferand (see n. 2) but is quite distinct from Tinctoris's terminology and definitions. How Tinctoris's own terms came to acquire new connotations in the sixteenth century remains to be investigated.

10. For a preliminary statement of this view see Margaret Bent, "Some Factors in the Control of Consonance and Sonority: Successive Composition and the Solus Tenor," in *International Musicological Society: Report of the Twelfth Congress, Berkeley, 1977,* ed. Daniel Heartz and Bonnie Wade (Kassel, 1981), pp. 625–33 <= Chapter 8>. The arguments will be developed at greater length in work in progress on *musica ficta* and mensural notation.

11. A modern singer receives a specification of the kind of fifth wanted by the composer, diminished, perfect, or augmented, but he will expect to tune it aurally without notated intonational aids. The medieval singer was expected to determine from his knowledge of contrapuntal rules what kind of fifth was required (and to know that with very rare exceptions, if any, it should be perfect) and to "tune" it accordingly without written signs. Even Aron, who seems to be asking for full notation of such signs in the *Aggiunta* to the 1529 edition of his *Toscanello in musica* (Venice, 1523; facs. of 1529 edition, Bologna, 1969), only in fact asks for simultaneities that could not be anticipated to be marked, regarding overnotation of the obvious as superfluous, even if he does not, with Tinctoris (*De natura et proprietate tonorum,* in *Opera theoretica,* ed. Seay, I, 74), call it asinine.

12. I do not mean to imply that *vulgariter* and *communiter* should themselves be distinguished. That they were interchangeable for Tinctoris is shown in *C,* where he defines the diatessaron in learned fashion, adding "et vulgariter quarta vocatur" (I.v.4), while writing in the next chapter "diapente . . . communiter quinta appellatur" (I.vi.4).

13. III.iv: "'³Sed ab hac regula eximuntur, qui magis contrapuncto dulciori ac venustiori student quam propinquiori. ⁴Quique pluribus super librum canentibus ut contrapunctum diversificent, eum cum moderatione instar quodammodo compositorum longinquum efficiunt, ut hic patet: [Example with tenor and two *contrapuncti* functioning as contratenor and discantus]." For I.x.10, see n. 18 below.

14. See p. 304 (*C* I.i.3). Singing and aural judgment figure importantly in counterpoint treatises from Prosdocimus through Zarlino; Tinctoris's definition is in no way unusual.

15. In this decision he has been followed by many standard reference works, including *Die Musik in Geschichte und Gegenwart* (Kassel, 1949–79), the *Riemann Musik-Lexikon,* Sachteil, 12th rev. ed. (Mainz, 1967), and *The New Grove Dictionary.*

16. *C* II.xxix, xxxii–xxxiii present manifestly incomplete two-voiced mensural excerpts from compositions by Domarto, Busnois, Ockeghem, Faugues, and Caron. *C* I.vii, xii, xvii (on the interval of the sixth and its octaves) include unmeasured examples of a *contrapunctus* added to an existing tenor and con-

tratenor framework, a combination which probably allows us to presume that they derive from a composition which would also have had a discantus. In the first of these, the colors are (mistakenly?) reversed, with only the tenor in black notes. Elsewhere the tenor is, as it should be, void. The starting-point for adding counterpoint to more than a monophonic *cantus firmus* could thus be either a tenor and contratenor from an existing composition or pre-arranged, successive contrapuntal combinations. Tinctoris gives us little help in trying to determine which of these might apply in a given case, because he is concerned with making counterpoint, not with diagnosing how results were achieved. The above examples may be added to the evidence of *C* II.xxii (see n. 27, p. 319 below) for the addition of counterpoint to existing polyphony.

17. Such distinctions made in the present paper should be taken to apply only to Tinctoris. In this case, they stand apart from the usage of, for example, Guilielmus Monachus, whose well-known chapters allegedly but not explicitly on improvisation deal with various aspects of composition and counterpoint without insisting on differences of nature between them or applying distinctions of voice-names or measure (Guilielmus Monachus, *De preceptis artis musicae*, ed. Albert Seay, Corpus scriptorum de musica, XI [n.p., 1965], esp. pp. 29–44). Part of Guilielmus's discussion of fauxbourdon, for example, takes place under the rubric of contrapuntal rules (p. 38), with the voice names supranus, tenor, and contratenor.

18. This example illustrates the use of the eleventh (*C* I.x); its accompanying text is:
"¹⁰Hinc a contrapuncto abiicitur nisi pluribus super librum cantantibus, unus eorum quintam sub aliqua tenoris nota, quod in penultima sepe fit, assumat. ¹¹Tunc enim ab alio undecima cantari poterit quam mox convenientior proximiorque concordantia sequetur, ut hic patet: [our example I follows]. ¹²In plurimis autem reifacte locis undecima admittitur, non solum ei quinta sed etiam tertia subiuncta, licet illius concordantie subiunctio magis quam istius asperitatem eius mitiget, ut hic probatur: [example with supremum, tenor, contratenor]." Similar explanations and examples are given for the fourth (I.v) and the eighteenth (I.xv).

19. III.i: "⁷Preterea nonnullli, quibus assentior, dicunt non esse vitiosum si multis super librum canentibus aliqui eorum in concordantiam desinant imperfectam. ⁸Quod tamen intelligendum censeo ubi plures fuerint concinentes quam concordantie perfecte vocibus eorum contente, ita etiam quod a sexta, tertiadecima, vicesimaque supra notam inferiorem abstineant. ⁹Sic enim nulla earum propter eius duritiem et precipue cum quinta, duodecima et decimanona perfectioni congruit, ut hic probatur: [example]."

20. III.ix: "³Sed profecto frustra nisi quisquis in ipsa arte preclarus evadere nitetur, diligenti cum assuetudine componat aut super librum canat. ⁴Nam, ut Cicero *Ad Herennium* ait, in omni disciplina infirma est artis preceptio sine summa assiduitate exercitationis. . . . ⁶Neque putandum est hos aut illos huiusmodi compositionis aut super librum cantationis assiduitati, a provecta etate velut Socratem fidium tractandarum immo a pueritia se penitus tradidisse. ⁷. . . nostra tempestate neminem prorsus cognovi qui si a vicesimo anno etatis eius aut supra sive componere sive super librum canere inceperit, eminentem aut clarum inter musicos locum sibi vendicaverit."

21. E.g., *C* I.x.12 (see n. 18 and p. 311), III.iii.3–4, and notably in III.ii, the permitting of parallel perfect fifths between parts other than the tenor in *compositio*, while it is better if similar consonances in succession are avoided in counterpoint between such parts (II.xx.8). III.ii: "³Verumtamen ubi compositio trium aut plurium partium fit, nonnulli unam partem cum alia inferiori duntaxat excepta, per easdem species concordantiarum etiam perfectarum ascendere descendereque permittunt. ⁴Immo si duarum partium ascensus aut descensus per concordantias perfectas eiusdem speciei fiat, dummodo aliqua intervenerit pausa, compositor a pluribus excusatur, ut hic: [example with (?), tenor, contratenor]."

III.iii: "³Attamen ubi alie concordantie possunt intermitti, huiusmodi contrapunctus super cantum planum canendo diligenter est evitandus. ⁴In refacta vero, precipue si imperfecte fuerint concordantie aliquando propter verba convenientissime admittitur."

See also II.xxii.7 (n. 27) and I.xv.6–8 (pp. 308–09, and 312 n. 26).

22. III.viii: "⁴Hanc autem diversitatem optimi quisque ingenii compositor aut concentor efficiet, si nunc per unam quantitatem, nunc per aliam, nunc per unam perfectionem, nunc per unam proportionem, nunc per aliam, nunc per unam coniunctionem, nunc per aliam, nunc cum syncopis, nunc sine syncopis, nunc cum fugis, nunc sine fugis, nunc cum pausis, nunc sine pausis, nunc diminutive, nunc plane, aut componat aut concinat. ⁵Verumtamen in his omnibus summa est adhibenda ratio,

quippe ut de concentu super librum taceam qui pro voluntate concinentium diversificari potest, nec tot nec tales varietates uni cantilene congruunt quot et quales uni moteto, nec tot et tales uni moteto quot et quales uni misse.

"[6]Omnis itaque resfacta pro qualitate et quantitate eius diversificanda est prout infinita docent opera, non solum a me, verum etiam ab innumeris compositoribus evo presenti florentibus edita."

23. For inventories and identifications of music examples in the manuscripts Perugia, Biblioteca Communale Augusta 1013 and Bologna, Civico Museo Bibliografico Musicale A 71, see Bonnie J. Blackburn, "A Lost Guide to Tinctoris's Teachings Recovered," *Early Music History* 1 (1981): 29–116. Her tables and findings support the impression that Tinctoris was careful to credit his occasional citations of other composers' work, and that most if not all other examples in *C* are by him.

24. Aron, *Toscanello* (1529 ed.), II.xvi, xxxi.

25. II.xx.6: three, four, or more singing *super librum*; .5: all parts of the *resfacta,* whether three, four, or more. *Multi* need not mean "many"; it is often used in the Middle Ages as a simple plural, i.e., more than one. "Unus eorum" (I.x.10, see n. 18) may mean that Tinctoris was assuming only one voice to a part. See also III.i.8 (n. 19).

26. I.ii: "[11]Multos etenim cantus composites totam manum continentes et quosdam excedere vidi, nonnullos etiam pueros ad tridiapason usque contrapunctum canentes audivi. [12]Quo fit ut concordantie nunc usitate 22 sint." Tinctoris expresses his disapproval of the use in composition of a wide interval (the eighteenth), but does not disqualify it (I.xv.8): "[7] . . . In refacta vero non numquam hec concordantia [the 18th] admitti poterit, si ei vel tertia vel quinta, qua dulcior efficitur, supposita fuerit. [8]Verumtamen huius modi compositionem ab optimo quoque compositore evitandam censeo, enim vero in ea modicum suavitudinis sensus auditoris percipit, ut hic probatur: [example with supremum, contratenor, and tenor]."

27. II.xxii: "Sunt autem et aliqui, quamvis rarissimi, non solum super tenorem, verum etiam super quamlibet aliam partem reifacte concinentes. [5]Talisque contrapunctus plurimum artis et usus requirit. [6]Hinc si dulciter ac scientifice fiat, tanto est laudabilior quanto difficilior.

"[7]Porro licet omnium premissorum modorum ad efficiendum contrapunctum tam super cantum planum quam super figuratum exempla sint contrapuncti diminuti, simpliciter tamen, hoc est nota contra notam eiusdem valoris in quovis modo, contrapunctus fieri potest."

28. "In contrapuncto vel refacta duarum partium," I.vii, xii, xvii; see n. 16.

29. Craig Wright, "Performance Practices at the Cathedral of Cambrai: 1475–1550," *The Musical Quarterly* 64 (1978): esp. 313–15. See also *idem*, "Dufay at Cambrai: Discoveries and Revisions," *JAMS* XXVIII (1975): 221, n. 222, on Tinctoris. Ronald Woodley, "Johannes Tinctoris: A Review of the Documentary Biographical Evidence," *JAMS* 34 (1981): 217–48, urges caution in identifications of the rather common name, but does not challenge that this one refers to the theorist (p. 230).

30. See II.xx.8 and II.xxii.6 (n. 27).

Bibliography

of works cited by author's name in Introduction and Annotations

Apel, Willi. 1938. "The Partial Signatures in the Sources up to 1450," *Acta Musicologica* 10: 1–13.

———. 1939. "A Postscript to 'The Partial Signatures in the Sources up to 1450,'" *Acta Musicologica* 11: 40–42.

———. 1953. *The Notation of Polyphonic Music 900-1600.* Cambridge, MA: The Mediaeval Academy of America, 4th ed.

Bent, Margaret. 1969. "The Old Hall Manuscript: A Paleographical Study." Ph.D. dissertation, University of Cambridge.

———. 1981. "Some Criteria for Establishing Relationships between Sources of Late-Medieval Polyphony." Pp. 295–317 in *Music in Medieval and Early Modern Europe: Patronage, Sources, and Texts*, ed. Iain Fenlon. Cambridge: Cambridge University Press.

———. 1990a. "The Yoxford Credo." Pp. 26-51 in *Essays in Musicology: A Tribute to Alvin Johnson*, ed. Lewis Lockwood and Edward Roesner. N. p. American Musicological Society.

———. 1990b with David Howlett. "*Subtiliter alternare*: the Yoxford Motet *O amicus/Precursoris.*" Pp. 43-84 in *Studies in Medieval Music: Festschrift for Ernest Sanders*: ed. Peter M. Lefferts and Brian Seirup (New York: Columbia University, 1990) = *Current Musicology* 45-47.

———. 1992. "The Late-Medieval Motet." Pp. 114-19 in *Companion to Medieval and Renaissance Music*, ed. Tess Knighton and David Fallows. London: Dent.

———. 1995. "The Limits of Notation in Defining the Musical Text." Pp. 367–72 in

Notazione e testo musicale. Tavola rotonda coordinata e introdotta da Margaret Bent, *L'edizione critica tra testo musicale e testo letterario,* ed. Renato Borghi and Pietro Zappalà. Cremona. Studi e Testi Musicale, Nuova Serie 3. Lucca: Libreria Musicale Italiana.

——. 1998a. "The Grammar of Early Music: Preconditions for Analysis." Pp. 15–59 in *Tonal Structures in Early Music,* ed. C.C. Judd. New York: Garland (Paperback reprint, 2000).

——. 1998b. "Early Papal Motets." Pp. 5–43 in *Papal Music and Papal Musicians in Late Medieval and Renaissance Rome,* ed. Richard Sherr. Oxford: Oxford University Press.

——. 1998c. "Ciconia, Prosdocimus, and the Workings of Musical Grammar." (Conference paper, Liège, in press.)

——. 2002a. "'Sounds Perish': In What Senses Does Renaissance Music Survive?" *The Italian Renaissance in the 20th Century.* Acts of an International Conference, Villa I Tatti, Florence, edited by Allen Grieco, Michael Rocke, and Fiorella Gioffredi Superbi. Florence: Olschki, forthcoming.

——. 2002b. "On False Concords in Late 15th-century Music: Yet Another Look at Tinctoris." *Théorie et analyse musicales 1450-1650 (Music Theory and Analysis),* ed. Bonnie J. Blackburn and Anne-Emmanuelle Ceulemans. 'Musicologica neolovaniensa Studia,' n° 9. Louvain-la-Neuve, forthcoming.

Berger, Karol. 1987. *Musica ficta: Theories of Accidental Inflections in Vocal Polyphony from Marchetto da Padova to Gioseffo Zarlino.* Cambridge: Cambridge University Press.

Blackburn, Bonnie J. 1987. "On Compositional Process in the Fifteenth Century," *Journal of the American Musicological Society* 40: 210–84.

——. 1995. "Petrucci's Venetian Editor: Petrus Castellanus and His Musical Garden." *Musica Disciplina* 49: 15–46.

——. 1998. Review of Thomas Brothers, *Chromatic Beauty in the Late Medieval Chanson: An Interpretation of Manuscript Accidentals. Journal of the American Musicological Society* 51: 630–36.

——. 2000. *Composition, Printing, and Performance: Studies in Renaissance Music.* Aldershot, UK: Ashgate/Variorum.

Blackburn, Bonnie J., Edward E. Lowinsky, and Clement A. Miller, eds. 1991. *A Correspondence of Renaissance Musicians.* Oxford: Oxford University Press.

Boorman, Stanley. 1990. "False Relations and the Cadence." Pp. 221–64 in *Altro Polo: Essays on Italian Music in the Cinquecento,* ed. Richard Charteris. Sydney, Australia: University of Sydney.

Bowers, Roger. 1999. "The Performing Ensemble for English Church Polyphony, c.1320–c.1390"; "To Chorus from Quartet: The Performing Resource for

English Church Polyphony, c.1390–1559"; "The Vocal Scoring, Choral Balance and Performing Pitch of Latin Church Polyphony in England, c.1500–1558" (chapters 1–3 in *English Church Polyphony*. Aldershot, UK: Ashgate/Variorum).

Bragard, Roger, ed., 1963. Jacobi Leodiensis, *Speculum musicae*. Corpus scriptorum de musica, vol. 3/4. [Rome]: American Institute of Musicology.

Brett, Philip. 1993. "Pitch and Transposition in the Paston Manuscripts." Pp. 89–118 in *Sundry Sorts of Music Books. Essays on The British Library Collections. Presented to O. W. Neighbour on His 70th Birthday*, ed. Chris Banks, Arthur Searle, and Malcolm Turner. London: British Library.

Brothers, Thomas. 1997. *Chromatic Beauty in the Late Medieval Chanson: An Interpretation of Manuscript Accidentals, c.1275–1450*. Cambridge: Cambridge University Press.

Bukofzer, Manfred F. 1950. *Studies in Medieval and Renaissance Music*. New York: Norton.

Caraci Vela, Maria. 1995. "Le specifità dei testi musicale e la filologia: alcuni problemi di metodo." Pp. 43–64 in *Filologia Mediolatina* II.

Cox, Bobby Wayne. 1982. "'Pseudo-Augmentation' in the Manuscript Bologna, Civico Museo Bibliografico Musicale, Q15 (BL)." *Journal of Musicology* 1: 419–48.

Crocker, Richard. 1962. "Discant, Counterpoint, and Harmony." *Journal of the American Musicological Society* 15: 1–21.

Cross, Lucy E. 1990. "Chromatic Alteration and Extrahexachordal Intervals in Fourteenth-Century Polyphonic Repertories." Ph.D. dissertation, Columbia University.

Dahlhaus, Carl. 1968a. *Untersuchungen über die Entstehung der harmonischen Tonalität*. Kassel, Germany: Bärenreiter. Translated by Robert O. Gjerdingen as *Studies on the Origin of Harmonic Tonality*. Princeton, NJ: Princeton University Press, 1990.

——. 1968b. "Zur Akzidentiensetzung in den Motetten Josquins des Prez." Pp. 206–19 in *Musik und Verlag: Karl Vötterle zum 65. Geburtstag am 12. April 1968*. R. H. Baum and W. Rehm. Kassel, Germany: Bärenreiter.

——. 1969/1970. "Tonsystem und Kontrapunkt um 1500." *Jahrbuch des staatlichen Instituts für Musikforschung Preussischer Kulturbesitz*: 7–18.

——. 1979. "Was heißt Improvisation?" Pp. 9–23 in *Improvisation und neue Musik*, ed. Reinhold Brinkmann. Mainz, Germany: Schott.

Davis, Shelley. 1967. "The Solus Tenor in the 14th and 15th Centuries." *Acta Musicologica* 39 : 44-64.

——. 1968. "The Solus Tenor: An Addendum." *Ibid.* 40: 176–8.

Dunstable. 1970. *John Dunstable, Complete Works*, Musica Britannica VIII, ed. Manfred F. Bukofzer, 1953. 2nd, rev. ed. by Margaret Bent, Ian Bent, and Brian Trowell. London: Stainer and Bell.

Earp, Lawrence M. 1983. "Scribal Practice, Manuscript Production, and the Transmission of Music in Late Medieval France: The Manuscripts of Guillaume de Machaut." Ph.D. dissertation, Princeton University.

———. 1993. Review of Daniel Leech-Wilkinson's Book and Edition of the Machaut Mass. *Journal of the American Musicological Society* 46: 295–305.

Ellsworth, Oliver B. 1973. "The Origin of the Coniuncta: A Reappraisal." *Journal of Music Theory* 17: 86–109.

———. ed. 1984. *The Berkeley Manuscript: University of California Music Library, ms. 744 (olim Phillipps 4450)*. Lincoln, NE and London: University of Nebraska Press.

———. ed. 1993. *Johannes Ciconia, Nova musica and De proportionibus*. Lincoln, NE and London: University of Nebraska Press.

Fallows, David. 1996. *Songs and Musicians in the Fifteenth Century*. Aldershot, UK: Ashgate/Variorum.

Grove: *New Grove* (=Grove VI) 1980. *The New Grove Dictionary of Music and Musicians*, ed. Stanley Sadie. London: Macmillan. 2nd ed (2001), ed. Stanley Sadie and John Tyrrell.

Haar, James. 1977. "False Relations and Chromaticism in Sixteenth-Century Music." *Journal of the American Musicological Society* 24: 391–418.

Harden, Bettie Jean. 1983. "Sharps, Flats, and Scribes: Musica Ficta in the Machaut Manuscripts." Ph.D. dissertation, Cornell University.

Herlinger, Jan W. 1989. Review of Berger, *Musica ficta*. *Journal of the American Musicological Society* 42: 640–47.

Herlinger, Jan, ed., 1984. Prosdocimo de' Beldomandi, *Contrapunctus*. Lincoln, NE and London: University of Nebraska Press.

Hirshberg, Jehoash. 1980. "Hexachordal and Modal Structure in Machaut's Polyphonic Chansons." Pp. 19–42 in *Studies in Musicology in Honor of Otto E. Albrecht*, ed. John Walter Hill. Kassel, Germany: Bärenreiter.

———. 1996. "The Exceptional as an Indicator of the Norm." Pp. 53–64 in *Modality in the Music of the Fourteenth and Fifteenth Centuries*, ed. Ursula Günther, Ludwig Finscher, and Jeffrey Dean. American Institute of Musicology, MSD 49.

HMT: 1972- . *Handwörterbuch der musikalischen Terminologie*. Ed. H.H. Eggebrecht. Wiesbaden, Germany: Steiner Verlag.

Holford-Strevens, Leofranc. 2000. Review of *Lexicon musicum latinum medii aevi*. *Plainsong and Medieval Music* 9: 181–5.

Hoppin, Richard H. 1953. "Partial Signatures and Musica Ficta in Some Early Fifteenth Century Sources." *Journal of the American Musicological Society* 6: 197–215.

———. 1956. "Conflicting Signatures Reviewed." *Journal of the American Musicological Society* 9: 97–117.

Hughes, Andrew. 1969. "Ugolino: The Monochord and Musica Ficta." *Musica Disciplina* 23: 21–39.

———. 1972. *Manuscript Accidentals: Ficta in Focus 1350–1450*. American Institute of Musicology, Musicological Studies and Documents 27.

Hughes, Andrew, and Margaret Bent, eds., 1969–73. *The Old Hall Manuscript*. 3 vols. Corpus Mensurabilis Musicae 46. Rome: American Institute of Musicology.

Judd, Cristle Collins. 1995. "Reading Aron Reading Petrucci." *Early Music History* 14: 121–152.

King, Jonathan. 1996. "Texting in Early Fifteenth-Century Sacred Polyphony," D. Phil dissertation, University of Oxford.

La Fage, Adrien de. 1864. *Essais de dipthérographie musicale*. Paris: Legouix.

Leach, Elizabeth Eva. 1998. "Counterpoint in Guillaume de Machaut's Musical Ballades." D. Phil. dissertation, University of Oxford.

———. 2000a. "Fortune's Demesne: The Interrelation of Text and Music in Machaut's *Il mest avis* (B22), *De fortune* (B23) and Two Related Anonymous Balades." *Early Music History* 19: 47–79.

———. 2000b. "Interpretation and Counterpoint: The Case of Guillaume de Machaut's *De toutes flours* (B31)." *Music Analysis* 19: 321–51.

Leech-Wilkinson, Daniel. 1984. "Machaut's 'Rose, Lis' and the Problems of Early Music Analysis." *Music Analysis* 3: 9–28.

———. 1989. *Compositional Procedure in the Four-Part Isorhythmic Works of Philippe de Vitry and his Contemporaries*. New York and London: Garland.

Lowinsky, Edward E. 1945. "The Function of Conflicting Signatures in Early Polyphonic Music." *The Musical Quarterly* 31: 227–60.

———. 1954. "Conflicting Views on Conflicting Signatures." *Journal of the American Musicological Society* 7: 181–204.

Memelsdorff, Pedro. 2000. "*Le Grant Desir*: Verschlüsselte Chromatik bei Matteo da Perugia." Pp. 55–83 in *Provokation und Tradition. Erfahrungen mit der Alte Musik* (Festschrift Klaus L. Neumann), ed. Regula Rapp and Hans-Martin Linde. Stuttgart, Germany: Metzler Verlag.

MGG: 1994–. *Die Musik in Geschichte und Gegenwart*, 2nd ed., ed. Ludwig Finscher. Kassel: Bärenreiter.

Milsom, John. 2000. "Analysing Josquin." Pp. 431–84 in *The Josquin Companion*, ed. Richard Sherr. Oxford: Oxford University Press.

Mixter, Keith. 1987. S.v. "Solus Tenor," *Handwörterbuch der musikalischen Terminologie*, ed. H. H. Eggebrecht. Stuttgart, Germany: Steiner Verlag.

Moll, Kevin N. 1997. *Counterpoint and Compositional Process in the Time of Dufay: Perspectives from German Musicology*. New York, London: Garland.

Nettl, Bruno. 1974. "Thoughts on Improvisation: A Comparative Approach." *The Musical Quarterly* 60: 1–19.

Otaola, Paloma. 1998. "Les *coniunctae* dans la théorie musicale au moyen âge et la Renaissance (1375–1555)." *Musurgia* 5: 53–69.

Owens, Jessie Ann. 1997. *Composers at Work: the Craft of Musical Composition 1450–1600*. New York, Oxford: Oxford University Press.

Page, Christopher. 1997. *Music and Instruments of the Middle Ages: Studies on Texts and Performance*. Aldershot, UK: Ashgate/Variorum.

Palmer, Jill. 1985. "A Late Fifteenth–Century Anonymous Mensuration Treatise." *Musica Disciplina* 39: 89–103.

Perkins, Leeman L. 1973. " Mode and Structure in the Masses of Josquin." *Journal of the American Musicological Society* 26: 189–239.

Pesce, Dolores. 1987. *The Affinities and Medieval Transposition*. Bloomington: Indiana University Press.

———. 1999. Review of Thomas Brothers, *Chromatic Beauty in the Late Medieval Chanson*. *Journal of the Royal Musical Association* 123: 283–88.

Petrucci. 1967. *Ottaviano Petrucci, Canti B Numero Cinquanta*, Monuments of Renaissance Music II, ed. Helen Hewitt. Chicago and London: University of Chicago Press.

Powers, Harold. 1992. "Is Mode Real? Pietro Aron, the Octenary System, and Polyphony." *Basler Jahrbuch für historische Musikpraxis* 16: 9–52.

Preece, Isobel Woods. 2000. *Our Awin Scottis Use: Music in the Scottish Church up to 1603*. Ed. Sally Harper, with additional contributions by Warwick Edwards and Gordon J. Munro. Studies in the Music of Scotland. Glasgow: the Universities of Glasgow and Aberdeen.

Randel, Don. 1971. "Emerging Triadic Tonality in the Fifteenth Century." *The Musical Quarterly* 57: 73–86.

Reaney, Gilbert. 1969. *Manuscripts of Polyphonic Music (c.1320–1400)*, *RISM B IV²*. Munich: Henle.

Rifkin, Joshua. 1995. "No Accident(als)." Pp. 407–18 in Notazione e testo musicale. Tavola rotonda coordinata e introdotta da Margaret Bent, *L'edizione critica tra testo musicale e testo letterario*, ed. Renato Borghi and Pietro Zappalà. Cremona, Italy: Studi e Testi Musicale, Nuova Serie 3. Lucca: Libreria Musicale Italiana.

RISM   *Répertoire International des Sources Musicales.* (See individual entries under Reaney, Wathey.)

Rohloff, Ernst, ed., 1943. *Der Musiktraktat des Johannes de Grocheo*, Media Latinitas II. Leipzig: Reinecke.

Russo, Marimichela and Dale Bonge. 1999. "*Musica Ficta* in Thirteenth-Century Hexachordal Theory." *Studi musicali* 28: 309–26.

Sachs, Klaus-Jürgen. 1974. *Der Contrapunctus im 14. und 15. Jahrhundert.* Wiesbaden, Germany: Steiner Verlag.

———. 1983. "Arten improvisierter Mehrstimmigkeit nach Lehrtexten des 14. bis 16. Jahrhunderts." *Basler Jahrbuch für historische Musikpraxis* 7: 166–83.

Scattolin, Pier Paolo. 1985. "Le *Regule contrapuncti* di Filippotto da Caserta." Pp. 231–44 in *L'Ars Nova Italiana del Trecento* V, ed. Agostino Ziino. Palermo: Enchiridion.

Schreurs, Eugen, ed. 1995. *An Anthology of Music from the Low Countries.* Leuven, Belgium: Alamire.

Scott, Ann Besser. 1970. "The Performance of the Old Hall Descant Settings." *The Musical Quarterly* 56: 14–26.

Seay, Albert, ed. 1967. *Johannes de Grocheo, Concerning Music.* Trans. Albert Seay. Colorado Springs: Colorado College Music Press.

Strohm, Reinhard. 1995. "Does Textual Criticism Have a Future?" Pp. 193–211 in *L'edizione critica tra testo musicale e testo letterario,* ed. Renato Borghi and Pietro Zappalà. Studi e Testi Musicale, Nuova Serie 3. Cremona, Italy: Lucca, Libreria Musicale Italiana.

Toft, Robert. 1992. *Aural Images of Lost Traditions: Sharps and Flats in the Sixteenth Century.* Toronto, Canada: University of Toronto Press.

Urquhart, Peter. 1988. "Canon, Partial Signatures, and 'Musica ficta' in Works by Josquin DesPrez and his Contemporaries." Ph.D. dissertation, Harvard University.

———. 1993. "Cross-Relations by Franco-Flemish Composers after Josquin." *Tijdschrift van de Vereniging voor Nederlandse Muziekgeschiedenis.* 43: 3–41.

———. 1994. "An Accidental Flat in Josquin's Sine Nomine Mass." Pp. 125–44 in *From Ciconia to Sweelinck: Donum natalicum Willem Elders,* ed. Albert Clement and Eric Jas. Amsterdam: Rodopi.

———. 1996. "Three Sample Problems of Editorial Accidentals in Chansons by Busnoys and Ockeghem." Pp. 465–81 in *Music in Renaissance Cities and Courts: Studies in Honor of Lewis Lockwood.* Warren, MI: Harmonie Park Press.

———. 1997a. "Calculated to Please the Ear: Ockeghem's Canonic Legacy." *Tijdschrift van de Vereniging voor Nederlandse Muziekgeschiedenis.* 47: 72–98.

——. 1997b. "Musica Ficta (15th–16th centuries)." *Die Musik in Geschichte und Gegenwart*, Ludwig Finscher, general editor. Kassel, Germany: Bärenreiter.

——. 1999. "False Discords in Busnoys." Pp. 361–87 in *Antoine Busnoys: Method, Meaning, and Context in Late Medieval Music,* ed. Paula Higgins. Oxford: Clarendon Press.

Walker, Jonathan. 1996. "Intonational Injustice: A Defense of Just Intonation in the Performance of Renaissance Polyphony." *Music Theory Online* 2.6. (http://www.societymusictheory.org/mto/).

Wathey, Andrew. 1993. *Manuscripts of Polyphonic Music: Supplement I to RISM B IV$^{1-2}$. The British Isles, 1100–1400.* Munich: Henle.

Wegman, Rob C. 1992a. "Music ficta." Pp. 265–274 in *Companion to Medieval and Renaissance Music*, ed. Tess Knighton and David Fallows. London: Dent.

——. 1992b. "New Light on Secular Polyphony at the Court of Holland in the Early Fifteenth Century: The Amsterdam Fragments." *Journal of the Royal Musical Association* 117: 181–207.

——. 1996. "From Maker to Composer: Improvisation and Musical Authorship in the Low Countries, 1450–1500," *Journal of the American Musicological Society* 49: 409–79.

Welker, Lorenz. 1993. *Musik am Oberrhein im späten Mittelalter: Die Handschrift Strasbourg, olim Bibliothèque de la Ville, C.22.* Habilitationsschrift, University of Basel.

Weller, Philip, and Andrew Kirkman. 1996. "Binchois's Texts." *Music & Letters* 77: 566–96.

Wibberley, Roger. 1996. "Josquin's *Ave Maria*: Musica Ficta versus Mode." *Music Theory Online* 2.5 (http://www.societymusictheory.org/mto/), and his response to my article: "'Mode versus Ficta' in Context," *ibid.*, 2.7, 96 (mto.96.2.7).

Widdess, Richard. 2001. "'Who Knows Who's Improvising?' Ethnomusicological and Related Perspectives." Paper delivered orally at a Royal Musical Association Study Day at Royal Holloway, 24 February.

Wilkins, Nigel. 1964. "Some Notes on Philipoctus de Caserta." *Nottingham Medieval Studies* 8: 82–99.

Zager, Daniel. 1987. "From the Singer's Point of View: A Case Study in Hexachordal Solmization as a Guide to Musica Recta and Musica Ficta in Fifteenth-Century Vocal Music." *Current Musicology* 43: 7–21.

Permissions

1   "Musica Recta and Musica Ficta" was originally published in *Musica Disciplina* 26 (1972), 73–100. © Hänssler. Reprinted with permission.

2   "Pycard's Credo No. 76" was originally appendix II to Chapter IV of *The Old Hall Manuscript, a paleographical study* (Ph.D. dissertation, Cambridge, 1969), pp. 266–76. Published here for the first time. © Margaret Bent.

3   "Renaissance Counterpoint and Musica Ficta" (1978) is published here for the first time. © Margaret Bent.

4   "Diatonic *Ficta*" was originally published in *Early Music History* 4 (1984), 1–48. © Cambridge University Press. Reprinted with permission.

5   "Accidentals, counterpoint and notation in Aaron's *Aggiunta* to the *Toscanello in Musica*" was originally published in *The Journal of Musicology* XII (1994), 306–44 (Festschrift issue for James Haar: *Aspects of Musical Language and Culture in the Renaissance*). © University of California Press. Reprinted with permission.

6   "Diatonic *ficta* revisited: Josquin's *Ave Maria* in context" was originally published in *Music Theory Online*, September 1996 (http://www.societymusictheory.org/mto/). © Society for Music Theory. Reprinted with permission.

7   "Editing early music: the dilemma of translation" was originally published in *Early Music* XXII/3 (August 1994), 373–94. © Oxford University Press. Reprinted with permission.

8   "Some Factors in the Control of Consonance and Sonority: Successive Composition and the *Solus tenor*" was originally published in *International Musicological Society: Report of the Twelfth Congress, Berkeley 1977*, ed. Daniel Heartz and Bonnie Wade, 625–34. Kassel &c, Bärenreiter, 1981. © Bärenreiter. Reprinted with permission.

9   "Pycard's double canon: evidence of revision?" was originally published in *Sundry Sorts of Music Books. Essays on The British Library Collections. Presented to O. W. Neighbour on his 70th birthday*, ed. Chris Banks, Arthur Searle & Malcolm Turner. London, The British Library, 1993, pp. 10–26. © Margaret Bent. Reprinted with permission of the British Library.

10   "Text Setting in Sacred Music of the Early 15th Century: Evidence and Implications" was originally published in *Musik und Text in der Mehrstimmigkeit des 14. und 15. Jahrhunderts: Vorträge des Gastsymposions in der Herzog August Bibliothek Wolfenbüttel, 8. bis 12. September 1980*, ed. Ursula Günther and Ludwig Finscher. Göttinger Musikwissenschaftliche Arbeiten, vol. 10, pp. 291–326. Kassel &c, Bärenreiter, 1984. © Bärenreiter. Reprinted with permission.

11   "*Resfacta* and *Cantare super librum*" was originally published in *Journal of the American Musicological Society* 36 (1983), 371–91. © American Musicological Society. Reprinted with permission.

Index